Postwar Austrian Theater

Text and Performance

Studies in Austrian Literature, Culture, and Thought

Postwar Austrian Theater
Text and Performance

Edited and with an Introduction
by
Linda C. DeMeritt and
Margarete Lamb-Faffelberger

ARIADNE PRESS
Riverside, California

Library of Congress Cataloging-in-Publication Data

Postwar Austrian theater : text and performance / edited and with an introduction by Linda C. DeMeritt and Margarete Lamb-Faffelberger.
   p. cm. -- (Studies in Austrian literature, culture, and thought)

Includes bibliographical references and index.
   ISBN 1-57241-107-4
   1. Austrian drama--20th century--History and criticism. 2. Theater--Austria--History--20th century. I. DeMeritt, Linda C., 1953- II. Lamb-Faffelberger, Margarete, 1954- III. Series.
   PT3821 .P67 2002
   792'.09436'09045--dc21
                                      2002071724

Cover:
Art Director: George McGinnis

Copyright ©2002
by Ariadne Press
270 Goins Court
Riverside, CA 92507

All rights reserved.
No part of this publication may be reproduced or transmitted
in any form or by any means without formal permission.
Printed in the United States of America.
ISBN 1-57241-107-4 (paperback original)

CONTENTS

Acknowledgments	v
Margarete Lamb-Faffelberger and Linda C. DeMeritt Text and Performance in Austria between 1945 and 2000: A Brief Introduction and Highlights	1
Katherine Arens The Persistence of *Kasperl* in Memory: H. C. Artmann and Peter Handke	33
Todd C. Hanlin Morality and Ambiguity: Fritz Hochwälder's *Der Befehl*	54
Jennifer E. Michaels The Treatment of Fascism in Post-World War II Austrian Theater	71
Roxana Nubert Fascination and Provocation in the Works of Thomas Bernhard	92
Rachel Freudenburg Masculinity as Performance in the Plays of Thomas Bernhard	114

Bernhard Doppler
The Return of the Kings: Peter Handke at the *Burgtheater*   133

Gerd K. Schneider
Social and Human Issues in Peter Turrini's Work   153

Kirsten Krick-Aigner
Staging a Legend: Claus Peymann's *Ingeborg Bachmann. Wer?*   170

Gerlinde Ulm Sanford
In the Beginning was the Word – And before That?
Theological Problems in Felix Mitterer's
Krach im Hause Gott   191

Dagmar C. G. Lorenz
The Issue of Male Violence in Dramatic Works of the
Two Austrian Republics: Veza Canetti and Felix Mitterer   213

Laura Ovenden
Body, Voice, and Text in Elisabeth Reichart's Dramatic
Monologue *Sakkorausch*   236

Linda C. DeMeritt
Staging Superficiality: Elfriede Jelinek's *Ein Sportstück*   257

Jutta Landa
Figure and Speech on Vienna's Major Stages
in the Nineties   277

Beate Hochholdinger-Reiterer
"Theater as a Form of Upscale Junkyard":
Werner Schwab's Plays: Nonsense That Defies Reason
or Disguised Morality?   300

Helga W. Kraft
Corpses and Gendered Bodies:
The Theater of Marlene Streeruwitz   328

Willy Riemer
Ocean Drive.: Marlene Streeruwitz's Fractal Mise-en-Scène   350

Contributors   364

Index   369

Acknowledgments

This volume has come together due to the efforts, expertise, and commitment of many people and institutions, and we wish here to acknowledge and thank them for all their help and support. Above all, we want to express our gratitude to our contributors for the opportunity to work together with them in this scholarly venture. Thanks also to those colleagues who gave so freely of their time and knowledge during the review process, providing us with invaluable commentary and advice about individual articles. Thus we offer our sincere gratitude to Beth Bjorklund, Geoffrey Howes, Michelle Geoffrion-Vinci, Regina Kecht, Jürgen Koppensteiner, Stephanie Libbon, Laura Quinn, Jochen Richter, Paul Schlueter, Helga Schreckenberger, Anne Ulmer, and Jackie Vansant. In addition, we want to single out and thank in particular George Byrnes for his literary insights as well as editorial suggestions concerning both individual essays and the volume as a whole. We are very grateful to Lafayette student Marc Ampaw who has helped us in various ways, including as research assistant, translator, and also in preparation of the Index. Finally, this volume would never have been completed without the expert help of Roz Macken, Allegheny secretary par excellence (!), whose attention to detail, patience, and ready smile accompanied and encouraged us throughout preparation of this manuscript.

There are also several institutions and organizations that have been instrumental in bringing this project to completion. Above all, we thank Allegheny College for its generous support of research initiatives over the past several years, both in terms of faculty development grants and leave time. We are also appreciative of the opportunity provided by the Literar-Mechana to engage in research directly in Vienna, which has meant that we have been able to witness on site a number of the theater performances discussed in our volume. Finally, thanks go to the Literaturhaus Wien for the use of its excellent library holdings on contemporary Austrian literature, in particular the numerous reviews contained in newspapers and magazines not readily available in the US.

Text and Performance in Austria between 1945 and 2000: A Brief Introduction and Highlights

Margarete Lamb-Faffelberger and Linda C. DeMeritt

Austria's theatrical life and in particular Vienna's theaters enjoy a rich and celebrated history. Theaters and theater-going have held a central place in Austria's public and political consciousness for the past three centuries. It is therefore not surprising that Austrian stages, especially the Vienna State Opera and the *Burgtheater*, have played an important role in formulating questions about and challenges to the shaping of individual and societal identity within the Second Republic.

The present volume offers an investigation of some of the most important voices from the theater world in that constantly evolving redefinition of a political state and its private citizens. They are for the most part critical voices, voices of provocation, voices that undermine the status quo and complacency. They include both the writers of the texts and the producers or directors of the performances, for the written word must take shape on stage, and the real debate of drama takes place in a public space. Today more than ever the making of theater includes the director, and the present volume, as expressed in its title, attempts to include issues of staging and reception where possible.

The essays included in this volume can make no claim to offering comprehensive or exhaustive coverage of Austrian theater between 1945 and today. What they can and, we hope, do in fact accomplish is to present some representative texts, playwrights, tendencies, and moments within that period. They offer a sampling of highlights that can serve to introduce the reader to contemporary Austrian drama, a sampling that may spark further interest and investigation of those highlights. Taken individually, the articles present both an introduction of important playwrights to an English-speaking audience as well as in-depth discussion of and new insights into those playwrights' work. Taken as a whole, the volume is intended to show the incredible richness and variety of the theater scene in Austria. At the dawn of the new millennium, theatrical life in Austria is anything but dull or stagnant.

The following introductory chapter is meant to provide a historical survey of postwar Austrian drama as well as an introduction to the country's most important playwrights. Summaries of the articles contained in the volume are included so as to contextualize subsequent discussions.

Performing Identity in the Postwar Years

The Vienna State Opera and the *Burgtheater* suffered immense damage during the last few months of the war: the Opera House was bombed on 12 March 1945, and fire destroyed the stage and the auditorium of the *Burgtheater* exactly one month later. Luckily, other important theaters fared better. Theatrical life in the *Akademietheater* and in the *Volksoper* resumed on 1 May 1945. The latter staged Mozart's *The Marriage of Figaro* as it temporarily assumed the role of Vienna's opera house. Also on 1 May 1945, the *Theater an der Wien* reopened with Beethoven's *Fidelio* and the *Theater in der Josefstadt* presented *Der Schwierige* (The Difficult One) by Nestroy. The *Deutsches Volkstheater* reopened in June 1945 with a performance of Grillparzer's *Des Meeres und der Liebe Wellen* (Hero and Leander).

The choice of these plays indicates that it was considered important to reclaim specifically Austrian/Viennese traditions and to reassert a continuity of artistic excellence that had been interrupted by the Nazi years.[1] The assertion of continuity is contrasted, however, on the political and socio-cultural front with the concept of a "zero hour," which was invoked to create a blank slate on which to shed the brown uniforms of Nazism and to rebuild a new and democratic Austrian Republic. The history of postwar theater in Austria, which in many ways reflects the country's search for identity, is marked by a fundamental tension between efforts to reclaim what was perceived as a glorious past and efforts to begin anew. That the tension was out of balance from the outset is indicated by the fact that, despite calls for cultural and political renewal, no serious attempts were made to bring back those many artists who had been forced into exile by the Nazi regime.[2]

Immediately after the war, leftist socio-critical theater was considered by many to be a meaningful display of Austrian patriotism. Several left-wing and communist directors, such as Günther Haenel, confronted Austro-fascism and Austria's involvement in World War II at the *Wiener Volkstheater* and the *Theater an der Scala*. For example, *Der Bockerer*, a political folk play by Peter Preses and Ulrich Becher, premiered at the latter stage in 1948.[3]

However, with the onset of the Cold War, the political and cultural climate shifted clearly to the right. Austria's orientation toward the West created a deceptive spirit of reconciliation which made possible the reintegration of former Nazis into mainstream Austrian society. Thus, leftist theory and practice on the Austrian stage were chastised,[4] and the general public soon rejected a social criticism that implicated Austria in Nazi atrocities. The topic of Austro-fascism was too vexing for most. It was more comforting to look towards a better future for oneself and the country and in doing so to remember only Austria's great past, to escape into a world untouched by the horrors of the Nazi regime. Hence, strong tensions arose between the reform-oriented writers, producers, and actors on the one hand and the restorative reconstruction movement on the other. The latter made use of traditional theater, staging many highly successful performances where the "brown smog" of Nazism still lingered on stage.[5]

The term "anti-fascist" also underwent radical change. "Anti-fascism" now meant to be essentially Austrian, by birth and by upbringing, as opposed to "Nazism" which was proclaimed as essentially "un-Austrian." This attitude, of course, excluded any self-criticism of Austria's involvement and participation in the Third Reich.[6] In order to establish a cultural identity distinctly different from Germany, Austria reactivated its cultural heritage by connecting the Second Republic of Austria to the myth of the Hapsburg Empire, an empire remembered and glorified as the golden era of mankind. The notion of Austrians as non-Germans replaced the myth of Austrians as the better Germans which was prevalent during the years of the destitute First Republic between 1918 and 1938. The role of the theater was to elevate Austria's status once again by staging these sentiments and by reflecting eternal values, and thus the theater became the place for individual morality, not for political rectitude.[7] Austria's political and cultural elite proclaimed the Second Republic as a modern continuation of Hapsburg Austria. The rallying call was to build a bridge to the past: "We only need to continue where the illusions of a mad man interrupted our dreams. In fact, we do not need to look forward but back," declared Alexander Lernet-Holenia.[8]

When, in 1955, Austria finally regained its sovereignty and the reconstructed great Viennese stages opened their doors to the public, the call was heeded. Vienna's State Opera performed – once more – Beethoven's *Fidelio* with its central theme of salvation and liberation. The *Burgtheater* presented Grillparzer's *König Ottokars Glück und Ende* (*King Ottocar, His Rise and Fall*) with its famous hymn to the glory of Austria. The question whether to perform Grillparzer's play or Goethe's *Egmont* was debated for months in the Austrian Parliament. In fact, the selection of the plays for the ceremonial opening of both state theaters was "the most studied example of the process of reconstructing a national cultural identity,"[9] a process which, furthermore, seriously undermined the "zero hour" concept in postwar Austria.

Promoting Performance for the Masses: The Festival Culture

During the 1950s, Austria's political and cultural conservatism encouraged the promotion of works that celebrated a certain national and cultural nostalgia for "what has since become known in literary history as the Hapsburg Myth."[10] Longing for "Kakania" (Robert Musil's extraordinary place in *The Man without Qualities*, 1933) dominated Austria's cultural policies, and the theater was the place where the "new" Austrians of the Second Republic could rediscover the essence of the "old" Austrian civilization. To cultivate the sentiment of continued greatness and cultural superiority, the state began to support a number of festivals. During the summer months, when the Viennese theaters are in recess, the Bregenz Festival (since 1946) and the Mörbisch Festival (since 1957) emphasize classical operetta. Both festivals cater to the audience's desire to be entertained, and thus offer extravagant shows which have developed into lavish tourist attractions.

The annual Vienna Festival during May and June (first held in the 1920s) was revived in 1951 in order "to document the unity of the capital ... and the cultural identity of Austria."[11] Its financial success enabled the renovation of the *Theater an der Wien*, which had been slated for demolition but instead reopened in May 1962 with Mozart's *Magic Flute*. The Salzburg Festival was originally founded in 1920 and celebrated its most brilliant seasons during the 1930s when Arturo Toscanini and Bruno Walter served as its principal conductors. Despite a marked decline after the Nazi annexation in 1938, it continued to take place until 1943 and was immediately revived after the Allies' victory in the summer of 1945. During the Herbert von Karajan years (from the late 1950s to the late 1980s) the festival gained a strong international recognition and became known for its elitist audience and traditional art performances of the highest quality.[12]

Today, festival activities have spread to every corner of the country. Not only the capital cities of the provinces but also small towns celebrate the arts, often presenting local talent together with world renowned artists. In addition to highly acclaimed music festivals, such as the Carinthian Summer and the Haydn Festival, the Graz avant-garde festival called *steirischer herbst* must be mentioned (founded in 1968), as well as the Viennale Film Festival. Moreover, the *Ars Electronica*, held annually in Linz since 1980, is the world's largest multimedia and computer-art festival.

Provincialism and the Rediscovery of the *Volksstück*

The Second Republic attempted to overcome the stigma of being a small and politically unimportant country by claiming centrality; it was the "heart of Europe," the bridge between East and West during the Cold War. By also claiming to be the inheritor of European civilization as well as the keeper of a simpler and uncorrupted rural life, the notion of *Heimat*-Austria was cultivated, as depicted in the many *Heimat*-films of the 1950s and 1960s featuring Austria's splendid natural beauty.[13] Provincialism and longing for *Heimat* were an essential part of the cultural atmosphere during the first two decades after the war.[14]

The mode of provincialism also paved the way for the rediscovery and popularization of the *Volksstück* and the distinctly Viennese *Volkstheater*.[15] "Born of a theater of tradition that thrived on the immediate dialectic of audience and tradition, the *Volksstück* [stays] close to the subject matter that is part of its designation: the struggles and joys of the underrepresented lower and middle classes."[16] Ödön von Horváth's plays were often heard and seen as radio and television productions during the 1950s and into the mid-1960s. His contributions to the renewal of the *Volksstück* were significant and carried important consequences for the development of the critical folk plays of Fritz Hochwälder, Felix Mitterer, Peter Turrini, Wolfgang Bauer, Heinz R. Unger, Gustav Ernst, and others.

Thus Austrian playwrights not only rediscovered the classic folk theater; more importantly, they consciously used its dramaturgy as an analytical tool directed against contemporary society. Many of the articles contained in this volume underline the importance of the critical folk play for postwar Austrian theater. In particular, the article by KATHERINE ARENS titled "The Persistence of *Kasperl* in Memory" traces the history of *Kasperl* in the 1950s and 1960s, focusing on two plays by H. C. Artmann and Peter Handke, *Kein Pfeffer für Czermak* (No Pepper for Czermak) and *Kaspar*, respectively. She convincingly argues that these works are not only to be understood within the tradition of language philosophy, but as "engaged black comedies criticizing the contemporary state at the dawn of the Cold War."

Fritz Hochwälder also makes extensive use of the folk play and has enjoyed popular success despite his biting social criticism. *Der Himbeerpflücker* (*The Raspberry Picker*, 1982), which was first broadcast on Austrian television on 9 April 1965 with Helmut Qualtinger playing the lead role, condemns Austrian complicity with the Nazi regime, the lingering effects of fascist attitudes, and the treatment of its Jewish and minority citizens. In his article analyzing Hochwälder's *Der Befehl* (1967/68, *Orders*, 1998), another play that directly confronts Austria's tainted past, TODD HANLIN compares the popular BBC version of this play to a little known version written for "'local' consumption" at Vienna's *Burgtheater*. The dramatist, known for his unambiguous presentation of moral themes, problematizes the issues facing his characters in the *Burgtheater* version, thereby burdening his specifically Austrian audience with questions of responsibility and culpability: What role can and should the ordinary person play when confronted with historical events as inhumane as those that occurred during the Third Reich?

Performance and Provocation

Despite widespread ignorance of and aversion to new art forms during the conservative restoration period of the 1950s and early 1960s, Austria's avant-garde and experimental art flourished. Young artists in two literary organizations in particular contributed to an aesthetic revolution – the *Wiener Gruppe* and *Forum Stadtpark*. The former included Friedrich Achleitner, H. C. Artmann, Konrad Bayer, Gerhard Rühm, and Oswald Wiener and lasted from about

1951/52 until the death of Konrad Bayer in 1964; the latter group was founded in Graz in 1958 and continues to this day.[17] Both avant-garde movements internationalized the form and content of their literature as a reaction against the traditional anti-modern sentiments that had destroyed the movement of the *Moderne* during the fascist years and that continued to persist after the war. Their artistically uncompromising work, their provocative and even absurd texts were soon noticed far beyond Austria's borders, while at home they met mainly with hostile rejection. The young artists of these alternative literary movements saw themselves as opposition to the prevailing conservative cultural trends and politics.[18] To counter the domination of *Heimat*-Austrianism, they began to stage readings as events or actions. The *Wiener Gruppe*'s concept of performance reached its peak in 1958/59 with the *Literarisches Cabaret*, where most of Konrad Bayer's mini-dramas were performed. In Graz, Alfred Kolleritsch, Barbara Frischmuth, Wolfgang Bauer, Gunter Falk, Hans Nurser, and Peter Handke staged their experimental readings as so-called *Dunkelkammer* events or happenings at the *Forum Stadtpark* between 1962 and 1965; and they were frequently joined by members of the Viennese literary avant-garde and *Wiener Gruppe* – Ernst Jandl in 1962, Friederike Mayröcker in 1964, Oswald Wiener and Achleitner in 1965.

One of these events, based on their manifesto *Happy Art & Attitude*, was performed by Bauer and Falk amidst pictures of icons of the new pop-culture and American comics – as well as free beer – at the university in Graz in 1965. *Happy Art & Attitude* presented "with mock-seriousness an ironic blending of banal and trivial elements with the earnestness of high art ... The seriousness of this unserious statement lay in the assertion of the human need to (re)establish art as a form of creative play."[19] The *Sprachspiel*-concept, i.e., the idea of the "language game" cultivated by the *Wiener Gruppe*, also exists as a fundamental structural element in Handke's early plays. *Publikumsbeschimpfung* (*Offending the Audience*, 1971), first staged under the direction of Claus Peymann at the *Theater am Turm* in Frankfurt as part of "Experimenta 1" in June 1966, has been recognized as a turning point in German-language theater.[20] By reversing the roles of reality and of style, understood as the linguistic realization of the mode of perception, and by reversing the role of actor and spectator, Handke undermined the conventional expectations of his audience. He hoped that the usual audience would become a different audience, one that would be "alert, keen of hearing, sharp-eyed, not only as theatergoers."[21]

Performance as provocation, i.e., the staging of literature as a shock-inducing happening, had been an essential feature of the work of the historical avant-garde; it now resurfaced in the events, performances, and happenings of the *Wiener Gruppe* and Graz avant-gardists. Another group called the Vienna Actionists[22] and including Otto Mühl, Günter Brus, and Hermann Nitsch,[23] radicalized this shock effect even further with their sado-erotic performances. Shock was valued as a means to renew the political dimension on stage, a critical thrust that competed with traditional theater concepts supported by conservative cultural politics, the bourgeois media, and the masses. The gap between the postwar avant-garde movements and the general public was a gap of political dimension, for experimental as well as socio-critical literatures challenged Austria's official self-projection as the "island of the blessed" located "in the heart" of Europe.

The concept of performance became absorbed by the "proliferation of large-scale counter-cultural events culminating in the student uprisings in 1968."[24] At the beginning of the 1970s, the socialist government under Bruno Kreisky (from 1970 until 1983) made possible a cultural modernization marked by openness towards contemporary art which brought forth a boom of free-theater projects with new forms of performance. The occupation of the St. Marx Arena by artists, intellectuals, and young people who hoped "to create an autonomous and self-administered center for culture and communication" marked the climax of this cultural explosion in 1976.[25]

Since 1970: The Politicization of Drama

By 1970, a radical redirection of literary dynamics had been achieved by the Austrian avant-garde. This new understanding of literature can be broadly characterized by several related developments. First, literature is emancipated from its obligation to tell a story. Language becomes its own subject; the sentence itself becomes the object of uncompromising scrutiny. Second, literature assumes a fundamental position of negativity. For example, the traditional folk play that is positively construed becomes its opposite, namely the socio-critical folk play that depicts the menacing aspects of the notion of *Heimat*. And finally, society and language become analogous, which means that social criticism can only occur through criticism of language.[26]

During the past three decades, playwrights such as Thomas Bernhard, Peter Handke, Elfriede Jelinek, Peter Turrini, and Felix Mitterer have staged their radically socio-critical and intellectually challenging plays. Their sophisticated aesthetics are combined with complex critical stances on public issues such as the notion of *Heimat*, collective memory, and cultural identity. In particular, Bernhard, Handke, and Jelinek "articulate a unique model of dissent, combining avant-garde and mainstream techniques of writing that cut across different modes of literary discourse and reception. Their literature exposes and attacks conventions of pre-arranged consensus and harmonization that block the ongoing negotiations necessary for the development of multicultural awareness."[27]

As outlined in the article by JENNIFER E. MICHAELS, one of the most pressing public issues that needed to be confronted was (and remains) Austrian culpability for Nazi atrocities. Beginning in the sixties with plays by Hochwälder and continuing throughout the next three decades with dramas by Turrini, Bernhard, Jelinek, and Felix Mitterer, Michaels traces voices of protest against the official stance of silence and proclaimed status as victim rather than perpetrator. In doing so, she refutes the commonly held perception that Austrian authors, in contrast to their West German colleagues, did nothing to promote public debate about the Nazi past and its lingering effects in the present.

Thomas Bernhard (1932-1989)

Thomas Bernhard wrote eighteen plays and a number of short dramas between 1967 and 1989, and had two unfinished plays on his desk when he died.[28] It has been said that Bernhard's theater texts actually constitute one large drama with recurring themes and self-quotations. Bernhard's dramas decry the deplorable condition of the world at the end of the twentieth century by utilizing contemporary Germany and Austria as models: "the small world-stage where the rehearsals of the large one take place."[29] Bernhard did not condemn Austria or the Austrians outright, but rather felt that the evils of the world were especially discernible in this country. For him, Austria's Second Republic was a hopeless venture, and this negative attitude is reflected in all of his writings.

Such negativity is the topic of ROXANA NUBERT'S article titled "Fascination and Provocation in the Works of Thomas Bernhard." Nubert describes the world constructed in Bernhard's dramas as being existentially threatened, obsessed with death, and fearful of destruction while nonetheless and inexorably leading to annihilation. She links her discussion of darkness as a thematic constant to a poetics of fragmentation, and notes that it is the very incomplete and artificial nature of Bernhard's dramatic language that provokes both fascination and repulsion in the audience. In a second article on Bernhard, RACHEL FREUDENBURG analyzes the apparent misogyny of Bernhard's dramas within the context of performance. The depiction of male and female roles is disgustingly negative and misogynistic, but through the self-consciousness of those playing the roles, i.e., through the performers' awareness of their performance, emerge opportunities for possible reinterpretations of the traditionally gendered script.

Bernhard relished hyperbole and confrontation and seemed to thrive on the controversy he generated.[30] His plays are "immediate and direct, sensational and spontaneous, tied to time, place, and even to particular actors";[31] they frequently have a connection to real life that increases their impact all the more and almost inevitably made them into media events. Even before the 1970 premiere of his first play *Ein Fest für Boris* (*A Party for Boris*, 1990), the author had a reputation for "cantankerous behavior" and outrageous satire.[32]

The premiere of Bernhard's last play *Heldenplatz* in November 1988 generated one of the most memorable scandals in Austrian theater history. It was staged in the *Burgtheater*, located only a stone's throw away from the actual Heldenplatz where Hitler gave his *Anschluß*-speech on 15 March 1938, and it grinds salt into the open wound of Austrian anti-Semitism. The production precipitated demonstrations and counter-demonstrations in the streets, heated exchanges in the media, and even death threats against Bernhard and *Burgtheater* director, Claus Peymann. Politicians of the conservative People's Party and the rightist Freedom Party fulminated against Bernhard's "anti-Austrian" play and against the "waste" of public funds on his works. President Waldheim, his own history a matter of controversy, denounced the play as "a vulgar insult to the Austrian people."

Bernhard's plays have been performed on nationally and internationally acclaimed stages in Austria and Germany. As early as 1972, *Der Ignorant und der Wahnsinnige* (The Ignoramus and the Madman) premiered at the Salzburg Festival. Three more plays were commissioned to be performed at the Salzburg Festival: *Am Ziel* (The Goal Attained) in 1981, *Der Theatermacher* (*Histrionics*, 1990) in 1984, and *Ritter, Dene, Voss* (*Ritter, Dene, Voss*, 1990) in 1986. Bernhard enjoyed a deep friendship and fruitful cooperation with Claus Peymann, who had premiered several of his plays in German theaters before he became director of the *Burgtheater* in 1986.

Bernhard skillfully used the media to promote his relentless cultural critique and in his literature exposed the politics of exclusion and the claim to a heterogeneous society as fascist. His commitment to "Austria's public sphere as its uncomfortable critical presence ... made him a powerful voice of constructive cultural dissent."³³

Peter Handke (1942-)

Whereas the degree of political clarity and engagement continuously intensified in Bernhard's work, the same cannot be said for Peter Handke's texts. While Bernhard rejected the telling of stories (like many others whose literature is influenced by the avant-garde), he nevertheless understood his protagonists as historically determined individuals. Handke, on the other hand, not only rejects the notion of the individual as a historical being, he rejects history itself as a classification system, as a system of patterns, standards, and canons used to institute order. He believes in the equation: "history = stories: history."³⁴ Handke's flight from history is a flight into an aesthetics of individuality and inward-looking that has been dubbed "new subjectivity." Yet, the author's subjectivity is not without political credibility. It is neither anti-realistic nor apolitical. Rather, he strives through his language to promote a mode of individual perception that can be considered political in that it challenges the predetermined images and discourse imposed by ideology:

> Handke wishes ... to engage language critically and aesthetically by exploring both its layers of sedimentation and its potential for liberating narratives. Individual perception ... is a quality through which Handke seeks to break beyond the predictability of conventional social discourse and its ideological perspectives.³⁵

To this day, Handke has written more prose than dramatic texts. He gained an international reputation for controversy early on when he contradicted the traditional literary establishment at a meeting of the Group 47 in Princeton in 1966. His play *Kaspar* premiered in 1968 in the *Theater am Turm* in Frankfurt and *Der Ritt über den Bodensee* in 1971 in Berlin *(The Ride across Lake Constance*, 1973). Both plays received much attention. Some of Handke's early success in the theater must be credited to director Peymann who, as was the case with Bernhard, understood and valued his literary program.[36]

In the 1990s, Peymann staged four Handke plays at the Burgtheater: *Das Spiel vom Fragen, oder, Die Reise zum sonoren Land (Voyage to the Sonorous Land, or, The Art of Asking,* 1996), *Die Stunde da wir nichts voneinander wußten (The Hour We Knew Nothing of Each Other,* 1996), *Zurüstungen für die Unsterblichkeit. Ein Königsdrama* (Preparations for Immortality: A Royal Drama), and *Die Fahrt im Einbaum, oder, Das Stück zum Film vom Krieg* (The Trip with the Outrigger or the Play for the Film about the War). These four plays are the topic of BERNHARD DOPPLER'S article, "The Return of the Kings," which focuses in particular on issues of aesthetic realization and political implications. Common to all four pieces is a distinctly non-dramatic tendency that renders staging difficult and reception problematic; underlying each is the author's belief in art as occupying a realm separate from the debates of mass culture. It is perhaps paradoxical that, for Handke, art's potential for opposition, the political engagement of literature so to speak, lies in this very separation, for in its difference it represents an alternative.

Peter Turrini (1944-)

Peter Turrini also writes relentlessly against an idealized and monolithic cultural heritage and stages his concerns about the lingering effects of fascist ideology. He makes use of the aesthetics of the critical folk play, which means that he frequently sets his plays in the milieu of the petite bourgeoisie or among minorities situated at the fringes of society. Using dialect as opposed to standard German, and combining tragicomical and farcical elements with mechanisms of violence, he depicts the family and its conflicts. His plays thus attempt to enlighten the audience about how brutality in the private sphere is a reflection of the institutionalized inhumanity in the public sphere of today's Austria. This is the topic of GERD SCHNEIDER'S essay titled "Social and Human Issues in Peter Turrini's Work," which investigates the gap between projected societal images on the one hand and lived reality on the other. As Schneider notes, Turrini's critical folk plays are highly political and are intended to contribute to political consciousness-raising. He uses the stage to challenge and question, perhaps even to change, a reality that we have created but no longer want to see.

Like Bernhard, Handke, and Jelinek, Turrini aims at stirring emotions and shattering attitudes of complacency:

> At the heart of our writing was and remains [the failed beginnings of Austria's Second Republic], and it affects everything else. It is a lifelong, incurable obsession: We live in this country but would like to create a different one – on paper, with composure and with agitation, with petitions and with protests, in a humble and a noisy manner, pleading and protesting.[37]

The dramatist pushes shock strategies of brutality, indecency, and filth to undermine the audience's expectations: "I want to reduce the discrepancy between reality and art in my play. And if the shock-level is high enough it will convince the audience."[38] Nevertheless, it is not the shock itself that is of interest but rather the stimulation of thought processes by means of shock. While Turrini initially welcomed scandal, his goal was never transgression alone: "Rather, the clue to all of Turrini's work ... is the author's obsession with the power of images ... By ceaselessly contemplating the theater's intervention in our visual culture, Turrini these days emerges not only as dramatist, but also as a cultural critic, who charts our very modes of public discourse."[39]

Peter Turrini was one of the first of the new generation of authors and playwrights to have his work performed at the *Volkstheater* in Vienna, namely *Rozznjagd* in 1971 (*Shooting Rats*, 1996) and *Sauschlachten* in 1972 (*Pig Slaughter*, 1993). Despite his initial success on stage, Turrini soon realized that he had to change his strategy in order to reach a larger audience. In the early 1970s, only about five percent of the Austrian population went regularly to the theater, and the vast majority who held *Burgtheater* subscriptions were over fifty years old.[40] Hence, Turrini began to write for television and demanded new media policies that would contribute to the emancipation of the individual and the humanization of society as a whole.[41] With his two TV series *Alpensaga* (1976-1980, Alpine Saga) – co-written with Wilhelm Pevny – and *Arbeitersaga* (1984-1990, Workers' Saga), Turrini revolutionized the *Heimatfilm* genre.

However, Turrini's frustration about his lack of control in television led him to return to the stage with *Josef und Maria* (*Joseph and Mary*, 1992), which opened in November 1980 at the *steirischer herbst* festival. Since then, he has become one of the most widely performed dramatists in Austria. During the Peymann years, three of his plays premiered at the *Burgtheater*. *Tod und Teufel* (Death and the Devil) in November 1990, *Alpenglühen* in March 1993 (*Alpine Glow*, 1994), and *Die Schlacht um Wien* in May 1995 (*Siege of Vienna*, 1996). In addition, the *Akademietheater* has staged many Turrini performances, including both *Endlich Schluß* (*Enough*, 2000) and *Die Liebe in Madagaskar* (Love in Madagascar) in 1997.

Whereas Turrini's early plays focus on individual case studies of societal oppression, beginning with *Alpine Glow* we detect a new direction. Although Turrini's critical thrust remains constant, the dramatist begins to thematize theater itself, focusing on the ever changing masks of society and the individual and asking where reality ends and appearances begin. At the same time, his characters gain a psychological profile that allows greater identification. According to Gerhard Fuchs's assessment of Turrini's literary development, the playwright seems to have embraced "a theater of emotion that allows for stronger self-identification." He explains further that "the playful relativism of identity and reality awareness, as well as the increased suspicion of political answers in the search for salvation," are new.[42]

In his most recent works, Turrini experiments with various dramatic genres. He was commissioned to write the "dance play" *Kasino* for the *Burgtheater*, which premiered on 22 January 2000, produced by Leonard Prinsloo. *Kasino* is a panoramic revue of the previous century of Austrian history, a "dance" leading to death on both the individual and state level. Turrini's latest piece, *Ich liebe dieses Land* (2000, I Love This Country), a comedy about racism and xenophobia, played at the *Berliner Ensemble* under Peymann in February 2001.

Two Excursions
The Peymann Years at the *Burgtheater*

Claus Peymann directed the *Burgtheater* from 1986 until June 1999. His tenure was a tumultuous one filled with conflict with the ensemble and scandals surrounding numerous staging and programming decisions. When Peymann first arrived in Vienna, he intended to inscribe the following words on the *Burgtheater* flag: "To truth, beauty, and rectitude." The inscription proposed by Bernhard instead is an ironic and exaggerated, but in some ways perhaps more accurate reflection of theater reality and reaction during the Peymann years: "To murder and death."

Peymann brought life and art into the "musty atmosphere"[43] of the *Burgtheater*. He was dedicated to staging contemporary Austrian dramatists, including not only Bernhard, but also Handke, Jelinek, and Turrini. In doing so, he transformed Austria's national theater, once more, into a site of contemporary national relevance and international acclaim. Peymann once said in an interview: "I unceasingly allow myself to dream that life is a fairy tale where good is still good and bad is bad. I allow myself this dream, which means also that I will safeguard it if necessary with all brutality and the greatest of finesse."[44]

Many of the articles in this volume mention the influence of Peymann on postwar Austrian drama, especially during his tenure at the *Burgtheater*. The article by KIRSTEN KRICK-AIGNER focuses in particular on the director, discussing Peymann's production titled *Ingeborg Bachmann. Wer?* (Ingeborg Bachmann. Who?). Krick-Aigner appreciates the service done by Peymann in making the works of Bachmann accessible to a broader audience, but notes that the performance omits much of the social and political criticism inherent to her work, thus presenting a depoliticized picture of the author. This is surprising considering Peymann's reputation and his stated intent to provoke and enlighten by means of theater.

Excursion to the Provinces: Felix Mitterer (1948-)

After the performance of his first play *Kein Platz für Idioten* (No Place for Idiots), which opened at the *Tiroler Volksbühne Blaas* in 1977, Mitterer stated: "I am really in doubt about the legitimacy of theater. However, in the provincial villages it is still important and useful."[45] Mitterer's plays are recognized as significant contributions to contemporary Austrian theater. They run not only in small provincial theaters, but are also performed on prestigious stages in towns and cities across Austria, Germany, and beyond. Moreover, Mitterer has created a number of successful television series that have earned him a reputation outside Austria's borders. In 1990, the Elysium Theater Company in the East Village in New York City staged two Mitterer plays, *Verbrecherin (Jailbird)* and *Man versteht nichts (Don't Understand a Thing)*.

Mitterer's dramas are set in the contemporary rural Tirolean landscape with all its customs, rituals, values, and folklore. He draws inspiration from the medieval passion play and the burlesque comedy of the *Bauernschwank*, and in particular from the theatrical traditions of the Viennese folk play. He weaves these different theatrical strands together to criticize the marketing of Austria's alpine regions as a picturesque *Heimat*-idyll to stimulate the tourist industry. His plays depict "Tirolism" – the tourists' desire to rest and relax in the villages of the Alps and the locals' willingness to cater to their every whim – as a deep social and moral morass for the people and their environment. Moreover, Mitterer's plays present a strong critique against the church and its moral apostles and against the powerful traditions of social and economic hierarchies that separate the population into rich and poor, into those who enjoy entitlement and those who do not.

Women comprise one group that has long been disadvantaged and suppressed by the structures of Church and State, and, as GERLINDE ULM SANFORD shows in her article about Mitterer's *Krach im Hause Gott* (1994, Discord in the House of God), Mitterer has written a number of dramas that foreground the lack of progress in the fight for women's rights and equality. Ulm Sanford traces the influence of feminist theologian Christa Mulack upon this recent play by Mitterer, showing how the playwright utilizes humor to voice what his audience may not want to hear, namely that patriarchal church hierarchies have brought about a reality that contradicts many Christian values.

DAGMAR LORENZ'S article compares dramas by Veza Canetti and Felix Mitterer, both of which thematize gender relations. Canetti's *Der Oger* (*The Ogre*) was written after World War I, Mitterer's *Die Wilde Frau* (The Wild Woman) after World War II; however, both depict male criminality and the brutal abuse of a woman in a male-dominated sphere. The comparison of dramatic works written during the First as opposed to the Second Austrian Republic reveals the radicalization of the gender discourse over time, the escalation of violence and oppression as portrayed in the later work.

Mitterer is a passionate advocate of the outsider and the disenfranchised. His plays depict the lingering effects of fascism in everyday Austria, especially where the private and the public spheres intersect. They must be added to the large corpus of "critical dramatizations of [rural] Austria's public sphere that expose society's dubious expressions of cultural narcissism, amnesia, and revisionism."[46]

Women and the Theater

According to Eva Brenner, women are not taken seriously by a male-dominated theater establishment:

> In the theater we are dealing with questions of representation. European theater is an art form in

which the bourgeoisie celebrates itself. Woman is traditionally excluded from this discourse. She might be allowed to work away in the seclusion of her home, to labor over her prose or poetry, but this retains a completely private character. She is not trusted to have any impact on public institutions, on public life. Accordingly, very few women have succeeded in the theater professions.[47]

Although there are exceptions to the above comment, most notably Elfriede Jelinek and Marlene Streeruwitz, they are recent and isolated. Thus the ProjektTheater Studio, founded as the new center for experimental theater and performance in May of 1998, is a welcome addition to Austria's theater scene. It grew out of Projekt Theater/Vienna-New York which was formed by Eva Brenner in 1991 to produce performances primarily based on texts by women writers on both continents, and Brenner serves the ProjektTheater Studio as its artistic director. The performance schedule for the next three years includes Elisabeth Reichart's *Aphrodites letztes Erscheinen* (Aphrodite's Final Appearance), Elfriede Jelinek's *Der Tod und das Mädchen* (Death and the Girl), Ingram Hartinger's *Texte zum Überleben* (Survival Texts), and Margit Hahn's *Das Theater mit der Liebe* (Love Theater).

Elisabeth Reichart has ventured increasingly into the world of theater after having made a name for herself through her prose works. In her article in this volume, LAURA OVENDEN analyzes the writer's first play, the dramatic monologue *Sakkorausch* (1984, *Foreign* 2000), exploring the ways in which female subjectivity is expressed in terms of body, voice, and text, and then considering the realization of the concept on stage.

Elfriede Jelinek (1946-)

Elfriede Jelinek has become one of those few women who does in fact have an impact on public institutions, who has indeed attained success on stage. Her theater debut occurred at the Graz

Schauspielhaus in 1979 with *Was geschah, nachdem Nora ihren Mann verlassen hatte, oder, Stützen der Gesellschaften* (*What Happened after Nora Left Her Husband or Pillars of Society*, 1994). The plays that followed – *Clara S.* in 1982, *Burgtheater* in 1985, and *Krankheit oder Moderne Frauen* in 1987 (Malady or Modern Women) – all premiered in Bonn, but also enjoyed successful performances in numerous Austrian theaters. Her sixth play, *Totenauberg* (*Death/Valley/Summit*, 1996) returned to Austria to celebrate its premiere with much success at the *Akademietheater* in Vienna during the 1991/92 season. Jelinek's literature is recognized as one of the most significant contributions to the contemporary literary scene in the German-speaking world. Her uncompromising texts – drama and prose – have brought her attention comparable in many ways to that provoked by Bernhard and his work. She too is often the center of scandals, and she too makes skillful use of the media to promote her socio-cultural critique.

Jelinek's relentless social and cultural iconoclasm is located within the language of postmodern society. Her texts are composed of the violent and corrupt language of the culture at large; they "pierce the ear like the screech of the cutting stone against glass"[48] and do not allow for mimetic interpretation. Moreover, as Matthias Konzett explains in a recent study, Jelinek "converts social icons into irreversible simulacra ... which is not only the site for unmasking post-industrial society and its radical instrumentalization of human practices; it is also a site of mourning for Europe's wholesale cultural disembodiment that culminated in the Shoah." Though Jelinek is generally not perceived as a Jewish writer per se, she "insists that her writing is profoundly Jewish in a critical and historical sense."[49]

Thus Jelinek's critical memory is directed against Austria's persistent cultural amnesia and entrenched cultural fascism. The illusion of *Heimat* and belonging, of authenticity and health is marketed as a commodity at the expense of minorities and the disenfranchised. In *Death/Valley/Summit* the author unmasks fascism as an everyday phenomenon in the rhetoric of consumerism, emphasizing the deceptive adaptability of fascism. In *Wolken.Heim*

(Cloud.Cuckoo.Land), which premiered in Hamburg in 1993, Jelinek penetrates the surface of the German cultural heritage to expose its nationalistic origins. Constructed as a philosophic-agitational debate, the drama traces the influence of the philosophy and literature of the eighteenth and nineteenth centuries on the idea of nationalism, the expansion of nationalist thought among academic youth through the writings of Fichte, and finally the *Weltgeist* ideology as purported by Hegel and then either supported or contradicted by his successors.[50]

Though Jelinek has threatened repeatedly to stop writing dramas – primarily as a response to the unduly polemic reception of her work – she continues to do so and her plays continue to be staged with success. *Raststätte oder Sie machens alle* (Truck Stop or Everyone's Doing It) with its *cosi fan tutte*-motif, premiered in 1994 at the *Akademietheater* with Peymann directing. *Ein Sportstück* (A SportsPlay), a study of fascistic and bellicose structures underlying the sports mentality, was the first of Jelinek's dramas to premiere on the grand stage of the *Burgtheater* in 1998 under the direction of Einar Schleef. The premiere was an enormous success, prompting standing ovations of nearly an hour. However, as LINDA C. DEMERITT points out in her essay titled "Staging Superficiality," Schleef's realization of the text's intended shallowness results in a questionable superficiality that fosters non-reflective audience identification. The hypnotic effect of the performance stands in direct opposition to the provocation of self-consciousness and critical awareness that is fundamental to Jelinek's dramatic concept in general.

Jelinek's play *Stecken, Stab und Stangl* (Stick, Staff, and Pole), based on the murder of four Romany gypsies in the east-Austrian town of Oberwart, deals with the problem of xenophobia as perpetrated in deed and through pulp journalism. It premiered in 1996 in Hamburg and was successfully staged in Vienna by George Tabori at the *Wiener Kasino am Schwarzenbergplatz* in 1997. Jelinek's mini-drama about Robert Walser as *leitfigur* of her own poetics titled *er nicht als er* (he not as he) constituted the center of the literary program at the Salzburg Festival in 1998.

During the past two years, two more plays were staged, but not in Austria. As a protest against inclusion of the right-wing Freedom Party in the new governing coalition, Jelinek has forbidden the performance of her dramas in Austria. The monologue *Das Lebewohl* (The Good-Bye) premiered at the *Berliner Ensemble* to rave reviews in December 2000 under the direction of Ulrike Ottinger. It is a text composed of Aeschylus's *Oresteia* and the farewell speech by Jörg Haider, pivotal figure in the Freedom Party, upon his decision to step down from the leadership of the national party. Jelinek's latest play, *Macht Nichts* (Never Mind) was also performed outside Austria's borders, this time at the *Schauspielhaus* in Zurich under the direction of Jossi Wieler on 11 April 2001. This play, subtitled "A little trilogy of death," is about power. In it Jelinek remains true to her thematic preoccupation with the "dead" and the "undead" that populate German and Austrian history, or in other words, with the cultural icons from the past that still have power over our present.

The Nineties: New Voices

According to JUTTA LANDA in her article on Austrian theater in the nineties, the distinguishing mark of recent drama – for all its variety and diversity – is the privileging of speech over figures, i.e., the reduction of dramatic characters to figures of speech, to mere speech machines. Landa explores the utilization of language in dramas produced on the first-rank Austrian stages during the past decade and finds that in works by Jelinek, Handke, Turrini, and newcomer Werner Schwab, language pushes itself to the foreground, obscuring the speaker behind it with force and sometimes violence.

Werner Schwab (1958-1994)

In only four years, Werner Schwab wrote over fifteen major plays that premiered either during his lifetime or shortly after his death of alcohol poisoning on New Year's Eve 1993/94. When, in 1990, the radicalism of his artistic expression was recognized as that of a great talent, Schwab was made, almost overnight, into the poet-genius of the German-speaking theater. In return, he repaid his admirers with an enormous output ("Project Schwab"). In 1991, the journal *Theater heute* gave him the Young Dramatist of the Year Award. In 1992, he received the prestigious Mülheim Award for Drama and was hailed as the "favorite 'brutalo' of the German feuilleton" and "the virtuoso of repugnance."[51]

Schwab's meteoric rise to international acclaim began with the remarkable premiere in 1991 of *Volksvernichtung oder Meine Leber ist sinnlos* (*People-Annihilation or My Liver Is Senseless*, 1995) at the Kammerspiele in Munich, directed by Christian Stückl. That opening was preceded in February 1990 by the Vienna premiere of *Die Präsidentinnen* (*First Ladies*, 1999), and it is this play that has become his most frequently performed one. Even after his death, his fame continued. During the 1999/2000 season the Vienna *Schauspielhaus* performance schedule was organized by themes, the first dedicated to Schwab's infamous saying that "Art is Dung" ("Kunst ist Notdurft") and opening with *Der Himmel mein Lieb meine sterbende Beute* (Heaven My Love My Dying Loot) on 11 September 1999. Schwab's collected works are published under the titles *Fäkaliendramen* (1991, Fecal Dramas) and *Königskomödien* (1992, Royal Comedies).

Schwab's plays revolve around themes of incest and child abuse, murder and manslaughter, rape and cannibalism. He stages the banality of evil and transposes the ugliness and vulgarity from the abyss of human existence into provocative pieces of art. Schwab's plays remind us of the shock-therapy performances of the Graz avant-garde and the Vienna Actionists. Though indebted to the critical folk play, these dramas also differ from most folk plays in that they refuse to impart a clear socio-critical message. The problem of interpretation is addressed in the title of BEATE HOCHHOLDINGER-REITERER'S article: "Nonsense That Defies Reason or Disguised Morality?" What meaning is to be gleaned from a theater that, in Schwab's own words, is reduced to a heap of scrap metal, a kind of junkyard, albeit an exalted one? Schwab's stage foregrounds not plot or character development, but language.

His scatological and sadistic rhetoric is not attached to a real person, but rather that person is "dragged about" by the rhetoric – like cans tied to the tail of a dog, as Schwab himself has stated. The protagonists do not engage in dialogue, but rather utter escalating verbal attacks consisting of slang and idiomatic expressions, conglomerates of neologisms, and linguistic paradoxes, a body of language so intense that it assumes its own corporeality.[52]

Today, Schwab's work is recognized far beyond Austria's borders. The prestigious Ambassador Theatre in London opened its season in June 1999 with the English premiere of *First Ladies*, and in Paris, Stanislas Nordey directed that same play in addition to three others at the Théâtre Gérard Philipe. Schwab's oeuvre has been translated into several different languages, including Chinese, and scholarly studies devoted exclusively to his work are appearing. Plays continue to be released posthumously, such as *Tierschädel* (Animal Skull) in October 1999.

Marlene Streeruwitz (1950-)

Like Schwab, Marlene Streeruwitz gained national and international recognition for her creative and provocative texts within a short period of time. She was recognized by the journal *Theater heute* in 1992 for her dramatic achievements through conferral of the Young Dramatist of the Year Award. Her breakthrough came with *Waikiki Beach.* in Cologne in 1992, which was followed by *Sloane Square.*, also in 1992, and *Ocean Drive.* and *Elysian Park.* in 1993. Next to Jelinek, Streeruwitz is seen as the most creative and provocative woman playwright for the German-speaking theater.[53]

Streeruwitz has a critical relationship to contemporary theater – to the institution as well as to the dramatic genre – for she sees it as a preserve of patriarchal thought. Her works are, she states, a challenge to the perspective of the traditional male order: "The object of the classic drama was death. The object of the modern drama was dying. I deal with life."[54] The images of "life" that the playwright presents on stage do not intend to reproduce or imitate reality, but rather to be their own reality, and in this way

Streeruwitz's notion of theater is similar to the non-realistic and non-dramatic theater of Jelinek: "We can observe our Now. Even in the theater. Yet, in order to become drama, it must be completely detached from realism. Form has to change time into presence. Why imitate actions if the drama itself can be action."[55]

In her article on Streeruwitz titled "Corpses and Gendered Bodies," HELGA W. KRAFT investigates the playwright's contribution to a new theater, stating that it can be found in her emphasis on the body. This is the "life" that replaces "death" in Streeruwitz's dramas as they strive to move away from the concept of the male-centered enlightenment subject to define and emphasize identity as corporal existence, materiality, the senses. However, the old system persists; the body continues to be determined and tortured by societal forces, leaving behind a stage strewn with corpses.

The titles of Streeruwitz's plays, which always end with a period as punctuation mark, suggest a holiday atmosphere at exotic locations. However, the protagonists find themselves instead in a decrepit building slated for demolition, a subway station, a men's public toilet, or a dead-end street. This is reality, and it stands in direct contrast to the sentimental dreams of romance and happiness as portrayed in movies and television, illusions which lie beyond the border of reality, on the other side of the period.[56] Streeruwitz's plays are located at the crossroads of today's media-induced multi-reality. The ambivalence between reality and artificiality is ever present in the broken speech patterns of her protagonists, who utter short sentence fragments interrupted by a sudden pause, staccato-like.

Streeruwitz, borrowing from the theater of cruelty and the critical folk play,[57] stages chaos and destruction in the attempt to shatter audience expectations. As seen in WILLY RIEMER'S article titled "Marlene Streeruwitz's Fractal Mise-en-Scène," which investigates *Ocean Drive.* within the context of chaos theory, the formal fragmentation of her theater prevents the closure of language and identity. It prevents the telling of grand narratives, and in doing so

Introduction 27

perhaps can avoid the dominance and exclusionary control inherent in paradigms claiming to be universal and final.

Her two latest plays, *Sapporo.*, a play against the manipulative banality of television realism, and *Boccaleone.*, which deals with the economic exploitation of asylum seekers, premiered at the *steirischer herbst* festival in the fall of 2000 and the Linz *Landestheater* in June 2001 respectively. Her text *The 1st 40 Years I Kept Looking for My God* was staged as part of the "Phantom: Love" cycle at the Projekt-Theater Studio under the direction of the American dancer and choreographer Mary Overlie.

Concluding Remarks

Text and performance – the writing of drama as well as its production – have enriched Austria's cultural life for centuries. During the past fifty years, Austrian theater has made significant contributions to the public discourse on issues of cultural and national identity. In particular, playwrights have felt a responsibility to address the cultural amnesia and historical revisionism that has characterized Austria's Second Republic. With varying degrees of intensity and on diverse aesthetic platforms, they engaged in the process of raising consciousness – and continue to do so today.

Notes

1. W.E. Yates, *Theatre in Vienna. A Critical History, 1776-1995* (Cambridge: Cambridge UP, 1996) 229.

2. Brigitte Bailer, "They Were All Victims," *Austrian Historical Memory and Identity*, ed. Günter Bischof and Anton Pelinka (New Brunswick, NJ: transaction publishers, 1997) 105-06.

3. Hugo Huppert, "'Der Bockerer': Uraufführung im Skala-Theater," *Dramaturgie der Demokratie. Theaterkonzeptionen des österreichischen Exils*, ed. Peter Roessler and Konstantin Kaiser (Vienna: Prometh, 1989) 145-47.

4. Evelyn Deutsch-Schreiner, "Bühnentradition und modernes Volksstück," *Modern Austrian Literature* 28.1 (1995): 83.

5. Hilde Haider-Pregler, "'Das Burgtheater ist eine Idee...' Die Jahre 1945 bis 1955 – eine Zwischenzeit des österreichischen Staatstheaters?" *Zeit der Befreiung. Wiener Theater nach 1945*, ed. Hilde Haider-Pregler and Peter Roessler (Vienna: Picus Verlag, 1998) 105.

6. Evelyn Deutsch-Schreiner 77-78.

7. Horst Jarka, "Der Kulturkampf auf den Bühnen Wiens vor 1939 und nach 1945," *Modern Austrian Literature* 32.2 (1999): 143.

8. Quoted in Wendelin Schmidt-Dengler, "Vorwort," *Literatur über Literatur. Eine österreichische Anthologie*, ed. Petra Nachbaur and Sigurd Paul Scheichl (Graz: Styria, 1995) 11.

9. Yates 231.

10. Frank Finlay and Ralf Jeutter, *Centre Stage: Contemporary Drama in Austria* (Amsterdam: Rodopi, 1999) 2-3.

11. Klemens Gruber and Rainer M. Köpple, "The Theater System of Austria," *Theatre Worlds in Motion; Structures, Politics and Developments in the Countries of Western Europe*, ed. Hans van Maanen and Steve E. Wilmer (Amsterdam: Rodopi, 1998) 41.

12. See Michael P. Steinberg, *The Meaning of the Salzburg Festival: Austria as Theater and Ideology, 1890-1938* (Ithaca: Cornell UP, 1990).

13. Margarete Lamb-Faffelberger, "Beyond *The Sound of Music*: The Quest for Cultural Identity in Modern Austria," *German Quarterly*, forthcoming publication, Spring 2003.

14. See Gertraud Steiner, *Die Heimat-Macher. Kino in Österreich 1946-1966* (Vienna: Verlag für Gesellschaftskritik, 1987).

15. See Herbert Herzmann, *Tradition und Subversion. Das Volksstück und das epische Theater* (Tübingen: Stauffenburg, 1997).

16. Lydia Katharina Kegler, "Defining the *Volksstück*," *Modern Austrian Literature* 26.3-4 (1993): 11.

17. Dagmar-Sonja Winkler, "Ideologische Ziele der 'Wiener Gruppe' und ihre Bedeutung für die Gegenwartsliteratur," *Zeitschrift für Germanistik* 1.3 (1991): 588-99.

18. Alfred Kolleritsch, "Marginalie," *manuscripte* 110 (1990): 4. "In Austria, one always has to fight for literature."
19. Simon Ryan, "Performance and Provocation in Graz," *Theatre and Performance in Austria*, ed. Ritchie Robertson and Edward Timms (Edinburgh: Edinburgh UP, 1993) 110.
20. Ryan 111.
21. Peter Handke, "Zur Publikumsbeschimpfung," *Stücke 1* (Frankfurt/M.: Suhrkamp, 1972) 203.
22. Rüdiger Engerth, "Der Wiener Aktionismus," *Protokolle* 1 (Vienna: Jugend & Volk, 1970).
23. Nitsch continues to arouse fierce public protest with the staging of his *Orgy-Mystery-Theater* every few years in his Prinzendorf castle. See Bernhard Doppler, "Hermann Nitsch's Festivals. Observations from the Prinzendorfer *Six-Day-Play* in 1998," *Literature, Film, and the Culture Industry in Modern Austria*, ed. Margarete Lamb-Faffelberger (New York: Peter Lang, forthcoming).
24. Ryan 114.
25. Gruber and Köpple 42. See Wendelin Schmidt-Dengler, *Bruchlinien. Vorlesungen zur österreichischen Literatur 1945-1990* (Salzburg: Residenz, 1995) 333-34.
26. Schmidt-Dengler, *Bruchlinien* 237-38.
27. Matthias Konzett, *The Rhetoric of National Dissent in Thomas Bernhard, Peter Handke, and Elfriede Jelinek* (Rochester, NY: Camden House, 2000) xi.
28. Stephen D. Dowden, *Understanding Thomas Bernhard* (Columbia, SC: University of South Carolina Press, 1991) 71.
29. Ernst Fischer quoted in Dirk Jürgens, *Das Theater Thomas Bernhards* (Frankfurt/M.: Peter Lang, 1999) 13.
30. Dowden 2.
31. Dowden 70.
32. Dowden 73.
33. Konzett 52.
34. Schmidt-Dengler, *Bruchlinien* 260.
35. Konzett 62.

36. Roland Koberg, *Claus Peymann. Aller Tage Abenteuer* (Berlin: Henschel, 1999) 138.

37. Peter Turrini, preface, *Gerald Szyszkowitz: Five Plays*, trans. Richard Dixon (Riverside, CA: Ariadne Press, 1990).

38. Turrini quoted in Alexandra Millner, "Scandalous Successes: The Reception of Peter Turrini's Plays in Austria," "*I Am Too Many People.*" *Peter Turrini: Playwright, Poet, Essayist*, ed. Jutta Landa (Riverside, CA: Ariadne Press, 1998) 44.

39. Jutta Landa, "Introduction," "*I Am Too Many People*" 3.

40. Yates 237.

41. Evelyn Deutsch-Schreiner 90.

42. Quoted in Gerhard Fuchs, "From Social Criticism to Emotional Romanticism? The Stage Plays of Peter Turrini," "*I Am Too Many People*" 81.

43. Bernhard quoted in Koberg 277.

44. Peymann quoted in Koberg 15.

45. Quoted according to Peter Turrini, "Ein neuer Volksstücke-schreiber," *Theater heute* 21 (1980): 23.

46. Konzett 26.

47. Eva Brenner, "Where Are the Big Topics, Where Is the Big Form?," *Elfriede Jelinek. Framed by Language* (Riverside, CA: Ariadne Press, 1994) 25.

48. Nancy Erickson, "Writing and Remembering – Acts of Resistance in Ingeborg Bachmann's *Malina* and *Der Fall Franza*, and Elfriede Jelinek's *Lust* and *Die Klavierspielerin*," *Out From the Shadows. Essays on Contemporary Austrian Women Writers and Filmmakers*, ed. Margarete Lamb-Faffelberger (Riverside, CA: Ariadne Press, 1997) 200.

49. Konzett 95-96.

50. Margarete Lamb-Faffelberger, "Auf dem "Holzweg des modernen Daseins." Überlegungen zu Elfriede Jelineks Kritik am Heimat-Mythos in *Wolken.Heim* und *Totenauberg*," *Modern Austrian Literature* 32.3 (1999): 135.

51. Jutta Landa, "'Königskomödien' oder 'Fäkaliendramen'? Zu den Theaterstücken von Werner Schwab," *Modern Austrian Literature* 26.3-4 (1993): 215.

52. Bernd Sucher, *Theaterlexikon* (Munich: Deutscher Taschenbuch Verlag, 1999) 2nd ed., 636.

53. Sucher 684.

54. Marlene Streeruwitz, *Und. Sonst. Noch. Aber. Texte. 1991-1996* (Vienna: edition, 1999) Interventionen 2, 26-27.

55. Marlene Streeruwitz, *New York. New York. Elysian Park. Zwei Stücke* (Frankfurt/M.: Suhrkamp, 1993) bookcover.

56. See Walter Grond, "Die mediale Multirealität als dramaturgisches Prinzip. Ein Wiener Personal an austauschbaren Orten," http://www.bildungsserver.at.

57. Alessandra Schininà, "Marlene Streeruwitz' Stücke: Vom Wiener Volksstück zum Theater der Grausamkeit," *Modern Austrian Literature* 31.3-4 (1998): 124.

The Persistence of *Kasperl* in Memory: H. C. Artmann and Peter Handke

Katherine Arens

Austria's literature had to rise from the ashes after the Second World War under different circumstances than did literature in Germany. Yet from literary history's point of view, the two postwar literatures are often distinguished only in cursory fashion, especially in light of Austrian authors' participation in Group 47. Nonetheless, no matter the commonalties among these germanophone cultures after the Second World War, the literatures of Austria and Germany took different routes to their engagement with history and the Cold War. A notable commentator on and contributor to Austria's literature in the era, Hans Weigel, pointed out that Austria did not have a *Stunde Null* (zero hour) after 1945, as Germany claimed to have had, but rather a *Nullpunkt im Imaginären* (null point in the imaginary).[1] Yet the German term "zero hour" anticipates the program of Group 47 which aims to reconstruct the German language and its literature through a return to human experience; the Austrian "null point in the imaginary," by contrast, outlines a search for an identity at a time when a previous identity has been exhausted.

The idea of a cultural "null point" rather than a "zero hour" guided many artists to their postwar engagement with Austria's cultural and political identities. This framework suggests that Austria's culture needed less to conquer its past – Germany's challenge of *Vergangenheitsbewältigung* – than to relocate that past. One specifically Viennese tradition within this process of recovery was the classic *Volkstheater*, the folk theater associated with Johann Nestroy and Ferdinand Raimund and still alive in the theater of Peter Turrini, among others.

Two of the most famous examples of this dramaturgy and its cultural-political traditions in postwar Austria will be the focus of the present discussion: H. C. Artmann (1921-2000), known more popularly as a dialect poet belonging to the *Wiener Gruppe*, and the more internationally famous Peter Handke (1942-). Artmann's best-known play in the folk theater tradition, *Kein Pfeffer für Czermak* (No Pepper for Czermak) from 1958, and Handke's *Kaspar* from 1968, I will argue, both use the dramaturgy of the folk theater consciously to enact specific political gestures aimed at Cold-War-era Austria. That is, Artmann and Handke do not only work within the traditions of the Austrian philosophy of language (including Wittgenstein), as most critics assume, but also within a very specific attitude towards the cultural history of Austria. Using this uniquely Viennese dramaturgy, as we shall see, allows both to offer a distinct critique of a class-bound European culture, a challenge to the high culture that was reestablishing itself as dominant in the first years of the independent German and Austrian cultures. Artmann and Handke adapt the classical folk theater as a very distinctive reference to the cosmopolitan Austrian culture of the nineteenth century, before the Nazi era. Seen as part of a tradition revalued, *Czermak* and *Kaspar* emerge not simply as existentialist or philosophical, but as engaged black comedies criticizing the contemporary state at the dawn of the Cold War.

From the *Wiener Gruppe* to *Forum Stadtpark*: The Avant-garde in Austria

The history of Austrian literature in the 1950s and 1960s parallels that of most Western nations: a small group of engaged intellectuals combat what they perceive as postwar conservatism and attempt to redefine high culture, especially in periodicals that functioned as the house organs for specific poetic and political agendas. Yet while the U.S. was becoming aware of the Beats and Germany followed Group 47 to its reconstruction of a humanistic culture, the first movement emerging to public prominence in Austria referenced in particular the European avant-garde of the prewar era, especially Surrealism, Dada, and what would become the French Theater of the Absurd. From about 1951 on, the *Wiener Gruppe* took center stage in Austria's counter-cultural intellectual world, especially through what English-speakers would call "happenings" such as public funeral processions that accompanied manifestos about art and politics.

The "members" of the group now deny that the *Wiener Gruppe* was ever a group in the formal sense,[2] although one of their number, Gerhard Rühm, helped to institutionalize it as such. And the press, of course, was willing from the first to unite under a single rubric these artists born in the 1920s and 1930s who had distinct memories of the war, although little direct culpability. Yet from the early 1950s on, the so-called group actually was comprised of major voices from all the arts, including architects and actors.[3] In reality, young artists with a shared interest in modern art trends from the West found themselves thrown together by circumstance and involved in experimental projects of all sorts. Today, the most publicly-remembered among them are perhaps Carl Merz and Helmut Qualtinger, whose infamous *Der Herr Karl* appeared on television in 1961 to lambaste the "golden Viennese heart." The *Herr Karl* monologue exposed the hypocrisy of an Austria that had, in the political negotiations leading up to the 1955 State Treaty, secured for itself a status not as perpetrator, but as the first victim of Hitler's aggression. This hypocrisy, the younger artists felt, also existed in the cultural realm. As part of a general anticommunist public debate, for instance, Brecht was tacitly banned from the Viennese stage until 1960.[4]

As Rühm summarized in his preface to the volume on the *Wiener Gruppe*: "it quickly became clear that the majority had a lot to object to about Nazi war politics, but very little to say, in principle, against its 'healthy' cultural politics."[5] The public was, in general, worried about being revealed as Nazis; by contrast, the younger generation was interested in preserving art as a social force in a climate that generally resisted such intervention. One of the first public acts of this younger generation, which was appalled at the politics and cultural politics of its elders, occurred in April, 1953: Artmann's "eight-point-proclamation of the poetic act" ("acht-punkte-proklamation des poetischen actes").[6] That proclamation defined a poetic act as an act of pure invention, designed to remain in its audience's memory so as to change their perception, not to be executed for profit – a gesture in the spirit of Don Quixote, not the modern literary marketplace, engaged but not tendentious.

Artmann wrote another, even more famous manifesto on 17 May 1955, in reaction to the founding of the new Austrian State on May 15. Twenty-five signatories to this document attest that these "existentialists" intended to be engaged in extremely political acts of art. The wording of this second manifesto is important here, especially for the movement's connection with the Viennese folk theater:

> MANIFESTO
> we protest with all emphasis
> against the macabre punch-and-judy show
> which will be played out
> with the reintroduction of an army,
> no matter how constituted,
> on austrian soil ...
> we all have had enough
> from the last time –
> this time, do it without us!
> it is temerity without end
> a shameless act without compare
> for ten years
> to spread anti-military propaganda
> while seeming holy, yowling about dirt
>   and degradation
> (the placards are still up ...)

and to declare all of it immoral
and then
in the first breezes of a so-called final freedom
that will draft a youth hardly old enough
   for school
to handle crap weapons
that is atavism!!!
that is neanderthal!!!
that is preparation
for legalized cannibalism!![7]

In this formulation, the "punch-and-judy show" of Austrian neutrality was a performance of national identity founded on a historical lie. With such public acts, the *Wiener Gruppe* became feared in Vienna as public gadflies, even if they remained largely unpublished. Members of the *Wiener Gruppe* followed in the footsteps of the creators of *Herr Karl* to help establish that distinctive Austrian phenomenon known in literary history as *Nestbeschmutzerliteratur* – literature that fouls its own nest. The first great published success of the group was Artmann's collection of Viennese dialect poetry from 1958 titled *med ana schwoazzn dintn* (with black ink). Unfortunately, that success branded them all as dialect poets, almost to the exclusion of other facets of their work. It also began to loosen Artmann's ties to the rest of the group, and by 1960 he left Austria.

While the aesthetic program of the *Wiener Gruppe* may be remembered somewhat falsely, there remains no doubt about their shared cultural politics. As the 1950s yielded to the 1960s, younger artists, including the *Wiener Gruppe*, began to feel alienated from a public that was increasingly conservative. Austria's postwar avant-garde had lost whatever cachet it had once enjoyed: "radio, television, press are ruled by an arrogant provincialism. 'avant-gardists' are suspect from the first – they should all go abroad, we don't need 'em in austria."[8] As Artmann summarized in a later interview: "Vienna is a murderous city. One has to know that. We are no operetta-everymen. We are good murderers."[9]

Such disillusionment with official cultural politics did not mean, however, that younger artists had no outlet. In 1959, the *Forum Stadtpark* was founded in Graz; it held its first major exhibition in November, 1960. *Forum Stadtpark* and its magazine, *manuskripte*, became the public face of 1960s artistic revolt in an Austria that would otherwise bypass the West's 1968 political turmoil. When, in the 1970s, a younger generation rose, they shared the platform of *Forum Stadtpark* with the *Wiener Gruppe*, just as they shared complaints about the cultural bureaucrats who were threatening to turn Austrian culture into an outdated museum. Significantly, *Forum Stadtpark* also nurtured Peter Handke, who had moved to Graz and had contacts with its artists since 1961, first reading there in 1964. *Forum Stadtpark* kept two generations of Austrian artists together in a specific time and place, an *Austrian* space.

To be sure, that Austrian space was tied to the Germanies, as later artists like Thomas Bernhard, Elfriede Jelinek, and Handke himself would freely exploit. As Rühm put it: "For me, the border between Austria and Germany does not exist. It is a purely political border. I consider it all a German-language region."[10] For Rühm, to assume the existence of such a border between the cultures is nonsense: "That would be provincialism! ... that would be catastrophic."[11] In this sense, these artists seek local engagement through the use of Western tradition, with a global vision behind it – long a hallmark of Austrian thought.

The Persistence of *Kasperl*

Given the political climate that made allies of the *Wiener Gruppe* and the *Forum Stadtpark* artists, it should come as no surprise that the Austrian stage also showed great continuity from before World War II to the present. No matter how many authors went into exile or collaborated with the right during the war, the Austrian stage cultivated traditions of drama and dramaturgy that were recoupable as modern and political innovation, as Gerhard Scheit documents through his study of various dramatists in the folk tradition from the nineteenth and twentieth centuries.[12] In fact, Austrian stage authors make a point of confronting traditions, just as the avant-garde was confronting history.

Here one uncovers a significant difference between the era's writers in Austria and Germany. Both groups were indeed interested in reestablishing their artistic traditions and continuity with the past, as the case of Günter Grass confirms. However, these avant-garde Austrians were at particular pains to take up traditions in relation to contemporary political and aesthetic issues. Again, Rühm frames this historical imperative succinctly: "... now I am of the opinion that there are two traditions. There is one tradition that Gustav Mahler has already called laziness. There is another that is progressive. And I declare total allegiance to my Viennese tradition."[13] This goal was overt in the generation of the *Wiener Gruppe* and emerged again in many of the authors of the younger Austrian generation whose works would be published by Residenz Publishers (including figures like Barbara Frischmuth). Their traditionalism is engaged, not passive.

These progressive traditionalists incorporated modern European art – especially Dada, Surrealism, and Existentialism – but they also tried to meet and subvert their own national traditions in a move that Caribbean theorists of the postwar era would call "cannibalism." Thus the *Wiener Gruppe* made early, specific attempts to draw on the West's literary traditions (such as montage and acoustic poetry), including Austria's own (most famously, dialect poetry). In addition, Artmann referenced world culture in its breadth: Hollywood movies and movie stars, the Baroque, American literature, and the Viennese folk theater. From the first, in consequence, critics have related Artmann's *Kein Pfeffer für Czermak* to Johann Nestroy, the most famous of the nineteenth century's folk theater authors and actors.[14] Similarly, Konrad Bayer's *kasperl am elektrischen Stuhl* (1962/63, kasperl in the electric chair) refers back to one of the tradition's famous early actors, Stranitzky.[15]

Viennese folk theater, the theater remembered today chiefly in plays by Ferdinand Raimund and Johann Nestroy, featured plays that grew out of the extemporizing theater tradition – the *commedia dell'arte*, brought to its greatest bloom in the sixteenth and seventeenth centuries throughout Europe. The *commedia dell'arte* was first a performing tradition in which great actors played a repertoire that included stock characters such as Pantalone, Harlequin, Columbine, Punchinello, and others. By the 1750s, however, and in the hands of famous masters like Carlo Goldoni (or perhaps even Beaumarchais and his *Figaro*), this performing tradition began to transform itself into a socially critical playwriting tradition. Goldoni draws on the Baroque convention of the *theatrum mundi*, a reference to a world in which not just tragedy or drama, but also comedy, could exercise a very specific social-moralizing function. Italian players brought this theater with them into the European capitals, and they left behind them the English pantomime and Punch and Judy puppet shows, as well as the French comic opera.

In his earliest German-language form, the main stock character of the tradition was the *Hanswurst*, who was then driven from the stage in 1743 by the German dramatist Gottsched in his search for a better-regulated theater without extemporizing characters. In Vienna, he assumed various forms, each a named variant of a figure called Kasperl evolved by a particular actor (the names range from Staberl through Thaddädl, up to the roles that Nestroy wrote for himself). In France, he was Punchinello; in England, his original stage brother, Punch, took center stage as an everyman.[16] Each figure was characterized by a costume type, often had a distinctive mask, and exercised a particular style of movement, gesture, and speech. Yet that theater was not intended to mirror faithfully the realities of everyday life as the audience knew it, but to represent the people one *might* meet – on the street set that was the standard stage backdrop.

Although critical literature about this theater tradition rarely traces it beyond Goldoni's inventive realism in Italy, the description of Goldoni's theater fits the Viennese folk comedy that came into its own around 1800: "Basically, Goldoni was concerned with bringing character, social criticism and moral purpose to the stage, and for the achievement of this objective he required a realist framework."[17] Even when it turned "realistic" by seventeenth- and eighteenth-century norms, then, the *commedia dell'arte* and folk theaters remained fundamentally a space that was non-realistic and non-propagandistic as compared with the later theaters of Ibsen, Hauptmann, or Brecht.

No wonder that the folk theater became a source for a twentieth-century Austrian avant-garde that was trying to combat the realistic theater favored by the dominant cultures (conservative or socialist) of post-World-War-II Europe. As a theater that drew the spectator into a common space, it shared many of the premises of the French Theater of the Absurd, made famous by Beckett and Ionesco.[18] In all cases, the theater's dramaturgy aimed at undercutting the dominant norm for the audience.[19] The postwar Austrian folk theater, like its predecessors, presented paradoxes of social morality in the stereotyped space of everyman, breaking the fourth wall to make an audience confront itself.

Kasperl, from Artmann to Handke

Artmann borrowed from many world traditions as he read extensively in literary history during the 1950s, but from early on his borrowings from the Baroque were evident. Part of this Baroque tradition was the *commedia dell'arte* and its Viennese stock figure, Kaspar (Caspar, or in the diminutive, *Kasperl*). Artmann used Kaspar as his everyman in many contexts, even political ones (as in his 1955 manifesto against state militarism); he also wrote a number of poems and short plays using the figure in various ways. The most overtly political of these was *die liebe fee pocahontas, oder kaspar als schildwache* (the dear fairy pocahontas, or kaspar as sentry), an explicitly anti-militarist play. Significantly, many of Artmann's Caspars are also characterized as "cannibals,"[20] as they are in the manifesto and as they will recur well into the 1970s.[21]

But the most playable, and hence the most significant of Artmann's Caspar plays is one using the form without the character name, a play very much in the style of a Nestroy play: *Kein*

Pfeffer für Czermak, subtitled a "Small Votive Offering to the Golden Viennese Heart." *Czermak* premiered in 1958 at the *Theater am Fleischmarkt* in Vienna just before *med ana schwoazzn dintn* made Artmann famous. *Czermak* takes us into the world of Grillparzer to a small store which turns out to be a chamber of horrors. The main figure is Gschweidl, a grocer (*Greißler* or *Kolonialwarenhändler*, a figure recalling Pantalone in the *commedia dell'arte*), whose store attracts the whole spectrum of Viennese society. We see him as a man who physically abuses his ward, Carolin, when she breaks a window she is cleaning. "Simply imposing just punishment, gentlemen!" he says when a police detective comes in looking for a suspect.[22]

The detective approves of Geschweidl's punishment of Carolin, then interrogates him as to the whereabouts of Czermak, a musician who lives across the street as a boarder and who is under surveillance. The grocer swears he would not sell that man the pepper he wanted, not in any form, and pleads with the policeman to note this in a formal statement: "I don't want people to go around saying that Gschweidl needs to sell his wares to just anyone, or otherwise his store will have to close" (37). The composer is a "Bohemian good-for-nothing" (*böhmischer Haderlump*, incorporating two senses of "Bohemian," 37), ripe for criminal prosecution. These stock characters – grocer, cop, ward, and artist – begin a cycle that takes the play through virtually all the stereotyped figures who can show "the golden Viennese heart."

Frau Godl, a poor seamstress aged twenty-nine, owes the grocer money but tries nonetheless to get some butter to entertain her guest, a man who might be her last chance at finding a bridegroom. Gschweidl's response is anything but golden: "Go back nicely up to your fourth floor and keep sewing" (38). She threatens him with ripping open her bodice and yelling that he is up to something. He tells her to go haunt the cemetery – at the very moment when an undertaker comes in demanding beer. Next a widow, Frau Hunger, enters, begging for a piece of blue paper to make a mustard plaster for her ill son. So poor that she rents a shift in a bed rather than a room, she cannot afford a doctor.

Naturally she, too, is thrown out. At that point, the audience finds out that Gschweidl has a drawer with two disembodied white hands in it that he treats like pets, feeding them more than his niece. The cast of old Viennese types, the kind who would appear in Spitzweg paintings, multiply further: a water-seller argues about a delivery; an old Viennese woman wants to hire – or is it buy – his niece. The proliferation of characters and action finally comes to an abrupt halt when Gschweidl has a stroke while tending his hands.

Artmann provides two different endings for *Czermak*, each straight out of old Vienna. In both, two angels appear, one good and one bad, speaking the Hapsburg aristocratic dialect. They watch the grocer have his stroke and then, to deck out the body as what is known as a *schöne Leich'* (an ostentatious funeral with mourners, far beyond the means of the deceased), they buy up all of Resi the flower seller's wares at a good price. In the first variant of the ending, a female thief enters the room as the grocer lies there disabled and steals the hands. The water-seller returns to continue the earlier argument and Gschweidl, who asks for water, is taken out to the well, presumably never to be seen again. In the second variant of the ending, Carolin finds him partially incapacitated while the two angels comment on her innocence and high color. The stroke has rendered the grocer partially blind, and so he begins to berate Carolin for poisoning him in the "best years of his life." The angels arrange for his second stroke and death, to the accompaniment of *Schrammelmusik*. This resolution, with a kind of *deus ex machina*, comes straight out of plays by Ferdinand Raimund, where the gods intervene to set the mortals right. But these angels speak Hapsburg, and they allow vengeance rather than justice per se.

If this had been the theater of Nestroy, fate would have intervened to punish the guilty to the point of making him change his mind, not murdering him. But this is not just literary mannerism; the *theatrum mundi* has been extended into the bizarre, where it converges with Merz and Qualtinger's *Herr Karl*, a famous monologue revealing the corruption of the "golden Viennese heart" after the Second World War. The grocer is grasping – why else does he feed extra hands? – and he exercises complete control over his ward, with more extreme abuse than even Dickens could imagine. In this world, widows and seamstresses live at the sufferance of their nominal betters; male tradesmen, gainfully employed, become the petty tyrants of their environment, demanding beer or setting terms just to show they can; the powers that be, including the police, run surveillance on anything different, without punishing real abuse or injustice – according to their concept of justice a Bohemian with no money and progressive artistic ideas has to be more dangerous than an abusive domestic tyrant. And only through money or sex can women exert any power at all.

Czermak shows the nightmare underbelly of the Vienna that Nestroy had satirized a century earlier: prejudiced, power- and money-hungry, hiding behind the façades of justice and religion. But where Nestroy allowed a clever servant to triumph and bring the social order of the *theatrum mundi* back into balance (or where Grillparzer allowed his *Poor Fiddler* to be mourned by a good woman), Artmann finds only domestic violence, closed spaces, vengeance, and small-mindedness. The "golden Viennese heart (and soul)" has only hands, no mind, and a bloodthirsty streak that does indeed allow the city to eat people alive, to consume their hearts and lives under the guise of quaint traditionalism. *Kein Pfeffer für Czermak* speaks for itself as a parody of the petit bourgeois mindset of a conservative era. Yet it is also a play written with the stock characters of the Viennese folk theater in a city that still knew the tradition, the plays by Raimund and Nestroy that rotate onto the playbills of the *Burgtheater* and the *Theater in der Josefstadt*, along with those of Horváth. Artmann's play therefore also represents a heightening of the critical potential that the culture bureaucrats of that Vienna were trying to bury under the myth of the "golden Viennese heart," under a vision of the Biedermeier as quiescent and picturesque. Artmann's Vienna is indeed a continuation of the Baroque and the Biedermeier – a creation of the Hapsburg avenging angels who appear in it – but as the murderous city he knows it to be, a place where a façade of forced quiescence cloaks domestic and political violence of all sorts.

Such an overt political message couched in traditional form seems at first glance to be miles distant from Peter Handke's *Kaspar*. Critics prefer to disassociate Handke from the progressive traditionalism of the *Wiener Gruppe*, despite his roots in the *Forum Stadtpark*. And despite the fact that Handke's debut falls in the same years as Artmann's various Kaspar- and *Volkstheater* work, he is usually seen in isolation from his Austrian contemporaries. Handke's most famous "speech play" (*Sprechstück*), *Publikumsbeschimpfung* (*Offending the Audience*), premiered in Frankfurt in 1966, the same year he denounced Group 47 at Princeton, and his own *Kaspar* followed closely in 1968. Where Artmann's Caspars can be called to witness political situations, however, Handke's have remained associated with the philosophy of language.[23] This despite the fact that *Kaspar* is followed by an overt contribution to the folk theater, his play of 1969 titled *Das Mündel will Vormund sein* (The Ward Wants to Be the Guardian), which also premiered in Frankfurt. More significantly, despite Handke's proclaimed allegiance to Brecht, his early theater manifestos strongly parallel the *Wiener Gruppe*'s analysis of the theater: "Since it is a social institution, the theater seems to me to be unusable for changing social institutions."[24] Thus Handke, like the *Wiener Gruppe*, was seeking to combat the aesthetics of the realistic theater. Like them, and following their attention to international dramaturgies like that of the Theater of the Absurd, Handke, too, has used the folk theater in the service of his own aesthetic revolution.

Kaspar is, most familiarly, an allusion to Kaspar Hauser, the famous orphan who had been imprisoned in isolation for years and who was therefore developmentally hindered. Yet the second face of this figure is more familiar from the context discussed in this article: Handke's Kaspar is dressed like a figure from the *commedia dell'arte*, i.e., in the baggy clothes characteristic of its everyman figures. Moreover, the appearance of the multiple Kaspars in the latter part of the play indicates Handke's awareness of the tradition's dramaturgical conventions, since Kaspar is the only figure in the Italian *commedia* who can be doubled, who can appear in more than one configuration on stage. And while the stage space in *Kaspar* appears to preserve the separation between the audience and the stage by allowing the auditorium to remain dark (unlike in *Offending the Audience*), the play's space is nonetheless anti-illusionary since voiceovers unite the audience with the stage in a shared third realm. In another sense, Handke's hero is also the *Kasperl* of the puppet theater, moved by others as he is by the voices of the announcers, the *Einsager* (a mix of *Ansager* – announcer – and *einreden* – to convince of). This *Kasperl* is, in yet another international allusion, a Frankenstein monster, other than human, yet created by the perverted desires of humanity.

First and foremost, Handke marks the stage itself as the kind of non-realistic space traditional to the *commedia dell'arte* and to the folk theater:

> The play *Kaspar* does not show how it REALLY IS or REALLY WAS with Kaspar Hauser. It shows what IS POSSIBLE with someone. It shows how someone can be made to speak through speaking. The play could also be called *speech torture*. To formalize this torture it is suggested that a kind of magic eye be constructed above the ramp. This eye, without however diverting the audience's attention from the events on stage, indicates, by blinking, the degree of vehemence with which the PROTAGONIST is addressed. The more vehemently he defends himself, the more vehemently the magic eye blinks.[25]

This space implicates the audience and Kaspar in a common speech torture, as the magic eye – a Masonic eye, perhaps? – looks down on them alike.

Handke also clearly marks his Kaspar as a *commedia dell'arte* figure in his dress and behavior, as an everyman:

> For example, he has on a round, broad-brimmed hat with a band; a light-colored shirt with a closed collar; a colorful jacket with many (roughly seven) metal buttons; wide pants; clumsy shoes; on one shoe, for instance, the very long laces have become untied. He looks droll. The colors of his outfit clash with the colors on stage. Only on second or third glance should the audience realize that his face is a mask; it is a pale color; it is lifelike; it may have been fashioned to fit the face of the actor. It expresses astonishment and confusion. (63)

This Kaspar confronts the announcers who say sentences over the loudspeaker until the point when six other Kaspars appear, at least one of whom is crippled. Over the course of the play, the announcers program Kaspar into platitudes of self-reference: "My love of order and cleanliness never give cause for rebuke" (56). The announcers only stop inculcating platitudes once the other Kaspars are there, once the original has, quite literally, become everyman.

Loudspeakers mark out another kind of space, shared by Kaspar and the audience alike. They provide a voiceover with fragments of social commonplaces, including fragments of rules of practice like table manners. Eventually, the Kaspars' masks are altered to take on an expression of satisfaction, and the central Kaspar's voice comes to resemble that of the announcers. He begins to comment on his own experience of being human: "I learned to fill / all empty spaces with words" (124). That this is to be understood as a negative, not positive, development, is signaled by the odd noises made by the other Kaspars: "no one / may miss the drill" (125). Ultimately the first Kaspar realizes he does not know what he is saying: "Every sentence / is for the birds" (132). He begins to look at himself retrospectively, providing a self-interpretation: "All at once I distinguished myself / from the

(137). What he has lost is a kind of innocence: "I no longer understand anything literally" (138), and his sense of security with it: "with each new sentence I become nauseous" (139).

His last lines are significant, much more so in the German than in the English translation. Kaspar utters each word seemingly disjointedly, probably with a distinct pause between them: "ich: / bin: / nur: / zufällig: / ich:"[26] which is inexplicably rendered in English as a repeated "Goats and monkeys" (140) instead of "I am myself only by chance." With this, Handke comes full circle on a link between social and linguistic relativism. The statement is uttered as six other Kaspars create an inarticulate din; the main Kaspar is not only a creation of linguistic relativism, but also a creation of mass culture.

In this, Handke takes on a message of 1960s Europe rather than the more specifically Austrian issues that concerned Artmann. His play becomes a critique of mass culture. The electronic announcers' voices that seem to guide this Kaspar into his purported identity actually only program him into the norms of mass culture and the whims of that culture. Handke has used an everyman from the folk tradition to critique the position of every-Kaspar in his Europe. This Kaspar is thrown into the media-governed space in which we all share (as spectators), under a watchful eye gauging the urgency of the public statements to which Kaspar must eventually conform. He comes to awareness not only of linguistic relativity, but also to the fact that he has been, in the worst-case scenarios familiar from the Frankfurt School, an object of the mass media, not a subject capable of self-determination. Since Kaspar is meant to be the little man, the conclusion is inevitable: this Kaspar is a member of the great, essentially inarticulate masses created by the media culture whose voices come over the loudspeakers that both he and his audience hear.

Handke's reference to the Viennese folk theater and its *commedia dell'arte* predecessors is thus undoubtedly as little an accident as was Artmann's: he, too, is able to use the form to address the here and now of everyday Europe (if not everyday Vienna). He is using the non-realistic space of that theater to recreate the fundamental reality of the late twentieth century, the dependence of all on mass media, on disembodied, electronic voices which organize our consciousness even before we know they are doing so. Handke's Kaspar, therefore, does not meet up with the cast of stock characters which Artmann was able to draw onto his stage, but rather simply internalizes the kinds of platitudes which they mouth, to their own destruction. Yet the audience will necessarily follow that Kaspar into his realization of how the system works to destroy individuals, just as clearly as Artmann's audience must see the violence concealed by the "golden Viennese heart." Both playwrights, therefore, see the continued potential of the folk theater for cultural criticism, even while they despair about the culture itself.

Some Conclusions

The dramaturgy of the Viennese *Volkstheater* and its antecedent *commedia dell'arte* puts another face on the borrowings of Austria's postwar avant-garde. From the first, that theater tradition cultivates subversive use of language in the mouths of stock social types, such as more famous truth-tellers like *Till Eulenspiegel*. Usually, an everyman character takes the stage as a representative of the lower classes, as a servant, a tradesman, or a laborer looking for work and for social advancement, and then his adventures reveal the social lies of purportedly benevolent social mores, especially through confrontations in language and willed misunderstandings.

The politics of the folk theater are indeed present in the plays discussed here. Artmann, starting from the reestablishment of the Austrian state into its role in the Cold War, uses his *Kasperl* and Caspars to critique the lies of that nascent state; his grocer Gschweidl, a linear heir of *commedia dell'arte*'s elder merchant, causes a necessary revolt of the younger generation. In this case, however, the younger generation kills him, rather than simply triumphing over his petty tyrannies. This is a fable of totalitarianism and violence, of a father generation slowly and deliberately killing its children by not admitting the skeletons (in this case, the grasping hands) in the closet. The traditionalism of the "golden Viennese heart" was itself theater of the absurd in a purportedly neutral country that ignored its Nazi past and was actively remilitarizing. This generation of evil fathers was quite literally threatening to eat its children.

A member of a younger generation, Handke nonetheless takes on the same critique of a generation eating its own children. His Kaspar is not just the figure of the folk comedy, but also the Kaspar Hauser of history, who may have been the heir to a throne, who was kidnapped so that scheming aristocrats could change dynasties. Handke, however, is also taking on the European politics of a generation later, a generation worried less about national identity than about media culture and the loss of individuality in a conformist Europe. Where Artmann and his colleagues denied that there is a cultural border between Germany and Austria, Handke, in addition, may have been exploiting that border in ways that playwrights like Thomas Bernhard would do a decade later: to craft a message learned in Austria and packaged in forms familiar to the Austrian tradition, but then to take those lessons into Germany and Europe in general.

Yet both Artmann and Handke, members of the respective avant-gardes of their generations, retain clear claims for being progressive traditionalists. They confront their audiences with revisionist uses of traditional dramaturgy in a modernist critique of conservative traditionalism that does not surrender those traditions to the past. *Kein Pfeffer für Czermak* and *Kaspar*, in the readings offered here, make the case that critical literary traditions need not lose their critical edge if they can be reclaimed from the functionaries of culture and media who have tried to tame them. Artmann and Handke hope to reclaim Austria by reclaiming one of its distinctive cultural traditions from the museum to which it was being relegated; they argue that traditions can persist as viable tools for critique, rather than as fossilized high culture that purports to overcome a past that needs examination instead.

Notes

1. Hilde Spiel, ed., *Kindlers Literaturgeschichte der Gegenwart (Autoren, Werke, Themen, Tendenzen seit 1945): Die zeitgenössische Literatur Österreichs* (Zurich, Munich: Kindler, 1976) 59.

2. For an exemplary disclaimer, see Peter Pabisch, *H. C. Artmann: Ein Versuch über die literarische Alogik* (Vienna: Verlag A. Schmidt, 1978) 23.

3. The *Wiener Gruppe*, Artmann said in a 1966 interview, included for instance Helmut Qualtinger, Peter Wehle, and Gerhard Bronner. See H. C. Artmann and Michael Krüger, "Wer es versteht, der versteht es: H. C. Artmann im Gespräch mit Michael Krüger," *H. C. Artmann* (Dossier, Bd. 3), ed. Gerhard Fuchs and Rüdiger Wischenbart (Graz, Vienna: Literaturverlag Droschl, 1992) 16.

4. Spiel 84.

5. Gerhard Rühm, "Vorwort," *Die Wiener Gruppe – Achleitner, Artmann, Bayer, Rühm, Wiener: Texte, Gemeinschaftsarbeiten, Aktionen*, ed. Rühm (Reinbek bei Hamburg: Rowohlt, 1967) 7. All translations from this preface are my own.

6. Rühm, "Vorwort" 9-10.

7. Rühm, "Vorwort" 18-19.

8. Rühm, "Vorwort" 33.

9. H. C. Artmann et al., "Xogt, gesoggt oder gsokt: Ein Gespräch zwischen H. C. Artmann, Friedrich Achleitner, Gerhard Rühm und Oswald Wiener, moderiert von Wendelin Schmidt-Dengler," *H. C. Artmann* 35.

10. Artmann et al., "Xogt" 32.

11. Artmann et al., "Xogt" 34.

12. Gerhard Scheit, *Hanswurst und der Staat – Eine kleine Geschichte der Komik: Von Mozart bis Thomas Bernhard* (Vienna: Deutike, 1995).

13. Artmann et al., "Xogt" 36.

14. See for example Peter O. Chotjewitz, "Der neue selbstkolorierte Dichter," *Über H. C. Artmann*, ed. Gerald Bisinger (Frankfurt/M.: Suhrkamp, 1972) 27.

15. Spiel 90. See also Gotthard Böhm, "Dramatik in Österreich seit 1945," Spiel 483.

16. Allardyce Nicoll, *The World of Harlequin: A Critical Study of the Commedia dell'Arte* (Cambridge: Cambridge UP, 1963) 87.

17. Nicoll 205.

18. Karl Riha, "Ein patagonischer Aviatiker: Zu H. C. Artmanns Dramen," *Über H. C. Artmann* 157.

19. Riha 159.

20. Josef Donnenberg, "Pose, Possen, Protest und Poesie – oder: Artmanns Manier," *Possen und Poesie: Zum Werk Hans Carl Artmanns*, ed. Josef Donnenberg (Stuttgart: Akademischer Verlag Hans-Dieter Heinz, 1981) 159.

21. Mechthild Rausch has done a marvelous job tracing how Artmann has adapted source materials into his *punch*. Yet her conclusion seems to ignore the continuity of the folk/*Kasperl* theater tradition. See "Punch und Putschenelle," *Über H. C. Artmann* 157-65.

22. Hans Carl Artmann, *Kein Pfeffer für Czermak, die fahrt zur insel nantucket* (Neuwied, Berlin: Luchterhand, 1969) 35. All translations are mine. Subsequent quotes from this text will be indicated by the page number in parentheses.

23. See for example Gotthard Böhm, "Dramatik in Österreich," Spiel 477-644.

24. Peter Handke, "Für *das* Straßentheater, gegen *die* Straßentheater," *Prosa, Gedichte, Theaterstücke, Hörspiel, Aufsätze* (Frankfurt/M.: Suhrkamp, 1969) 305.

25. Peter Handke, *Kaspar and Other Plays*, trans. Michael Roloff (New York: Farrar, Straus and Giroux, 1969) 59. Subsequent quotes from this text will be indicated by the page number in parentheses.

26. Peter Handke, *Kaspar* (Frankfurt/M.: Suhrkamp, 1968) 84-85.

Morality and Ambiguity:
Fritz Hochwälder's *Der Befehl*

Todd C. Hanlin

Fritz Hochwälder was for at least a quarter of a century the leading postwar Austrian dramatist. His plays attracted an international audience "beyond the borders of Austria, Germany, and Switzerland to other European countries, to the Middle East, and to North and South America."[1] Such interest in Hochwälder's plays can be attributed to a great extent to the moral dilemmas they presented: "the awakening of man's conscience under the pressure of adversity and criminality, the problem of achieving justice in the world, the corruption of power in the belief that might makes right, and the conflict between personal inclination and obedience to authority, or in other terms the conflict between conscience and following orders."[2] Born in Vienna in 1911, he became a master upholsterer under his father's tutelage and first began writing plays in the 1930s. When Hochwälder had to flee Vienna in 1938 because of his Jewish origins, he illegally entered Switzerland. As an emigrant, he could not obtain a work permit, so he turned necessity into a virtue: he sat down and spent his days writing plays. His first works in Swiss exile were premiered at a minor Swiss theater in Biel-Solothurn since as a Jew he was forbidden to be performed on Austrian or German stages. At that time he was befriended by the renowned Expressionist dramatist Georg Kaiser;[3] international recognition and acclaim soon followed. As a result of his parents' deaths in the Treblinka concentration camp, Hochwälder remained in Switzerland after the war until his death in 1986.[4] Typical of Hochwälder's work is a traditional, conservative approach to theater. As the Hochwälder scholar Donald G. Daviau notes, the dramatist's oeuvre consists of "logical, contrived plays written in traditional three- or five-act form, with exposition, rising action, climax, falling action, and dénouement, and observing the Aristotelian unities of time, manner, and place."[5] Throughout his dramatic career – Hochwälder wrote only plays, no poetry or prose fiction – the aspect of morality was foremost in his works. As Daviau writes: "He eschews ambiguity and consciously utilizes strong theatrical effects, while developing a clear theme, with relevance to his audiences, which he leads to an inexorable conclusion."[6] Hochwälder's first plays were semi-historical pieces, such as *Das heilige Experiment* (1943, *The Holy Experiment*, 1998), *Meier Helmbrecht* (1947), *Der öffentliche Ankläger* (1948, The Public Prosecutor), and *Donadieu* (1953). But by the mid-1950s he had begun to write more contemporary pieces: *Die Herberge* (1955/56, The Inn); an up-dated morality play for the Salzburg Festival, *Donnerstag* (1959, *Thursday*, 1998); and his first plays dealing explicitly with the Nazi past, *Der Himbeerpflücker* (1965, *The Raspberry Picker*, 1982) and *Der Befehl* (1967/68, *The Order*, 1998).

In his autobiographical essay "Über mein Theater" ("About My Theater"),[7] Hochwälder asserted that there have been two theatrical venues for his plays, emphasizing London and Paris as major European cities which have featured his works. Given that he had rarely had contacts with German or Swiss theaters, Vienna, of course, became *the* Austrian outlet for his works. Hochwälder's plays were generally premiered at the leading Austrian houses, such as at the *Burgtheater* in Vienna, and often written specifically for those audiences. Hochwälder always considered himself Viennese and gladly admitted his theatrical debt to the Austrian *Volkstheater*, a robust tradition with elements of the Baroque theater as well as the Italian *commedia dell'arte*. In other words, his stylistic goal involved popular entertainment with a moral focus.

In only two instances did he write for the growing medium of television, and one of those plays was *The Order*,[8] a piece which piques our interest not only because of its topic – Hochwälder's recurring treatment of the moral dilemma surrounding orders and blind obedience[9] – but also because of Hochwälder's execution: he wrote one version for European distribution via the BBC, another for "local" consumption in Vienna at the *Burgtheater* which has, thus far, escaped critical scrutiny. Hochwälder's original German script was translated into English as *The Order* by Patrick Alexander for the Eurovision Series "The Largest Theater in the World," originating January 1967 on BBC Television and broadcast by a majority of European television stations.[10] The stage version was first performed in March 1968 at the *Burgtheater* in Vienna in a second, altered rendition. Both versions share a common theme and similar structure; however, there exist obvious and interesting differences as well. It is the focus of this article to compare these two versions, a comparison that will show the accent on the theme of morality and the appearance of unexpected ambiguity within Hochwälder's theatrical world.

BBC Version[11]

The play begins in the Mittermayer kitchen on a sunny, cheerful morning. His wife is watering flowers as birds sing in the background – all in all, an optimistic beginning. However, Mittermayer has no appetite, fearing that he may be forced into retirement because of a nervous breakdown fifteen years ago. His wife, as his former nurse, assures him that his trouble had been an "after-effect of the war."[12] Nevertheless, she reminds him that his greatest weakness is that he is only interested in "orders, obedience, work ... You always have to do what's right ... as if the world hasn't had enough of that lately" (244-45).

Arriving at police headquarters, Mittermayer is summoned to a meeting with the Chief and ordered to investigate a war crime – the 1942 murder of a young girl, the daughter of a trade representative from Amsterdam named de Goede who is currently in

Morality and Ambiguity: Fritz Hochwälder's *Der Befehl* 57

Vienna. Twenty years before, de Goede and his sixteen-year-old daughter had been members of the Dutch resistance, distributing anti-German leaflets. When the German occupation police (then known as "Greens," from the color of their uniform) came to arrest them, the father fled, but the daughter was caught. Resisting arrest, she was struck by one of the policemen and drowned in a nearby canal; bystanders identified the "Green" from his accent as Viennese. De Goede emphasizes that he wishes neither to exact revenge nor to prosecute the crime, but simply to confront the Viennese perpetrator. During the recounting of the murder, Mittermayer is stunned, gradually feeling that he could have committed the crime and that he has repressed all memory of it in the intervening years. Nevertheless he obeys the Chief's order to solve the crime.

At the beginning of the second act, in an attempt to resolve his confusion, Mittermayer visits the psychiatrist who treated him during his nervous breakdown. Conjuring up a hypothetical "friend," Mittermayer attempts to understand how someone could possibly have repressed any memory of such a horrific deed. The doctor gives a plausible medical explanation, in essence blaming such amnesia on shock. Meanwhile, at police headquarters in Vienna, detective Poslanetz has stumbled onto a likely suspect whom he intends to frame, in a desperate bid to gain credit and thus a promotion for solving the case. While brooding about the case, Mittermayer ostensibly hears a voice and becomes inexplicably agitated in the presence of his two colleagues, Poslanetz and Dwornik. As a result of Mittermayer's unusual behavior, detective Dwornik begins to suspect Mittermayer.

Acting on a suggestion by Dwornik, Mittermayer visits his former commanding officer who confirms the deed and recalls that he had ordered Mittermayer to forget it; the man now repeats his original order and commands Mittermayer to get drunk and forget the whole episode. But Mittermayer continues his private investigation, seeking out his partner on that fateful day. The partner now runs a rural bar and is himself drunk upon Mittermayer's arrival. Roused, he recounts the incident anew – how they were ordered to conduct themselves and how they were exemplary models of aggression and brutality. Mittermayer is shocked and pronounces that if that is the way he was, then that is the way he still is today. Returning home drunk, Mittermayer brutally repulses his wife, and then recounts the murderous incident, word for word, admitting his guilt in front of his wife. Again he concludes he is the same man today that he was in the past.

As in the first act, the final act begins at the Mittermayers' breakfast table. Mittermayer attempts to console his wife with the thought that in a few hours he will interrogate a suspect, exact a confession, and then be a different man. During the interrogation itself, it is learned that the suspect could not have committed the crime. Since the three detectives have thus failed to solve the case, the Chief orders them to resolve it. Alone with Mittermayer in the ensuing silence, Dwornik suggests that he himself may have stumbled onto a suspect, an honorable civil servant that no one would have connected to the crime had that person not so obviously drawn attention to himself. The perpetrator was no fanatic, no sadist – and Dwornik procedes to recite Mittermayer's dossier, including a suspicious recent visit to his former commanding officer. Mittermayer silences him, saying that it is Dwornik's duty to take this evidence to the Chief.

But, risking his own career, Dwornik emphatically defies orders, obedience, and duty, and assures Mittermayer that he will tell no one what he knows. Instead, he begs Mittermayer to go to de Goede – since *both* are suffering as a result of the past – and confess that he was the one who committed the crime but that he is not the same person any more. Mittermayer counters with the assertion: "I was the one. And I'm still the same man today" (308). When Dwornik suggests that it was the times that caused the atrocities, Mittermayer insists that it was not the times, "It was the people" (308). When Mittermayer's death is reported the next day – he was killed by a local gangster, apparently in the line of duty, though he was not assigned to that case – the Chief and Dwornik regret the death of such a wonderful policeman, speculating that the accident was perhaps due to a nervous relapse that caused Mittermayer to come in harm's way. Still, the Chief feels they owe de Goede a report and orders Dwornik to make it.

In the final scene of the play, Dwornik visits de Goede and privately confesses that he has found the murderer; it is someone much like Dwornik himself: "It's not to my credit that I'm not the actual murderer. The times back then, the people ... The uniform, the rifle, the mission, the orders, the excitement, the fear, the blind rage ... and last but not least, the profound cowardice which leads to excesses against the defenseless" (313). Under such circumstances an average citizen could easily become a monster. Addressing de Goede – but clearly the audience as well – Dwornik insists we should make certain that such times, such circumstances are never repeated. And, equally important, we should be extremely grateful that we were not placed in similar circumstances where we might have become equally culpable.

The BBC version is written as a classic tragedy and, appropriate to its audience, focuses on one specific "European" moral question. As the epitome of a dedicated public servant, Mittermayer is compelled to carry out his order to solve the crime and thus bring about his own downfall. While various orders, to which the title alludes, are given and obeyed throughout this version, there are no sub-plots that might divert the audience's attention: there is no preoccupation with various characters' longing for the "good old days"; the police are competent and, with the exception of the ambitious Poslanetz, conscientious and decent.

In this version, Mittermayer's crime becomes known to several: to his psychiatrist, his former commanding officer, a former accomplice, a fellow police officer Dwornik, and eventually to his wife. Mittermayer's wife in particular is stunned to discover the brutal aspect of her husband's past, and the audience might wonder how their relationship would have continued had Mittermayer not met his death prematurely. But even this possible ambiguity is minimized, as the wife does not appear on the stage after the beginning of the third act. In general, the reactions of the minor characters to Mittermayer's deeds are of less significance to the audience than in the later version. And, likewise, the lives of other possible war criminals are shown more as comparisons with Mittermayer than in explicit judgment of their actions, since they each appear on stage only once in a sort of cameo role and then are forgotten. Mittermayer's life thus takes on a new dimension when we are shown the others' more or less successful attempts to overcome their past. The former commanding officer appears to have no qualms about his former life and has adjusted to democratic capitalism with the same aggression and cleverness that had helped him succeed as an officer; the former accomplice daily drinks himself into a stupor, hinting that he has not been able to dismiss his past so effortlessly, that he too may be haunted by his wartime acts; Poslanetz's possible suspect, so brutal during the war, now raises rosy little pigs and cannot bear to slaughter them himself.

As we have seen, the ambiguities are minimized here – there is but one overarching question of orders and obedience: the initial order to solve the case indeed leads to its ultimate resolution. On the other hand, Dwornik's refusal to follow orders and expose Mittermayer's complicity is to be seen in sharp contrast, not as disobedience or complicity in a cover-up, but as an act of wisdom and humanity. Dwornik refuses Mittermayer's order to turn him in, as he is seemingly more interested in healing than in some abstract form of justice. He proclaims that both de Goede and Mittermayer – both victim and perpetrator alike – are sick from the past (as many in the European audience must have been in those days). With his appeal for humane understanding and healing, Dwornik is almost an Expressionist "new man," a dramatic resolution which would have made Hochwälder's old mentor, Georg Kaiser, extremely proud.

The explanation for the murderous crime is clearly plotted throughout the play. Mittermayer is obviously tormented by his guilt and insists that justice be done; though he cannot face de Goede, it is clear that his death at the hands of a gangster is meant as atonement in the line of duty for a crime that was originally committed also in the line of duty. Thus, Mittermayer is to be seen as a decent, conscientious man who was not strong enough to resist his "time."[13] In summation, Hochwälder has reduced the play to a humane equation: according to Dwornik, it was the times; according to Mittermayer, it was the people. Both are correct, for in the ultimate scene Dwornik pleads with de Goede to help make certain that the "times" never return, because too many "people" could incur guilt if given the proper opportunity or circumstance. This, then, is a "European" solution – Hochwälder does not ask his audience to forget or forgive the past, but to understand why it happened and why basically decent people committed inhuman crimes. This conclusion underscores the mature Hochwälder's conviction that "justice is to be found within the heart and mind of man rather than in the courts."[14]

Burgtheater Version[15]

Despite his self-imposed, lifelong exile in Switzerland, Hochwälder maintained that his inspiration for the theater derived from the Austrian tradition of the *Volkstheater* of his childhood. Out of modesty and a strong sense of tradition, Hochwälder expressly distanced himself from the experimental playwrights of the twentieth century, the absurdists and the proponents of epic theater, and especially from those who aspired to be great literary figures. Instead, Hochwälder insisted on his own humble status as an "illiterate – unliterary, unpretentious, close to the common man."[16] He characterized his plays as "catholic," that is, traditional in the nonsectarian sense, or as one scholar expressed it, "straightforward, economical, well-constructed plays."[17] Another writes:

> In his hands the theater remains a moral institution with an obligation to entertain and also to edify and instruct. Writing in the tradition of the Viennese folk theater as he does, Hochwälder is usually less interested in the psychological development of his characters than in illustrating the central problem per se. As is appropriate to the

> entertaining plays he wished to produce, his characters are usually stereotypes who enunciate a fixed position and undergo little psychological change or development in the course of the action.[18]

The exposition for this second version is identical to that of the BBC version. Mittermayer is ordered to investigate a war crime involving de Goede and his teenage daughter. Here, again, de Goede's intention is not to extract revenge or to prosecute the crime, but merely to confront the perpetrator. And here, again, after Mittermayer realizes that he committed but repressed memory of the crime, he visits his former commanding officer who advises Mittermayer to get drunk and again try to forget the whole episode. Under the influence of alcohol, Mittermayer recounts the murderous incident word for word, in essence admitting his guilt but consoling himself with the fact that he could stonewall the investigation and remain beyond suspicion. Returning home drunk, Mittermayer is confronted by his alter ego, a vision of himself as a cynical and brutal "Green" policeman who tells Mittermayer to find a scapegoat, someone who has a shady past and can easily be framed for the murder.

Act Two opens with Mittermayer at breakfast with his mother. She is concerned about his drunken behavior the night before and reminds him that his father died in an institution as an alcoholic. His mother then leaves for church, to pray for her son, while Mittermayer blames the alcohol for his haunting vision of the "Green." Immediately thereafter, Mittermayer is sent to Holland to interview witnesses. But the interrogation only intensifies his sense of guilt and he nearly betrays himself; in yet another confrontation, the "Green" suggests Mittermayer plunge into the water of the canal and drown himself as the only resolution to this crisis.

Back in Vienna, Detective Dwornik had suspected Mittermayer for some time. Alone now with Mittermayer, Dwornik proposes that the crime was committed by someone much like himself, caught up in the turbulence of the times – and under orders. Dwornik suggests that the murderer should go to de Goede and confess that he was the one who did it, but that he is not the same person any more. Since de Goede only wants satisfaction, not a conviction, it would clear the conscience of the perpetrator without criminal consequences and the case would be closed, once and for all.

The third act begins with Mittermayer's visit to de Goede; he privately admits he committed the murder in an attempt to atone for his guilt. But de Goede will not accept this confession, suspecting instead that Mittermayer has been ordered by his superiors to confess, to appease de Goede because they have not been able to solve the crime. Mittermayer leaves, gets drunk again, and after nightfall wanders down to the river where he is haunted by the voice of himself as the "Green." Attempting to strike the apparition, he falls off balance into the water and drowns. When Mittermayer's death is reported the next day – in the play's final scene – the Chief of Police regrets the accidental death of such a wonderful public servant:

> I have sad news to tell you. Chief Inspector Franz Mittermayer had a fatal accident last night under strange circumstances. The mortal remains of the deceased were recovered early this morning from a tributary of the Heustadel. According to a report from the Forensics Institute, no crime was committed. In order to prevent possible rumors, I declare on the basis of this personnel file that Mittermayer's incomprehensible confession, according to testimony by Mr. de Goede, is without any validity. We lament the dearly departed, a scrupulous civil servant who, his whole life long, never veered one iota from decency and humanity. We will always preserve an honorable remembrance of him.[19]

Though the Chief does not understand Mittermayer's confession to de Goede, he vaguely excuses it as some sort of personality defect and resolves to maintain the memory of Mittermayer as an example of decency and humanity.

In this version of the play, the "order" referred to in the title is but one of many. In some instances, orders are obediently followed, in others they provide an excuse for personal weakness: in 1942 Mittermayer's commanding officer is ordered to apprehend Dutch citizens from the resistance; he then gives the order to Mittermayer who serves throughout the play as the epitome of the man who follows orders with unquestioning dedication. After the death of the girl, Mittermayer is ordered to forget the crime – which he does, conscientiously and completely. When he is given the new order to solve the crime, he dedicates himself to that end, again because it is an order from his superior. But what moral judgment is an audience to draw from these circumstances? That one should not blindly obey orders? Such a moral imperative might have prevented Mittermayer's murder of the girl, but obviously would have prevented the discovery of the crime years later.

The theater audience here is also left in doubt as to whether Mittermayer's death is intended as suicide and escape, as an act of insanity, an attempt at redemption, or as merely a drunken accident resulting from his hallucinations of the "Green." In the abstract, the audience could consider the guilty punished and justice served. But as for the initiator of the case, de Goede, such a resolution becomes problematic: he simply states that he wishes the case closed, and it is unclear whether he finally accepts Mittermayer's confession, whether he believes that the case will remain unsolved, or whether he is simply disgusted with the political machinations and bureaucratic intrigue surrounding his initial request.

The Viennese theatergoer, accustomed to Hochwälder's transparent style, would be stunned by the present version of *The Order* and its numerous ambiguities. What could Hochwälder have intended for his "local" audience? The insight that, on an individual level, this is the human condition – that normal citizens are momentarily capable of heinous crimes which on sober reflection would shock even themselves? Or that people can overcome their failings – that Mittermayer *was* a murderer, but is not the same person today? That, in moral terms, individual human beings must continually practice personal responsibility to accept and atone for their misdeeds?

By emphasizing the Viennese venue in locales, flavor, and characters, the Austrian production of *The Order* offers another striking contrast to the BBC version. Scenes are now located in the Prater, at the Imperial Hotel, and in the Konstantin Hills. Vocabulary is spiced with particularly Austrian terms, such as *salvieren* (21), *tunken/eintunken* (34/55), *Klamsch* (49), *Werkelmänner* (50), and *eruieren* (77). In addition, there are stock characters recognizable from the *Volkstheater* tradition: a semi-invisible alter ego or *Doppelgänger* in the person of the "Green," a youthful Mittermayer in the service of the Third Reich in occupied Amsterdam who represents his past deeds as well as his conscience. The audience would also be amused – and troubled – by the figure of the Mother running off to church to pray for her errant son (who, by now, is almost sixty years of age!); furthermore, the fact that the middle-aged Mittermayer is not married hints that possibly something is wrong in his life, that he may still require "mothering." There is also a typical shady character, a suspicious criminal element, described as "Balkan" in nature and, for good measure, an actual character named Death, replete with scythe.[20]

Hochwälder's utilization of the *Volkstheater* tradition and employment of Austrian trappings are tailor-made for this specific audience – the Austrians are to recognize the milieu and themselves in this play. Unlike his earlier "European" solution, Hochwälder clearly insists that nothing has changed in Austrian society – that orders are still given and carried out without heeding the human consequences. In this light, and in consideration of their recent past, he thus renounces the titular "order" and emphasizes that Austrians as individuals should practice selective obedience. Furthermore, this is also a critique of the traditional Viennese insistence on appearance over truth – that Mittermayer will henceforth be remembered as a decent human being and not exposed as a murderer. In broader terms, the dramatist insists that Austrian society is unrepentant, content to forget the past and enjoy the current blessings of peace and prosperity. To this end, several minor characters in the play indicate that they used to be persons of power or influence during the Nazi years, but now, in "normal" times, have sunk to the level of lowlife on the fringes of society. This exemplifies a direct critique of Austrian brutality during the war years, of their willing complicity in the war, their attempt to exonerate themselves as "Hitler's first victims" and exploit today's democratic society. Ultimately Hochwälder disallows them any possibility of denial and threatens the Viennese with the force of some invisible but omnipresent universal justice if they fail to acknowledge their complicity.

More troubling, Hochwälder also suggests that even the younger generation of Austrians, innocent of war crimes by virtue of their age, can be just as cold and calculating as their parents were during the Third Reich. One gratuitous example occurs in the play's penultimate scene. Mittermayer's plunge into the water is witnessed by two young lovebirds in the bushes. In a brief dialogue, the girl warns her beau that someone has fallen into the water. He replies that it is just a drunk and that he does not want to get involved. They leave abruptly, without attempting a rescue.

The dramatist's theatrical focus relative to the punishment of war criminals changed subtly over the years. Whereas Hochwälder originally argues for their dogged prosecution, by the time he wrote *The Order*, he "advocates the cessation of hunting and prosecuting war criminals because of the passage of time ... Although he had believed in strict justice, he became convinced that harmonious order in society is more important than justice. Hence it is better to close one's eyes to crimes of the past for the sake of the present."[21] This, clearly, is the focus of the BBC version – but not that of the Vienna text. In the latter, Hochwälder returns to his earlier stance, that justice must prevail: regardless of Mittermayer's actual motivation, he dies as a direct result of his earlier crime, and his drowning only parallels the young girl's drowning twenty years earlier. Too, the Austrians themselves will not be permitted to escape culpability – released by some Dwornikian "new man" as portrayed in the BBC version – but will have to struggle with the many troubling questions posed above.

At the outset of this investigation I quoted critic Donald G. Daviau, who emphasized Hochwälder's enduring commitment to moral issues: "[Hochwälder] eschews ambiguity and consciously utilizes strong theatrical effects, while developing a clear theme, with relevance to his audiences, which he leads to an inexorable conclusion." To be sure, these insights pertain to Hochwälder's entire oeuvre – with the exception of the *Burgtheater* version of *The Order*. Though Hochwälder retained the title of the BBC version, this play no longer focuses our attention on that previous theme, namely the decent though imperfect human being as a victim of treacherous times. Fritz Hochwälder was a sophisticated dramatist who would neither intentionally bludgeon his audience with a simple moral nor confuse them with extraneous subplots. He was a moralist who seldom equivocated or posed questions he was not prepared to answer. Thus, the intended ambiguities only make this version more provocative, more controversial. We can only speculate that this unique version was intended as Hochwälder's dramatic revenge on his native land for his own permanent exile and the execution of his parents.

Notes

1. James Schmitt, "The Theater of Fritz Hochwälder: Its Background and Development," in *Modern Austrian Literature* 11 (1978): 49.

2. Donald G. Daviau, "Fritz Hochwälder," *Major Figures of Modern Austrian Literature*, ed. Donald G. Daviau (Riverside, CA: Ariadne Press, 1988) 242. See also U. Henry Gerlach, "Das Motiv des unterdrückten Gewissens in den Dramen Fritz Hochwälders," *Modern Austrian Literature* 16 (1983): 53.

3. For a brief background of Hochwälder's friendship with Kaiser, see Schmitt 52-53.

4. Hochwälder, while maintaining his Austrian citizenship and writing primarily for the Austrian stage, resided in Zurich for almost fifty years, though he always considered himself an outsider in Swiss literary circles. He was for the entire time a contemporary and "neighbor" of both Friedrich Dürrenmatt and Max Frisch, the two giants of twentieth-century Swiss drama. There is no evidence that they were in close contact with each other, in spite of thematic similarities between several of their plays. While there have been only a few, isolated comparisons of Hochwälder and Dürrenmatt or Hochwälder and Frisch, an extensive study of the dramaturgical interrelationship between the three would be highly instructive. For a brief overview, see Donald G. Daviau, "Fritz Hochwälder's Range of Theme and Form," *Modern Austrian Literature* 18 (1985): 38.

5. Daviau, "Fritz Hochwälder's Range of Theme and Form" 31.

6. Donald G. Daviau, "Afterword," *The Holy Experiment and Other Plays* (Riverside, CA: Ariadne Press, 1998) 317.

7. Fritz Hochwälder, "Über mein Theater," *Der Befehl* (Graz: Stiasny Verlag, 1967) 88-107. This version, dated April 1966, supercedes an earlier draft of 1956.

8. Interestingly, the play written just before *The Order*, namely *The Raspberry Picker*, was also a dual presentation, but the national venues were reversed: it was first shown on Austrian TV, and then six months later enjoyed a staged premiere in Zurich. See the "Fritz Hochwälder Bibliography," compiled by James Schmitt, *Modern Austrian Literature* 11 (1978): 63-73.

9. Hochwälder turned to variations of this theme in several plays, such as *The Holy Experiment*, *Der Flüchtling* (*The Fugitive*), *The Public Prosecutor*, as well as *The Order*.

10. I am indebted to Bernadette Donaghy of BBC Information and to Susan Knowles of the BBC Written Archives Centre for details regarding this production.
11. Originally published as *Der Befehl* in *Stücke* (Berlin: Henschel, 1968).
12. This and all following translations of this version are by Todd C. Hanlin, *Orders, The Holy Experiment and Other Plays* (Riverside, CA: Ariadne Press, 1998) 244.
13. Alan Best argues convincingly that Mittermayer is to be considered a representative "decent" European, with Oedipus and Max Frisch's Biedermann as predecessors. Best also posits an etymological derivation of the main character's name, implying an average citizen: "Shadows of the Past: The Drama of Fritz Hochwälder," *Modern Austrian Writing: Literature and Society after 1945*, ed. Alan Best and Hans Wolfschütz (London: Oswald Wolff, 1980) 58.
14. Ian C. Loram, "Fritz Hochwälder," *Monatshefte* 57 (1965): 13.
15. Published in 1967 as *Der Befehl* (Vienna: Stiasny).
16. "… mit Vergnügen bleibe ich Analphabet … unliterarisch, unprätentiös, volkstümlich," *Über mein Theater* 99.
17. Loram 8. Yet Daviau points out that "not many of his plays feature a *Hanswurst* [clown] nor do they display other characteristics of the Volkstheater tradition, such as interludes of singing and dancing," from "Fritz Hochwälder's Range of Theme and Form" 41.
18. Daviau, "Fritz Hochwälder" 242.
19. From an unpublished translation by Lisa Exey.
20. Hochwälder's black-comedy Death is pessimistic and discouraged, longing for the good old days when people truly feared him; here he has been relegated to a sideshow performer who cannot even frighten little children. How quickly the Austrians, in just one generation, have conveniently forgotten their gruesome past is revealed by a comparison with Wolfgang Borchert's

unforgettable portrait of Death who suffered indigestion from "over-eating," in *Draußen vor der Tür* (Outside the Door) from 1946.

21. Daviau, "Fritz Hochwälder's Range of Theme and Form" 37.

The Treatment of Fascism in Post-World War II Austrian Theater

Jennifer E. Michaels

Kurt Waldheim's election to the presidency of Austria in 1986 and the fiftieth anniversary of the *Anschluß* in 1988 led to wide public debate in Austria about its role in and culpability for Nazi atrocities, a debate in which Austrian writers took a leading part. Before this time, Austrian writers were often criticized, rather unfairly, for their silence on this topic. In 1984, for example, Ute Nyssen expressed a commonly held view that, unlike such dramatists in the Federal Republic as Rolf Hochhuth, Peter Weiss, and Heinar Kipphardt, Austrian authors had been remiss in discussing their country's Nazi past.[1] In the years after the war this topic was not, however, ignored. A number of Austrian writers, including Ilse Aichinger and Ingeborg Bachmann, urged their fellow citizens to reflect on their behavior during the Nazi years, although their works failed to reach wide audiences. Some of Austria's most popular and successful postwar dramatists, as well as some of its most controversial ones, also confronted the Nazi past. Through their works, these dramatists tried to promote public debate about Austrian complicity during this period and to voice their concern about the lingering effects of Nazi ideology in the present. In the following I will give an overview of some of these different treatments of fascism in plays by Fritz Hochwälder, Peter Turrini, Thomas Bernhard, Elfriede Jelinek, and Felix Mitterer, whose works span over thirty years of postwar theater in Austria.

In three of his plays written after the war – *Holokaust* (1961/1998, Holocaust), *Der Himbeerpflücker* (1965, *The Raspberry Picker*, 1982), and *Der Befehl* (1967/68, *Orders*, 1998) – Fritz Hochwälder, one of Austria's most popular postwar dramatists, confronts his country's Nazi past. *The Raspberry Picker* and *Orders* are among his most successful plays. In his essay "Über mein Theater" (1966, "About My Theater"), Hochwälder expresses his concern about the continuing presence of Nazi ideas in Austria and the nostalgia that some still have for the "good old days" of the Nazi past.[2] In his plays, he scrutinizes such attitudes under the magnifying glass[3] and unmasks what lies beneath people's façade of respectability. Today, he observes, if one were to meet an officer who had callously herded people into the gas chambers, one would be surprised to find a civilized man with perfect manners and normal habits, untroubled by any feelings of guilt.[4] What one was then and what one is today is a central question in Hochwälder's plays.[5]

Because he was Jewish, Hochwälder had to flee to Switzerland in 1938 and he continued to live there after the war as an Austrian citizen until his death in 1986. Despite his years first in forced and then in chosen exile, Hochwälder considered himself Austrian, specifically Viennese,[6] and he credits the atmosphere in Vienna for giving him clarity of thought, a sense of form, and theater blood. He views himself not as a theoretician but rather as a man of the theater,[7] whose works are unliterary, unpretentious, and popular.[8] Hochwälder admires the Viennese folk theater and its leading practitioners, such as Nestroy and Raimund, and he draws on this rich tradition in many of his works. Like all great theater, he writes, the Viennese theater has its roots not in gray theory but in fairs, the farce, and the *commedia dell'arte*.[9] With its wide appeal, the folk play, he believes, "embodies a living tradition and one particularly suited to the contemporary world."[10]

Like many of Hochwälder's plays, *Holokaust*, written in 1961 but published only recently, uses the structure of the well-made play to explore questions of responsibility and guilt. He bases his play loosely on the case of the Hungarian Jew, Dr. Rudolf Kastner, who negotiated with Eichmann about Himmler's offer to free a million Hungarian Jews in exchange for 100,000 trucks.[11] When this plan failed, Kastner bargained with Eichmann to allow some Hungarian Jews to emigrate to Palestine in return for his help in maintaining peace in the transit camps and preventing the remaining Jews from resisting deportation to the gas chambers. Kastner, who was later shot on a street in Israel, managed through this collaboration to save nearly 1,700 out of the around 476,000 Hungarian Jews, and those he saved were prominent people and members of Zionist organizations.[12]

Hochwälder's fictional treatment of this event employs the dialectic structure of a trial to examine the painful moral dilemma of a man who had to choose who should be saved and who should die. He sets the play twelve years after the war in a country house on the Côte d'Azur. Roberts, a rich Jewish emigrant living in the United States, has finally tracked down Victor Glaser, the Kastner figure in the play, and has gathered three survivors to confront him with his collaboration with the Nazis. Glaser does not deny the charge but believes he will be pronounced innocent. He paints a grim picture of the hopelessness of the situation when the Hungarian Jews, who were being deported daily to Auschwitz, felt abandoned by all. Since many were old and sick there was little chance of resistance, and the allies were deaf to pleas to bomb the rails leading to the camps. Roberts considers Glaser responsible for the lack of resistance because he knew that the Jews were being deported to their deaths and yet did not warn them. Glaser defends himself by saying that he tried at first to warn them, but nobody wanted to believe him. In this desperate situation, Glaser chose to collaborate with the Nazis to save at least some Jews and through unscrupulous methods succeeded in raising enough money to purchase the lives of two thousand Jews, all of whom belonged in some way to a cultural elite. During the trial, Roberts concludes that he too would have acted like Glaser because he would have managed to save at least a few people. Glaser, however, can no longer live with the knowledge that he had actively participated in mass murder and he forces the former policeman Berek to kill him. By selecting which Jews were to be saved, he realizes, he had accepted Nazi racial thinking. Like the Nazis, he had decided who was worthy to live and who should die.

Hochwälder wrote *Holokaust* before Hochhuth's *Der Stellvertreter* (1963, *The Deputy*, 1964) and Peter Weiss's *Die Ermittlung* (1965, *The Investigation*, 1966). The play, which was not performed at the time, showed Hochwälder to be a pioneer in confronting the Nazi period in the postwar German-language theater.[13] Although the play deals with the deportation of the Hungarian Jews, Hochwälder does not emphasize the Hungarian setting except for brief references to railroad stations in Budapest[14] because he wants to confront his audiences with the enormity of the Holocaust as a whole rather than with one specific example. As in many of his plays, Hochwälder examines here individual and collective responsibility. Although Glaser saved two thousand Jews, he realizes that at a time when all values had disintegrated he too became a traitor, a murderer, and a blackmailer, and he accepts responsibility for his actions. The play is bitterly ironic since Glaser, one of the victims of Hitler's regime, is brought to trial, yet no mention is made that those responsible for the situation which forced Glaser to act unethically are wrestling with their own consciences or being brought to justice.

Hochwälder's next treatment of this topic, *The Raspberry Picker*, was broadcast as a television play in April 1965, an indication of his desire to reach a wide audience, and premiered as a drama at the *Schauspielhaus* in Zurich on 27 September 1965. This play, which draws on the tradition of the critical folk play that he so admired, examines how the Nazi past lives on in postwar provincial Austria. Hochwälder draws attention to this continuity by setting his play in the small but thriving town of Bad Brauning to remind his audience of Hitler's birthplace Braunau. The inn where the action takes place is called the White Lamb to underscore how the characters play the role of innocent victims and whitewash the past.

Hochwälder observes that his play is unfortunately not invention but rather reportage.[15] From the beginning he makes it clear that the town's leading citizens are unreformed Nazis who are anti-

Semitic and racist and who, like the retired doctor Schnopf, long nostalgically for the "glorious" time of the Hitler past. As the play opens, Schnopf is reading in the paper about a jewelry store robbery, and the headmaster Huett shows that he is still a Nazi at heart when he remarks that in the past they would have sent such "riffraff" to a concentration camp or cut their heads off. Like the others, the builder Ybbsgruber is an avid reader of the Old Comrades paper. The paper is indignant about the plight of a war criminal who, even though his "misdemeanors" took place years ago, is being sought on the basis of "underhanded accusations" and "lying statements by witnesses." Showing his anti-Semitism, Ybbsgruber terms this "Old Testament vengeance," and he hopes to help such war criminals escape. One fugitive from justice is Ernst Meiche, called the Raspberry Picker because he ordered prisoners in the near-by concentration camp to pick raspberries and then amused himself by using them as target practice. In this way he was responsible for the murder of between six and eight thousand prisoners.

In their zeal to help fugitive war criminals, the townspeople mistake the crook Kerz for the Raspberry Picker. At first the innkeeper Steisshäuptl, who was the former local Nazi group leader and who is now mayor of the town, is afraid that if the Raspberry Picker is arrested it will be bad for the town's tourist business. Most of all he fears that the Raspberry Picker will demand the return of his two boxes of gold fillings from the teeth of camp inmates. Steisshäuptl was supposed to keep the gold for the Raspberry Picker but used it himself, the reason he is now prosperous. He soon takes the position that he is proud that this "hero" has come to stay at his inn. The townspeople treat the supposed mass murderer with respect and give him money, and they intrigue against each other to take advantage of the situation. Only the threat of the Nazi hunter Brischa brings them together to whitewash the past. They discover that the supposed Raspberry Picker is in reality the petty criminal Kerz, who happens to be Jewish, and who is quickly arrested. The real Raspberry Picker, they learn, was arrested and committed suicide, to the relief of the innkeeper who no longer has to account for the boxes of gold.

Through the device of mistaken identity, Hochwälder unmasks the Nazi attitudes that continue to shape the present behavior of these seemingly respectable citizens, and shows their refusal to accept any responsibility for the past. He underscores the ease with which former Nazis were integrated into postwar Austrian society where they became leading citizens as doctors, lawyers, teachers, and mayors. The innkeeper minimizes the thousands killed by the Raspberry Picker as a few dark patches in an otherwise heroic past and asserts that if Hitler had not lost the war, he would still consider him his *Führer*. All these citizens were involved to some degree in Nazi crimes. The doctor participated in euthanasia in the Old Age Home; the lawyer profited from the aryanization of Jewish property; the police inspector was in a special duty squad in Vilna; and the headmaster killed forced laborers in his native Germany. As the play ends, it is clear that the characters will continue to survive and flourish, untroubled by any sense of horror at their deeds.

Hochwälder's play was very popular, but its macabre humor left him open to the charge that he trivialized the past.[16] Hochwälder does not make light of the past but rather uses biting satire to strip off his characters' hypocritical masks. Esslin, who points out the play's similarities to Gogol's *The Government Inspector*, argues that the differences between the works are especially revealing. In Gogol's play, the people are afraid of the supposed virtue of the man they mistake for a government inspector, sent to investigate their corruption. In Hochwälder's play, however, the supposed Raspberry Picker inspires respect not because he is virtuous but because he is a mass murderer. As Esslin observes: "No more bitter, no more telling satire could be imagined."[17]

Orders, Hochwälder's next treatment of the Nazi past, was produced first as a television play in 1967 and later revised for the stage. It was performed on 3 March 1968 at the *Burgtheater*. In the play, which takes place in Vienna in the present, Chief Inspector Mittermayer is assigned to find the Viennese military policeman responsible for killing the young daughter of de Goede, a Dutch resistance fighter, during the war in Amsterdam. Hochwälder points out that this is not, however, an example of Austrian zeal to confront its past. The investigation occurs only because de Goede is now a member of a Dutch economic delegation to Austria, and the Austrians do not want to offend him. Mittermayer is assigned the case because he appears to be a decent, ethical person with a spotless record. He refuses to allow his colleague Poslanetz to pin this "trivial" incident on someone as a scapegoat. As Mittermayer investigates, he realizes with horror that he is the person who killed the girl, a guilt that he had repressed through excessive drinking after the murder took place. His record is spotless only because his former commanding office has expunged the murder from his file. When he visits his wartime comrade Hainzl, Mittermayer learns that he committed other crimes. Hainzl, who is not troubled by conscience, remembers how he and Mittermayer brutally rounded up Jews and deported them to concentration camps. Because of this they were held up as models for the other policemen to emulate. Mittermayer accepts responsibility for his crimes and, in the stage version of the play, commits suicide by forcing a criminal to shoot him.

Hochwälder calls this play the tragedy of the little person who has to follow orders.[18] The play was controversial because some thought it tried to exonerate the guilty by "rationalizing their behavior simply as a manifestation of the times."[19] Although Hochwälder sympathizes with Mittermayer, he does not exonerate him but rather uses him as an example of the complicity of ordinary Austrians in the Nazi years. Now as then, Mittermayer is interested only in "orders, obedience, work."[20] His colleague Dwornik tells de Goede that the perpetrator was an animal back then but today is a normal average man, and he tries to rationalize the crime by saying that the perpetrator lost control at a time when there was a bonus for every criminal act and punishment for humane behavior (313). Mittermayer represents the many solid citizens who committed and then covered up their crimes and now lead respectable lives. He is different only because he accepts responsibility for his actions while the others, such as his former commanding officer, who dismisses the past by saying they were just carrying out orders, do not. Dwornik urges Mittermayer to tell de Goede: "I was the one, but I'm not the same man today" (308). Mittermayer believes, however, that he is the same man today. Unlike Dwornik he insists that people, and not the times, were responsible. As in *The Raspberry Picker*, Hochwälder stresses here that not only monsters like the Raspberry Picker but also ordinary citizens like Mittermayer had within themselves the potential for brutality and were responsible for crimes.

Like Hochwälder in *The Raspberry Picker*, Peter Turrini draws on the tradition of the critical folk play to point to the continuity of Nazi thinking in postwar Austria. *Sauschlachten* (1974, *Pig Slaughter*, 1993), which was first performed at the Munich *Kammerspiele* on 15 January 1972, shocked the audience and the critics. Turrini has long been outspoken about Austria's Nazi past. In the essay, "Ich bin ein Gefangener meiner Biographie" (1986, "I Am a Prisoner of My Biography"), Turrini describes the complacent faces of the village notables he saw around the *Stammtisch* when he was growing up. In these faces Turrini detected no trace of sorrow about the Nazi years. Instead of confronting the past, those responsible for the horror moved quickly into positions of power in postwar society. The Nazi group organizer became the new mayor, for example, and the Nazi teacher became the new school director, a comment that echoes Hochwälder's criticism in *The Raspberry Picker*. Later in Vienna, Turrini encountered the same faces from which all guilt and sorrow had been banned, and among these faces he includes Kurt Waldheim's. Although these people have learned to liberalize their language, they have not liberalized their being.[21] By reminding his readers that many Austrians were active in the SS, Turrini tries to dispel the myth of Austria as the first innocent victim of Nazi aggression. He notes that Austrians such as Eichmann, Kaltenbrunner, and Globocnik played a leading part in constructing and running the concentration camps.[22] Although fascism was officially ended in 1945, Turrini observes, it continued unofficially as a state of mind, as a poisoning of the spirit.[23]

In *Pig Slaughter*, which was written in dialect, Turrini shows how this continuing fascism poisons the present and leads to violence. The play, dedicated ironically to Turrini's "all too beloved country," is set on a farm and depicts the increasingly vicious treatment that Valentin, called Volte, the farmer's oldest son, is forced to endure. Volte refuses to speak and only grunts like a pig. Spurred on by Volte's illegitimate brother Franz, who wants to inherit the farm, the family members and the farmhand sadistically enjoy tormenting him: his father hits him because he will not speak; they try to make him sing patriotic songs, filled with Nazi clichés about *Heimat*; they brutally force him to eat pig swill; and finally, urged on by the doctor, the priest, the teacher, and the lawyer, they slaughter him like a pig. Turrini included in the program notes for the play graphic descriptions about how pigs are slaughtered.

Turrini shows here how society treats individuals and groups whom it perceives to be different, how it strips them of their humanity and sadistically destroys them. Although the play focuses on the present, Turrini makes clear that Volte's treatment is caused by the same Nazi thinking, racism, and intolerance that led to euthanasia and the murder of the Jews. In the "unregenerated society"[24] of the play, the characters are still warped by the Nazi past and feel no remorse for their actions during the war. The farmhand does not regret his brutal treatment of prisoners-of-war, and the farmer and his wife still use patriotic slogans from the Nazi period. The lawyer makes veiled references to euthanasia when he observes that thirty years ago the doctor could easily have dealt with the problem of someone like Volte. Because he refuses to speak, Volte is regarded as sub-human and unworthy of living. Through his characters' references to "worthless life" and "extermination,"[25] Turrini explicitly draws connections between Volte's slaughter and the final solution. This brutal play gives insight into Turrini's view of the theater. The stage is for him a place where he can make the terrible more terrible in order to deter.[26]

Thomas Bernhard, like Turrini one of Austria's most prominent and controversial playwrights, addresses his country's Nazi

80 Jennifer E. Michaels

past and its continuing legacy in *Vor dem Ruhstand* (1979, Eve of Retirement) and *Heldenplatz* (1988). Bernhard, who enjoyed his reputation as a troublemaker, is known for his scathing attacks on wide-ranging aspects of Austrian culture and society and for his "cantankerous behavior and a scorched-earth tactics in satirical writing,"[27] but he was also a "powerful voice of constructive dissent."[28] Bernhard was sharply criticized in Austria during his lifetime but became respected once he was safely dead. Turrini gives an ironic portrait of Bernhard returning to the *Burgtheater* as a ghost. The ghost relates his astonishment at the unexpected praise and respect he has enjoyed in Austria since his death and recommends that all living Austrian writers follow his example as quickly as possible.[29]

In *Vor dem Ruhstand*, first performed on 29 June 1979 at the *Staatstheater* in Stuttgart, Bernhard attacks the fascist ideology that continues to poison the present. The play was written for Claus Peymann, who at that time was artistic director of the *Staatstheater*. Conservative politicians in the Christian Democratic Union had long criticized Peymann for his avant-garde artistic policies and they forced him to resign. One of his severest critics was Hans Karl Filbinger, Minister President of Baden-Württemberg at that time. It came to light that Filbinger had been a naval judge under the Nazis and in this capacity had sentenced numerous people to death, and he first denied and then trivialized his past. As his last play, Peymann planned to put on Hochhuth's *Juristen* (1979, Lawyers) but when Hochhuth could not finish the play on time, he chose Bernhard's play instead. Unlike Hochhuth, Bernhard does not deal directly with the Filbinger scandal, but instead caustically analyzes the continued adherence to Nazi ideology in the postwar years.[30]

Like many of Bernhard's plays, this one has little action and few characters. The three characters here are Rudolf Höller and his sisters Vera and Clara. Höller, a former concentration camp commandant and now a chief justice of a German court, demonstrates the ease with which war criminals moved into leading positions in the postwar years. For decades, Vera and Rudolf have celebrated

Himmler's birthday, which for Rudolf is the highlight of the year. For this occasion, Rudolf puts on his SS uniform, which Vera has lovingly ironed, and they reminisce about the past. As part of the previous year's celebration they forced their crippled sister Clara to play a concentration camp inmate. They shaved her head and made her wear concentration camp clothes. To end the celebration Vera and Rudolf go to bed together, an incestuous relationship that has continued for many years, and through which Bernhard casts light on the moral depravity of Nazism.

Rudolf, who claims he just did his duty, has no feelings of shame or regret for what he did. Instead he is proud that the camp he ran was a model operation and he still believes that the task he fulfilled benefited the entire German people. He is grateful to Himmler for preventing a poison gas factory being built on the location of their home and for providing him with a false passport so that he could escape at the end of the war. As Rudolf and Vera look nostalgically at the photos of the past, Vera ignores the brutality of the camp and sees only that the trees were pretty and the landscape was charming. This grotesque family album includes snapshots of Hungarian Jews, of Ukrainians Rudolf has shot, and of the gas chambers at Auschwitz.

Not only do Rudolf and Vera have no regrets about the past, but their Nazi views shape their attitude to the present. Rudolf brutally tells his crippled sister Clara, for example, that in the past people like her would have been gassed. Rudolf, who is strongly anti-Semitic, holds Jews and democracy responsible for everything he considers wrong in present-day society. Rudolf and Vera have turned Nazism into a perverted religion that includes the millenarian belief that it will soon return. They mythologize the past into a Golden Age, peopled with archetypal figures like Himmler.[31] In his play Bernhard suggests that this "addiction to National Socialist thinking" still lurks not only "within the modern German psyche,"[32] but also within the Austrian.

As was typical for Bernhard's plays, *Vor dem Ruhstand* outraged the public, but this reaction was mild in comparison to the uproar that greeted *Heldenplatz* when it was produced by Peymann on 4 November 1988 at the *Burgtheater*. Bernhard wrote this play for the centennial anniversary celebration of the *Burgtheater*. The year 1988 was also the fiftieth anniversary of the *Anschluß*. The play caused an enormous scandal and it was harshly denounced by the media, the government, and by Austrian citizens, all of whom were outraged by "Bernhard's latest blasphemy against his country and countrymen."[33] It turned "Austria temporarily into a *Staatstheater*."[34] Although Bernhard's sharp criticism of Austria in the play is similar to that expressed in his earlier works, people were particularly offended because the play was written for the centennial of the *Burgtheater*, the symbol and pride of the Austrian cultural establishment. Bernhard believed, however, that this was precisely the right time and the right setting to hold up a mirror to his fellow citizens and to remind them of the *Anschluß*.[35]

The play raises a variety of sensitive issues. Its title recalls the jubilant response that greeted Hitler's speech on the Heldenplatz on 15 March 1938. Bernhard addresses the complicity of Austrians during the Nazi years and discusses the widespread anti-Semitism that he sees as an integral part of Austrian nature. In the play, he depicts the lasting effects of the *Anschluß* on the disrupted lives of one Jewish family. The family fled from the Nazis but returned to Vienna after the war. Before the play opens, Josef Schuster has committed suicide by jumping out of their apartment near the Heldenplatz. As the family and the servants look back at his life since the *Anschluß*, they, and particularly the dead man's brother Robert, sharply criticize Austrian politics, culture, and society. The family members feel threatened by increasing anti-Semitism that shows itself openly, and they sense that Austrians would like the Nazis to return to power. In every Viennese, Robert provocatively claims, there is hidden a mass murderer.[36] Josef's widow cannot forget the past. In her mind she hears the voices of the mob from the Heldenplatz triumphantly greeting Hitler. At the end of the play the jubilant screams get louder and louder in her head and she collapses. For her, as for Bernhard, "these terrible experiences are just as present as if they had been only yesterday."[37]

Fascism in Post-World War II Austrian Theater   83

Like Hochwälder, Turrini, and Bernhard, Elfriede Jelinek also examines the unconfronted past and points out how the past continues to shape the present. In *Totenauberg* (1991, *Death/Valley/Summit*, 1996), for example, a fictive encounter between Hannah Arendt and Martin Heidegger, Jelinek underscores her critique of Austrian chauvinism and the tourist industry by juxtaposing films of a tourist landscape, littered with dead mountain climbers, with clips from old documentary films showing the deportation of Jews. Like Bernhard's *Heldenplatz*, her play *Burgtheater* (1985), which she terms a burlesque, caused a scandal when it premiered in Bonn in 1985. As in the case of Bernhard, many Austrians were offended by her criticism of their national theater.

The characters in the play are the married couple, Käthe and Istvan, their three daughters, Istvan's brother Schorsch, his sister Resi, a dwarf, and the Alpenkönig. The first part of the play, set in 1941, depicts the three *Burgtheater* actors as vain anti-Semitic, pro-Nazi opportunists, who have easily adapted to the new times. They are pleased that the *Führer* admires them and proud of their roles in Nazi propaganda films. Schorsch hopes that members of the Hitler Youth will come to see the *Burgtheater* as their theater.[38] In an allegorical interlude, the Alpine King (Alpenkönig), a figure out of Austrian folk theater, visits them to collect money for the resistance, but they abuse him and tear him apart. In the second part of the play, set in 1945 shortly before the liberation by the Soviets, the three actors try to cover up their complicity in the Nazi period and their participation in Nazi propaganda. When they discover that Resi has hidden a dwarf, also an actor at the *Burgtheater*, they demand that he testify to the Soviets that they rescued him from euthanasia. Since Schorsch has managed to get himself arrested and can thus play the role of a Nazi victim, the dwarf's testimony is no longer needed. The play ends with slogans from Viennese culture mixed through with Nazi ideology.

Jelinek's play is both a linguistic satire and a criticism of how the *Burgtheater* betrayed its role as a moral institution and then suppressed its past after the war. She stresses that her play is primarily a critique of language. She intends it to denounce Austrian provincial language that was never de-Nazified and still reflects Nazi attitudes. This chauvinistic language, she writes, was taken over by the *Heimat* kitsch of the 1950s.[39] Jelinek uses in her play quotations from such Nazi films as *Heimkehr*, in her view the worst Nazi propaganda film, in which admired actors of the *Burgtheater* starred.[40] She also denounces both the hypocrisy of the *Burgtheater*, which on the day after the *Anschluß* did not allow Jewish actors to enter the theater,[41] and its actors, who refused to be held accountable for their complicity after the war. Although she does not name specific actors in her play, she mentions in an interview Paula Wessely. Wessely, who starred in eleven Nazi propaganda films including the notorious *Heimkehr* (1941), continued her success as an actress after the war.[42] The play contains obvious parallels between the stage characters and real people and was condemned as a vicious attack on the Austrian actors Paula Wessely and Attila Hörbiger.[43] Despite such criticism, the play succeeds in making an important contribution to confronting Austria's past and it helps to demythologize "a form of blind patriotism and arrogant chauvinism encapsulated in the concept of the Austrian *Heimat*."[44]

Felix Mitterer, one of the most popular playwrights writing in the German language today,[45] uses the critical folk play to confront his country's past and hopes, by using this genre, to reach as wide an audience as possible.[46] Mitterer believes that the theater can play a key role in making people aware of important issues and promoting discussion and self-examination. In *Kein schöner Land* (1987, There's No Finer Country), which premiered at the *Tiroler Landestheater* on 12 April 1987, Mitterer combines elements of the peasant farce, popular in Tirol, with the folk play to confront his audience with Austria's persecution of its Jewish citizens in the Nazi period. Mitterer, who is almost fanatical about researching his projects,[47] carefully researched the Nazi persecution of the Jews in Tirol for his play.[48]

Mitterer bases his play on the case of Rudolf Gomperz, who was active in developing tourism and skiing in St. Anton and who was later murdered in a concentration camp. Mitterer investigates how Nazism, opportunism, cowardice, and self-interest flourish in what seems to be a tranquil, and typical, village in the Tirolean Alps. Although not all in the village are actively involved in Adler's persecution, most do nothing to prevent it and look on as it occurs. By using the village setting, Mitterer intensifies the horror of the persecution. Adler, its target, who has tried to hide his Jewish ancestry and has assimilated successfully, as he mistakenly thinks, into village society, has been for many years a respected member of the community. Neighbors, whom he has always treated kindly and fairly, suddenly turn on him. All are aware of the persecution and cannot hide behind the excuse that they did not know what was going on. Mitterer shows the enthusiasm of the young people for Nazi ideas and stresses that Nazism was not imported from Germany but was present in Austria long before the *Anschluß*.

Mitterer raises other troubling issues in the play, such as the collaboration of the Catholic Church with the Nazis and Austrian complicity in the Nazi euthanasia program. At the end, the village priest tries to help Adler and he too is killed, but he was earlier a religious anti-Semite who preached against Jews in his sermons. He thus encouraged the anti-Semitism of his congregation that led them to acquiesce in Adler's persecution. Toni, the mentally handicapped son of the rabidly anti-Semitic Nazi teacher Hopfgartner, is one of the few people in the village who tries to protect Adler. Because of his handicap, he is first sterilized and later murdered by lethal injection.

Of all the characters in the play, the mayor demonstrates most clearly the shaky foundation on which Mitterer believes postwar Austrian identity rests. Mitterer depicts him as a typical opportunist and conformist, who cunningly goes along. As the name of his inn, the White Lamb, suggests, he intends to whitewash the past. The mayor supported Dollfuss, later the Nazis, and now the postwar government. At the conclusion of the play, he shows his determination to rewrite history and suppress the past and he absolves the Nazis and opportunists from all responsibility for their crimes. Mitterer believes that the mayor's lack of remorse and his refusal to wrestle with ethical and moral issues are typical of Austria's attitude to its Nazi past. The complicity of the villagers in the murderous persecution of Adler and the killing of Toni and the priest expose the hollowness of the mayor's claim that they were all innocent victims. Mitterer insists in the play that it is essential to learn from the past because, as the quotation from George Santayana's *Life of Reason* that opens the play suggests: "Those who cannot remember the past are condemned to repeat it."

In his recent play *In der Löwengrube* (1998, In the Lion's Den), which premiered at the Vienna *Volkstheater* on 24 January 1998, Mitterer again uses the folk play to address the Nazi past. The play is based on the story of the Jewish actor Leo Reuß. After the Nazis came to power in 1933, Reuß lost his engagement in Berlin. He returned to Vienna but was unable to get work there. In the summer of 1936 a Tirolean peasant dressed in Tirolean costume, and supposedly named Kaspar Brandhofer, came to Max Reinhardt and said he wanted to be an actor. Reinhardt was impressed with his talent and recommended him to the *Theater in der Josefstadt*, where Ernst Lothar hired him for the role of the voyeur Dorsday in the dramatization of *Fräulein Else*. His performance was an enormous success and the critics, including the Nazi ones, hailed this "natural talent," who turned out to be Leo Reuß. This story became a legend in the Viennese theater. Mitterer was fascinated by this story of a Jewish actor, who through play-acting unmasks the absurdity of Nazism. Although Reuß played his peasant role in Vienna where nothing much could happen to him at the time, Mitterer believes that it was Reuß's dream to appear on the Berlin stage as an Aryan "natural" and thus attack Nazism in the lion's den. In his play, Mitterer lets Reuß fulfill this dream.[49]

In the first two scenes, which take place in Berlin in 1933, Mitterer depicts the humiliations Jewish actors endured. Arthur Kirsch, the Reuß figure, is playing the role of Shylock in *The Merchant of Venice*, but his excellent performance is disrupted by protests organized, he learns later, by the Nazi actors in the play. After the Nazi takeover, Reuß is no longer allowed to play Shylock, but the play is still performed, now with an anti-Semitic focus. One Nazi actor makes Kirsch scrub the stage, a reminder to the audience of how the Nazis forced Jews to scrub the streets of Vienna after the *Anschluß*. Only one of the actors, Olga, has the courage to protest against Kirsch's treatment. The others are intimidated and remain silent.

The rest of the play takes place a year later when Kirsch returns, disguised as the Tirolean peasant Benedikt Höllrigl, wearing *Lederhosen*, a long thick beard, and carrying a copy of the Nazi paper, *Völkischer Beobachter*. He plays his role as a pro-Nazi, anti-Semitic Tirolean peasant superbly. When he performs Tell, the Nazis, including Goebbels, praise Kirsch as the model of the pure Aryan hero. Although Kirsch lacks the nerve to unmask himself at the height of his Aryan triumph and thus mock the Nazi system openly, as he had originally planned, his very presence on the stage shows the absurdity of Nazi ideology. In this very funny play, Mitterer not only criticizes Nazi racial ideology but also, like Jelinek in *Burgtheater*, shows how actors opportunistically used the Nazi regime to further their careers. Kirsch's wife Helene is one such example of an actress whose career is flourishing under the Nazis and who calls Goebbels her friend. In the play, Goebbels emphasizes the importance the Nazis place on the theater as a vehicle for Nazi Aryan propaganda (93), a comment that underscores Mitterer's conviction that these actors played a crucial, and indefensible, role in supporting National Socialism.

For more than thirty years, some of Austria's most popular and influential dramatists have discussed such important and sensitive issues as Austria's complicity during the Nazi period and its treatment of its Jewish citizens, and have raised concerns about how thinking instilled in the Nazi years continues to pervade the present. They were successful in reaching wide audiences. Because of the controversies surrounding their plays, issues that Turrini, Bernhard, and Jelinek raised were discussed widely. Hochwälder and Mitterer were adept at using humor to force their audiences to examine the past, and they enjoyed popular success, partly because of their use of the tradition of the folk play, which has proved in Austria to be an effective genre for addressing such serious concerns. These dramatists have been voices of conscience and have played an active and important role in encouraging their fellow citizens to confront their past.

Notes

1. Ute Nyssen, "Nachwort," Elfriede Jelinek, *Theaterstücke*, ed. Ute Nyssen (Cologne: Prometh Verlag, 1984) 160.
2. Fritz Hochwälder, "Über mein Theater," *Im Wechsel der Zeit: Autobiographische Skizzen und Essays* (Graz: Styria, 1980) 100.
3. Fritz Hochwälder, "Vom Versagen des Dramas in unserer Zeit," *Im Wechsel der Zeit* 67.
4. Hochwälder, "Versagen" 66.
5. Hochwälder, "Über mein Theater" 100.
6. Fritz Hochwälder, "Als Bühnenschriftsteller im Exil," *Im Wechsel der Zeit* 27.
7. Fritz Hochwälder, "Kann die Freiheit überleben?" *Im Wechsel der Zeit* 103.
8. Hochwälder, "Über mein Theater" 93.
9. Hochwälder, "Über mein Theater" 90.
10. Alan Best, "Shadows of the Past: The Drama of Fritz Hochwälder," *Modern Austrian Writing: Literature and Society after 1945*, ed. Alan Best and Hans Wolfschütz (London: Oswald Wolff; Totowa, NJ: Barnes and Noble, 1980) 45.
11. Heinar Kipphardt also treats this topic in his documentary play *Joel Brand* (1965). Unlike Kipphardt, Hochwälder does not use historical figures but rather fictional characters and a fictional setting.
12. Wilhelm Bortenschlager, *Der Dramatiker Fritz Hochwälder* (Innsbruck: Universitätsverlag Wagner, 1979) 147.
13. Martin Esslin, "Nachwort," Fritz Hochwälder, *Holokaust (Totengericht)* (Graz: Styria, 1998) 95.
14. Esslin 93.
15. Hochwälder, "Über mein Theater" 100.
16. Bortenschlager 156-57.

17. Martin Esslin, "Introduction," Fritz Hochwälder, *The Public Prosecutor and Other Plays* (New York: Frederick Ungar, 1980) xii.
18. Hochwälder, "Über mein Theater" 101.
19. Donald G. Daviau, "Fritz Hochwälder," *Major Figures of Modern Austrian Literature*, ed. Donald G. Daviau (Riverside, CA: Ariadne Press, 1988) 258.
20. Fritz Hochwälder, *Orders*, trans. Todd C. Hanlin, *The Holy Experiment and Other Plays* (Riverside, CA: Ariadne Press, 1998) 244. Future references appear in the text.
21. Peter Turrini, "Ich bin ein Gefangener meiner Biographie," *Liebe Mörder! Von der Gegenwart, dem Theater und vom lieben Gott*, ed. Silke Hassler and Klaus Siblewski (Munich: Luchterhand, 1996) 9-10.
22. Peter Turrini, "Die touristische Bananenrepublik," *Liebe Mörder!* 19.
23. Peter Turrini, "Wir sind Kinder der postfaschistischen Provinz," *Liebe Mörder!* 66.
24. Margarita Pazi, "Peter Turrini," *Major Figures of Contemporary Austrian Literature*, ed. Donald G. Daviau (New York: Peter Lang, 1987) 373.
25. Peter Turrini, *Sauschlachten: ein Volksstück* (Wollerau, Vienna and Munich: Georg Lentz, 1974) 54-55.
26. Peter Turrini, "Schrecken und Optimismus," *Liebe Mörder!* 92.
27. Stephen Dowden, *Understanding Thomas Bernhard* (Columbia, SC: University of South Carolina Press, 1991) 73.
28. Matthias Konzett, "*Publikumsbeschimpfung*: Thomas Bernhard's Provocations of the Austrian Public Sphere," *The German Quarterly* 68.3 (1995): 268.
29. Peter Turrini, "Die Geister des Burgtheaters," *Liebe Mörder!* 134.
30. Dowden 77.

31. Joseph A. Federico, "Millenarianism, Legitimation, and the National Socialist Universe in Thomas Bernhard's *Vor dem Ruhestand,*" *The Germanic Review* 59.4 (1984): 147.

32. Federico 147.

33. Donald G. Daviau, "Thomas Bernhard's *Heldenplatz,*" *Monatshefte* 83.1 (1991): 29. Daviau gives a detailed analysis of this scandal.

34. Konzett 266.

35. Daviau 32.

36. Thomas Bernhard, *Heldenplatz* (Frankfurt/M.: Suhrkamp, 1988) 118.

37. Cited in Dowden 79.

38. Elfriede Jelinek, *Burgtheater, Theaterstücke* 106.

39. "Elfriede Jelinek im Gespräch mit Adolf-Ernst Meyer," *Sturm und Zwang: Schreiben als Geschlechterkampf* (Hamburg: Klein, 1995) 44-46.

40. *Sturm und Zwang* 46.

41. *Sturm und Zwang* 46. Turrini makes a similar critique of the *Burgtheater.* See Peter Turrini, "Die Geister des Burgtheaters," *Liebe Mörder!* 133-34.

42. *Sturm und Zwang* 46-47.

43. Allyson Fiddler, *Rewriting Reality: An Introduction to Elfriede Jelinek* (Oxford: Berg, 1994) 102-04.

44. Fiddler 110.

45. Karl E. Webb, "An Introduction to Felix Mitterer and his Critics," *Felix Mitterer: A Critical Introduction,* ed. Nicholas J. Meyerhofer and Karl E. Webb (Riverside, CA: Ariadne Press, 1995) 1.

46. Mitterer also addresses this topic in his television film script *Verkaufte Heimat* (1989, Homeland, Sold Out). Mitterer is interested in working in television because it offers the possibility of reaching millions of people. See Nicholas J. Meyerhofer and Karl E. Webb, "Felix Mitterer Interview," trans. Nicholas J. Meyerhofer, *Felix Mitterer: A Critical Introduction* 26.

47. Webb and Meyerhofer, "Felix Mitterer Interview" 36.

48. The first edition of the play contains documents used by Mitterer. See Felix Mitterer, *Kein schöner Land: Ein Theaterstück und sein historischer Hintergrund* (Innsbruck: Haymon, 1987).

49. Felix Mitterer, *In der Löwengrube: Ein Theaterstück und sein historischer Hintergrund* (Innsbruck: Haymon, 1998) 9-11. Future references are given in the text.

Fascination and Provocation in the Works of Thomas Bernhard

Roxana Nubert

The present study approaches the plays of Thomas Bernhard through an exploration of the playwright's fascination with illness, focusing in particular on *Die Jagdgesellschaft* (The Hunting Party), which was written in 1973 and premiered at Vienna's *Burgtheater* a year later. Bernhard considered this play to be his best, and it is representative of both earlier and later treatments of illness. Thus it serves as the focal point for my discussion of thematic as well as formal tendencies within the playwright's dramatic oeuvre.

Bernhard's interest in the theater was deep-rooted: "And theater in itself has always fascinated me, even as a child."[1] He worked as a theater critic for the Austrian weekly *Die Furche* and wrote a study on Brecht and Artaud when he was a student. Apart from economic reasons, Bernhard pursued his interest in the theater for the human contact it provided: "For me, the theater is a means ... by which I maintain my friendships, and in addition it brings people in general into contact with each other. You cannot but help meet other people at the theater."[2] And yet, despite the self-proclaimed importance of drama for the author, Bernhard's plays have been largely neglected by critics. This lack of debate can be attributed to the perception that his dramas are the same as his fiction, just not as good. Supposedly Bernhard wrote his plays only for recreation, as a "means to relax."[3] His plays have been criticized due to a perceived "loss of authenticity,"[4] as expression of an outdated utopian outlook,[5] and as a "trivialization of initially great contents."[6]

Christian Klug shows that Bernhard approaches subjectivity differently in his plays than in his prose. The escape mechanisms of his early work are laid bare, stripped of their magic and contrasted to complementary behavioral patterns that are, however, equally deficient.[7] Concomitant with this change, Bernhard switches from a poetics of reflection to a kind of reductionist poetics. The viewer is no longer invited to lose him- or herself in the abundance of analogies and meanings contained in the linguistic material. Instead, the audience has its attention drawn to a truth content by means of dramatic irritation, similar in a sense to Kierkegaard's "indirect communication."

Clear structural parallels exist between Bernhard's epic and dramatic texts due to the very nature of his writing. His novels are staged more than they are told, their various settings are arranged as theatrical scenes, and his main characters tend to speak in monologue form. In addition, theater itself, or the art of acting, represents an important thematic complex of images within the author's fiction as well as drama, serving as a model or possible way in which to experience the world and reality:

> When you open the pages of my works, you should imagine that you are at the theater. You lift the curtain with the first page, the title shows up, total darkness sets in, and slowly words come forth from the background, from the darkness, words that slowly become acts of outer and inner nature, words that, precisely because of their artificiality, clearly become such nature themselves.[8]

Language rather than action lies at the center of Bernhard's plays, and his characters live through their words, not acts. Wendelin Schmidt-Dengler terms Bernhard's language a "language of exclusivity." In other words, at the very moment something is barely intimated it also begins simultaneously to undergo a process of becoming absolute, for it is immediately endowed with an expression of totality or exclusion.[9] Thus everything becomes an extreme. All human action is subject to the paradox, practically a Bernhardian principle, expressed by the painter Strauch from the novel *Frost*: "One has to do exactly what one always dreaded; one has to be exactly what one always rejected."[10] Whether the imperative derives from destiny or a request remains a matter of indifference. What is decisive is the absolute as expressed in the words "has to."

Bernhard's plays, like his prose, construct a universe that consistently and thoroughly self-destructs. Content consists primarily of catastrophes or fantasies of catastrophes, of the fear of destruction and the will to annihilation, of a world that is existentially threatened. Here is an author who embraces negation without compromise or apology, and it is this negativity which lends his work that unique combination of fascination and provocation. He is a representative of "reactionary thinking," as Emil Cioran described him,[11] a faithful successor to Eugen Ionesco and Samuel Beckett.

Due to his general obsession with death and the senselessness of human existence, Bernhard ignores the traditional distinction between comedy and tragedy. The writer explores this theoretical position in his short story "Ist es eine Tragödie? Ist es eine Komödie?" (Is It a Tragedy? Is It a Comedy?), which appeared in the volume *Prosa* (Fiction) in 1967. He explains that the old categories "comedy" and "tragedy" are not appropriate for present-day plays because either one on its own fails to capture the senselessness of contemporary reality, which is both tragic and comic at the same time and yet neither one nor the other completely. In this text the narrator, a young medical student, is prevented from going to the theater by an old man who killed his wife years ago, served his time, and is now out and about wearing her clothes. During their conversation the stranger deduces on the basis of the student's conduct and mood that a comedy is playing. The student hates a world full of the falsity of performance but remains captured within it. The contrast between theater and reality is obvious, but not real. Whereas the narrator hates the theater in actuality, the wife-killer loves it, and whereas the latter's own rather theatrical performance might be a scene from a comedy, the murder of his wife falls undoubtedly within the realm of tragedy. In the end, it remains unclear whether the murderer's life can be called tragic or comic and whether a tragedy or a comedy was being played: the difference between the two is nullified.

Bernhard's first plays were written between 1956 and 1969. The topic of death is central to such dramas as *Der Berg* (The Mountain) from 1956, *Die Totenweiber* (Death Women), the librettos *Rosen der Einöde* (Roses of Loneliness) from 1959 or *Köpfe* (Heads) from 1960, and numerous one-act plays. The allegorical situation drama titled *Ein Fest für Boris* (*A Party for Boris*, 1990), which was written in 1967 and premiered in 1970 in Hamburg, continues this motif. An old woman who has lost both legs in an accident lends meaning to her life as a cripple with a gruesome hobby: Under the guise of tolerant kindness she bullies and plagues her nurse Johanna as well as her invalid husband Boris, thereby hoping to satisfy her craving for power. The old woman, cynically called The Good Woman, bombards and controls her servant by means of incessant language, so that her helplessness ultimately arouses not compassion but hatred. Living in total solitude, she speaks into a cold empty space to an almost silent Johanna. She remains incapable of dialogue and instead skips associatively from one topic to the next, beginning over and over again, simultaneously astute and singularly obsessed. Her directions for a forthcoming ball with "high society" alternate with preparations for a party with the inhabitants of the near-by asylum.

This action, if it can be called such, is interrupted repeatedly by self-observations, accusations, and outbursts of fear and hatred, all of which echo one another in almost ghost-like fashion as if spouted each day with renewed but ever weakening power. Existence as a cripple narrows the experiences of life, a limitation reflected in language, but such an existence also reveals that everyone in fact leads a crippled life, even apparently healthy people.

The old woman experiences fear, insight, and existence itself with greater intensity than others. And sometimes, in between her demonstrations of domination and despair, of verbosity and speechlessness, there are signs that she accepts her destiny, that she agrees with a life that has become nothing more than a rehearsal for death by paralysis: "It's a good thing / that I put a stop to it / a stop / [very softly] a stop."[12]

Boris invites thirteen fellow cripples from the asylum to his birthday party, yet he himself does not survive this macabre celebration of humiliation. They sit around the table, eating, drinking, talking, singing. The party of cripples becomes a dance of words, some absurd, others tragic, their tempo and senselessness constantly intensifying. Boris speaks less than any of them, but toward the end of the party he punctuates their feverishly hectic sentences with drumbeats to the point of collapse and death.

The Good Woman forces her servant Johanna to wear the mask of a pig's head, while she herself is dressed as a queen. Adorned as such, she launches into a tirade about her role as the leg-less ruler in this party of amputees, about the ridiculous games of vanity and of empty sociability: "People keep trying again and again / Costume balls / Parties balls / are the saddest affairs" (30). The position of dominance she plays while wearing her costume as queen becomes reality. She creates beings who must submit to her power, for their existence is just as futile as hers. She has freed Boris from the asylum, but her words reveal that she did so only to exert control over someone with no will of his own.

The atmosphere of violence and repression that surrounds the old woman right from the start explodes into wild curses against the asylum, the doctors, nurses, and the asylum regulations, none of which, of course, is intended as concrete or productive social criticism. Human mortality, the drive of society to self-destruct, and the monomaniacal death wish of the individual dominate her long monologues: "Every day everything is everyday / a repetition of repetitions" (8). A despotic dominance mechanism – distrust and fear, a threatening hatred – typifies her relationships to others and ultimately leads her to confine even Johanna to a wheelchair, for she knows and cannot bear that the latter's health necessarily reverses the master/servant constellation. In contrast, Boris serves The Good Woman as a test case for man's inexorable decline. Helmut Motekat believes that such a chaotic world can be conceived as a "model for contemporary mankind, for its present state and conduct, and for the relations obtaining in it." He maintains further that the "absurdity of this existence, of man's unstoppable fall into death," might even be perceived affirmatively.[13]

Shortly after Boris's death, The Good Woman bursts into "horrible peals of laughter" (71). It is a contradictory laughter, for it signals the attempt of the old woman to escape her sudden desperation and shock, to in fact confront or even stand up to death. Bernhard's twinning together here of death and laughter should not come as a surprise, for it constitutes the core premise underlying many of his works: humanity's fear of death on the one hand and on the other its ridiculous attempts to control this fear through taboos or mental rejection. In his speech upon receiving the Büchner Prize in 1970, Bernhard stresses the creative potential of this most basic of human experiences: "We are (and this is history and this is history's state of mind): fear, bodily fear, spiritual fear, and fear of death as the creative principle."[14] He also underlines the ambiguity of this core situation for his plays: "It is a theater of bodily fear and also, though less so, a theater of spiritual fear and therefore of fear of death ... We do not know if it is about tragedy for comedy's sake or about comedy for tragedy's sake, ... but it is always about horror, misery, and lack of accountability ..."[15] It is a premise that demolishes the traditional understanding of the comic and the tragic.

The baroque metaphor found in much of Bernhard's prose of the world as a stage on which people play out their death roles is also expressed in the realm of his theater, specifically in the play *Der Ignorant und der Wahnsinnige* (The Ignoramus and the Madman) which premiered at the Salzburg Festival in 1972. This play seems to have little in common with *A Party for Boris*. It is not about the depressing world of the crippled, but rather the spheres of artistic perfection and scientific conquests. It explores the denial of the possibility of a meaningful world – a central topic of contemporary literature – but Bernhard develops it in original fashion. He lends the individual an energy, an existential will, that manifests itself in the attempt to create, albeit inevitably without success, a counter-world. The radicalism of this pessimistic-nihilistic outlook, which aims ultimately at the standstill of history, results in an extreme reduction of stage dynamics for the play. The characters prefer to speak in monologues in which they enlarge upon their obsessions. In this way, Bernhard's plays take on the character of a monotonous speaking score, while simultaneously effecting provocation in their function as the opposite of dialogue.

The central event of this drama is the fascinating interaction between its characters: a *prima donna de coloratura*, her blind father, a dresser, and the doctor on duty. Their engagement with and against each other takes place behind the curtain, before the beginning of Mozart's *Magic Flute*, and it comes to symbolize the meaninglessness of life. The first part of the story consists almost exclusively of a monologue delivered by the doctor, a widely recognized authority in the field of anatomy, to the singer's father, an alcoholic since the beginning of his daughter's career. The doctor (the madman in the title) explains in excruciating detail the dissection of the human body to the alcoholic (the ignoramus in the title). He intersperses his explanation with remarks about the career and artistry of the Queen of the Night, attempting it seems to dissect art with the same precision with which one dissects a corpse. The analogy suggests that the theater, or in this case the opera, is nothing more than a pompous celebration of corpses, of art machines or coloratura machines, one of whom appears in the latter part of the first act as the famous singer, the drunkard's daughter, the Queen of the Night: "Your daughter's voice / the most perfect on the one hand / beyond reproach on the other."[16] The overture has already started by the time she enters the dressing room. Like an unfeeling puppet, she is dressed and made up with white powder, which accentuates her artificiality even further, before she hurries onto the stage. For the doctor, she embodies his conviction that art must be radically artificial. Only through such artificiality can it offer salvation from the threat of nature's destruction. At the same time, however, this state of extreme alienation from the pleasures of ordinariness necessarily annihilates the artistic, artificial being, who is unable to reflect upon its own condition or on the condition of art. This then is the task of the doctor, a man of science, who is bound to art in a type of love-hate relationship and who dissects its corpse during and by means of his never-ending stream of words. Despite their many points of agreement Art and Nature remain separate for him, with nature representing an inferior mode of existence, whereas art, despite being generally scorned, and precisely because of its extreme artificiality and unnaturalness, offers a place of refuge from barbarism. With the certainty of utter exhaustion in the end, the artist swings perpetually back and forth between ignorance and madness.

After the performance the three characters have dinner, during which the artist radically changes her conduct. In a sudden moody outburst she decides to cancel her coming engagements in Stockholm and Copenhagen and go to the mountains. We do not find out if the singer possesses the inner strength to quit or if her deadly illness – she is coughing more and more – forces her to do so. After the doctor completes his dissection of both life and art, the stage is plunged into darkness – as will happen later in the play *Die Jagdgesellschaft*. In other words, the completion of the body's dissection also brings to an end all further debate on life and art. The artist utters the closing words of the play: "Exhaustion / nothing but exhaustion" (121).

The darkness that descends upon the three characters at the end of the play, almost like their damnation, is qualitatively different than that darkness in which, according to the playwright himself, his texts typically take place, a general darkness from which the characters and sentences break loose only to founder within it again. The darkness in this play is deeper; it resembles more a spiritual dimming, an obscurity that serves as refuge for protagonists who can no longer bear the super-clarity of their minds, who can no longer endure their heightened and thus painful ability to know and suffer, and who therefore glide into "the second, the final darkness."[17] The doctor describes this "final" darkness, which is embodied throughout the play by the drunkard father, as a worthy goal. The motif of total darkness, then, represents nothing more or less than the hopelessness of human existence. This being the case, the scandal which was precipitated opening night of the play – the management refused to turn off the emergency lighting and the play was struck from the repertory of the Salzburg Festival – reflects the widespread lack of understanding that accompanies Bernhard's texts.

It is obvious that such a play has less to do with theater than with philosophy and literature. Yet this philosophical drama, which describes an existence devoted solely to the intellect and art, offers little comfort to intellectual man. Ignorance is no alternative for the intellectual, but neither is madness. Nor is there solace in simply squandering time, and ultimately even all spiritual attempts fail. Such a philosophy of life, or to be more precise, such a philosophy of art is dark, but it is not new for Bernhard. The Queen of the Night personifies here the artist's destiny and the doctor's philosophy. She has turned into a "coloratura machine" due to her uncompromising passion for art. Her coloraturas control her, not she them, and the musical score for *The Magic Flute* drowns out all other thought. For this reason she hates art. She lives on the verge of a breakdown but fears nonetheless that her art might become mere routine and lose its spontaneity, a fear that drives her to strive for ever greater perfection. Her existence is therefore a deadly process, not all that different than an autopsy.

Die Macht der Gewohnheit (The Force of Habit), written in 1973 and opening at the Salzburg Festival in 1974, can also be considered a tragic comedy. Set in a small circus, the action consists of daily rehearsals of Franz Schubert's *Trout Quintet*. To be more precise, the ringmaster Caribaldi attempts desperately to rehearse this music with his Granddaughter, his nephew the Lion-Tamer, the Clown, and the Juggler, but whereas the quintet represents great art for the ringmaster, the bored and pained members of his ensemble react with indifference and even aggression. Caribaldi knows full well that the music cannot and will not be performed, but he refuses to abandon the ritualized rehearsals, which become increasingly grotesque, ridiculous, and tragic. It is not so much Caribaldi as the force of habit that brings everyone together again and again. Caribaldi does possess a type of "force" or power over these four failed lives and he torments them in various ways, especially with his concept of great art, but they in turn torment him with their lack of sensitivity and brutality. The master/servant relationship is thus revealed and developed along the lines of this dialectic. The Juggler says: "You dominate your nephew / like your granddaughter / The clown only clowns about / Because you force him to / All these people / are at your mercy."[18] But the same holds true for the ringmaster: "But of course you suffer too / in this typical / megalomaniac approach of yours / from your own ruthlessness" (17-18). Although the Granddaughter becomes the passive object of his exhortations to practice, Caribaldi himself is sickened by the coarseness of the Lion-Tamer, his nephew, who accuses his uncle of treating the Granddaughter "like an animal." The nephew passes on the humiliations he incurs from Caribaldi to the Clown who, as the weakest member of the quintet, must bite his tongue and save his jokes for the ring.

Throughout the play, the wretchedness of reality is contrasted to the unfulfilled yearning for a perfect art. Whereas the pursuit of art means only pressure and senseless torment for Caribaldi's performers, for the ringmaster himself it offers the possibility to dream at least of perfection: "If we succeeded just once / just one single time / in completing / the Trout Quintet / one single time perfect music" (9). In this way the daily rehearsals remain ambiguous: on the one hand they function solely as a means to derive masochistic pleasure and are thus rendered absurd; on the other hand Caribaldi, aware of the transitory nature of existence, persists precisely for this reason, just as all of them, actors and viewers alike, persist in the torment and futility of their lives.

This play, and indeed most of Bernhard's dramatic work, is built upon a paradox or contradiction between content and form. While it speaks of artistic failure and lifelong dilettantism, it does so in a language that is nothing short of masterful: *The Force of Habit* is distinguished by its richness of images and metaphors, precision of thought, the intertwining of pantomime and language, and suggestive character constellations.

Bernhard's play titled *Die Jagdgesellschaft* is written "in three movements," the third being the "slow movement."[19] Thus the play is structured as an analogy to music, to a sonata or symphony, where the adagio, however, breaks the classical mold and stands at the end, "after the hunt." Through the suicide of the main character it turns into a funeral march. Thematically, Bernhard develops the motif of sickness to death as an allegory for the destruction of identity.[20] The role which Bernhard ascribes to writer and literature within this process of destruction serves simultaneously as a reflection upon his own aesthetics.

Die Jagdgesellschaft commences with the writer recalling an instance of past irritation where he could remember only the beginning of an aphorism on silence. He portrays the general's wife who was made restless by this incident. The first movement of the play conveys an atmosphere of ambivalence, of vacillation back and forth between diversion and presence, between arbitrary memories and attempts to forget. The present action on stage repeats previous gatherings in the hunting lodge to a significant but indeterminable extent. The narration slips from the past tense into the narrative present and then back again. The conversational game of question and answer is frequently mere show, for the person asking the question already knows the answer. The days spent together during the hunts of bygone days must have elapsed similarly. Inviting the writer and the complex preparations for his visit have become a ceremony, a ritual.

The dialogue fills in the missing details. Despite the monotony of the repeated scenes the tone in the first scene of *Die Jagdgesellschaft* is considerate. The writer resists the temptation of being distracted by card playing, and the language of both characters expresses their willingness to listen for the more subtle echoes of their words and memories. The conversation between the writer and the general's wife serves less to communicate news than to get into tune or to synchronize with each other by referring briefly to known people and common memories. The figures bring up the events preceding the action of the play in fragmentary fashion, including a characterization of the writer and the reconstruction of the fatal illness from which the general is suffering. They reconstruct the past by means of hints and allusions, referring only to the symbolic value of objects, no further explanation of the shared experience needed. Thus the exposition sets the tone, i.e., it strives to assure the "harmony" of the expressive means used. For example, the fact that it is normally not clear if it is snowing or not has no relevance for the musical accord of these meteorological indications. Within Bernhard's semiotic system, the weather and cold are stereotypically associated situations that do not need confirmation.[21]

Decline and death prevail. The general suffers from cataracts and a fatal kidney condition. The ministers effect his fall from a publicly important political office. The forest, which in many ways represents the objectification of his life story, is infested by bark beetles and must be felled. His physical decline and the threat to his social position are part of the general's "sickness unto death," which is more than merely a fatal illness; it is a disease of his spirit, of his psychological state. Death images have haunted him since the battle for Stalingrad, where he lost his left arm. The conversations between the writer and the general's wife, as well as the general's statements about himself, point to the conflict that is taking place in this ambivalent figure. The memories and experiences of death that plague him with increasing force and frequency threaten his identity, the role that he defends compulsively, that he neither can nor wants to give up. The writer, too, speaks almost incessantly of death and dying. With his keen intelligence he reminds us of the doctor in *Der Ignorant und der Wahnsinnige*, and he uses his knowledge about the general to destroy him. At the end of the play, as the writer continues his conversation with the hunting party, the general leaves the room without a word and shoots himself. Outside, as dawn breaks, the woodcutters begin their work.

The writer has the final word, just as he spoke the first word and in fact the majority of the text. The distance afforded him through his role and his intelligence allows him to depict with biting acidity the fragile private and collective state, a condition of frailty and weakness which must be borne without any hope of improvement. It further enables him to perceive the general's destiny as comedy, not without indicating the gap between reality and reality as depicted here, transformed into comedy (104-105). The general suspects this: "The curtain goes up / there we sit / a comedy" (96). There is of course nothing to laugh about, or if we do laugh, then it resembles the laughter of the old woman in *A Party for Boris*. The people prepare themselves to die, but only the writer is in a position to see the garments as funeral clothes and the activity as that of an undertaker.

Critics have pointed out that the basic concept behind *Die Jagdgesellschaft* might have been influenced by an idea from the philosopher Blaise Pascal,[22] whom Bernhard mentions as one of his teachers along with Michel de Montaigne and Arthur Schopenhauer. Pascal describes an important politician who is distracted all day long by various pursuits and people and who suddenly finds himself in the situation of having to think about himself. In the case of Bernhard's general and president, their fall from power instigates for the first time fear of losing a hard-won position. On the one hand, political office and military rank require extraordinary discipline and submission to the demands of one's role, but on the other hand this position of power offers unique possibilities of eliminating both inner and outer sources of irritation with force and "extreme ruthlessness." The general lives utterly shielded from the outer world. As an authoritarian figure and like most Bernhardian characters with the exception of intellectuals such as the writer, the general has a very low "tolerance point for ambiguity."[23] He cannot bear the least irritation.

What irritates the general about the writer and the "theater of high art" (94) is the existential reflection imposed on him by the sheer doubling effect of the stage. The writer serves as a commentator from "another world" (79) who brings onto stage what he observes. He has already dramatized and performed his previous encounter with the general. The general must flee at the sight of the mirror that is held up before him by the mere presence of the writer and, even more so, by the dramatization of his life. The threat of reflection is heightened even further by the fact that his existence appears as a comedy under the writer's lens. The general refuses to see his life as reflected from the outside, but for Bernhard the comic is exactly this outside perspective on the tragic. The general is already threatened to the breaking point by those "irritations" and contradictions that are located within himself, in particular his war experience, which he relives through never-ending dreams, hallucinations, and obsessive-compulsive behaviors.

The immense forest now infested by bark beetles holds special significance for the general's lived history. After the war, he and his wife hid in the woods, for to stay in the hunting lodge would have meant discovery and certain death. Thus for the general the forest evokes feelings of shelter and mortal fear simultaneously, and it serves as a visible manifestation of his past life. It is not only the location of important experiences, but also represents, together with his mother (59) and war wounds (58), the entity that will determine his future path.

Whenever Bernhard uses the metaphor of the forest, and he does so with particular frequency in his works prior to 1975, it functions as an allegorical location. Mainly at night, in darkness, the forest is the locus for self-experience, involuntary remembrance, and contemplation of being, as well as for loss of orientation and existential threat. Usually this experience ends in hopeless and even deadly confusion, but now and then mystical clarity might result. Even when the complexities of the forest as allegory are not fully worked out, its metaphorical meaning evinces a clear relationship to a place of transcendental experience. The allegorical and causal correspondences between the forest and the "darkness metaphor" so typical of Bernhard can also be explained by means of the forest's function as a location of experience and knowledge. Dusk is shorter in the woods and darkness sets in suddenly, as is repeatedly emphasized in *Die Jagdgesellschaft*.

The forest is a place for remembrance and as such it epitomizes a retrospective experience of historicity. Death, visible throughout the forest, is historical death in a double sense: first as phenomenal image, since its concrete shape was produced by war; and second as determining factor for the general's life story. In addition, the forest in *Die Jagdgesellschaft* is a projection framework and place of action for paradoxical acts which correspond to Pascal's "confused drive." In all of these paradoxical performances and roles, however, the forest does not assert Bernhard's poetic metaphysics, rather it is the place where his protagonists act out themselves and their existence. The paradoxical over-determinations, which represent the main character's affective relationship to the forest, cannot be explained as a particular role, but only as a concretization on the horizon of a dialectics of self-awareness. Thus the forest is paradoxically over-determined in the sense that it becomes the scene of the general's contradictory and symbolic actions. Seen in relation to the existence and fatal illness of the general, the forest has the following multiple functions, according to Klug: place that recalls the battle of Stalingrad; refuge during the war; place to collect his thoughts and draw motivation; recreational site for the hunt; cause of sudden darkness; background visible through the window for happenings in the lodge; concrete embodiment of the general's life story, infested first by beetles and ultimately felled.[24]

The paradoxical fashion in which the general infuses the woods with symbols is apparent, as mentioned above, in the sense of both mortal fear but also shelter it evokes in the general. A further contradiction exists between the care the general provides for the forest and the fear that the foresters employed to give such care will cheat him. The owner lives in constant fear that what he owns will be taken from him. Even before any evidence of his own mortal illness or the infestation of the forest, the general mentioned bark beetles, obviously deeply concerned about the health of his forest (23-24). In literal as well as symbolic terms, the fortune contained within the forest is a "monstrous fortune" (38).

The forest is also the scene of escape mechanisms such as the hunt. Bernhard borrows a motif from Blaise Pascal who saw in the hunt the essence of recreational distraction and its dialectic relationship to disquiet or worry: The unique dynamic of recreation consists of seeking the activity and not its end effect, the hunt itself and not the booty. The hunt represents a typical form of recreation in that it avoids the sight of death and misery while paradoxically and simultaneously causing both. Within the context of the hunt, the general's poor eyesight is ascribed a particular meaning. To hunt can be seen as a defiant rebellion against disease, be it cataracts or his mortal illness, for the general must aim as if looking "through a veil" (62). We have here another example where the action itself, not its result, where the shooting itself and not actually hitting the prey, is the purpose behind this form of recreation. The general regenerates himself while hunting. The diversion offered him through the hunt is not distraction from something, but rather "distraction for concentration,"[25] a concentration that allows him to fend off sources of irritation and confirm identity. Hunting is therefore not just one form of distraction among many for the general; it is the compulsive repetition of Stalingrad.

Finally, the chainsaw used to fell the infested forest has allegorical value. The general's symbolic attempt to "carve" the signs of his life story into a history of violence, both suffered and inflicted, is revealed as self-contradictory. The desire to annul one's own history is itself annulled as a result of this history. This is why the symbolic deed becomes self-maiming in actuality: the general saws into his own leg.

In this play the author groups two complementary male characters around a female mediator. The writer, a sort of philosophizing family friend and ladies' man, is an indifferent relativist, whereas the general embodies the apocalyptic character type, someone who lives in constant and conscious desperation, who is incapable of distance. While the writer understands despair as a quasi-ontological prerequisite, the general feels that his fatal illness is a scandal, a permanent devaluation of his life. The writer is an observer, while the general cannot stand the naked sight of the abyss of existence and for this reason he takes refuge in symbolic substitute actions. The contrast between the two types is made even clearer by the fact that both have had similar experiences. Both have survived only by chance; both have existed ever since in full awareness of the omnipresence of death. For the writer, the only certainty in life is his eventual death. His fatalistic mindset is expressed in an excerpt from Lermontov's *A Hero of Our Times* which he reads to the general's wife before the hunt (82). The writer holds a more abstract view of death than the general, whose perspective is more personal, closer. Although both men nearly died, the nature of the two similar experiences was nonetheless very different. Whereas the general almost bled to death at Stalingrad, the writer was a mere onlooker in Warsaw as a falling icicle killed a woman six or seven steps ahead of him. Thus the reasons behind the two men's differing existential attitudes – on the one hand individual disposition, on the other blind fate – are held in balance by Bernhard (57-58).

The writer and the general hate each other, as the two competitors themselves admit (60). They meet only when necessary. The general's wife, who feels both disgust and fear toward her husband, invites the writer to the lodge so that she has company during the hunt, which she abhors. In *Die Jagdgesellschaft* then, too, the basic model of interaction is the triangle. Like the doctor in *Der Ignorant und der Wahnsinnige*, here it is the philosophical type who threatens an already extant relationship between two persons. Three character types always play the leading roles in Bernhard's triangles, which are used by the author to speculate on problems of identity and subjectivity: the successful but compulsive neurotic, the mediator who can at times reflect upon the situation but is incapable of making a decision, and the intellectual free thinker. As a consequence of the logic of these triangular relationships, life becomes a zero sum game in which the price for compromise and success is neurosis and anxiety. The powerful have to pay for their position, and one such price is precisely the intrusion of the writer into their marriages.

In the play, the general and the writer fail to communicate directly. Instead they speak about each other, explaining the other man's character to bystanders. The writer does this indirectly at first. The intended target of his lecture on mortal illness and difference in principle is obvious but not directly expressed. Both men despise any form of distraction preferred by the other. The general hates cards, writing, and all forms of influence the writer exerts over his wife. Conversely, the writer is repulsed by hunting. However, whereas the general interprets the other's presence and manner of passing the time as a threat, the writer gives himself up to the repulsive element, as it were, for purposes of study. The general's wife is aware of a similar contradiction in her own feelings, for she esteems the writer's very dreadfulness and ruthlessness. Her opinion of the writer is not, in fact, all that different than her husband's. The difference lies in how the characters deal with a perceived threat. Whereas the general would simply like to avoid all contact with the writer, his wife's paradoxical attitude can be best termed "lust for fear" – an attitude which typifies the relationship of all Bernhardian female characters to their religious or philosophical family friends. The symmetrical contradiction is apparent in one further respect: The general interprets the writer's art existentially, whereas the writer sees the general's Stalingrad experience aesthetically, as "his best story" (57). The complementary conduct of the characters as a whole illustrates another essential principle of Bernhard's dramatic texts: the suspension of opposites, whereby each sentence negates the preceding one, only to be negated in its turn by the next, thereby provoking extreme audience uncertainty.

By the end of the play we still do not know the "real" causes of the general's fatal illness. Bernhard presents the allegorical connections not as reality, but as a possibility. In the end, the ending is not certain. With the clearing of the forest the setting of the existential comedy is also cleared away, just like props in a drama. The entire drama is dominated by a theatrical aspect: the surroundings become scenery, the world becomes theater, and the characters become artificial, an artificiality which precludes comparisons with reality. Even where the degree of factuality encourages decoding, the radical stylization of the play rejects all attempts at identification with a historical personality.[26]

Die Jagdgesellschaft depicts a situation that both perplexes and attracts the viewer, and the primary reason for both the fascination and provocation is the fragmentary nature of his works. The viewer is left with a sense of incompleteness, with more questions than answers. According to critic Schmidt-Dengler, "Bernhard frustrates the possibility of seeing in his work a perfect work of art – impossible in reality – by raising the fragment to the status of a principle ... On the other hand, [he] insists on an artwork whose perfection is anything but fragmentary, thereby and in totally consistent fashion again negating his demand for fragmentation."[27]

Bernhard's poetic theory corresponds to a "Poetics of Artificiality," whereby he sends his characters to a place beyond the social realm, to a place of total darkness where they can unveil their alienating prop-like forms. The author describes his work with these words:

> In my books everything is artificial, that is, all the characters, events, incidents take place on stage, and that stage is completely dark. The characters perform on a darkened stage, within a stage square, and their outlines are more clearly distinguishable than when they appear in the natural lighting typical for traditional fiction. In the dark everything becomes clear. And this is true not only for the apparitions, for images, it is also true for language.[28]

Darkness as a poetic principle that bans his figures from the sphere of living social relationships, from life under natural lighting, stands for the final darkness of death, that point of reference from which the world appears as an artificial scene, as a theater play and mask.

Critic Marcel Reich-Ranicki labels Bernhard "the darkest poet and bitterest prophet of German literature," and notes that opinion is split between fascination and repulsion: "Whereas some reproach him for overflowing talkativeness and extraordinary monotony, others praise his virtuosity of eloquence and irritating suggestiveness. If some condemn his dreadfulness and beastliness, others praise his lack of compromise and his radicalism."[29] Bernhard himself talks about the fascination of that which is empty and lifeless. It is the task of the artist as observer and creator to give shape to the "monstrous movement" of things: "When one looks at a white wall one notices that it is not white and smooth. ... one discovers cracks, small rifts, roughness, mites. There is a monstrous movement on those walls."[30] His plays must be perceived as a challenge, as provocation, according to Schmidt-Dengler:

> The uncertainty conveyed by Bernhard's works should not be negatively assessed, let alone used to condemn his work. His works should not be thoughtlessly read as a game to be played within language. Instead, they must be seen as a means to promote insight by abandoning the traditional concept of smoothness, a smoothness attained through polishing, one which simulates results and finality and thereby merely reinforces the pretense of the work of art. A work of art does not resolve contradictions; it sharpens them. Thomas Bernhard creates under the sign of these contradictions. He refuses to compromise with the public, but this very refusal serves ultimately to attract us all the more.[31]

The experience of the paradoxical situation as a writer is a painful one for Bernhard: "Only by resisting myself, only by always being against myself, am I able to be at all."[32]

Translated by Linda C. DeMeritt and Sorin Ciutacu

Notes

1. Kurt Hofmann, *Aus Gesprächen mit Thomas Bernhard* (Munich: Deutscher Taschenbuchverlag, 1988).
2. Hofmann 91.
3. Thomas Sorg, *Thomas Bernhard* (Munich: Beck, 1977) 189.
4. Erich Jooß, *Aspekte der Beziehungslosigkeit. Drei Studien zum Monolog des Fürsten in Thomas Bernhards Roman Verstörung* (Selb, 1975) 11.
5. Herbert Gamper, *Thomas Bernhard* (Munich: Beck, 1977) 160.
6. Sorg 160.
7. Christian Klug, *Thomas Bernhards Theaterstücke* (Stuttgart: Metzler, 1991).
8. Thomas Bernhard, *Drei Tage, Der Italiener* (Frankfurt/M.: Suhrkamp Taschenbuch, 1989) 83.
9. Wendelin Schmidt-Dengler, *Der Übertreibungskünstler. Studien zu Thomas Bernhard* (Vienna: Sonderzahl, 1986) 7-8.
10. Thomas Bernhard, *Frost* (Frankfurt/M.: Suhrkamp, 1963) 154.
11. Emil Mircea Cioran, *Über das reaktionäre Denken* (Frankfurt/M.: Suhrkamp, 1980) 43.
12. Thomas Bernhard, *A Party for Boris, Histrionics: Three Plays by Thomas Bernhard*, trans. Peter Jansen and Kenneth Northcott (Chicago: University of Chicago Press, 1990) 23. Subsequent references to this translation will be cited in the text by page number.
13. Helmut Motekat, *Sinnlosigkeit als Thema: Das zeitgenössische Drama des Absurden* (Stuttgart: Metzler, 1977) 131-32.
14. Thomas Bernhard, "Büchnerpreisrede," *Büchner-Preis-Reden: 1951-1971* (Stuttgart: Metzler, 1972) 215-16.
15. Bernhard, "Büchnerpreisrede" 215.
16. Thomas Bernhard, *Der Ignorant und der Wahnsinnige* (Frankfurt/M.: Suhrkamp, 1972) 112. Subsequent references to this work will be cited in the text by page number. Translations by DeMeritt and Ciutacu.

17. Bernhard, *Drei Tage* 161.
18. Thomas Bernhard, *Die Macht der Gewohnheit* (Frankfurt/M.: Suhrkamp, 1974). Quotes are taken from the translation: *The Force of Habit*, trans. Neville and Stephen Plaice (London: Heinemann, 1976) 17. Subsequent references to this work will be cited in the text by page number.
19. Thomas Bernhard, *Die Jadggesellschaft* (Frankfurt/M.: Suhrkamp, 1974) 112. Subsequent references to this work will be cited in the text by page number. Translated by DeMeritt and Ciutacu.
20. Klug 260-97.
21. Klug 263.
22. Klug 264-65.
23. Lothar Krappmann, "Neuere Rollenkonzepte als Erklärungsmöglichkeit für Sozialisationsprozesse," *Seminar: Kommunikation, Interaktion, Identität* (Frankfurt/M.: Suhrkamp, 1976) 320.
24. Klug 269-70.
25. Klug 273.
26. Schmidt-Dengler 107-08.
27. Schmidt-Dengler 109.
28. Bernhard, *Drei Tage* 150-51.
29. Marcel Reich-Ranicki, *Thomas Bernhard* (Zurich: Ammann, 1990) 45.
30. Bernhard, *Drei Tage* 152.
31. Schmidt-Dengler 111.
32. Thomas Bernhard, *Der Keller: Eine Entziehung* (Munich: Deutscher Taschenbuchverlag, 1990) 73.

Masculinity as Performance in the Plays of Thomas Bernhard

Rachel Freudenburg

> Thou wert better in a grave
> than to answer with thy uncover'd body
> (*Minetti* 50)

To write a gender-based interpretation of Thomas Bernhard's plays seems, at first, to be a task doomed to failure. Where does one begin when this author's texts are so rife with misogyny? When one must admit that the novel *Das Kalkwerk* (1970, *The Lime Works*, 1986), in which a husband shoots his wife, is typical? It might seem that the only possible result of such an investigation would be a superficial recapitulation of the ever so obvious hatred of women exhibited in Bernhard's texts. It might furthermore appear that traditional modes of inquiry, which examine the nature of art, knowledge, and the person, would bear more fruit. However, these literary themes are connected to the theme of gender in Bernhard's works, and in order for Bernhard research to progress, we must begin to tie these two areas of investigation together.

Questions such as, "What is the nature and function of art?" or, "How is a person fashioned?" and "How do we come to know the world?" are certainly helpful in guiding us through Bernhard's labyrinthine creations. But these questions and the answers to them are usually cast in gender-neutral language. Recent research in gender studies has shown that such "universal" language pertains to men, and that gender figures largely in aesthetic, ontological, and epistemological inquiries. Drawing on the work of Judith Butler, who articulates the performative nature of gender, I unite both thematic clusters under the umbrella concept of performance: "The acts by which gender is constituted bear similarities to performative acts within theatrical contexts."[1] I begin with a play which overtly thematizes masculinity as theatrical: *Minetti: Porträt des Künstlers als alter Mann* (1976, Minetti: Portrait of the Artist as an Old Man), and continue my discussion with examples and counter-examples from other dramas that also address issues of performance, gender roles, role-playing, directing, producing, and writing drama: *Immanuel Kant* (1978), *Der Weltverbesserer* (1980, The World-Improver), and *Der Theatermacher* (1985, *Histrionics*).[2] For Bernhard, identity is both performative and always gendered: "Men are theater."[3]

To date, there are only three scholarly works which analyze Bernhard's works via the critical category gender.[4] The most important of these is Ria Endres's book *Am Ende angekommen*, which reads as an *Abschiedskuß*, or parting kiss, from Bernhard the woman-hater. Her first words are: "Before I never again open the books of the author Thomas Bernhard, I will repay an old debt."[5] She proceeds to situate Bernhard in a long tradition of patriarchal-misogynist writers whose constant themes are death, tragedy, and the repression of women. Her thesis is that, because men are unable to bear children, they turn their creativity instead to male, patriarchal culture. Born of men's terror at their own inability to bear live young, this tradition is a grandiose expression of the patriarchy's fear of and obsession with death: "The great universe that is the masculine genius's world is a landscape of death."[6] True, in Bernhard's works, which announce themselves as belonging to canonical literature, death and misogyny are central obsessions.

Admission that misogyny is present in Bernhard's writing need not, of course, imply that the author himself was a misogynist. Bernhard and those who knew him consistently distinguished between the man and his texts. Gitta Honegger wrote: "From his work people expected him to be a forbidding, brooding figure. But he was a very kind, charming, polite gentleman with a great sense of humor and a ready laugh. 'I get rid of my misery in writing. I don't have to live it,' he once told me."[7] Not only his listener, but Bernhard himself drew a bold line between what he wrote and what he lived. Instead of reading the misogyny represented in Bernhard's dramas as an unreflected expression of the playwright's attitudes, I shall explore its construction within the texts as performance. In taking this approach, we open up new angles of interpretation. We begin to see that the dramatist may be distancing himself from his imagined figures. Is he perhaps poking fun at his women-hating men, exposing their frailties and criticizing their faults? And in exposing the misogynist's faults, is he not also taking issue with the misogynistic role-assignment propagated in our cultural tradition?

Minetti. Ein Porträt des Künstlers als alter Mann is a fitting starting point in the search for answers to these and other related questions because it dramatizes an ideal of masculinity which has become standard for Western culture. According to this ideal, men are rational, and due to their superior reason they occupy the seat of power. Men rule both themselves and others, and as rulers they occupy the public realm. Their acts in this realm are meaningful and define reality. Thus the world is created in the image of man. Men are valued as active members of society; they are praised as creators in the fields of art, science, history, and politics. The perfect reason by which men create and rule the world is expressed through the perfection of the male body. The "chaste" statues of male nudes that populate museums and other public spaces are meant to express the harmony and perfection of a masculinity that is guided by rationality and self-control. Contemporary men's studies points out that the overemphasis on power, control, reason, and public activity has led to an imbalance because it failed to address men as sexual or emotional beings. And indeed, present-day accounts of male emotionality constantly point to a perceived deficiency. Furthermore, to admit to having physical needs was tantamount to an admission of weakness, a giving in to the body. In the end, this has resulted in a polarization of masculinity as representations of physical perfection existed alongside diatribes against the body.⁸ Bernhard stages and explores such contradictions within the cultural representation of masculinity.

Bernhard dedicated two plays to the actor Bernhard Minetti: *Minetti. Ein Porträt des Künstlers als alter Mann* and *Die Macht der Gewohnheit* (*The Force of Habit*). The actor starred in many productions of the dramatist's plays and over time was identified with the playwright Thomas Bernhard, just as Claus Peymann became known as the one and only director of Bernhard's work. The logical riddle posed by the title of the play under discussion here is not to be unraveled: a play called Minetti was written for an actor named Minetti, who also played the central role of Minetti. To what extent is reality a role? In a short reflective piece on Bernhard, Minetti answered this question for himself:

> I never had the feeling that I was playing myself in *Minetti*. ... Again and again I am asked whether I am the Minetti that Bernhard formed there. When that happens, I can only answer with a fleeting smile and think that large parts of my life do not even appear in Bernhard's plays. On the other hand, he puts his finger on the core of my being as an actor.⁹

Although the person, Minetti, realizes that the role does not encompass all of who he is, it does nevertheless express a part of himself. Although one cannot play oneself, one can, it seems, play oneself as an actor. It is the theatricality of gendered personality, rather than any notion of an essentially male or female character, which I attempt to bring forward here.

Throughout the play, Minetti's sad biography emerges in bits and pieces. His father had been a magician, and Minetti, too, began his career as a performer making people disappear on stage. But suddenly, a wrist inflammation made it impossible for him to continue and he took up dramatic acting instead. Forty years prior to the present moment of the play, he was successfully employed as the manager of the Lübeck theater, where he also starred in the title role of *King Lear* and received rave reviews in the newspapers. Thirty-two years ago, he played Lear in Rotterdam and met with a man by the name of James Ensor, who agreed to make him a mask of the lunatic king.[10] This meeting seems to mark the onset of Minetti's dementia, for he remembers seeing Shakespeare himself in the room talking with Ensor. Then about thirty years ago, he decided to abstain from all "classical" art because it leaves its audience "unmolested" (*Minetti* 48). He finally understood that the task of art is to trap, wound, and mock its audience. As a result of this change in attitude toward art's purpose and its relationship to the audience, he struck all "classical" pieces from the program except for *King Lear*. This programming change was apparently quite unpopular with both the public and the government of Lübeck and a suit was brought against Minetti. After a trial, he was removed from his post as theater manager, and at some point he was diagnosed with insanity (*Minetti* 52). He retreated to Dinkelsbühl, where he lived with his sister and grew onions in a little garden: "Lear hid himself" (*Minetti* 36). Every day, though, in his sister's attic where he lived, he would put on the Lear mask and look at himself in the mirror. And on the thirteenth of every month at eight o'clock in the evening, he donned the mask and recited the entire play, in German and in his own English translation (?!), just to keep in practice. Now, in the present of the play, he is waiting in a hotel lobby in Oostende, the very same hotel lobby where he met with James Ensor some thirty years ago, where he first asked for the Lear mask, and where he had the vision of Shakespeare. Throughout the course of the play, he is waiting for the director of the theater in Flensburg, who has allegedly agreed to direct Minetti in a new production of *King Lear*, but unfortunately he cannot find the telegram in which the director asked him for a meeting to discuss his part. He waits and waits. He has spent every last cent on the train ticket to Oostende. Once he realizes that the director is not coming, he goes out into a snowstorm, puts on the Lear mask, ingests a bottle full of pills and dies.

For those of us versed in world literature, Minetti's biography reads like a collage of snippets from famous works and biographies. The title of the play is a reference to Joyce's *Portrait of the Artist as a Young Man*; he waits in vain like the characters in *Waiting for Godot*; nor is the presence of King Lear as mask, subtext, and role to be overlooked. Less obvious references conjure up German rather than English-language literature. Thomas Mann was from Lübeck, where Minetti worked for a time, and is identified in two biographies as a magician.[11] Minetti's trial, or *Prozeß*, calls to mind Kafka's major novel, *Der Prozeß* (*The Trial*). Finally, the approximately thirty years of insanity spent pursuing activities which are both harmless and irrelevant are reminiscent of Hölderlin, or perhaps even Nietzsche, both of whom lived out the end of their days in the abyss of mental illness.

To be sure, these myriad allusions are typical of Bernhard's writing, and this technique has generated several essays on Bernhard's so-called postmodernity. In an article on *Histrionics*, Steven Joyce writes, "Bruscon [the central character] ambitiously entertains the idea of performing a grandiose intertextual work," yet simultaneously gestures toward the "essential futility of his task."[12] Bernhard's particular version of postmodernity, then, involves lavish quotations from texts of the past, but these literary allusions and the sense of futility that emerges when one attempts to knit them all together also contribute to the representation of masculinity. Minetti's entire life is a reenactment of many, many male roles written down in world literature. Lear, like Minetti, lost his kingdom (theater) and went mad. Like K. in *The Trial*, he is accused, tried, and sentenced for something he does not fully comprehend. Like Tonio Kröger in the novella of the same name by Thomas Mann, he leaves the city of Lübeck. Even Minetti's decision to abstain from classical literature, which fails to attack its audience as he thinks it should, can be understood as a reference to Peter Handke's *Publikumsbeschimpfung* (*Offending the Audience*). The border between man and literature is blurred by the many allusions included in the play, revealing manliness as a construction, as a collection of roles that are gleaned from cultural products. It is a composite role, one we write for ourselves by grabbing at scraps of stories, biographies, and characters who have become famous in our minds. In this sense, Butler writes of gender at the social level as a "sedimentation."[13] Yet if gendered identity is sedimentary, like limestone, it is also profoundly irrational and beyond individual control because it predates the individual. It is there before and informs the individual man's life in ways he is incapable of comprehending. This structure emphasizes the futility of reason's attempts to comprehend everything and reverses the traditional ideal of masculinity as rational, self-aware, self-controlled, or even self-created.

Handed-down ideals of masculinity are incommensurate even with themselves, and this is doubly true where the body is concerned. Minetti's body is in a state of decline: he is a certified lunatic; he cannot dress himself properly, requiring the help of the hotel porter; and he is suicidal. Most of Bernhard's male characters are insane (Minetti), or ill (the World-Improver), or even amputees like the legless Boris in Bernhard's first play, *Ein Fest für Boris* (*A Party for Boris*). Again, as a point of contrast, we may imagine the male nudes of the ancient Greek sculptural tradition which were appropriated by male culture as a symbol of masculine perfection. For Bernhard, masculinity is damaged, sickly, and crazy, but veiled in performance. Minetti's quotation from *King Lear* captures this strategy. Twice, he quips: "Thou wert better in a grave than to answer with thy uncover'd body" (*Minetti* 50, 51). The quote comes from Act III, Scene iv, in which Lear is out in a dangerously strong storm and disrobes. The human body is insignificant and vulnerable without its coverings, without the cultural, historical, social, and personal meanings we attribute to it. More pointedly, the male body can never attain the perfection and grand stature ascribed to it through a phallocentric tradition.

Ironically, Minetti, a deluded old man, aspires to play the role of King Lear, a deluded old man, but never gets the chance to do so, is barred from greater meaning and cuts a decidedly insignificant figure.[14] Yet he, and a host of other male characters in Bernhard's plays, desire global relevance because our culture tells them that this is the locus of true manhood. While femininity resides in the private sphere, masculinity shapes and controls the public arena. Though he is never given the chance to play the role of Lear on stage, he does recite it every month, but only to himself in the attic of his sister's house in front of a mirror. In this performative context, what Minetti himself terms the "most significant dramatic work in all of world literature" (*Minetti* 11) becomes nothing more than an expression of one particular, private body's deterioration. The scene of Minetti, masked as Lear and declaiming the part all alone, expresses the inappropriateness of inherited masculine roles in the present-day world. But is this not at least one of the messages of Shakespeare's Lear: that the role one plays is perpetually out of sync?

In order to cover the deficiencies of their bodies and their entire persons, men have learned to use language strategically. Instead of expressing the self, this strategic language cloaks it.[15] While he is waiting, Minetti strikes up monologic, and strategic, conversations with two different women. The first is an older lady who plans to retreat to her hotel room on this New Year's Eve, don her monkey mask, empty two bottles of champagne in one enormous gulp, and pass out. The other is a young girl who is waiting for her boyfriend. Minetti's cornered audience will hear his life story, whether they want to or not, and throughout the play he subjects them to tales of his fame and significance. He shows off newspaper articles celebrating him in his heyday, explains that *King Lear* is "the most significant dramatic work in all of world literature," and then proceeds to identify himself with Shakespeare's play. To Bernhard readers, the scenario is a familiar one: man dominates woman with stories of his own greatness. Yet the mistake many readers make is to try to understand the content of such speeches without simultaneously analyzing their context. The speeches are given by a frail old man whose physical infirmities are all too apparent to his listeners. The women indulge him, help him dress himself properly, and then go about their business. The idea that masculinity, as embodied by the character Minetti, aspires to global significance is made light of throughout the play through the creation of dissonance between Minetti's performance and the stage on which it is given: party-goers celebrating the new year pass through the lobby and largely ignore the actor. Thus the tales Minetti spins appear as empty posturing, as reiterations of a masculine role which is terribly out of step with its setting. As mentioned, Minetti's conversations are monologic, but they are not monologues in which the character speaks to himself and the audience. Instead, he talks with women, but he does all the talking. The primarily monologic structure constructs a "self-sufficient shell," while the need for a listener gives the lie to the appearance of autonomy.[16] The ideal man is self-sufficient and exists independently of others, but the reality of the situation is loneliness and an intense need for others. Minetti desires the presence of his female listeners and yearns for the director, a long-lost friend from his youth, to appear. Thus Bernhard unmasks the autonomy of masculinity as merely a performance, while in actuality "the significant psychological unit for Bernhard is less an individual than a dyad."[17] In other words, men who appear to be independent are in fact reliant upon others.

If masculine autonomy is all an act, then it is a misogynistic construct that veils its own reliance on women. Perhaps because of such veiling, Bernhard's works have been read as literature in which women do not exist.[18] If they are seen at all, it is generally as "part of the man," rather than as characters who are interesting in their own right.[19] In the play *Histrionics*, Bruscon, the central character (a playwright, director, and actor) explains: "But what would a comedy like mine be / without female performers / we need them / If our comedy is to flourish / we need women in our comedy / that's the truth / however bitter it may be" (*Histrionics* 202). Even the staging of masculinity requires females. Later on in the play, Bruscon indulges in his own Lear-like moment of self-aggrandizement when he asks his daughter: "What is your father?" But when she responds with a very matter-of-fact, "Herr Bruscon," he flies into a rage and demands that she identify him as "The greatest actor / of all times" (*Histrionics* 235). The performance of masculine superiority requires an oppressed, yet admiring, female audience.

The *Weltverbesserer* provides a distressing example of how Bernhard typically connects the public, autonomous man to the private female while also stressing that masculinity and femininity are inseparable from one another. In this play, an author is about to receive an honorary doctorate from the university for his tract on "The Improvement of the World." But while waiting for the mayor, the president of the university, and other dignitaries to arrive, he orders his housekeeper/lover around as a slave; he insults her, yet because his health is so poor, he is completely dependent upon her. Indeed, it is doubtful that the pamphlet itself could have been written without the domestic services of this woman. Here, Bernhard is using an essential insight from feminist thought, namely that the public and private are interdependent. In other words, behind the great works of philosophy and literature, which appear in a public space, lurks the oppression of women in private. The role of the great man of letters, the enlightened man who guides the world toward goodness and right through his reason, is unmasked by Bernhard as being a cover-up for a character who is in fact a misogynistic tyrant. The traditional emphasis on the public character of masculinity blinds men to their own roles within the so-called private sphere and their reliance on women, but Bernhard shows us the man at home, thus exposing the "slippage," or should one say "canyon," between masculinity's public persona and its domestic one.[20]

The distribution of gender roles in *Der Weltverbesserer* is typical of Bernhard's most unpleasant depictions of misogyny. It is this dyadic configuration which prompts Endres and others to conclude that women are absent from Bernhard's works. While far from absent, they are usually depicted as the passive objects of male domination. Indeed, this is the *Urszene*, or originary dramatic script of misogyny: "Just as a script may be enacted in various ways, and just as the play requires both text and interpretation, so the gendered body acts its part in a culturally restricted corporeal space and enacts interpretations within the confines of already existing directives."[21] While Bernhard himself returns to the misogynistic dyad – a "culturally restricted corporeal space" – again and again, he also varies or "interprets" it and through such interpretation allows for something more than the domination of women by men.

The play *Immanuel Kant* provides an interesting variation on the misogynistic dyad. Here, Bernhard mixes up historical times and places Kant on a steamship headed for New York where he believes he will be delivering a lecture at Columbia University and undergoing eye surgery to restore his vision. In actuality, however, he is being delivered to a mental hospital. More interesting even than Bernhard's witty critique of Kant is his portrayal of Mrs. Kant. As it turns out, she is the one who has organized the philosopher's passage to America, and she is the one who is responsible for upholding his delusions of himself as the great thinker who brings "reason to America" (*Immanuel Kant* 125). She even pays off the ship's steward to help her more successfully stage the illusion. At the lantern party, on the last night of the journey, Kant receives a telegram that is probably a prop created by Mrs. Kant herself. She arranges with the steward to have "the telegram" delivered into her hands and then "reads" it to the assembled party: "A telegram from Columbia University ... We welcome Kant to America, the event of the twentieth century" (*Immanuel Kant* 125). After having pulled off the deception, "Mrs. Kant whispers something in the steward's ear and slips him a large bill" (*Immanuel Kant* 130). It is Mrs. Kant who produces, directs, and acts in the drama that is Professor Kant's life. Though he plays the starring role, Immanuel is an unwitting participant and even states: "my wife is the victim of the deadly science" (*Immanuel Kant* 127). Outwardly, this may seem to be true, but the Kants' marriage only loosely resembles the relationship between the World-Improver and his female domestic; here, the philosopher is duped by his wife.

In *Immanuel Kant*, Bernhard asks an intriguing question: to what extent do women profit from the staging of their own supporting roles, even of their own victimization? To what extent do women benefit from the great men with whom they associate? Mrs. Kant, while posing as the servant-wife, actually controls the situation in order to reap the benefits of having a celebrity husband. She is surrounded by servants and enjoys a lavish dinner party with a millionairess, a cardinal, an admiral, the ship's captain, and an art dealer. Clearly, she is the one who gains by maintaining the illusion of Kant's greatness. For Mrs. Kant, the performance of traditional gender roles is a strategic move by which she secures her own luxurious standard of living. Though part of an insane production of male-female polarization, traditional gender roles may contain potential benefits for women as well as men, and the mere existence of such benefits may help to explain why society is so slow to change. The status associated with the great male minds of history, such as Kant and even Bernhard himself, accounts for a general reluctance on the part of universities and scholars of both genders to give up these figures in favor of female ones. Furthermore, such considerations may help to explain our difficulty in generating new roles, or even redistributing the old ones.

In *Histrionics* we witness a role reversal that does not fundamentally change anything. The male lead, Mr. Bruscon, has written a play called "The Wheel of History" in which great men such as Churchill, Napoleon, and Stalin take center stage. Interestingly, Bruscon casts himself and his own family in these and other roles, thus allowing private-feminine and public-masculine roles to confront one another in various ways. Alas, again the actual performance never takes place. As the auditorium fills in the moments before the curtain is to go up, a thunderstorm breaks out. When lightning strikes the parsonage and sets it on fire, the audience runs out of the theater to tend to the emergency. In the play's ending, theater and the exigencies of real life seem to have no connection at all to one another. However, as Bruscon's casting choices indicate, private family roles are nevertheless intertwined with theatricality. Bruscon, the male head of the household, has taken his family, which is also his acting troupe, on tour. Though we never see the play they were to perform, we do see Bruscon directing the family drama. While Mrs. Bruscon is confined to her bed with a cough, Mr. Bruscon prepares the "house," or theater, for the show. As a part of these preparations, he organizes lunch for all, *Fritattensuppe*, a lightly seasoned broth garnished with julienned crèpes. It is the perfect meal for someone who is ailing, and Mr. Bruscon makes sure that his wife partakes of it. He also performs several other "feminine" functions, such as redecorating, having new curtains hung, cleaning the windowsills (which he explicitly calls women's work), and fussing over clothing (costumes). He even tells his daughter not to pick her nose, applies his wife's makeup and fixes her hair. While Bruscon himself assumes the feminine role of household manager, the role his wife plays is reminiscent of the World-Improver. She is a professional actor, just like her husband, but is largely confined to her bed due to illness. Here, it is she who depends on the domestic services of a man.

Both members of this couple play roles which are at once public and private, masculine and feminine. But if the role assignment has become more egalitarian, some fundamental principles of performance remain unchanged. Here, we turn our attention to the authoring of roles as represented in *Histrionics*. Bruscon has written a script for his family to act out on stage, casting his son as Churchill and Metternich and his daughter as Churchill's wife and Metternich's mistress. In the play Bruscon writes, as opposed to the drama of his own life, women stay in their traditional roles. Mrs. Bruscon, who is cast as Madame Curie, would seem to represent the exception to this rule and to embody the liberation of women from their roles as wives and courtesans. However, Mr. Bruscon makes up his wife's face "to the point where it is almost entirely black" and says to her: "Atomic age my dear / the whole atomic age / must be in this face / (terrible thunder) / More or less / the end of the world / in your face / (making up her face so that it is finally completely black)" (*Histrionics* 276). Clearly, in Mr. Bruscon's play, the opening up of traditionally male roles to women is a less than salutary development leading to the end of the world. He spares no effort to "blacken" the reputation of women who have, like his own wife, stepped out of bounds and become "a disgrace to the feminine gender" (*Histrionics* 280).

In *Histrionics*, the performance of gender is profoundly strategic, but also petty and comic. Indeed, one is left with the impression that Bruscon turns Madame Curie into a monster because he resents the control his wife exerts over him. He claims that she is not ill, but only acts ill in order to be pampered by him, when really he is the one who is sick and in need of special treatment. Furthermore, her pretended illness was the reason they went on this disastrous tour in the first place; he never wanted to go on tour but did it for her, because the doctor said she would benefit from the fresh country air (*Histrionics* 214-215). In an act of revenge, Bruscon has written a part for her in which she stands for ultimate destruction. In his relationships with his children as well, he attempts to write over any visible influence that she may have had on them. He claims to have taught them everything they know, from the art of the theater to that of massage and even tries to inscribe his own thoughts into his son's mind: "Swear to me / that from this day on you will read / what I order you to / that you will think / what I tell you to" (*Histrionics* 253). In the end, though, education as a means of writing over and thereby repressing the mother's influence is bound to failure: "The father can say what he likes / it's no use / The mother spoils everything / that the father has accomplished" (*Histrionics* 214). His son will no more think what he is told than his daughter will speak her lines the way he intends them to be spoken. As indicated earlier, Bruscon forces his daughter to tell him that he is the "greatest actor of all time," which she initially tries to avoid doing. When she does finally recite her father's text, she does so "reluctantly" (*Histrionics* 235). Similarly, Mrs. Bruscon seems in the habit of sabotaging the lines written for her with coughing: "Such beautiful lines / such a magnificent passage / and she coughs it all away" (*Histrionics* 228). Frustrated that his players fail to indulge him in the performance of his own megalomania, he denounces all actors as untalented: "When we write a comedy / and even if it is the so-called world comedy / we have to take full account of the fact that it will be performed by dilettantes / by anti-talents" (*Histrionics* 220). While Mr. Bruscon claims over and over that his wife lacks both talent and understanding, she may simply be attempting to play the part her way, to create a performance which subverts the misogynistic text written by her husband.[22]

In contrast to the impression given by secondary literature, gender is a significant analytic category for Thomas Bernhard's dramas. When the issue has been addressed, Bernhard's work has been viewed as a straightforward document of misogyny. However, his depiction of masculinity and femininity as roles to be performed encourages a more critical understanding of the topic. The roles themselves, scripted by generations of cultural products and reenacted by generations of people, are fairly predictable. Masculinity is public and therefore significant, but also domineering and tyrannical, while femininity is just the opposite: private, meaningless, subservient, and victimized. This is the situation depicted in *Der Weltverbesserer*, where the male performs publicly recognized intellectual work while the female toils as his servant and sex object. However, the same drama may be enacted very differently by another set of individuals, such as Mr. and Mrs. Kant. Here, the age-old script appears to harbor hidden benefits for the right woman. Finally, in *Histrionics*, the script itself has been modified to include men playing women's roles and vice versa and even allows for a single character to play different roles at the same time. Ultimately, the roles themselves are revealed as preposterous. Lear is the character Minetti's most significant work perhaps because the role of king (the male as ruler of the world) is an insane one. Mad as they may be, the roles become interesting when we can ask questions pertaining to the individual performances themselves, such as who is performing which role(s)? How are these roles being modified and why? Does the performance include a self-critical or ironic element? And who ultimately benefits from performing these roles in this particular way?

The misogyny in Bernhard's plays is not to be confused with the author's own attitude. Bernhard himself clarified this when asked in an interview for Germany's prestigious news weekly, *Der*

Spiegel, what he thought of Endres's accusations and her criticisms that his texts depict women as stupid, groveling victims of tyrannical men. Bernhard responded: "Many such women also exist in reality; they are happy when they are allowed even just to wipe up the vomit of the socially impaired."[23] This is vintage Bernhard: scandalous, ridiculous, but determined to rub his audience's noses in their own filth. The gender roles that surround us – the socially impaired, vomiting male and the vomit-wiping female – are, in a word, sick. Significantly, Minetti calls classical literature, which does not molest and attack us in the way Bernhard's texts and interviews do, *zum Kotzen*, "vomitatious" or nauseating (*Minetti* 48). And this is precisely the point – literature which unreflectedly represents misogyny is just as nauseating as the inherited roles themselves. Although Bernhard's dramas do not offer an escape from prescripted roles of masculinity and femininity, his depiction of gender as performance allows for a certain distance from this nauseating cultural legacy, and perhaps even grants individual actors the power to reenact the script in new and less offensive ways. Through an awareness of the many different people involved in any performance, from the actor to the writer, from the director to the audience, Bernhard allows us to see the many opportunities for a reinterpretation and readaptation of an age-old script.

Notes

1. Judith Butler, "Performative Acts and Gender Construction. An Essay in Phenomenology and Feminist Theory," *Writing on the Body: Female Embodiment and Feminist Theory*, ed. Katie Conboy, Nadia Medina, and Sarah Stanbury (New York: Columbia UP, 1997) 403.

2. Dates indicate performances. Publication information for these plays is as follows: Thomas Bernhard, *Minetti. Ein Porträt des Künstlers als alter Mann* (Frankfurt/M.: Suhrkamp, 1977); *Immanuel Kant. Komödie* (Frankfurt/M.: Suhrkamp, 1978); *Der Weltverbesserer*

(Frankfurt/M.: Suhrkamp, 1979); *Der Theatermacher* (Frankfurt/M.: Suhrkamp, 1984). Of the plays discussed here, only *Der Theatermacher* has been translated into English: *Histrionics*, trans. Peter Jansen and Kenneth Northcott (Chicago: University of Chicago Press, 1990). Also included in this collection are: *A Party for Boris* and *Ritter, Dene, Voss*. Subsequent references to these plays are indicated in the text. All translations of passages from *Minetti* and *Immanuel Kant* are my own.

3. In the translation by Jansen and Northcott, "Männer sind Theater" is rendered as "Men are the scene" (*Histrionics* 213). This is a fine translation, but in order to emphasize theatricality I have, in this instance only, used my own translation of the line.

4. Renate Latimer, "Thomas Bernhard's Image of Women," *Germanic Notes* 8 (1977): 25-27; Claudia Öhlschläger, "'In den Wald gehen, tief in den Wald hinein': Autoerotische Phantasmen männlicher Autorschaft in Thomas Bernhards *Holzfällen. Eine Erregung*," *Auto(r)erotik. Gegenstandslose Liebe als literarisches Projekt*, ed. Annette Keck and Dietmar Schmidt (Berlin: Erich Schmidt, 1994) 119-31.

5. Ria Endres, *Am Ende angekommen. Dargestellt am wahnhaften Dunkel der Männerporträts des Thomas Bernhard* (1980; Vienna: Bibliothek der Provinz, 1994) 9.

6. Endres 92.

7. Gitta Honegger, "Thomas Bernhard," *Partisan Review* 58.3 (1991): 503. Similarly, Krista Fleischmann, who produced a television show about Thomas Bernhard, claims that although he had a reputation for being difficult, he was in truth kind and friendly. Krista Fleischmann, "Kein Problem mit dem Schwierigen," *Thomas Bernhard. Portraits*, ed. Sepp Dreissinger (Weitra: Bibliothek der Provinz, 1991) 203.

8. George Mosse, *The Image of Man* (New York: Oxford UP, 1996); Victor J. Seidler, "Rejection, Vulnerability, and Friendship," *Men's Friendships*, ed. Peter M. Nardi (Newbury Park: Sage Publications, 1992) 15-34; Victor Jeleniewski Seidler, *Man Enough. Embodying Masculinities* (London: Sage Publications, 1997).

9. Bernhard Minetti, "Ein Autor namens Bernhard. Erinnerungen eines Schauspielers," *Thomas Bernhard. Portraits* 220.

10. James Ensor is the name of a nineteenth-century artist who created images of human heads attached to insect bodies. What this might imply for the construction of masculinity must remain, for the time being, unexplored.

11. Erika Mann, *Mein Vater der Zauberer*, ed. Irmela von der Lohe and Uwe Naumann (Reinbek bei Hamburg: Rowohlt, 1996); Peter De Mendelssohn, *Der Zauberer. Das Leben des deutschen Schriftstellers Thomas Mann* (Frankfurt/M.: S. Fischer, 1975).

12. Steven Joyce, "Kismet and Continuities. Postmodernism and Thomas Bernhard's *Der Theatermacher*," *Colloquia Germanica* 24.1 (1991): 24.

13. Butler 407.

14. Catharina Wulf, "Desire for the Other: Obsession as Failure / Failure as Obsession. Beckett's *Krapp's Last Tape* and Bernhard's *Minetti*," *Beckett in the 1990s*, ed. Marius Buning and Lois Oppenheim (Atlanta, GA: Rodopi, 1993) 90.

15. Seidler 1997, 135.

16. Wulf 91-92.

17. William E. Gruber, *Missing Persons. Character and Characterization in Modern Drama* (Athens, GA: The University of Georgia Press, 1994) 113.

18. Endres 93.

19. Stephen Dowden, *Understanding Thomas Bernhard* (Columbia, SC: University of South Carolina Press, 1991) 35.

20. Significantly, the dictionary designates "Weltverbesserer" as satirical in tone: "spött." *Duden. Das große Wörterbuch der deutschen Sprache*, 6 vols., ed. Wissenschaftliches Rat (Mannheim: Bibliographisches Institut. Dudenverlag, 1981) 6: 2865.

21. Butler 410.

22. Gruber points out that because Bernhard includes very few stage directions, actors must generate their own interpretations

of the roles he has written (124). Unlike his character Bruscon, the dramatist allowed for the creative input of others.

23. Thomas Bernhard, "Ich könnte auf dem Papier jemand umbringen," *Spiegel* 23 June 1980: 182.

The Return of the Kings:
Peter Handke at the *Burgtheater*

Bernhard Doppler

In 1966, upon production of his first and programmatic drama titled *Publikumsbeschimpfung (Offending the Audience)*, Peter Handke captured public and scholarly attention through provocation of the theater establishment. Now, by contrast, it seems he has become an official author of the *Burgtheater*. Handke wrote four dramas between 1989 and 1999, all of which were premiered at Austria's national theater with great fanfare. Assuming the continued significance of the *Burgtheater* as Austria's foremost theatrical institution, the result has been the consecration of Handke, this former *enfant terrible*, into one of the "classics" of contemporary Austrian literature.

Ridicule of the playwright as a reactionary "poet-priest"[1] began as early as the 1980s; and especially after his defiant commitment to the Serbians and against NATO air raids, his attitude or stance as a writer elicited fierce attacks in the *feuilletons*. But does not Handke, as sociologist Peter Straßer maintains in his book from 1990, have the right as an author to remain distanced from "the battlefield of conflicting opinion"? According to Straßer, Handke is neither "a spokesman of opinion nor a conveyor of world views; on the contrary, he is a significantly-natural or naturally-significant person of stature."[2] The four rather singular plays by Handke that premiered at the *Burgtheater* posit art as a world separate from and in opposition to the debates determined by mass media and public opinion. The following investigation attempts to reconstruct and comprehend this position. In discussing such a claim for these plays, the venue and director of the premieres are not at all insignificant for their status as works of art.

The Dramatist and his Director

At the end of the twentieth century, the concept of a representative state theater or an Austrian national theater appears to be an anachronism. Yet Claus Peymann, director of the tradition-rich *Burgtheater* for more successive seasons than anyone else, supported exactly this idea. Not only did he extol the *Burgtheater* as the preeminent theater in Austria and declare its artistic quality to be without rival, he also took the educational mission of the theater as a state institution seriously. In a commentary titled "Abrechnung" (A Reckoning) which Peymann delivered toward the end of his tenure in Vienna, the director states that his intellectual origins in the student movement of 1968 led him to pursue theater in the tradition of Lessing, Schiller, or Brecht.[3] He recognizes that the pursuit of art – of the classical triad of truth, goodness, and beauty – is an undertaking which in today's society might be considered a presumption of quixotic proportion, but nonetheless he sees the *Burgtheater* as a bastion against an all-pervasive pragmatism that rules the world. Peymann maintains that the art of theater will write history. Even now, he contends, the faces of actors such as Attila Hörbiger or Bernhard Minetti shown on television for only a second are infinitely more significant than all the appearances of Austrian politicians taken together. But, Peymann continues, Austrian dramatists in particular will outlast history: "Thomas Bernhard will remain in our memory, but who this cardinal was or that minister is, will soon be forgotten forever."[4] This perspective, i.e., an existence as idealistic dreamer as opposed to practical politician, serves Peymann as legitimization of his own task as a theater producer.

Despite the fact that historically most directors have come from Germany, Peymann suffered continual discrimination as a

German, as a *Paradepiefke* at the helm of the *Burgtheater*. Yet despite his Northern German heritage he cultivated above all *Austrian* literature, and Austrian literature in a very representative sense. He emphasizes in this connection that it is not the job of the *Burgtheater* to discover young Austrian talent; that is a task left to other less important stages. But during his term at the *Burgtheater*, Peymann brought to the stage and, as a rule, personally directed premieres of well-known and generally established Austrian playwrights such as Thomas Bernhard, Elfriede Jelinek, Peter Handke, and Peter Turrini. He did so unless performance bans levied by the authors themselves prevented staging in Austria, for instance Bernhard's will or Jelinek's decree after the xenophobic murder of four Romany gypsies in Burgenland.[5] Of course every canon can be criticized. The choice of Bernhard, Jelinek, Handke, and Turrini as canonical authors, as a quartet of representative Austrian dramatists, excluded others like Werner Schwab, who attained *Burgtheater* status only posthumously, or Felix Mitterer. Nevertheless, the canonization process at the *Burgtheater* reflects the attitude of literary studies toward contemporary Austrian literature, which when dealing with recent works also concentrates on those that have already gained acceptance and recognition by the literary establishment.

At the beginning of Peymann's tenure in Vienna, Thomas Bernhard stood unchallenged among the four *Burgtheater* dramatists as *primus poeta Austriae*. Both the dangers and privileges of this position, the ease with which public reverence can become outrage and rejection of the national poet, are demonstrated in Bernhard's exclusive relationship with Peymann. As early as 1970, while Peymann was still in Germany, Bernhard authorized the director to premiere many of his dramas, and Peymann states in his "Abrechnung" that Bernhard even formulated press releases for him. During Peymann's final season at the *Burgtheater* in 1998, and after moderation of the performance ban for Bernhard's plays in Austria, three Bernhard mini-dramas featuring Peymann himself as a stage character were rehearsed.[6] Yet, Bernhard's privileged position with Peymann did not translate into public acclaim until after the playwright's death. Just months before he died, conservative cultural forces unleashed a vociferous and decidedly raucous protest against him and the production of his *Heldenplatz* by unloading manure in front of the *Burgtheater*. Several months later, however, countless flowers adorning the writer's grave corresponded in size and importance to the manure heap. Within a matter of months, the smear campaign against the writer had been transformed into an outpouring of respect.

In January of 1990, one year after Bernhard's death, the *feuilletons* proclaimed Peter Handke his successor,[7] a role he was able to fill at least in terms of becoming the theater's most important author. Even though the relationship between Peymann and Handke was not as close as that between Peymann and Bernhard, both Handke and Peymann had promoted each other's careers as early as the 1960s. In 1966 at the *Theater am Turm* in Frankfurt, Peymann staged the first performance of a Handke play, *Offending the Audience*. With the success of this production, additional Handke premieres followed, such as *Kaspar* in 1968. Seen from today, these plays impress not so much because of their defiant revolutionary attitude, but rather because they experiment and play with the possibilities of the theater. Early Handke works such as *Offending the Audience*, *Selbstbezichtigung* (*Self-Accusation*), and *Weissagung* (*Prophecy*) have been newly produced for the *Burgtheater*, allowing a kind of reassessment thirty years after their premieres.

Compared to the ideological attitudes of the student movement of the late 1960s, Handke held an uncompromisingly individual position even at the beginning of his career. He criticizes the cliché-ridden conventionality of the 1968-generation and goes so far as to question the validity of Bertolt Brecht, one of the hallowed pillars of theater at that time, by stating: "His works are idylls. My reality mocks them at every moment. His disillusionment is one more illusion and even more dangerous than naïve illusion."[8] After successes in the late 1960s and 1970s, Handke's dramatic career floundered in the 1980s. The image he had created of the isolated individual became an irritant; his solitary stance now announced itself with a pompously solemn, declamatory tone. His

Peter Handke at the *Burgtheater* 137

"dramatic poem" *Über die Dörfer* (*Walk about the Villages*), produced by film director Wim Wenders and premiered 8 August 1982 at the Salzburg Festival, was butchered by critics as being hopelessly obsolete and sentimental, although literary scholars have devoted a fair amount of attention to the play subsequently.[9] After such harsh criticism Handke wanted nothing more to do with the theater. In this respect the performance of the four Handke plays in the 1990s at the *Burgtheater* is also a new beginning.

Handke and Peymann share a number of attitudes and opinions, most notably a belief in the possibility of creating "great" art and a passion for that art. Probably the greatest difference between the two men lies in Handke's skepticism toward the theater as a moral institution. In contrast to Peymann, the author refutes the pedagogical responsibility of theater, stating that such theater "gets on his nerves because he considers it to be a kind of cabaret."[10] Thus Handke has little use for the humanizing educational objectives of plays by Peter Turrini, the other Austrian writer most frequently premiered by Peymann. But theater director and writer are in agreement when it comes to the assessment and expectations of art, and both make claims that are immodest enough to sound decidedly pretentious and arrogant. For example, Handke said in reference to his play *The Art of Asking* that he had written nothing less than a *Faust*, a claim which was bound to irritate members of the already critical public discussing the performance with him in the *Burgtheater* lobby.[11] Peymann has also frequently mentioned Goethe and Handke in the same breath.

Yet, the relationship between Handke and Peymann has not always been without conflict or tension. In the 1970s Handke distanced himself from Peymann's theater productions, and in a 1988 interview with the weekly newspaper *Die Zeit*, Peymann criticized the writer who was to become his "house author" a short time later: "I think his books are a kind of self-therapy where he brings order to his life. Some of what he is writing now is completely unbearable to me. It is almost touching how reactionary his thoughts are. At that point, I cannot always follow him."[12] Handke makes a politically reactionary impression above all at public appearances where he has been known to react with extreme impatience or even anger. Readings and discussions often degenerate into public insults, which are frequently misogynistic as well. For instance, Handke's public attitudes toward the situation in Serbia were avidly discussed and scathingly criticized in the German and Austrian presses.[13] His criticism of the hypocrisy of the student movement and his praise for long-lost values have occasionally caused comparisons with Botho Strauß and attacks as a "new Rightist." However Handke, in contrast to Strauß, never allowed right-wing political factions to use or instrumentalize him. In his holy wrath, Handke also seems more interested in continuing the "passions" expressed earlier by Thomas Bernhard than those of Strauß or the political right.

Handke in the 1990s

The four Handke pieces staged at the *Burgtheater* during the 1990s represent a challenge for the business of theater. The non-traditional nature of the plays' scenic structure is demanding for any stage and difficult to categorize, as is already suggested in the doubled titles and the proliferation of subtitles: *Das Spiel vom Fragen, oder, Die Reise zum sonoren Land* (1989, *Voyage to the Sonorous Land, or, The Art of Asking*, 1996); *Die Stunde da wir nichts von einander wußten. Ein Schauspiel* (1992, *The Hour We Knew Nothing of Each Other*, 1996); *Zurüstungen für die Unsterblichkeit. Ein Königsdrama* (1997, Preparations for Immortality: A Royal Drama); and *Die Fahrt im Einbaum, oder, Das Stück zum Film vom Krieg* (1999, The Trip with the Outrigger or the Play for the Film about the War).[14] Handke has explained repeatedly in interviews that he wanted to present to the theater completely non-dramatic texts that would be impossible to perform. The texts more closely resemble unwieldy essays, collections of aphorisms, or anecdotal sketchbooks than dramas. Even the seemingly endless pages of stage directions are unable to breathe dramatic life into the plays. With figures such as the People or the Wall Watcher, the audience mistakenly believes that technical theater terminology is intended and does not expect to see actors performing the roles of people made of flesh and blood.

Handke's claim that his works continue the traditions of the theater is justified then not so much through dramatizations of character or plot, but through a great number of quotes and references. These quotes and references fall into two primary categories. First, Handke quotes himself. For example, the character Parzival in *The Art of Asking* represents a continuation of the fool or clown from Handke's early play *Kaspar*. Another example is the absence of speech in *The Hour We Knew Nothing of Each Other*, which corresponds to and quotes the silence from the earlier piece *Das Mündel will Vormund sein*. More importantly, however, Handke quotes classical writers to whom he wants to pay homage. Both Handke and Peymann draw numerous connections between the dramatist's works and the classics of the world theater tradition. For example and as mentioned before, director and playwright alike compare Handke's *The Art of Asking* with Goethe's *Faust*. Such provocatively lofty connections remove Handke from comparisons or competition with his contemporaries. The dedication for *The Art of Asking* is typical in its staggering immodesty and hence in its ability to irritate as well: "For Ferdinand Raimund, Anton Chekhov, John Ford, and all the others."

In the dedication above, Handke positions his play first in the tradition of Ferdinand Raimund, a well-known Austrian dramatist, but one whose melodramatic pathos frequently gives rise to a smile of condescension. *Zurüstungen für die Unsterblichkeit* offers an additional example with its stated allusion to Raimund's allegorical *Original-Zauberspiel, Die gefesselte Phantasie* (Original Magic Play: Fettered Fantasy) (*Zurüstungen* 47). This Raimund play attempted to blend features of the folk theater with those of a drama of ideas, but without success at least as far as audience appeal was concerned. Raimund's often melancholic attempt to create poetry is considered by many literary historians to be the conservative antithesis of Nestroy's intellectual cynicism. But Handke at times borrowed popular figures from Raimund's magic plays in order to create a sense of place, to provide local soil under the feet of characters whose stories take place in a mythological and distanced realm. Examples include Papageno in *The Hour We Knew Nothing of Each Other*, the Local in *The Art of Asking*, and a Raimund-like Alpine King and misanthrope, as well as the People in *Zurüstungen für die Unsterblichkeit*.

Handke's dedication of the play to Chekhov is more complex. Critic Thomas Hennig has identified a subtext that alludes to and quotes Jewish tradition in Handke's texts, and he perceives the dramatist's works as a possibility beyond the impossibility of writing stories after Auschwitz. Hennig discerns in Handke's *The Art of Asking* an echo of Chekhov's *The Cherry Tree*, where Jewish musicians play in the background. These musicians literally evoke the subtitle of the Handke play, *Voyage to the Sonorous Land*, for they produce "a distant sound, as if from heaven, the sound of a string breaking, a sad sound," which calls to mind the "sonorousness" of the journey.[15] Cabala, as well as texts by Kafka and Jabes (for example the latter's *The Book of Questions*), even though Handke might not have been familiar with them, provide poetic parallels for Hennig between the contemporary playwright and Jewish tradition, while also lending Handke's mystical course of inquiry depth and background.

Handke has been repeatedly accused of sanctifying his material, of rendering it holy or sacred. This tendency derives from an attitude that sees "all things as being symbolical, valuable, and meaningful" and that portrays them "in specific moments and views, as something timeless and eternal." With such an attitude it is only natural that Handke's texts tend toward the religious and the sacred.[16] The theater, however, relativizes such dangers. A careful reader of the author's prose works can detect a subtle humor. For example, Handke's three *Versuche*[17] (*Essays*) demonstrate numerous moments where the holy wrath of the author suddenly tips into a humorous situation – right in the middle of cutting wood the author begins to curse, or at the peak of inspiration his pencil breaks. In his dramatic works, such sudden shifts into humor characterize all of Handke's figures. Moreover, Handke's perspective is not fixed upon one narrator, but rather split into various ambivalently portrayed characters whose roles psychologize and relativize the stage reality. Thus in *The Art of Asking*, Handke is on the one hand the Wall Watcher and at the same time the Spoil-Sport, and these two figures act as counterpoints to each other. Whereas the Wall Watcher celebrates everything laboriously and obsessively in a romantically depressed poetic language, the know-it-all Spoil-Sport is an essentially positive critic who goes so far as to criticize his own criticism. When yet another character from *The Art of Asking*, the Actor, proclaims that he "finally wants to be serious for longer than a few seconds" (25), the seriousness of the proclamation itself is left open to question. Is this a pose on the Actor's part? Are we to take it as coquetry, play acting, or is it indeed meant seriously? By questioning seemingly unquestionable pronouncements in this fashion, the theater is able to counteract the proclivity for the religious or sacred. Due precisely to their faithful renderings of Handke's original text, Peymann's premieres brought out the subtle humor and latent comedy of the characters.

Interpreting Handke

If literary critics were to respect and adhere literally to Handke's own stated requests, they would not attempt to explain his works analytically. The playwright demands not answers, but rather hopes to provoke in his audience what he terms questions of wonderment; he wants the viewers to continue spinning the fantastical tale in their imagination, not explain it or comment upon it. The motto of *The Hour We Knew Nothing of Each Other* is: "Do not betray what you have seen. Stay in the picture." Each drama is to be experienced as a finely woven work of art, and Handke has frequently stated that the key to real comprehension of his dramas lies in attending multiple performances of them, not in dissecting a single performance intellectually. The female narrator of *Zurüstungen für die Unsterblichkeit* explains that distance is no longer the most difficult stance to attain; rather, "simple observation is most difficult. But only through the ability to see, to look at something, will you make war impossible" (99). This is the same attitude that

Handke used when undertaking his reports on Serbia, and it was rebuked by numerous critics as being an aggressive flight from reality into the paradise of childhood.[18] Handke insists on a double meaning of perception: on the one hand there is a "seeing that merely registers," on the other hand there exists a "higher, intensified kind of seeing."[19] Gerhard Melzer has shown that this opposition can be traced to the earliest works by Handke. Such proclamations by Handke, in conjunction with his disavowal of opinions or analytical thought, have split both the scholarly and more popular reception of his work into two factions – the followers and the opponents.

Handke's play *Voyage to the Sonorous Land, or, The Art of Asking* premiered in 1990. Despite the fact that it is the most logical of the four plays under discussion here, it met with the most vehement protest – with the exception of the politically motivated reactions to his play about the war in Bosnia, *Die Fahrt im Einbaum*. Although reaction was not as scathing as the attacks on *Walk about the Villages* had been in the early 1980s, *The Art of Asking* was bitterly denounced as being "reactionary and grandly pretentious kitsch" and as "chic shit."[20]

The Art of Asking is a station-drama that involves eight travelers: the Wall Watcher and the Spoil-Sport who call themselves Raimund and Chekhov at one point,[21] an autistic youth called Parzival, a Local, a pair of young Actors, and finally an Old Couple. These eight figures make their way through the forest in pursuit of the correct path of inquiry or questioning. Each station occurs at a grouping of trees, and the tree-ensemble of the previous picture, i.e., of the previous station, remains visible on the stage horizon, reduced in perspective. The thought processes of the characters revolve around questioning as wonderment, questioning as an act of goodness, around the desire to be questioned, and around questioning as an end in itself without an answer. On the surface, the characters appear to be positive and idyllic; however, during the course of the play they are revealed as being deeply ambivalent. The Old Couple, for instance, have spent their entire lives together and frequently utter sentences in unison, thus reminding us of Philemon and Baucis. However, their togetherness is suddenly exposed as being involuntary. They do not depict a harmonious world. The Old Woman grumbles: "It's a disgrace that we're still together" (109). Even the rhapsodic Wall Watcher, who in contrast to the nearly paranoid Spoil-Sport advocates a return to "healthy stupidity" (an especially attractive Handke-esque ideal!), is not an unambiguously positive character. The opposition between Wall Watcher and Spoil-Sport serves to mitigate at least to some extent the former's effusiveness, as do the humor and irony of some of his lines: "... in between I was once clever, I was in fact once sick from so much cleverness and intelligence, but through my gaze, through quiet observation, I have become as dumb and carefree as a child" (77). On the other hand, that somewhat ponderous Handke-esque wrath still comes through in his depiction of the Young Couple. Here the Woman's fashionable chatter about emancipation is countered by the "heavy seriousness" "in which lust occurs" and by the "effervescence of desire" (96). These lines, themselves pompous and laden with clichés, do little to relativize the Woman's talk of liberation.

Of the four Handke pieces staged in the 1990s, *The Hour We Knew Nothing of Each Other* was performed most frequently on international stages. It is a drama in which not a single word is spoken. The concept underlying such wordlessness is that the word – the gossipy self-portrayals forced upon everyone every evening by TV talk shows as well as clever prattle and verbose reflections – all forms of the word have killed the silent happiness of the seer. More than anything else, the word kills the secret of a person, a secret that remains preserved only so long as no one opens his or her mouth. This is just as true for the theater as it is for everyday life, according to Handke, and he has criticized performances or dramatic texts for just such proliferation of words and speech, as for example on the occasion of a Heiner Müller performance: "You were depressed because you knew the words would start up again at any moment. There was scarcely any time to draw a breath and just look."[22]

The Hour We Knew Nothing of Each Other is a play about seeing and perceiving, and the object of the audience's gaze is a market place with various people hurrying by. This requires a tremendous effort from the costume designers and stage managers; the ensemble has to transform itself into 300 different people within a period of an hour and a half. At times, a story seems to emerge between the various figures, but these potential stories disappear again and again as new and surprising effects grab our attention for a fleeting moment. Characters like Moses with the Ten Commandments or Peer Gynt blend without notice into the passersby, the policemen, a roller skater, the village idiot, businessmen, and many many others. Impressionistic snapshots of everyday life mix wordlessly, as well as effortlessly, with great myths. Papageno with his birdcage quotes the Viennese theater where Mozart's *Magic Flute* was first performed (*Theater an der Wien*). But at the same time, the audience casually witnesses a fatal heart attack, parodied by the Local Idiot, and has opportunity to hear the first speech sounds attempted by a mute – a Pentacostal miracle! and the sole utterance of the entire play. No matter how carefully and even dramatically the production may be constructed, the play requires the active participation of an audience willing to infer and play along. If the audience does not want to get involved, it will have no problem identifying pious kitsch in Handke's undertaking.

Handke's "drama of kings" titled *Zurüstungen für die Unsterblichkeit*, which at first might seem most similar to a traditional drama, is however unique as well within the theater establishment at the end of the 1990s. Here too, the playwright strives to avoid an intellectuality that would reduce the poetry of the work. He expresses this sentiment in the following journal note: "There should be no distracting thoughts and no ulterior thoughts; instead, just tell the story, tell it with power and in passing."[23] The story told in the drama centers on a people called the Enclavepeople due to the fact that their territory is surrounded by that of another people, the Space Restrictors, who – again true to their name – have long suppressed and repressed the minority group in their midst. The Enclavepeople are now awaiting a king, Pablo Vegas, born of a daughter of the First Ancestor who was raped by a Space Restrictor. He is to avenge the Enclavepeople. The drama traces Pablo's childhood, his return, and his struggle with the Space Restrictors. Pablo is accompanied by his wife, the Story Teller, whose job it is to "tell the story away and tell the story about it."[24] Pablo's brother Felipe functions as a parallel character and complementary figure to Pablo. Outwardly a failure, he is married to the Refugee, who serves in turn as the parallel character to the Story Teller.

Handke's royal drama quotes Ferdinand Raimund's play *Unheilbringende Krone* (Crown of Misfortune). Raimund attempts to combine Shakespeare and the Austrian theatrical tradition, thereby mixing kings with fairytale and allegorical figures, an attempt that in its naïve seriousness elicited a smile of condescension from Raimund's contemporaries. Similarly, Handke's *Zurüstungen für die Unsterblichkeit* can be seen as the anachronistic attempt to write a popular royal drama in the tradition of Shakespeare, but in the twentieth century. Though set in a fairytale world with a Spanish flavor, the action and figures of the play easily lend themselves to contemporary interpretation. Thus the Enclavepeople can represent Austria, with the figures of the People and of the Idiot opposing in stereotypical Austrian ambiguity and untruthfulness the aspiring royal candidate Pablo. But on the other hand the Enclavepeople can – especially via the motif of rape – represent Bosnia or even Serbia. The figure of the king himself is by no means constructed as a hero who will bring prosperity. Instead, Handke draws him as the torn and irresolute Alpine King, at odds with himself, a "lonely bumbler." Handke describes him in his notes as a character "who can be joyously happy and yet simultaneously stand at the brink of the abyss."[25]

The drama thematizes the act of restoring that which was lost, be it restoration of what the Space Restrictors have destroyed or restoration of language – for example, the change from *Zähre* (tear drop) to the more fashionable *Thräne* is lamented (53).[26] Yet with all its restoration of the old, the play does not exhibit any monarchical or anti-democratic contours. That which is royal, and the concept of a kingdom itself, are evoked as an existential experience. This becomes even clearer when one compares Handke's play to the successful premiere of Botho Strauß's *Ithaka* a few months earlier. Like Handke's drama, it too ends with the reinstatement of a king. At the conclusion of *Ithaka*, which was not much more than a dramatization of the nineteenth song of Homer's *Odyssey*, King Odysseus has successfully cleared out the "democratic pigsty" of the "suitor business" and founded the old Reich anew – an irritating allusion to present-day Germany. *Ithaka* ends with the reinstatement of a purified order, and Strauß seems to be postulating this final picture as an ideal to be emulated by the new Berlin republic: a new German Reich cleansed of all revolutionary and democratic sentiments as propagated by the generation of 1968. In contrast, Handke imbues his King with ideologically less alarming sentiments. The first sentence of King Pablo's constitution reads: "Face to face with a foreigner, consider your own foreignness!" (123).[27]

Handke's plays are anything but non-political or an escape from reality into art. The author notes: "Of course political relevance is an integral part of any work of art, but it is one part among many others; it is one part *next to* many others."[28] For his farewell performance from the *Burgtheater*, Peymann chose Handke's Serbian piece, *Die Fahrt im Einbaum, oder, Das Stück zum Film vom Krieg*. Political relevance and everyday reality seem to lie at the core of this play, especially considering the fact that one day after the premiere, on 12 June 1999, the war ended and Belgrade promised to accept the conditions set by NATO. In interviews before the war ended, particularly in the Munich-based newspaper *Die Süddeutsche Zeitung*, Handke had repeatedly and vociferously criticized NATO bombings and the military actions of the American and German governments, thereby isolating himself in German *feuilletons*. The drama, of course, does not portray direct political engagement. Handke's dedication of the play to the "theater as a free medium" (5) is in fact meant as opposition to journalistic war reporting, which he had already condemned with full wrath in his travel narrative and political essay *Eine winterliche*

Reise zu den Flüssen Donau, Save, Morawa und Drina oder Gerechtigkeit für Serbien (1996, *A Journey to the Rivers or Justice for Serbia*). He posits the perspective of a poet, a perspective that merely looks and observes the things of the world, as an alternative to the journalistic tendency to immediately categorize and order that world.

The play is set in the year 2005 in a dilapidated hotel located in the Balkans. Two film producers, one American and one Spanish, conduct casting try-outs among the local citizens for their war film. Handke utilizes the role of the Greek, an ostracized and isolated journalist, and his confrontations with the three Internationals as a pro-Serbian mouthpiece within the play, even though the Internationals themselves are perhaps less reminiscent of NATO officials than of the fairytale Space Restrictors from *Zurüstungen für die Unsterblichkeit*. Reviews of the premiere from the summer of 1999 expressed skepticism toward Handke's attempt to posit poetry as a counterweight to journalistic opinion, and they judged the underlying conceptual model of nature as opposed to destructive Western civilization untenable. The Spanish film director describes the one side of the opposition, namely the barbarism of civilization, with the words: "The hordes no longer form separate cliques, but rather stick together as one massive clique; and this clique then calls itself 'the world' and it is the new 'world community.' In truth it is a horde of pure money and mongers, and behind their oozing charm lies complete brutalization. An outrageous, unheard-of time. The end of society!" (123). This historical pessimism is countered by a utopia as conceived by the Fur Lady, namely a journey in an outrigger canoe through the Serbian landscape. The idealization of Serbian naturalness might border at times on kitsch, but upon closer examination such passages are seen to be ironic and ambivalent. Thus in this drama as in those already discussed, the surface idyll is broken and relativized. In addition, Handke's characters are not just theater figures, but rather theater figures playing on the stage, for they are local inhabitants playing themselves as well as their counterparts in front of film producers during casting.

The American director O'Hara states: "It is still too early for a film. ... In fifty years, perhaps, or a hundred ... But for this story we have to find a different breath of life than that of film" (122f.). Perhaps 1999 was too early for a drama about the story as well. The contradiction between the play's contemporary relevance on the one hand and the author's claim to a literature or drama that is free of direct reference to reality on the other is not productive in *Die Fahrt im Einbaum*; the opposition seems to pose an unresolved dilemma for the author. Nevertheless the play's appeal and effect seem to have transcended its specific and actual political reference. Though it will undoubtedly never resonate with the audience as did Handke's most popular *Burgtheater* play, *The Hour We Knew Nothing of Each Other*, it was staged in both Hamburg and Düsseldorf during the 2000/2001 theater season.

The relative infrequency of Handke performances by no means refutes the playwright's elitist claim. His allegorical "thought plays" (*Denkspiele*) do not really fit within the theater landscape of the 1990s, sharing more traits – including the rarity of their production – with the "idea dramas" (*Ideendrama*) from the beginning of the twentieth century, dramas such as Werfel's *Spiegelmensch* or Strindberg's *To Damascus*. The ability of Handke's dramas to provoke and irritate the audience seems to lie in their anachronistic claim to greatness, in their high and lofty literary pretensions, just as Peymann irritates and provokes in his claim that the theater is a representative place. Peymann could have, he has stated, staged Handke's plays as true "thought plays" lacking all props and theatricality, but it was his intent to support the playwright's literary and poetic aspirations with his own artistic methods on stage. More than any other single factor, this understanding of himself and his own role in the world of theater, an understanding of self that was often misunderstood by Austrians as being arrogant, made Peymann into a nuisance and annoyance in public opinion. On the occasion of Peymann's farewell performance in the *Burgtheater*, Handke wrote a dedication in which he poetically ennobled the director's role as provocateur. In doing so, he transfigures even the agitator into a revered "evocator," thereby stripping him of his destructive potential and intent: "C.P. [Claus Peymann], the provocateur, provider of light (not glare), the story teller. C.P., the provocateur? The evocator."[29] The question remains: Are Handke's *Burgtheater* plays in fact such very great art that they justify the high and lofty claims made about them? The playwright provides the following reflection in his notes accompanying *Zurüstungen für die Unsterblichkeit*: "Great literature is just a breath away from kitsch, be it religious kitsch or some other kind of kitsch. *But it is precisely this breath that matters.*"[30]

Translated by Linda C. DeMeritt and Jaclyn R. Kurash

Notes

1. Ulrich Holbein, "Dichterpriester-Humor und Hordenclown-Mystik," *Text und Kritik* 24 (1999): 110-24. All translations by DeMeritt and Kurash.

2. Handke is "kein Ansichtenvertreter und kein Weltanschauungsagent; vielmehr ist er eine bedeutsam-natürwüchsige, natürwüchsig-bedeutsame Größe." Peter Straßer, *Der Freudenstoff. Zu Handke eine Philosophie* (Salzburg: Residenz, 1990) 7.

3. Claus Peymann, "Die Abrechnung. Claus Peymann und Wien," *profil* 13 December 1998.

4. Peymann, "Abrechnung."

5. Jelinek's play *Stecken, Stab und Stangl* (1996, Stick, Staff, and Pole), based on this murder, premiered in Hamburg for this reason.

6. This production, called *Claus Peymann kauft sich eine Hose und geht mit mir essen* (Claus Peymann Buys Himself a Pair of Pants and Goes Out to Dinner with Me), traveled with Peymann to his new theater, the *Berliner Ensemble*, Brecht's stage in the 1950s.

7. The discussion concerning who would become Bernhard's successor determined both tone and substance of many reviews of the premiere of Handke's *The Art of Asking* in January 1990, one year after Bernhard's death.

8. Peter Handke, "Horváth und Brecht," *Ich bin ein Bewohner des Elfenbeinturms* (Frankfurt/M.: Suhrkamp, 1972) 63f.

9. See Karin Kathrein, "Die herbe Lust, kein Wiederholungstäter zu sein. Einige Überlegungen zur Rezeption von Peter Handkes Bühnenwerken in den achtziger Jahren," *Peter Handke*, ed. Gerhard Fuchs and Gerhard Melzer (Graz: Droschl, 1993) 155-64; Karl Wagner, "Ohne warum. Peter Handkes *Spiel vom Fragen*," *Text und Kritik* 24 (1999): 201-14; Ellen Hammer, "Rätsel erfunden fürs Fest. Zu Peter Handkes dramatischem Gedicht *Über die Dörfer*," *Die Arbeit am Glück*, ed. Gerhard Melzer and Jale Tükel (Königstein: Athenäum, 1985) 99.

10. From the program for Handke's play *Zurüstungen für die Unsterblichkeit* (Vienna: Burgtheater, 1997), *Programmbuch* 174, 54.

11. Peter Handke, "Nichts begriffen, setzen, sechs!," *Presse* 22 May 1990.

12. André Müller, *Im Gespräch* (Reinbek bei Hamburg: Rowohlt, 1989) 178.

13. Bitter criticism of Handke has been collected in *Die Angst des Dichters vor der Wirklichkeit. 16 Antworten auf Peter Handkes Winterreise nach Serbien*, ed. Tilman Zülch (Göttingen: Steidl, 1996).

14. For this paper I use the following publications of the dramas discussed: *Das Spiel vom Fragen, oder, Die Reise zum sonoren Land* (Frankfurt/M.: Suhrkamp, 1989); *Die Stunde da wir nichts voneinander wußten. Ein Schauspiel* (Frankfurt/M.: Suhrkamp, 1995); *Zurüstungen für die Unsterblichkeit. Ein Königsdrama* (Frankfurt/M.: Suhrkamp, 1997); *Die Fahrt im Einbaum oder Das Stück zum Film vom Krieg* (Frankfurt/M.: Suhrkamp, 1999). The first two of these dramas have been translated into English: *Voyage to the Sonorous Land, or, The Art of Asking, and, The Hour We Knew Nothing of Each Other/Peter Handke*, trans. Gitta Honegger (New Haven, CT: Yale UP, 1996). All quotations in this article are taken from the German editions and translated by DeMeritt and Kurash.

The cover blurb itself for *Spiel vom Fragen* thematizes the question concerning genre: "A comedy? A dream? A Singspiel? An expeditionary report? A live reportage? A cheap romance? Or a drama after all is said and done?"

15. Thomas Hennig, *Intertextualität als ethische Dimension. Peter Handkes Ästhetik "nach Auschwitz"* (Würzburg: Könighausen & Neumann, 1996) 73-86; here 84.

16. Franz Josef Czernin, *"Die Wiederholung* und *Am Felsenfenster morgens.* Zum Verhältnis von Erzählung und Weltanschauung," *Text und Kritik* 24 (1999): 44.

17. Peter Handke, *Die drei Versuche* (Frankfurt/M.: Suhrkamp, 1998). This collection contains the three prose essays: *Versuch über die Müdigkeit, Versuch über die Jukebox,* and *Versuch über den geglückten Tag.* All three have been translated: *The Jukebox and Other Essays on Storytelling,* trans. Ralph Manheim and Krishna Winston (New York: Farrar, Straus and Giroux, 1994).

18. Frauke Meyer-Gosau, "Kinderland ist abgebrannt. Vom Krieg der Bilder in Peter Handkes Schriften zum jugoslawischen Krieg," *Text und Kritik* 24 (1999): 3-20.

19. Gerhard Melzer, "Lebendigkeit. Ein Blick genügt. Zur Phänomenologie des Schauens bei Peter Handke," *Die Arbeit am Glück. Peter Handke,* ed. Gerhard Melzer and Jale Tükel (Königstein: Athenäum, 1985) 127.

20. *Die Arbeiterzeitung* of Vienna opens its biting review with the words "Schicke Scheiße," or "chic shit," in reiteration of audience catcalls at the premiere: "Des Dichters Nabelschau im Bambuswald," *Die Arbeiterzeitung* 18 January 1990. Peter Iden's review is also extremely negative: Peter Iden, "Qualvolle Reise in den grünen Kitsch," *Frankfurter Rundschau* 18 January 1990.

21. The Actress also makes the reference explicit when she takes leaves of the Wall Watcher and the Spoil-Sport with the words: "Much time, Anton Pavlovich! Much time, Ferdinand!" (147).

22. Program for *Die Stunde da wir nichts von einander wußten* (*Schaubühne* performance in Berlin, 1993) 18.

23. Program for *Zurüstungen*, 7. The original German is: "Nur keine Neben- oder Hintergedanken; einfach mächtig und beiläufig voranerzählen."
24. *Zurüstungen* 133: "die Geschichte weg- und dazu zu erzählen."
25. Program for *Zurüstungen*, 18.
26. Handke is probably using a word play or association here: *Zähre* even in the nineteenth century was considered old-fashioned and very poetic, but Handke seems to prefer it because it evokes the German *sich verzehren*, which means "to consume oneself."
27. "Bedenket vor jedem Fremden die eigene Fremde mit!"
28. Program for *Zurüstungen*, 21. Emphasis in the original.
29. Hermann Beil et al., *Weltkomödie Österreich*, vol. 2 (Vienna: Zsolnay, 1999) 169. "C.P., der Provokateur, der Beleuchter (nicht Blender), der Erzähler. C.P., der Provokateur? Der Hervorrufer."
30. Program for *Zurüstungen*, 49: "Was die Großen geschrieben haben ist nur einen Hauch verschieden vom Kitsch, religiösem oder sonst einem. *Aber dieser Hauch ist es.*"

Social and Human Issues in Peter Turrini's Work

Gerd K. Schneider

Peter Turrini can be considered one of the best chroniclers of contemporary Austrian society. His plays, performed mainly in Vienna's *Burgtheater* under the directorship of Claus Peymann, show how present-day reality affects our social and personal lives, i.e., how societal structures determine and frequently dehumanize the individual. Turrini, however, makes us aware of these problems in a sometimes shocking and provocative way because, as he has stated, "... the world is shocking. The situation in which we live is, to be sure, appalling."[1] This approach has earned him the reputation of *Nestbeschmutzer* (someone who fouls his or her own nest), pornographer, and labor activist with socialist or even communist leanings. Yet Turrini's "shock therapy" is not only negative; it is not only meant to criticize. The playwright wants to transform attitudes. The intent of his theater is to change the way people perceive and treat their fellow human beings, and to achieve this goal he employs shock and exaggeration. He de-masks his contemporaries and reveals what he considers to be the reality behind the surface.

For Turrini, literature is an ideal vehicle to effect change in society. In this belief he reminds us of Marat in Peter Weiss's play *Marat/Sade*: "I don't watch unmoved / I intervene and say that this and this are wrong and I work to alter and improve them."[2] Turrini expresses a similar view in an interview from 1977 with Lutz Holzinger:

> Every literature – even conservative and reactionary literature – intends to move something. There is no writer in this world who sits down and says: I am writing something so that nobody will be touched or moved. On the contrary. Everyone wants this. The only question is what direction do we move in and whom do we touch or how many. We believe in getting rid of the dominance of man over man. We simply want, expressed poetically, to live more happily. And this is the reason we write.[3]

Thus the societal chronicles offered by Turrini, however negative and depressing they may be in and of themselves, possess critical and even transformative intent for his audience.

Turrini combines illusion with disillusionment, or fantasy with reality, in an attempt to provoke from the viewer a process of questioning that will eventually or at least potentially open the way to change. As a playwright, he is able to use his stage to undermine contemporary perceptions of reality which might tend to gloss over its ugly and brutal side. The stage setting itself can become a silent, but powerful, dramatic co-player, contrasting starkly with audience expectations. One of the most striking examples is the setting for *Alpenglühen* (1992, *Alpine Glow*, 1994) where the rising curtain reveals a scene of such ravishing beauty "that it could only occur in popular sentimental movies or on the pages of tourist brochures."[4] This is the idyllic Austrian landscape, complete with rising sun, towering mountains, and the human habitat snuggled peacefully within nature. The beauty of this "brilliantly bright stage set"[5] is misleading, however, because Turrini immediately negates viewer anticipation of harmony. The rising sun reveals a sleeping old man to whom the beauty of the sunrise is irrelevant because he is blind. Furthermore, all of the animals who once inhabited this natural landscape have since been eliminated. Their songs, still resounding throughout the mountains, are in actuality reproduced by the blind old man, an employee of the Austrian tourist industry. The discrepancy between *Schein und Sein*, or reality and appearance, is immediately obvious: there is no natural beauty, no unity between man and nature, but rather only dominance and deception motivated by greed. Here, and in many of Turrini's plays, such contrast or clash serves to criticize social conditions as well as change them perhaps.

The playwright takes his audience on an emotional roller coaster ride, thereby creating an intense atmosphere in which we are asked to look for the truth behind the pictures. The result might well be that the viewers look within and ask themselves: Is it really so? Why? What would I have done, or what should I do, in this specific situation? The following essay will investigate some of these characteristic moments of deception within contemporary society where illusion and reality simply do not gel: the way society treats the elderly, the effect of job loss on the individual, the spread of the porno industry, and Austrians' hostile prejudices toward foreigners. Turrini's dramas are an attempt to focus attention; they force us to observe on stage the consequences of our otherwise often unreflected views. In this way, we come face to face with the reality we ourselves have created. Seeing the various instances of the "dominance of man over man" personified and dramatized, in a situation that shocks because of its stark, frequently repulsive exaggeration, could be the first step toward the intended process of personal and societal questioning.

Societal attitudes toward the elderly are castigated in *Josef und Maria* (1980, *Joseph and Mary*, 1992). In this play, Mary, a sixty-five-year-old cleaning woman who is employed part-time in a department store, meets Joseph, a sixty-eight-year-old security guard who works there too. It is Christmas Eve, celebrated traditionally as a time of love and compassion, but perverted in our time into a commercial festival, with material goods replacing spiritual values. For instance, the personnel director announces that the store's employees, with the exception of the sales clerks in the book division, the part-time cleaning women, and the foreign co-workers, will be given a small bottle of brandy as a token of the director's appreciation. It is exactly these outsiders, excluded from the festivities and the well-to-do community, whom Turrini portrays in this play. He shows that behind the mask of seemingly convivial altruism is a political separatist view which stands in direct contrast to a Christmas message supposedly inclusive of all human beings.

Mary and Joseph live, like their biblical counterparts, on the periphery of society, considered outcasts even by members of their own family. Mary's daughter-in-law does not want her around, not even in this time of love and caring, and Joseph's socialist comrades have passed away or are too young to have shared his life experiences. The primary cause for the status as social outcast suffered by both Mary and Joseph is their advanced age. Turrini shows the de-personalization of a human being who is no longer young in the fate of Mary's old neighbor:

> When my neighbor died, they put her things out on the sidewalk. I looked to see if there was anything I could use. There were old report cards from elementary school, some good grades, too. Letters from her husband from the first World War. There was nothing interesting in them, just love stuff. The next day the garbage men took it all away. What's left of you when there's nothing left of you? I'll tell you – it's just better to go when you can ... (72)[6]

Mary repeats the last sentence when she reminisces about her son: "Sometimes I think it's better just to go ... that you just go away. People don't worry about you, it's the truth. I'm tellin' it like it is" (61). The underlying problem Turrini addresses in the play is the aging of society – both in terms of exclusion of the elderly by others and of their own feelings of worthlessness.[7] The elderly are, according to Margarita Pazi, "an underprivileged minority,"[8] subjected to societal prejudice.

Thus Turrini's play, to use Mary's words from above, "tells it like it is," or in other words, the play sheds light upon a hidden ill and forces the audience to see and hear something typically overlooked and hushed. In doing so, Turrini holds out the possibility and hope to shake up the status quo and bring about change. The playwright, in accepting the Gerhart-Hauptmann-Prize of the *Freie Volksbühne* in 1981, comments on this:

> I put up a fierce resistance against this new attitude [of being inactive], because it deprives man of the possibility of interpreting the world. ... I am someone who firmly believes that everything has its origin in man and that all can be referred back to man ... A literature that shows man in a world where nothing can be gained, only lost, brings forth exactly those horrors from which that world suffers.[9]

Joseph and Mary illustrate the above thought; they both gain insight and develop tolerance; they change regardless of their advanced age, which many see as an impediment to change and transformation. Thus this work ends with a ray of hope, which is unusual for Turrini who usually "depicts a society which functions on pervasive mutilation, with people mutilating each other or themselves."[10] Here, in contrast, the playwright shows that love and understanding are still possible in our time. Despite the many obstacles and very different biographies that separate these two old people, a Christmas miracle happens: they find a way to overcome the distance between them through their sense of human loneliness and compassion for others.

Interpersonal relations between the sexes is also a core topic of Turrini's play titled *Grillparzer im Pornoladen* (1993, Grillparzer in the Sex Shop), but in this more recent play the outcome of the encounter between man and woman is not as hopeful as in the earlier one. *Grillparzer im Pornoladen* premiered February 1993 at the *Berliner Ensemble* and in September 1994 at the *Theater im Rabenhof* in Vienna. The title reveals the mixture of the sublime and the economic because it combines the name of one of Austria's best-known dramatists with a business venture where sex paraphernalia are displayed, demonstrated, and sold. Already in the title then we have the type of clash typical for Turrini, one whereby the reality of business transactions will be shown to have a very direct impact upon our typically romanticized notions of love, one whereby the interplay between theater and life, between *Schein und Sein*, or mask and the face behind it will be thematized.

The play features two nameless people, a man and a woman, who have widely different life experiences, as did Joseph and Mary, but who also have loneliness in common. The man, who lost his job as a prompter at the *Burgtheater* in Vienna to a woman, manages a porno shop. The woman comes into the shop for obvious reasons but pretends to have done so just by chance. She has been separated from her doctor/husband for four years and now works as ORF-editor in the Austrian media world. She trusted her husband, but he betrayed her with a female student. She hates and distrusts men just as the man hates women, although for different reasons. This hatred toward the opposite sex takes the form of hurting each other under the pretext of sex, and they enter into a sado-masochistic relationship resulting in a near-deadly outcome. The end of the play remains open; it is not clear whether the relationship between these two people will ever change for the better or even continue. Wolfgang Kralicek notes: "This short piece about love in our cold times tells us the heart-moving story of two lonely souls, who fail to find each other (or still find each other) at the end."[11]

Layered on top of this picture of power relations between the sexes are questions concerning the theatrical mask versus the real nature of the two figures – their desires, wants, fears, and hopes. It is no accident that Turrini makes his male character a former prompter in the theater. In addition, the dramatist incorporates quotes from Grillparzer's play *Des Meeres und der Liebe Wellen* ([1840], *Hero and Leander*), which translates literally as Waves of the Ocean and of Love. The man quotes from this, the last play which he in fact prompted, reciting lines spoken by the young priestess Hero:

> You, ... must watch for that man's every glance,
> Your husband and your master; must not speak,
> Must hold your tongue, or whisper, though you're right.[12]

In Grillparzer's play, it is clear that these words of Hero to her mother are meant ironically, that she does not agree with the view that a woman has to be dependent on her husband. The words of the mother to the daughter – "A woman's happy only at a husband's side" (19) – belong to a concept that lost its relevance and meaning for contemporary society long ago. Yet Turrini's modern man thoroughly believes in the concept and words. Convinced that men will be displaced from their seemingly secure jobs and positions by overly eager and aggressive women, he fears the revolution of the sexes: "The obliteration of man began in the sixties."[13] On the other hand, the female protagonist, who was originally betrayed for having expected protection and security at the side of her husband, now does in fact assume her role as liberated woman, albeit with resentment and frustration, both existentially and sexually.

Turrini shows his audience the reality of sexual politics in today's society. In addition to revealing the human calamity, his criticism is directed at the underlying reasons for the proliferation of the porno industry. Fear of human contact, of closeness, and of intimacy has become so great in both sexes that a whole industry has sprung up with mechanical gadgets that allow the individual to satisfy himself or herself without a human partner. In an interview about this play Turrini remarked, "And my characters will have to find a way to get through these sexual devices."[14] Although the play shocks its audience, it also reflects contemporary Austrian reality.

The themes of *Grillparzer im Pornoladen* are sex, violence, employment insecurity, and above all the human suffering created by these societal conditions. We find the same themes in Turrini's play *Die Minderleister* (1988, *The Slackers*, 1992), and it is therefore not surprising that reference is made to the same Grillparzer play here,

Des Meeres und der Liebe Wellen.[15] The term "slackers" refers to steel mill workers whose productivity has decreased. Turrini shows that in a capitalist society oriented toward the values of profit and meeting consumer demand, the actual producers of wealth get short-changed and are subjected to inhuman treatment. This is what happens to Hans and Anna Freiberger, the couple in the play. Hans works in the nationalized steel industry. Because of falling demand and cheaper production abroad, the steel industry is downsized and workers are dismissed. Hans is among those laborers, and the lay-off damages his self-esteem, or as Turrini said in an interview with Uwe Jens Jensen: "A man who does not work is no man."[16] This happens at an unfortunate time because his wife, who works at a factory that manufactures washing machines, also loses her position and for similar reasons – cheaper production costs abroad. The loss of family income results in a weakening of love between Hans and his wife.

Turrini shows how degrading social conditions dehumanize interactions between people, both on a familial and a work level. Hans is re-employed in the steel mill through the intervention of a minister, but only on the condition that he record the suppposed slackers so that they can be dismissed. His wife helps to augment the family income by starring in a porno film, directed by a Yugoslav. Hans, who watches porno films in his free time, happens to see her, and he and his comrades release their aggression in a most brutal way by welding the Yugoslav's penis into a heated steel tube. Hans's situation at the plant also eventually changes since his comrades, with whom he enjoyed a good working relationship, now ostracize him for spying on them. Hans feels isolated from his former friends, his workplace, and his wife, and in his frustration he hurls himself into the fiery furnace.

Turrini describes a situation with which Europeans as well as Americans are quite familiar. Industry downsizes in order to increase the profit margin, and not only "slackers" fear losing their job but also highly productive workers. Nobody can be sure of employment security in this capitalistic, competitive world, not even the producer of porno films. In reality, the condition of the

Yugoslav is not so very different from that of Hans and his friends. Hans recognizes before his death that the Yugoslav was only a scapegoat for the frustration he and his comrades felt, and he apologizes to him: "I really hated you. I'd like to apologize / For that now" (218). Turrini also criticizes the media and the underground video porno market, as Jutta Landa points out: "Moreover, the play castigates the coopting of the media in the political, social, and psycho-sexual exploitation of the worker: videos, game shows, porno movies, etc. destroy what little political consciousness and power of resistance is left after an excruciating shift at the blast furnace."[17]

Turrini paints a pessimistic picture which leaves little hope for change. The factory librarian in the play, named Shakespeare, can be interpreted as Turrini's alter ego. He was born in 1944, the same year as Turrini, and when the actor playing Shakespeare in the Viennese *Akademietheater* became ill, Turrini himself played the role. Shakespeare, who does not actually participate in the manufacturing process at the furnace, is in charge of the books which nobody loans or reads, as he laments:

> I have the treasures of the soul
> At my disposal.
> Why does no one approach me
> And touch a book?
> Your heart is a desert
> The whole country is a desert . . .
> The truth is –
> Nothing has really affected me.
> No story no book
> I turned to sand long ago
> And now I crawl on all fours
> Through my own desert. (150-51)

His world of books is not the world in which the workers fight for their existence. Shakespeare, the educated individual, is useless in the competitive struggle for survival and his only way to belong is by drinking beer, for which the men pay. Thus the hopeless tone of this play raises the question concerning the ability of literature to change the dehumanizing conditions in which people live and work. Although Turrini elsewhere expresses belief in the power of the word to change present social injustices, he does not give an answer here. He does, however, present a situation so shocking that it might force his audience to reflect on what they have seen or read and to search for an answer to the key problem of this play, which Turrini formulated in an interview from 1988: "The drama of my play, the desperate actions of my characters, are determined by the fact that they cannot understand, and do not want to understand, why the few things they want from life no longer are available to them."[18]

The central problem of Turrini's play *Die Schlacht um Wien* (1995, *The Battle for Vienna*, 1996) is Austrian xenophobia, and the playwright draws parallels between contemporary treatment of foreigners and past instances of hatred and genocide. The title of the work recalls previous battles for Vienna, such as the attempted invasion by the Turks in the sixteenth and seventeenth centuries. The enemy remains the same, but the battle now takes place not outside the city gates, but within the capital itself. Reference to the Holocaust is bluntly evident in the central passage uttered by the old man to the young woman, representative of the continuity between generations: "Calm down now, Miss. In this country there will always be people who want to burn up other people. Sometimes more, sometimes fewer. It's just in their blood."[19]

Jewish identity and the recording of that identity under past and present racism is also thematized by Turrini. While in a Nazi concentration camp, a Jew was forced to change his name from "Bleibtreu," meaning literally "stay faithful," to "Froehlich" or "cheerful," a change that is of course both ironic and tragic. After the war the Jew retained the Nazi name and invented a "Nazi-resume" to go along with it (151), because he finds that prejudice and bigotry against the Jew in postwar Austrian society still run rampant. Now, a very old man, he wants to write down the story of his life using a laptop computer. This act implies the rediscovery and preservation of Jewish identity; furthermore, the story becomes a record of the terror and violence committed against Jews in the recent past. The difficulty of the task for the old man is made apparent in his inability to figure out the "delete" as opposed to the "save" commands on the laptop: "What do I have to do so that my stories and I don't get erased as easily as that sentence?" (158). It is also a dangerous task: A young gang-leader shows him how to control the computer functions, and immediately thereafter crushes his skull with an immense stone. Such a document is not wanted in a society that perpetuates the attitudes and behaviors of Nazi Germany.

The Battle for Vienna starts in the tradition of a mystery play: the stage is dark, God appears, and creation starts. First, light emerges, then a star-filled sky, next inorganic life, and finally organisms. God commands animals into existence without difficulty, but his powers prove inadequate to create man in his image. Something has gone wrong with his divine plan and it seems during the course of the play that the Devil, his metaphysical opponent, wields more power than he.

Eight characters from various strata of life now merge in a hotel parking lot in response to a newspaper ad that called on people to form a "group called Murderers." The aim of this group is to burn down the refuge of asylum seekers and kill them. For some members of the group, this is a last attempt to re-create law and order and return to the *status quo*, or as the woman explains it: "There are so many strange people in the world. More and more are coming to our country every day. On a single day sometimes it's as high as five hundred or a thousand. A thousand new people every day. It can't go on like this. That's why we've joined this group; they've got guns" (124). But the original intention to kill foreigners is not realized; instead, most of the potential murderers are killed themselves. The theater director, who wanted more realism on stage, is killed by a real bullet fired from a theater revolver. An unsuccessful journalist suffers a similar fate. Wanting to record a realistic event for his newspaper, he encourages the cellist to commit suicide. When a gang of murderous teenagers enters the scene, the journalist sees the opportunity to record an event of even greater realism and tells the cellist: "We'll turn it all around. We won't do a suicide. We'll do a murder. You'll be shot by someone else while the camera's rolling. From off-screen" (167). The gang-leader, however, shoots the journalist instead.

Such ironic and paradoxical reversals provoke questions: Why do these people who gathered to kill foreigners end up being killed instead? What is real and what is mere theater? What happens when the mask is taken for reality? While the primary intent of the play was to comment on the killing war in Yugoslavia, the emphasis shifted to the xenophobic attitude of the Austrians, an attitude which, considering the history of the country, is contradictory and a paradox itself. Austria is, as Turrini states in a *Spiegel* interview from 1995, a multicultural country integrating immigrants from Hungary, Czechoslovakia, Yugoslavia, and other regions, a mixture which Austrians of German descent sometimes find unacceptable today, yet a reality that can be denied only by denying one's own identity. Thus killing foreigners from these countries can be looked on as almost suicidal, as actually self-destructive: "This country is a European mixture with a strong Slavic bent. This mongrel pretends to be a purebred shepherd dog and Haider is the self-acclaimed top dog. This is the true Austrian tragedy, which of course is also a comedy. If Austria could love its muddle [*Durcheinander*], the other in itself, it would be a beautiful country."[20] The same criticism of his countrymen is voiced by Turrini in a speech of 1994 in which he says that in "no other country of Europe is xenophobia more widespread and more idiotic than in Austria."[21]

The Austrian hatred of foreigners and the aggression against them can be attributed to a misunderstood *Heimatliebe*, which can be translated roughly as "love of one's country." Turrini's work strongly criticizes and condemns a national pride that has become dangerous and exclusionary due to the lack of critical reflection upon its implications for others, i.e., due to an unwillingness to question or scrutinize its various manifestations. His skepticism toward the concept of *Heimatliebe* prompts the following sarcastic characterization of himself as a *Heimatdichter*, or as a "writer of the homeland," in an interview with Franz Wille: "You want to make an Austrian *Heimatdichter* out of me. Well, so be it."[22] Turrini writes in his essay "Heimat" that *Heimat* and family originally were a unit, where all goods were manufactured in a region in which one lived. "Life was predictable," he continues, "the moral and economic relations were hierarchical, but stable."[23]

Heimat then is a place filled with personal memories and charged with emotions. It is therefore perhaps not surprising that Austrians defend what they understand to be their *Heimat* with irrational aggression against anything and anyone who threatens this seemingly holy place in today's fast-paced and often frightening world. Turrini is aware of this troublesome attitude in his fellow Austrians; he understands it, but never condones it. During the rehearsals of *The Battle for Vienna* in 1994 he wrote the following sardonic text:

> I understand these people. They only have culture left. The First World War took the monarchy away from them. This man Hitler took away the gold and foreign currency deposits from the National Bank. After the war the Americans declared Austria to be the Hawaii of central Europe, and the Germans have again invaded the country and bought up the most beautiful places surrounding the Austrian lakes. And now a German [Claus Peymann] takes away the last value: the *Burgtheater*.[24]

Turrini's biting humor epitomizes his social criticism, his relentless attempt to undermine the glossy surface of reality and provoke reflection and question.

Only in *Joseph and Mary*, where the two main characters find each other and come together despite their obvious differences, does Turrini show a ray of hope. Only in this play, which one critic considers to be among the best Turrini ever wrote,[25] can the individual defy social circumstances that otherwise lead to the dehumanization and brutality so typical of the playwright's dramas. In both *Grillparzer im Pornoladen* and *The Slackers*, Turrini reveals the consequences of a capitalist economy for the individual, where profit and greed destroy human relations. In the former, the need for human intimacy is manifest only as fear of others – fear for one's job, fear of closeness – and this fear perverts interpersonal relationships into self-satisfaction or sado-masochistic interaction. In *The Slackers* Turrini shows the problem of job insecurity, a problem which is not restricted to Austria alone, but can be found in almost all countries making up the new global economy. The author does not offer a solution to this problem, but by presenting it he makes us reflect and ask ourselves what could be done. Similarly, in *The Battle for Vienna* the playwright portrays Austrian prejudice against foreigners. Again he cannot offer a solution: xenophobia is integrated deeply within the historical and political past of the country and change does not come easy. He can, however, force us to confront the issue and, ideally, also gain insight into the paradoxical nature of such an attitude for a country of immigrants like Austria.

The plays of Peter Turrini chronicle important social issues that plague contemporary society, ills that are covered up and hidden from view and that are accordingly allowed to continue. The dramatist uses the theater to de-mask the illusion, to reveal the ugliness behind the pretty pictures propagated by those in power. He hopes that through painting the darkness of reality, through exaggerating an inhumanity we do not want to see, his plays will force the audience to at least acknowledge the existence of that reality as well as the necessity for change.

Notes

1. Peter Turrini, "Provokation," *Liebe Mörder! Von der Gegenwart, dem Theater und dem lieben Gott* (Munich: Luchterhand, 1996) 91-92; here 91.

2. Peter Weiss, *The Persecution and Assassination of Jean-Paul Marat as Performed by the Inmates of the Asylum of Charenton under the Direction of The Marquis de Sade* (New York: Simon and Schuster, Pocket Books, 1973) 46.

3. Lutz Holzinger, "Wilhelm Pevny/Peter Turrini. Die eigene Betroffenheit ist entscheidend," *Kürbiskern* 1977.4: 129-34; here 133-34. Translation mine.

4. Peter Turrini, *Alpenglühen* (Hamburg: Luchterhand, 1992). The play premiered in 1993 at the *Burgtheater*. Translated as *Alpine Glow* by Richard S. Dixon (Riverside, CA: Ariadne Press, 1994).

5. Paul Barz, "Großes Schauspieltheater für Primadonnen. Triumph für Claus Peymann mit Turrinis *Alpenglühen* im Thalia-Theater," *Welt am Sonntag* 21 March 1993: 99. Joachim Kronsbein, reviewing Turrini's play under the title "Lügner mit Charakter" in *Der Spiegel* 47 (8/1993), refers to the set as "ein beeindruckender Schnellkurs in bühnentechnischer Landschaftsmalerei" (223) (an impressive, quick course in theatrical landscape painting). Similarly, in an interview with Christine Dössel in the *Süddeutsche Zeitung* 20-21 May 1995: 15, the stage designer Hermann compares the design of his stage set with the mountain paintings of Caspar David Friedrich.

6. Peter Turrini, *Joseph and Mary, The Slackers and Other Plays*, trans. and afterword by Richard S. Dixon (Riverside, CA: Ariadne Press, 1992) 72. All other page references to this text refer to this edition and appear in parentheses after the quote.

7. The increase of the elderly as a percentage of the total population is a pressing issue for advanced industrialized societies. In Austria, according to Leopold Rosenmayr, the age category of people over seventy-five will increase more than any other category. This group now numbers 500,000 in a total population of 7.5 million; by 2030, with the total population having shrunk by an estimated one million, it will number between 600,000 and 700,000. See Rosenmayr, *Altenhilfe: Ein soziales Anliegen der Jahrhundertwende* (Wiener Journal Zeitschriftenverlag: Hotel Atelier, 1991) 10-11. See

also Rosenmayr, "Keine Nähe ohne Streit," *Presse* 3 January 1998: Spektrum III.

8. Margarita Pazi, "Peter Turrini," *Major Figures of Contemporary Austrian Literature*, ed. Donald G. Daviau (New York: Peter Lang, 1987) 387.

9. Peter Turrini, "Gerhart-Hauptmann-Preis," *Mein Österreich. Reden, Polemiken, Aufsätze* (Darmstadt: Luchterhand, 1988) 78, 81. Translation mine.

10. Gabrielle Robinson, "Slaughter and Language in the Plays of Peter Turrini," *Theatre Journal* 43 (1991): 195-208; here 195.

11. Wolfgang Kralicek, "Sex, Gewalt und Rätselhaft," *Theater heute* 35 (1994): 32-34; here 34. Translation mine.

12. Franz Grillparzer, *Der Meeres und der Liebe Wellen*, *Grillparzers sämtliche Werke in zwanzig Bänden*, ed. August Sauer, vol. 7 (Stuttgart: Verlag der J. G. Cotta'schen Buchhandlung, n.d.) 36. Translated as *Hero and Leander* by Henry H. Stevens (Yarmouth Port, Mass.: The Register Press, [1938]) 18. All other page references to this text refer to this edition and appear in parentheses after the quote.

13. Peter Turrini, *Grillparzer im Pornoladen. Nach dem Bühnenstück Love Boutique von Willard Manus* (Vienna: Thomas Sessler, neue Edition, n.d.) 36.

14. Elisabeth Hirschmann-Aitzinger, "Interview mit Peter Turrini," *Bühne* 9 (1994). Quoted in program notes, *Grillparzer im Pornoladen* at the *Rabenhof Theater* (3). Translation mine.

15. Peter Turrini, "The Slackers," *The Slackers and Other Plays* 182. Page references to this play are taken from this edition and appear in parentheses after the quote.

16. Uwe Jens Jensen, "Die Minderleister I. Interview mit Peter Turrini," Turrini, *Liebe Mörder!* 74-81; here 78. Translation mine.

17. Jutta Landa, "*Minderleister*: Problems of Audience Address in Peter Turrini's Plays," *Modern Austrian Literature* 24.3-4 (1991): 167.

18. Jensen 80. Translation mine.

19. Peter Turrini, *Siege of Vienna*, in *Shooting Rats, Other Plays, and Poems*, trans. and with an afterword by Richard S. Dixon (Riverside, CA: Ariadne Press, 1996) 155. In my article, I use the translation title *Battle for Vienna* because it expresses the violence more clearly. All subsequent quotes are taken from this translation and appear in parentheses in my text.

20. Peter Turrini, "Wir sind explosive Wesen," Interview with Hans-Peter Martin, *Der Spiegel* 18 (1995): 192-98. Rpt. in Turrini, *Liebe Mörder!* 156-64; here 159. This passage has been translated by Hermann Schlösser, "The Reception of Turrini's *Die Schlacht um Wien*," *"I Am Too Many People": Peter Turrini: Playwright, Poet, Essayist*, ed. Jutta Landa (Riverside, CA: Ariadne Press, 1998) 147.

21. "Wie verdächtig ist der Mensch?" Speech of 11 September 1994 for the opening of the Bruckner Festival in Linz, *Liebe Mörder!* 48-55; here 50. Translation mine.

22. Peter Turrini, "Die letzte Liebesgeschichte findet im Theater statt." Interview with Franz Wille in *Theater heute* 4 (1995): 4-13. Rpt. in *Liebe Mörder!* 135-52; here 147. Translation mine.

23. Peter Turrini, "Heimat," Turrini. *Mein Österreich. Reden, Polemiken, Aufsätze* (Darmstadt: Luchterhand, 1988) 66-68; here 67. Published first as foreword to the book edition of the TV-series *Alpensaga* in 1980. Translation mine.

24. Peter Turrini, "Die Schlacht um Wien." Unpublished text, recorded at the rehearsal for the play at the *Burgtheater*. In *Liebe Mörder!* 128-131; here 130-31. Translation mine.

25. Bernd Fischer, rev. of *"I Am Too Many People," German Quarterly* 72.4 (1999): 419.

Staging a Legend:
Claus Peymann's *Ingeborg Bachmann. Wer?*

Kirsten Krick-Aigner

> It is inside that all dramas take place.
> (Bachmann)[1]

Within the framework of this anthology on Austrian theater, I will explore how Ingeborg Bachmann's work has experienced a renaissance on stage at the national *Burgtheater* under the direction of Claus Peymann, its director from 1986 to 1999. In order to portray the life and works of this post-World War II author more than two decades following her death, Peymann's production titled *Ingeborg Bachmann. Wer?* (Ingeborg Bachmann. Who?), which premiered on 11 November 1995, is a patchwork of biographic fragments comprised of citations from poetry, prose, and Bachmann's public life. This biographic tapestry of the once typically private author is an identity construction, and as such, just one possible response to the question of who Bachmann really was, or is. Peymann's production, in an effort to make Bachmann's complex work more palatable to an audience beyond academic circles, depoliticizes her writings by underrepresenting the criticism of political and social reality inherent to her work.

Bachmann, born in 1926, was both revered and rejected by Austrian society during her lifetime for her individualistic writing style as well as for her biting portrayal of postwar Austrian society. Since her untimely death in 1973, Bachmann's work has been read with renewed interest and it continues to elicit both outrage and delight. Her works have been translated, interpreted, and reedited; painters, composers, and film directors have created works of art inspired by her words; and books about her life have been published for an audience eager to learn her most intimate secrets.[2] Throughout her lifetime and following her death, Bachmann has been portrayed by the Austrian media as a myriad of conflicting identities: as a lonely woman suffering from romantic rejection and depression, a well-respected intellect who dedicated her life to writing, a fashionable woman so shy that she could only read her works in public in a low whisper, and a sexually liberated woman whose secrets were indiscreetly chronicled in Adolf Opel's book about his trip with the author to Egypt.[3] Many scholars have attempted to define Bachmann's identity through the female protagonists portrayed in her last volume of short stories from 1972, *Drei Wege zum See* (*Three Paths to the Lake*), and her unfinished novel cycle, *Todesarten* (Death Styles). It is evident by the steady stream of scholarly studies on Bachmann's writings and numerous creative interpretations of her work that her legacy continues to fascinate and inspire readers at the turn of the twenty-first century.

Peymann's *Ingeborg Bachmann. Wer?* makes use of both biographical facts and rumors about Bachmann's life to portray the author, as well as to interpret the female protagonists of the *Todesarten* novel cycle and other fictional works. The production interprets the author's life as emotionally tumultuous, yet manages to portray the sometimes girlish and humorous side of the Austrian writer, otherwise known for her battle with depression and her tragic death from the complications of burns suffered in her apartment in Rome. Although *Ingeborg Bachmann. Wer?* tends to oversimplify the complexity of the author's work, Peymann has nevertheless brought Bachmann to prominence. His production never paints a definitive portrait of Bachmann's life; but instead, situates her work in an intertextual context that adds a novel and often refreshing dimension to her life and work. Peymann illustrates that Bachmann's life can only be portrayed as a fragmented montage of extracted passages from her published works that are reformulated as a narrative representative of her personal life.

Peymann's collage of Bachmann's oeuvre, a co-production written by Hermann Beil and Jutta Ferbers, draws from the author's novel cycle *Todesarten*, written in the 1960s and 1970s, with a strong emphasis on the novel *Malina* from 1971, and the two poetry collections *Die gestundete Zeit (Borrowed Time)* and *Anrufung des Großen Bären (Invocation of the Great Bear)*, from 1953 and 1956 respectively. Other lesser-known poems, written between the late 1960s and 1973, such as "Keine Delikatessen" (No Delicacies), "Exil" (Exile), and "Enigma," are also prominently featured. When Peymann first conceived of the production, he explained that instead of being a "biography" of Bachmann, it would portray "ten to twelve exemplary moments from the life of a creative woman."[4] These "moments" can be likened to the recollection of public memory that is recreated on stage as an identity construction of the public figure of Bachmann. The production, which lasts two-and-a-half hours without intermission, immerses the audience in Bachmann's world by demanding an uninterrupted focus on the span of the author's life and work.

The printed theater program captures the collage-style structure of the performance. A green portfolio, tied together with an elegant black band, holds facsimiles of black and white photographs of a smiling Bachmann, either playing chess or strolling fashionably in front of the Spanish steps in Rome. The photographs depict Bachmann as one whose private persona counters her more popular media image as a reclusive woman suffering from depression. The assorted collection of photographs reminds the viewer that these "moments" of Bachmann captured on film can be rearranged haphazardly to create a certain image of the author. In other words, each individual member of the public is able to revise and reconstruct his or her own perception of Bachmann. The photographs chosen for the program of a cheerful Bachmann, however, also predetermine the image that Peymann prescribes for the viewer. The director wishes to create a context for the performance in which Bachmann, despite her battle with depression, is portrayed as a hopeful romantic who shares her sense of humor with the audience.

Also enclosed in the program is a small assortment of text passages from Bachmann's work, including a biographical fragment about her childhood in Klagenfurt and a typescript of the poem "Böhmen liegt am Meer" (Bohemia Lies on the Ocean) with Bachmann's scrawled notations. The selection of publications provides a framework for the collage of Bachmann's life that spans her childhood full of hopeful and romantic dreams to her adult life, in which she took it upon herself to work through her experiences of war and her reactions to the Holocaust. Therefore the folder represents more than just a visitor's memento of "an evening at the *Burgtheater*" as the front cover suggests; rather it is an artist's portfolio, containing the most striking photographs taken of Bachmann and a selection of those gripping passages of her writing emphasized in Peymann's production.

A page from the program folder lists the seven scenes that comprise the performance: "Time Today," "Hell and Heaven/Klagenfurt," "Love in Vienna," "My Firstborn Country/Italy," "Everywhere and Nowhere/The Third Man," "About Fear," and "Enigma." The titles of these segments refer to phrases from Bachmann's work that capture various geographic locations (Klagenfurt, Vienna, and Italy) the author knew and emotional states (love and fear) that are frequently addressed in her writing. Peymann does not portray Bachmann's work chronologically; instead he highlights persistent central themes in the author's writings that meld the various genres and styles of her artistic expression. The production begins on a darkened stage, on which an actress recites "I cannot tolerate slavery" and continues with a monologue that twice repeats the phrase "I am always myself." This self-reflective statement emphasizes the fragmented nature of the following production that portrays the many – and often contradictory – facets of the author's personal and public persona. Before running off stage, the actress continues: "I am always myself. When I climb, I climb high; when I fall, I fall completely."

Here the hopeful and "high-climbing" image of Bachmann is juxtaposed with both the author's emotional demise and the "murders" and deaths suffered by the female narrators of *Todesarten*. The montage of Bachmann's life culminates in the recitation of Bachmann's poem "Böhmen liegt am Meer" that highlights the tension between the hope and hopelessness of humankind's existence as exemplified in Bachmann writings. The central line of the poem, "Completely destroyed, I calmly get up. Fundamentally I know now, and am 'un-lost,'"[5] emphasizes the persistence of hope throughout Bachmann's work. The final stanza of the poem also embodies the end of the play: "I am talented by way of the ocean that debates whether or not it is the country of my choice."[6] Here, the ocean is Bachmann's "country of choice," rather than any specific country or nationality that is defined by its borders. In "believing the ocean," she can "hope for land," and therefore hope for salvation. Peymann's production emphasizes this vision of hope in the wake of Bachmann's reaction of horror and shocked silence to the events of the Third Reich. At the conclusion of the novel *Malina,* for instance, the female narrator laments that poetry will no longer exist and that "no day will come."[7] Instead, "a day will come" on which "only Malina's dry, cheerful voice will exist," and no longer a "beautiful word" from her.[8] In an interview about *Malina*, Bachmann stated that there is hope even within this "capitulation" and that this mark of hope is intrinsic to the human experience.[9] It is precisely this tension between the "dry voice" and the "beautiful word" that is the focus of Peymann's performance.

The production has no intention of presenting a linear narrative of Bachmann's life. Instead, it is a montage of fragments selected from Bachmann's poetry, prose, personal essays, and interviews, read either by an individual Bachmann-character or by a chorus of seven actresses. A pamphlet among the folder's contents lists a selection of musical pieces Bachmann treasured and referred to in her writings. It features diverse composers such as those of the Vienna School (*Wiener Schule)*, Alban Berg, Anton Webern,

Gustav Mahler, and Arnold Schoenberg, as well as other popular composers such as Giuseppe Verdi, whose *La Traviata* is sung by Bachmann's favorite opera star Maria Callas, and American jazz artist Miles Davis. The music, which is recognized by a broad cross section of the population, allows the audience entry into the author's work through more familiar artists.

The montage of Bachmann's life unfolds on a spacious stage with minimalist features. Devoid of realistic references to actual geographic locations, the set transports the viewer to the various stages of Bachmann's life, which are played out as scenes from her childhood in Klagenfurt, her move to Vienna as a student, her relocation to Italy, and her death. The vast set, devoid of cluttered props, enables the audience to imagine the changing scenes of Bachmann's life and to experience her words as they fill the *Burgtheater*. The bare stage draws attention to the sounds of Bachmann's poetry. Peymann has taken his cues from the novel *Malina*, in which Bachmann's "stage directions" in the novel's introduction state that the time is "today" and the place is "Vienna."[10] For the spectator, time is always lodged in the present. This emphasis underscores the viewer's realization that Bachmann's life and work can always only be approached from the perspective of the present. In other words, Bachmann's life, as it is portrayed on stage, is constructed from her publications and the public memory of her life.

Critics, however, no doubt expecting a more traditional and ornate set, called it "a multi-portaled, arched bunker"[11] and described it as a "waiting room in a train station."[12] Both the set design by Peter Schubert and the selection of stage props make reference to the novel and film *Malina*. By recalling Werner Schroeter's 1991 film, the play confines the audience to a predetermined, one-dimensional reading of Bachmann's novel that ignores the complex and often dreamlike, multileveled narrative structure of her work. Stage props, described in the novel and familiar to the film, include an old travel typewriter, an old-fashioned telephone, a transistor radio, and a suitcase. Frequent images of fires burning throughout the film, and references to fire in the novel, inspire a blaze in a trunk as the performance draws to a close. Props emphasize what one critic describes as Bachmann's "inner process" that "becomes scenic material."[13] Such blunt references to poetic metaphors, however, fail to capture the underlying complexity and dimension of Bachmann's word choice. The multifaceted image of fire in the novel *Malina* as anger, hatred, passion, (self-) destruction, and creative inspiration is lost in the play to an oversimplified, visual special effect.[14] Stage-right, the male alter ego of the female protagonist in the novel, Malina, sits at a piano. Stage-left, the public is confronted with a life-size wall opening, reminiscent of that more metaphorical crack in the wall into which the female protagonist of *Malina* disappears at the conclusion of the novel. Throughout the performance, physical references to the novel and film, such as rose petals, manuscript pages, and charred sheets of paper, blow through the crack onto the stage. At one point during the performance, an actress representing Bachmann recites that she will "go into the wall" as she disappears into the opening in the wall. Such simplified physical acts on stage cannot do justice to the cyclical movement of the novel *Malina*. For instance, whereas the female narrator is silenced at the close of the novel, her *Doppelgänger* Malina is able to answer a ringing telephone. The reader of the novel is, however, propelled to the beginning of the narrative where the female narrator has not yet been silenced and tells her story.

Perhaps it is the narrator's "split personality" in *Malina* – the intuitive, lyrical feminine and the logical, rational masculine – that inspires Peymann to portray Bachmann by a chorus of seven actresses. Bachmann herself intended for her novel's readers to view Malina and the female narrator as *one* being, in which he functions as her *Doppelgänger*.[15] In an interview from March 1971, Bachmann stressed that the female narrator's lover Ivan may also be read as a "double figure" or even a "triple figure."[16] Peymann's chorus of actresses, dressed in various shades of blue, attempts to capture the essence of Bachmann's different personalities familiar to the public, which include the inquisitive child, the chain-smoking intellectual artist, the ardent feminist, and the hopeful lover.[17] The blue color of the costumes recalls the ethereal blue that marks the longing of the German Romantic period, as well as the melancholy blue of Picasso's "blue period" paintings. The color also points to Peymann's frequent references to Bachmann's poem "Böhmen liegt am Meer," in which the ocean is an expression of artistic freedom, unburdened by nationalities and borders. The vocalizations of the actresses simultaneously present on stage, however, capture more than just the role of the *Doppelgänger* in *Malina*. The multiple voices are also able to depict the diverse and frequently overlapping voices in Bachmann's work. In another April 1971 interview, Bachmann stated that she had to write from the perspective of both the male and female and that the male voice had to "weigh more heavily" while "not denying" the female voice.[18] Disenchanted with Peymann's fragmented portrait of the author, critic Arnd Wesemann describes this portrayal of Bachmann as that of "a sevenfold zombie" and comments that after a few minutes the play becomes a "Viennese death dance of zombies on the stage-cemetery of her [Bachmann's] literature."[19] This reference to "the walking dead" emphasizes the difficulty of capturing the aura of the private individual Bachmann, especially when her multifaceted public identity has been constructed by the media. The sevenfold Bachmann-creation on stage is, however, neither "zombie" nor "monster." Instead, it is the embodiment of the different roles that Bachmann has played in public and the multiple poetic styles explored in her writing.

The innovative impulse of Peymann's production, as evident in the sevenfold Bachmann or the use of montage, is in many ways characteristic of his productions during his tenure at the *Burgtheater*. In an interview with Peter Iden, Peymann defines his dramatization of Bachmann's work not as a traditional play but rather as "an evening in the *Burgtheater*," stating that the production represents a means of exploring forms outside of theater literature. Referring to Bachmann as "possibly [the] most important poet of the German language," the director asserts that her stage persona is "woven together" with her writings. He claims that Bachmann "brought herself into a situation" in Rome "that [did] not exclude death," reasoning that she suffered from depression because she had failed to complete her opus, "of which *Malina* has remained a fragment."[20] Thus we see that Peymann regards Bachmann's depression as a result of her inability to finish her novel cycle, instead of considering that she may have been emotionally incapacitated by the difficult and frequently horrendous content with which she was dealing in her work. Bachmann herself stated in an interview in May 1973 during a trip to Poland that her reactions to the Holocaust and her visit to Auschwitz and Birkenau had "made her speechless."[21] It is this historical and political relevance of Bachmann's writing that is strangely absent from Peymann's direction. Instead, the focus of the production is aimed at celebrating the lyrical beauty, the musical composition, and the humor integral to Bachmann's work.

The omission of the political is even more surprising when one considers the production at the *Burgtheater* of such controversial and critical dramas as those by Thomas Bernhard, Elfriede Jelinek, and Peter Turrini.[22] Peymann has maintained that such twentieth-century writers are capable of predicting the future, proclaiming that the public "need[s] visionaries for the stage."[23] When asked why he chose to open the newly renovated *Burgtheater* in 1995 with a "collage of texts by Bachmann," Peymann stated that his preoccupation with Bachmann had the "characteristics of a demonstration," that he wanted to show that "enlightened literature" has a definite role to play at the *Burgtheater*.[24] The fact that Peymann likens Bachmann's work to a "demonstration" shows just how controversial Bachmann's work has been in the eyes of the Austrian public. The staging of Bachmann's "great voice" was conceived by Peymann as an antidote to the media rampage, fueled by the rightest Freedom Party and Jörg Haider, directed against the avant-garde and Austria-critical performances at the *Burgtheater*. In a November 1995 interview with Iden, Peymann stated that the predictions and warnings contained in Bernhard's dramatic comedies concerning Austrian National Socialist and right-wing tendencies were "already too insignificant," and that an individual such as Haider would prove to be a greater "threat."[25] Although Peymann had intended to provoke the Austrian media with a "demonstration" of Bachmann's texts, he nonetheless failed to address Bachmann's passionate attack on the political right in postwar Austria or make clear his own misgivings about the Freedom Party in his production.

Prior to Peymann's dramatization of Bachmann's life and work at the *Burgtheater*, numerous independent theaters and film directors aimed to bring public attention to Bachmann's work by staging her writings, or by interpreting her works within the context of her public identity constructed by the media. The overwhelmingly negative criticism by the media in the wake of some of these productions seems to be a reflection of the public's dissatisfaction with interpretations of Bachmann's life and work that do not seek to recreate a linear biography of the author's life or to fill the void of the seemingly mysterious circumstances surrounding her death.[26] Bachmann was one of Austria's most well-known public figures of the postwar period and became the country's claim to fame in the literary world of the second half of the twentieth century. Austria has maintained a love-hate relationship with Bachmann because she intentionally chose to leave the Austrian for the German publishing world and lived outside of Austria for the bulk of her career as a freelance author, with a critical eye on Austrian postwar politics. Few public interpretations of Bachmann's work have allowed audiences to come to terms with the image of Austria as Bachmann portrays it, nor have they been able to approach her work in a public setting such as the national theater *Burgtheater*.

The German-speaking public was reintroduced to the author's 1971 novel *Malina* through Schroeter's 1991 controversial film, based on both the novel and Elfriede Jelinek's screenplay from the same year. Schroeter's film merges the novel's references to the mental unraveling of the female protagonist with rumors and clichés of Bachmann's own battle with depression. This emphasis on the female protagonist as an unstable and hysterical woman seems to squelch any motivation for most audiences, unfamiliar with Bachmann's work, to come to terms with other more sociohistorical subjects addressed in her writings. Schroeter's film, like Peymann's staging of Bachmann's work, largely omits references to the author's keen and critical observations about Austria's involvement in World War II and the Holocaust.[27]

Concurrent with Peymann's Bachmann dramatization at the *Burgtheater*, however, several smaller independent theaters managed to win over audiences with productions that underscored the author's sharp criticism of the social and political situation of postwar Austria. In September 1995, for instance, Brigitte Antonius produced one of the few stagings of Bachmann's work that addresses the author's historical and political discussions about fascism and war. The performance, an interpretation of Bachmann's short story "Unter Mördern und Irren" (Among Murderers and Madmen), explores the characteristics of murderers and victims and was "highly acclaimed" by critics.[28] Another example is afforded by the 1995 production of *Malina* by Berlin actress Blanche Kommerell, who was heralded by the media for presenting "this grandiose woman's novel" in a "lively" fashion to a broad audience beyond a limited circle of readers familiar with Bachmann's work. Kommerell's one-woman act grapples with social issues such as the battle of genders, and it places the father figure on stage as a murderer and metaphor for fascist destruction. The play attempts to set the author's work apart from Bachmann's own life, although critic Willgruber-Spitz could not help but remark on the "uncanny biographical proximity."[29] The text used by Vienna's *Theater Brett,* which also staged the novel *Malina* in December 1995, directed by Klaus Fischer, was cited as a "well conceived scenic collage," enabling viewers to relate to "one of the most difficult prose works of the modern era."[30] That same month, the International Ensemble Projekt Theater/Vienna-New York, directed by

Eva Brenner, staged the short story fragment "Gier" (Greed), which one critic, aware of the sudden influx of theatrical interpretations of Bachmann and the media spectacle surrounding Peymann's production, dubbed "the other Bachmann this theater season."[31] In situating Bachmann's work within the framework of the social and political, the productions by Fischer and Brenner redirect the viewer to appreciate Bachmann's writing in a larger cultural context.

Although Peymann does not emphasize the political in his production of Bachmann's life and work, the author herself was adamant about her political awareness and involvement. In a 1971 interview, following the publication of her first novel *Malina*, Bachmann states her intention to portray the socio-historical reality of the Austrian postwar period through the female narrator. In an effort to "describe all of society" and "the state of consciousness of one time period," Bachmann believed that, in order to portray the current time period, "it [had] to be shown in a radically different way." Bachmann hoped that her novel *Malina* would capture the hypocrisies of Austrian postwar culture: "the illness of the world and the illness of this person [female protagonist in *Malina*] is the illness of our time for me. And if one cannot see it this way, then my book [*Malina*] has failed. But if it can be seen, then perhaps not."[32] Whereas Bachmann's novel conveys the relationship of the female narrator's mental state to the ills of postwar Austrian society, it is precisely this reciprocal relationship of the individual to society and history that is markedly absent from Peymann's staging of Bachmann's work.

Current Bachmann scholarship supports the thesis that the author's work is socially and politically relevant by featuring her writings in studies concerning Austrian women's literature and history.[33] Most recently, Bachmann scholars such as Hans Höller, Sigrid Weigel, and Karen Remmler have begun to cast the author's writings in the context of Austrian twentieth-century history.[34] Höller's 1998 study of the author's final, unpublished poems, for instance, allows a more socio-historical reading of precisely some of the poems featured in Peymann's production, such as "Böhmen liegt am Meer," "Keine Delikatessen," and "Enigma," written during her stay in Berlin from the spring of 1963 to the end of 1965. Höller compares the multiple variations and revisions of the poems to the pluralistic unity of prose variations in *Todesarten*.[35] Bachmann's collection of shorter poems addresses more urgently her coming to terms with the history of the Holocaust in her fictional work. For example, the poem "In Feindeshand" (In the Hands of the Enemy) describes the violence of war and recalls images of the Holocaust by directing the voice at a reader who is an unwilling target of the hatred by an unidentified perpetrator: "You are in enemy hands, / they are already grinding your / bones, they are stomping out / your vision / they are stepping on your vision / with their feet / trill in your ear / with alarm whistles / Alarm." This image of the tortured victim is a reoccurring subject throughout *Todesarten*, her short story "Three Paths to the Lake," as well as her poem "Keine Delikatessen."[36] Höller's recent Bachmann biography also explores the author as a person acutely aware of her integral role in history.[37]

A further study emphasizing Bachmann's political involvement, Weigel's 1999 *Ingeborg Bachmann*, reveals surprising and fascinating evidence of Bachmann's relationships with Jewish intellectuals and Holocaust survivors during the postwar period. Weigel was able to trace Bachmann's correspondences to the posthumous collections of scholars such as Gerschom Scholem, Theodor Adorno, Hannah Arendt, and Wolfgang Hildesheimer. Weigel makes evident that Bachmann's work is a result of a vibrant exchange of ideas that challenge the concepts of victimhood, punishment, and justice in the wake of World War II and the Holocaust. Although many of these political issues were discussed during her lifetime, such as the statute of limitations on murder committed by Austrian and German Nazi war criminals, Bachmann questioned many contemporary perceptions of the time by emphasizing that history is a continuous span of actions by individuals in the past, present, and future.[38] These recent scholarly studies emphasize that Bachmann's fictional writing has become accepted as literature with historical and cultural value. It is, however, precisely the absence of this discussion about war crimes and postwar politics in Peymann's production that has enabled the director to revive Bachmann's work at the close of the twentieth century. The apolitical staging has taken the edge off of Bachmann's biting commentary about contemporary Austrian culture and has given the public an opportunity to experience her words in a less controversial light that emphasizes her humor, her love of music, and her intellect.

Despite his failure to highlight the political and socio-historical dimensions of Bachmann's literary writings, Peymann has been lauded by the majority of critics for bringing Bachmann's work to the national stage.[39] Whereas Bachmann's writings have continued to be a popular topic among academics, it is Peymann's production that has brought her work to a general audience. As Reinhold Reiterer gratefully notes: "It is thanks to the *Burgtheater*, under the direction of Claus Peymann, that this great Austrian writer has been elevated to the stage."[40] Karl Löbl, well-known and respected Austrian television critic of theater and music, describes Peymann's production as "an extraordinary, an unusual, a beautiful evening," and states that the event has given him the motivation to "now also read Bachmann."[41]

Peymann's production *Ingeborg Bachmann. Wer?* is exemplary for his initiative to bring contemporary and often controversial theater to the Austrian national stage. In doing so, Peymann has reintroduced Bachmann to Austria as a public figure by presenting her works in a new contextual and contemporary setting. Bachmann demonstrated foresight when she said that texts such as her own were to be interpreted differently by every generation: "In any case, one has to be able to read a book in different ways and to read it differently today than tomorrow."[42] Having accomplished this, Peymann has also achieved Bachmann's most sincere wish that her works be read and function as tools of positive transformation. In her acceptance speech for the Anton Wildgans Prize,

Bachmann expressed that she "just wanted her works to be read; read like those books that had transformed her and others."[43] Peymann's production has given the public the incentive to read or re-read Bachmann's works and discover for themselves *who* the author is through her texts, beyond her public image. To be affected by her words, however, to be perhaps even "transformed" by them, remains a rewarding challenge for both the viewer of Peymann's production and the reader of Bachmann's work. Bachmann once remarked in a May 1965 interview that she felt it was impossible to imagine or portray life's most important moments in the form of a play: these critical scenes begin only after the curtain has fallen.[44]

Notes

1. Citation taken from the title of the article: "Vom Denken, das zum Sterben führt. 'Denn es ist das Innen, in dem alle Dramen stattfinden' – Ingeborg Bachmanns 'Todesarten'-Projekt," *Neue Presse* [Coburg] 29 November 1995.

2. In Austria a train line now bears Bachmann's name, carrying passengers across a country that could not fully appreciate her work during her lifetime. In her hometown of Klagenfurt, *The Klagenfurt Jergitsch Gymnasium* was recently renamed the *Ingeborg Bachmann Gymnasium*, at last honoring its citizen who dared to criticize Austria's willing participation in the Third Reich and poked fun at a society in which atrocities were committed during times of peace. In celebration of her poetic words and love of music, the contemporary musician Friedrich Cerha composed the instrumental work entitled "Für K.," inspired by Bachmann's short story "Ein Wildermuth." Cerha's composition premiered in St. Pölten, Austria on 25 September 1993, and is in honor of the seventieth birthday of his friend, Karl Prantl.

3. Adolf Opel, *Ingeborg Bachmann in Ägypten: "Landschaft, für die Augen gemacht sind"* (Vienna: Deuticke Verlag, 1996).

4. Wolfgang Kralicek, "Peymann kann nicht tanzen," *Falter* [Vienna] 14 November 1995: 64.

5. "Zu Grund gerichtet wach ich ruhig auf. Von Grund auf weiß ich jetzt und bin unverloren." Bachmann, *Böhmen liegt am Meer*, *Werke*, ed. Christine Koschel, Inge von Weidenbaum, and Clemens Münster, vol. 1 (1978; Munich: Piper, 1993) 167-68.

6. Original: "... begabt nur noch vom Meer, das strittig ist Land meiner Wahl zu sein." Bachmann, *Böhmen liegt am Meer* 168.

7. Bachmann, *Malina* 303.

8. Bachmann, *Malina* 326.

9. Ingeborg Bachmann, *Wir müssen wahre Sätze finden*, ed. Christine Koschel and Inge von Weidenbaum (Munich: Piper, 1983) 128.

10. Bachmann, *Malina* 12.

11. Ronald Pohl, "Schöne Texte, neue Bühne, alte Kiste," *Der Standard* [Vienna] 13 November 1995: 9.

12. Paul Kruntorad, "Nachhilfe für eine Dichterin," *Rheinischer Merkur* [Bonn] 17 November 1995.

13. Hilde Haider-Pregler, "Burgtheater: Claus Peymann fragt 'Ingeborg Bachmann. Wer?' Die gestundete Zeit wird sichtbar ...?" *Wiener Zeitung* [Vienna] 14 November 1995: 5.

14. For Bachmann, the all-consuming fire is also a metaphor for creative inspiration in *Malina*. In an interview, she explained that she had quoted a phrase from Flaubert: "I write about the nature of fire with my burned hand" in her novel *Malina* "because before burning one's hand, one cannot write about it." Bachmann, *Wir müssen wahre Sätze finden* 71.

15. Bachmann, *Wir müssen wahre Sätze finden*, 87 and 100.

16. Bachmann, *Wir müssen wahre Sätze finden* 88.

17. The seven Bachmann characters are played by *Burgtheater* actresses Therese Affolter, Krista Birkner, Kirsten Dene, Ursula Höpfner, Anja Kirchlechner, Julia von Sell, and Ute Springer.

18. Bachmann, *Wir müssen wahre Sätze finden* 100.

19. Arnd Wesemann, "Auf dem Friedhof der Literatur," *Weser Kurier* [Bremen] 13 November 1995.

20. Peter Iden, "Ein Theater muß ein Brennpunkt sein," *Frankfurter Rundschau* [Frankfurt] 17 November 1995.

21. Bachmann, *Wir müssen wahre Sätze finden* 142.

22. In his interview with Iden, Peymann wrote: "texts such as those by Elfriede Jelinek and Peter Turrini interest me." He also recalls that when Bernhard's *Heldenplatz* premiered, it initially caused a scandal due to its critical view of Austria during the events of 1938. In the course of one hundred performances, the production would become the *Burgtheater*'s most successful tragicomedy, in which the "audience roars with laughter": Iden, "Ein Theater muß ein Brennpunkt sein."

23. Iden, "Ein Theater muß ein Brennpunkt sein."

24. Iden, "Ein Theater muß ein Brennpunkt sein." The media reaction to the production *Ingeborg Bachmann. Wer?* is just one example of how Peymann has cleverly used the media to his advantage since his relationship began with the *Burgtheater*. Hilde Haider-Pregler, Chair of the Institute for Theater Arts (*Institut für Theaterwissenschaften*) at the University of Vienna, calls Peymann a "PR-machine," and states that it was the continual presence of the media brought on by Peymann's provocative productions that made the *Burgtheater* a topic of discussion, reaching far beyond Vienna. See Barbara Petsch, "Claus Peymann ist weder Zerstörer noch ein Revoluzzer – aber ein genialer Medienstratege," *Die Presse* [Vienna] 29 June 1999: 25. Peymann himself states in a 1999 interview that the popular belief that he is a "PR-genius" is untrue. He admits turning down "95-98 percent of the interviews" requested of him, claiming that his "strategy is to resist" and that a "deficit leads to need." See Wolfgang Kralicek and Armin Thurnher, "Ich zahle gern zurück," *Falter* [Vienna] 2-8 July 1999: 24. Haider-Pregler believes that it is Peymann's ability to discover the "comical potential of texts" and produce "astounding images" that has contributed to his fame. Peymann's work, for example, with

Bernhard plays, from the premiere of *Ein Fest für Boris* (*A Party for Boris*) at the Hamburg *Schauspielhaus* theater in 1970 to the *Heldenplatz* premiere in 1988, brought him much recognition in the German-speaking media.

25. Iden, "Ein Theater muß ein Brennpunkt sein." Haider has been governor of Carinthia since the beginning of 1999, and was briefly the leader of the second largest party, the Freedom Party, winning 27% of the votes in the election for the Austrian National Parliament. In an August 1999 interview with the Viennese culture newspaper *Falter*, Peymann stated that he considered Haider "only an actor" and recalled that the *Burgtheater* had denied free passes for Haider at a performance of Bernhard's *Heldenplatz*. Kralicek and Thurnher, "Ich zahle gern zurück" 23.

26. In 1993, Andreas Staudinger staged a performance of Bachmann's life named after the poem "Schatten Rosen Schatten" (Shadows Roses Shadows) at the *Laibacher Cankar-Zentrum* in which the author's existence was portrayed as torn between the everyday and art by way of fragmented sentences and broken telephone conversations. The production also emphasized Bachmann's double life as an author in residence in the German-speaking countries of Germany, Switzerland, and Austria on the one hand, and Italy on the other, by featuring a stage language that alternated between German and Italian. The production was not well-received by critics, who felt that Staudinger's staging of Bachmann's work was inaccessible to those not studying German literature, prompting a further critic to call the author a "dead idol" and her glory "faded." See Mira Miladinovic, "Bewegende Annäherung," *Kleine Zeitung* [Klagenfurt] 1 October 1993: 106. Another reviewer denounced the piece as a drama portraying Bachmann as "a master of secretive banalities." Ingomar Robier, "Bachmann zweigeteilt," *Kärnter Tageszeitung* [Klagenfurt] 7 October 1993: 16.

27. Perhaps little known due to its limited distribution as a television production and film in the film festival *Welser Filmtage*, is Margareta Heinrichs's 1993 film adaptation of Bachmann's short

story "Ihr glücklichen Augen" (Oh Happy Eyes), a co-production of ORF, the Austrian National Radio and Television Broadcast, and ZDF, a German television network. Director Heinrichs examines the life of the near-sighted Miranda who opts to experience the world without her glasses in order to shield herself from the ugly realities of life, her impaired vision the symptom of a psychosomatic reaction to her environment. Even lesser known is Heinrichs's film *Zwielicht* from 1976, which is also based on a Bachmann short story. This information was taken from a written review of *Ihr glücklichen Augen* in the ORF *Programm*, ORF 2, 19 June 1993.

28. "Brigitte Antonius spielt Ingeborg Bachmann," *Vorarlberger Nachrichten* [Bregenz] 14 September 1995: C 6.

29. Elisabeth Willgruber-Spitz, "Eine Frauenfigur durchlebt Ingeborg Bachmanns 'Malina,'" *Neue Zeit* [Graz] 15 March 1995: 29.

30. Eva-Maria Mantler, "Wachsende Ängste der Namenlosen," *Wiener Zeitung* [Vienna] 2 December 1995: 4.

31. Anita Prammer, "Ingeborg Bachmann's 'Gier' für das Theater entdeckt," *Neue Zeit* [Graz] 22 December 1995: 19.

32. Bachmann, *Wir müssen wahre Sätze finden* 72.

33. Allyson Fiddler's volume *'Other' Austrians. Post-1945 Austrian Women's Writing* from 1996; Günter Bischof, Anton Pelinka, and Erika Thurner's volume *Women in Austria* from 1998; and David Good, Margarete Grandner, and Mary Jo Maynes's volume *Austrian Women in the Nineteenth and Twentieth Centuries* from 1996, are representative of this trend.

34. A recent study by Karen Remmler explores the dilemma of remembrance and representation in Bachmann's *Todesarten* by drawing on Walter Benjamin's concept of "insightful remembrance," which calls for the interrelationship of collective history and personal experience. Karen Remmler, *Waking the Dead: Correspondences Between Walter Benjamin's Concept of Remembrance and Ingeborg Bachmann's Ways of Dying* (Riverside, CA: Ariadne Press, 1996).

35. "Enigma," for example, has at least twelve versions and was revised over a period of three years. Hans Höller, *Ingeborg Bachmann. Letzte, unveröffentlichte Gedichte, Entwürfe und Fassungen: Edition und Kommentar von Hans Höller* (Frankfurt/M.: Suhrkamp, 1998) 12.

36. Höller, *Ingeborg Bachmann*, 20, 35, and 36-37.

37. Hans Höller, *Ingeborg Bachmann. Monographie 50545* (Reinbek bei Hamburg: Rowohlt Taschenbuch Verlag, 1999).

38. Sigrid Weigel, *Ingeborg Bachmann. Hinterlassenschaften unter Wahrung des Briefgeheimnisses* (Vienna: Paul Zsolnay Verlag, 1999).

39. Critics, however, have also pointed out that Peymann's production fails to address more serious questions raised in Bachmann's work and leaves the query of his production, *Ingeborg Bachmann. Wer?*, largely unanswered: see Pohl, "Schöne Texte, neue Bühne, alte Kiste" 9. Haider-Pregler questions Peymann's failure to cultivate new and previously unknown talents at the *Burgtheater*. Aside from already well-known Austrian dramatists and writers such as Bernhard, Handke, and Turrini, only Jelinek's *Totenauberg* and *Sportstück* could be considered new and revolutionary. Nationality has seemingly always been a point of contention at the *Burgtheater*. In November 1995, Robert Meyer, the speaker of the theater ensemble of the *Burgtheater*, accused Peymann of producing "Austrian evenings," featuring works by Handke and Bernhard without, however, employing any Austrian actors, and stepped down from his position. Haider-Pregler, however, states that the much-discussed critique of Peymann's German nationality as head of an Austrian theater is a "superficially constructed phenomenon," and that the quality of his work is unrelated to his national origin. Nevertheless, it is of note that the new director of the *Burgtheater*, Klaus Bachler, former director of the Viennese *Volksoper*, is Austrian. Barbara Petsch, "Claus Peymann ist weder Zerstörer noch ein Revoluzzer" 25.

40. Reinhold Reiterer, "Ingeborg B., Dichterin," *Neue Vorarlberger Tageszeitung* [Bregenz] 14 November 1995: 42.

41. Gerd-Eckard Zehm, "Bachmann auf der Bühne: Peymann fasziniert mit inszenierter Lyrik," *dpa* [Hamburg] 12 November 1995. Critic Bernd Sucher praises Peymann for reminding viewers of Bachmann's work: C. Bernd Sucher, "Ihr Worte, auf, mir nach!" *Süddeutsche Zeitung* [Munich] 13 November 1995: 12. There have also been dissenting views. Some critics have viewed Peymann's production as oversimplified and rigid, describing it as a "tutoring" lesson in Bachmann's literature for the audience. Others call Peymann's production "flat," "no evening in the theater," and "harmful to theater," because of its lack of typical *Burgtheater* drama. See Hans Haider, "Nachhilfe im Burgtheater," *Die Presse* [Vienna] 13 November 1995: 20; and Paul Kruntorad, "Nachhilfe für eine Dichterin," *Rheinischer Merkur* [Bonn] 17 November 1995.

42. Bachmann, *Wir müssen wahre Sätze finden* 100.

43. Ingeborg Bachmann, "Anton Wildgans Preisrede," *Werke*, ed. Christine Koschel, Inge von Weidenbaum, and Clemens Münster, vol. 3 (1978; Munich: Piper, 1993) 296.

44. In a May 1973 interview, six months before her death, Bachmann stated that Gerhard Klingenberg, at that time director of the *Burgtheater*, had commissioned her to write a play about Sarajevo. She writes: "I have never written a play, and it could fail completely. It seems wrong to say anything about it beforehand." See *Wir müssen wahre Sätze finden* 56. Although Bachmann wrote only one (stage) play during her lifetime – *Carmen Ruidera* (1942) – Peymann would transform her entire life and work into a play.

In the Beginning was the Word – And before That? Theological Problems in Felix Mitterer's *Krach im Hause Gott*

Gerlinde Ulm Sanford

Let me begin by explaining the significance of this essay's title. The first chapter of The Gospel According to John starts out with: "In the beginning was the word." John identifies Jesus Christ as "the Word" (in Greek *logos*) incarnated, or made flesh. The concept of *logos*, however, goes back to Philo of Alexandria, a Jewish philosopher from the first century B.C. He taught that the *logos* was the intermediary between God and the Creation. The *logos*, according to Philo, is both the agent of the creation as well as the agent enabling the human being to apprehend and comprehend God. Christa Mulack, primary source for the theological topics explored in the play discussed here, refers to theories showing that as early as the Babylonian Creation myth Enuma Elish, male intellectual power suppressed female creative power. According to Mulack, the Judeo-Christian Creation myth then expresses such patriarchal, anti-woman attitudes in many ways and to an even more pronounced degree, and especially in the formulation "in the beginning was the word." Since a man cannot procreate with his body, he has to procreate with his word, with his intellect. Mulack shows how, over the course of human history, the *male* word developed into the Word of God, while female intellectual power, the female word, became more and more suppressed.[1] It is this male dominance as expressed by "in the beginning was the word" which is questioned by Felix Mitterer. Led by feminist theologian Christa Mulack, he asks: Was male dominance really at the beginning of everything? Is it possible that something different, something better, existed before? Something that might teach us a valuable lesson?

The works of Mitterer often address controversial issues of contemporary society or problematic situations of former times that might still be relevant for the present. The playwright speaks up for a mentally handicapped boy in *Kein Platz für Idioten* (1977, No Place for Idiots), for a guest worker in *Munde* (1990), for victims of aids in *Abraham* (1993), for people persecuted by racial prejudice in *Kein schöner Land* (1987, There's No Finer Country) and *In der Löwengrube* (1998, In the Lion's Den), and for the elderly in *Sibirien* (1989, Siberia) and *Die Frau im Auto* (1998, The Woman in the Car) – to name just a few of the people and causes he has championed. Two further concerns have consistently attracted Mitterer's attention: women's rights and religious freedom. These two issues form the basis of his play from 1994 titled *Krach im Hause Gott* (Discord in the House of God).[2]

In many of his plays, Mitterer espouses women's rights and women's equal status in society. He often shows the unfair conditions to which, even today, they are at times submitted. The female character in the one-act-play *Besuchszeit* (1985, Visiting Hours), for example, does not have a name and is called only "She" to indicate the stereotypical and impersonal patterns of communication that dominate relationships between man and woman. Mitterer's interest in women's rights and his high esteem for women in general are, moreover, demonstrated by his portraying several female characters as superior to their male counterparts: e.g., the Hind (Hirschkuh) in *Drachendurst* (1986, Dragon's Thirst), the title character of *Die Wilde Frau* (1986, The Wild Woman), or the Mother of God (Muttergottes) from the play discussed in this essay.

Born in Tirol, Mitterer grew up in an environment and a society strongly influenced by the structures, institutions, and thoughts of the Catholic Church. Without adhering to a specific religious confession, Mitterer nonetheless believes that the Creation, and in particular the fate of a human being, is guided by a benevolent power. In a number of his plays he depicts deeply religious characters from the countryside, suggesting a certain respect for the strength of faith one can still find in rural Austria. Not withstanding this, he criticizes the misuse of power by the church, e. g. in *Stigma* or in *Die Kinder des Teufels* (1989, Children of the Devil), and he defends the right of religious freedom in particular in *Verlorene Heimat* (1992, Lost Homeland) and *Kein schöner Land*. Mitterer's seemingly contradictory attitude toward religion might in some ways be compared to that of Goethe who also can be considered as being deeply pious but whose work frequently criticizes the Catholic Church as an institution of religious power. Furthermore, Goethe's esteem for the *Eternal-Feminine* as expressed in his *Faust II* might well be compared with Mitterer.[3] Just as, at the end of *Faust II*, Faust is redeemed and lifted upward toward the *Mater Gloriosa*, i.e., toward the *Eternal-Feminine*, we encounter in several plays by Mitterer female characters who bear the characteristics of mother deities, the most prominent of such examples being the Hind in *Drachendurst*, the female character in *Die Wilde Frau*, and especially the Mother of God in the play discussed here.

Years before writing *Krach im Hause Gott*, Mitterer became aware of the strongly patriarchal structure of the Catholic Church. As the dramatist relates in the afterword for the book edition of his stage play, for a number of years he sensed that something was lacking in Christianity and he identified this absence as "the feminine. Where is the woman? Why is there only a God the Father (Lord-God)? Do we not also have a very essential need for a mother, if indeed we need someone above us at all?"[4] He started to ask himself what roles are assigned to women in the Bible. If it is true that we need a higher authority, do we then not need a God the Mother just as much as a God the Father? As a consequence of such questioning, Mitterer returned to studying the Bible and developed an interest in feminist theology, in particular as investigated by theologian Christa Mulack. Her books, above all *Maria – die geheime Göttin im Christentum* (Mary – the Secret Goddess of Christianity)[5] and *Jesus der Gesalbte der Frauen* (Jesus the Women's Anointed),[6] were of great help to him because they treat in detail the questions he raised.

In 1989, Mitterer wrote a new version of the *Everyman* subject matter in which he was able to begin to explore his interests in the lack of a feminine principle in modern Christianity. Following tradition, Mitterer began his play, which he titled *Ein Jedermann* (1991, An Everyman), with a prologue in which God the Father, God the Son, God the Holy Ghost, the Devil, and Death discuss Everyman's downfall. Although this prologue was eventually cut in half for the performance, it serves as the nucleus of a radio drama and the full-length stage version of the play under discussion here. *Krach im Hause Gott* was commissioned for the Bregenz Festival. In Austria, it was produced first on 2 August 1994 under the direction of Bruno Felix. The German premiere took place on 16 December 1994 under the direction of Edith Koerber at the *theater-tribüne* in Stuttgart.

Mitterer, on the suggestion of his friends, the actor Charly Rabanser and the stage director Maurus Mosetig, takes up in this play the theological problems and the consequences of monotheistic religion. Mitterer in a sense uses the play, particularly its second half, to expand his perception of the underlying theological problems inherent in contemporary religion. He attempts to treat feminist theological thinking as he encountered it in Mulack's work in a manner that will be effective on stage, in a manner that will speak to and provoke contemporary theater audiences. This essay addresses these two issues. First, I explore what specific ideas from Mulack's theories Mitterer incorporates in his play and, second, I investigate how those ideas are realized on stage, focusing on the playwright's utilization of humor.

Before continuing with a discussion of the play, let us look briefly at the arguments of Mulack that found direct or indirect expression in Mitterer's play. The validity of Mulack's and other feminist theologians' theories and theses is not under discussion in this essay. My intent is to show what kind of resonance or treatment some of these basic tenets received on stage.

Mulack claims that patriarchy suppressed and eventually overcame a previously existing matriarchal societal order. The Judeo-Christian religious tradition has been dominated and shaped by patriarchal structures of thought and organization. Jesus Christ's message, however, is seen as pro-women in principle, as an attempt to gain back recognition for certain ideas that were valid during the time of matriarchy. She alleges that "brotherly love" and charity, as propounded by Jesus Christ, are really more kin to the female nature than to the male. According to Mulack, such aspects of Jesus's message were first misrepresented through the patriarchally oriented Evangelists and, throughout subsequent centuries, through the church hierarchy and its almost exclusively male authorities. Thus Mulack maintains that the institution of the Church spread the essentially pro-women message of Jesus in a manner that stands in crass contrast to its original intent. As examples for the misuse of Jesus's message, she lists the flagrant crimes committed in the name of Jesus during the Crusades and during the Inquisition. She furthermore states that certain texts that bear evidence of the initial matriarchy were never accepted into the Church Canon and, therefore, disappeared. Only more recently have some of these lost or suppressed texts become accessible again through the discovery of early Christian writings as well as through more sophisticated methods of textual analysis.

Numerous contradictions in the Bible can, according to Mulack's theory, be traced back to the fundamental conflict between matriarchal and patriarchal attitudes. The examples selected here correspond to examples that Mitterer incorporates into his play: In Genesis 1.28, God calls upon man to subdue the earth "and have dominion … over every living thing that moveth upon the earth." This conflicts with Jesus's message in Matthew

22.39: "thou shalt love thy neighbour as thyself." Similarly, in John 1.1, we read: "In the beginning was the Word, and the Word was with God, and the Word was God." Thus, one could interpret, in the beginning was God's command – his Word – for Creation to come into being. This, however, according to Mulack, is only the patriarchal version of the act of Creation. In the beginning was not the "Word" of God, but rather matriarchal systems that followed much friendlier principles, principles namely that were inclined toward life, love, and happiness, whereas patriarchal principles are characterized by authority and obedience.[7] Matriarchal as opposed to patriarchal myths of the Creation form the central themes of Mulack's books, as typified in the following quote:

> In older matriarchal myths of Creation it is the Goddess who gives birth to light from out of her womb. ... [In the Biblical Genesis], the feminine act of birth is replaced by the masculine Word. Yet in the Old Testament too, the feminine spiritual principle precedes and hovers as Ruah over the feminine primordial waters, over the Tehom. ... Spirit and Water, physically expressed: energy and matter as two sides of the same coin from which all building stones of life originate. The creating God, therefore, is the creation of these primordial feminine forces – mythologically speaking, he is the son of the goddess.[8]

As Mulack points out, in the patriarchally oriented Jewish and Christian religions there are still rudiments to be found of a previously existing matriarchy.

In Mitterer's play, some of these theories, in particular those centered on the suppression of the feminine principle by patriarchal structures, are taken up explicitly. However, theological-philosophical topics, even if carefully selected, cannot be turned easily into an engaging stage play. At this point allow me to reiterate the central question of my essay and the central difficulty faced by the playwright: How can Mitterer convey such a serious and controversial topic in a convincing fashion, i.e., in such a way that his audience will not automatically reject it? How can he encourage his audience to rethink or at least question its ingrained attitudes toward religion and the role of women in the church and in fact in society generally? And finally, how can he render such serious content entertaining and indeed dramatic? I claim that Mitterer found his answer to these problems in the use of comedy. The entire play is characterized by humor, by a kind of playful irony or tongue-in-cheek stance that serves to communicate Mitterer's societal criticism in an entertaining form. Mitterer's use of exaggeration, which at times borders on the ridiculous and the hilarious, creates enough distance that it allows the public to laugh, and it is only later that the audience realizes it is laughing at itself. The comic effects of the play soften the barb of his biting sarcasm to the point where it is palatable, though never harmless.

Already the play's title, *Krach im Hause Gott*, which can be translated as Discord in the House of God, alerts us to Mitterer's intentions, even though the English word "discord" might not cause quite the same reaction as the German expression "Krach," which in addition to "discord" connotes a loud and disorderly household row. In short, the informality suggested by the title does not seem proper to the setting in which the action takes place, i.e., in the House of God. Thus the title serves to personalize and humanize the Heavens, to bring them down to a level that can be understood by mortals and accordingly can also be criticized. This comic technique characterizes the entire play: Mitterer transforms the holy Christian Trinity and the Devil into fallible beings who, like humankind, make mistakes. Omnipotence is revealed as a man-made construct, and if humankind erected the structures in the first place, then it is not only possible for us to question and even change those structures when needed, it is in fact our responsibility to do so. Mitterer's comic effects are achieved especially through the characteristics and demeanors attributed to the Holy Ghost and to Satan, but even God the Father and Jesus display comic traits. This kind of humorous, rather than moralizing, presentation renders the controversial topics of *Krach im Hause Gott* more palatable even to those readers or spectators who do not wish to question the integrity of the Bible or established Church precepts. With his seemingly innocuous humor, Mitterer in fact indicts Christianity and indicates that the contemporary Church is in dire need of reform.

Comedy and humor through the revelation of human fallibility marks the plot development throughout the play. There are five characters in the play, and Mitterer assigns them all very human and accordingly also comical traits. Already in his characterizations, then, we see clearly how the playwright proceeds in a light and humorous, rather than a moralistic tone. The clash, however, between our perception of traditionally venerable religious figures and the iconoclastic, irreverent treatment these figures receive at the hands of Mitterer allows us to question those seemingly intractable perceptions. The first character is God, actually God the Father, who in the stage directions is always simply called God. He has the look "of a conservative businessman"(9). His son Jesus, simply referred to as Son, is a relaxed Hippie type who carries his crown of thorns around in a plastic bag. The Holy Ghost, referred to as Ghost, is described repeatedly as effeminate, a personality trait that will be discussed in more detail later in this essay. The fourth character is Satan, who appears in a yellow-and-black combat uniform, which however conceals a smart modern suit underneath. The fifth character is the Mother of God ("Muttergottes"), Mary (Maria).

This is the "family" living in the House of God, and it is no accident that Mitterer clothes them in human-like garb. They could be any family, albeit a somewhat eccentric one, and the conflict to come is foreshadowed in the different types they represent. There is bound to be discord between a "conservative businessman" and his Hippie son, especially when the son treats religious symbols as casually as does Jesus. Similarly, the effeminate ways of the Ghost will most certainly rouse the ire of a God who so identifies with the traditional male role. In addition, both parental and filial relationships within the House of God are everything but clear, and while confusion about father- and motherhood might not be uncommon among humankind, such a situation within the House of God causes the spectator to smile. Finally, a further comical predicament is introduced when the male trinity is suddenly and severely questioned upon advent of the female principle represented by Mary.

Mary, the Mother of God, in contrast to the male figures, has multiple personalities. To gain access to the male-dominated Last Judgement conference, she appears as five different types; first as secretary, then as foreign cleaning woman, as Marilyn Monroe (who uses her body to apply for a receptionist position), as an addicted punk-girl, and finally as the Madonna of Lourdes, dressed in white and blue and surrounded by an air of regality (50). Thus the Mother of God appears first in the role of servant: secretary, cleaning woman, and even Marilyn Monroe, who is seen here not as the famous star adored by men, but rather as a woman willing to serve men with her body in order to obtain a menial job. Then the Mother of God appears in the role of an outcast, namely as the addict for whom there seems to be no place in the world. Finally, however, she reveals herself regally dressed as Madonna of Lourdes, who tries to move God, although in vain, to consider her as his companion, as equal to him and not as his servant (59). The first four roles might be considered representative of the roles women have traditionally assumed in society, ones that they continue to assume even today despite progress made by the women's movement. Mitterer thus points here to the fact that many women are restricted to service positions, that they have to market their body to advance in society, and that they become outcasts if they refuse to abide by these conventions. With the fifth role, that of regal mother, Mitterer not only indicates the position that the Mother of God should rightfully hold within the Christian religion, but also the position that women should be accorded in contemporary society.

Mitterer subtitled his play *Ein modernes Mysterienspiel* (A Modern Passion Play). Critic Robert Mitscha-Eibl considers this subtitle more than justified and maintains that Mitterer's play is in no way inferior to popular passion plays of the Middle Ages; in terms of both the theological debate and coarse bluntness it rivals its historical model.[9] The play's plot runs as follows: God the Father calls for a conference in order to inform his son and the Holy Ghost that he intends to destroy mankind, which has not improved in the two thousand years that have passed since Jesus's sacrifice. Stormy discussions arise between the members of the Holy Trinity, which has shed any pretense of unity, and also between the Holy Trinity and Satan. Whereas God the Father and the Holy Ghost advocate annihilation of mankind, Satan does not see the necessity for a Last Judgment since mankind will self-destruct at some point in the near future anyway (35). Jesus attempts to function as the savior of humankind, thereby continuing his Biblical role, and he defends humankind. Moreover, he demands that Mary, the Mother of God, be allowed to participate in the conference. Despite God the Father's objections, Mary finally arrives on the scene and unmasks the patriarchal power structure of heaven. Jesus tries to negotiate the reestablishment of the appropriate place for the "mother," i.e., for the feminine principle at the side of God the Father. Most likely, however, God the Father will not be able to overcome his age-old fear (61) of the feminine and will, therefore, continue to insist on its exclusion. Thus, patriarchy, and with it the problems of this world, will most likely continue to exist. In the end, Jesus questions the meaning of Christianity altogether within the framework of such a patriarchal power structure. Perhaps, he argues, humankind would fare better if God were to annihilate himself and his Holy Trinity (64 f.). Upon that suggestion, God the Father leaves, and all decisions – concerning the Last Judgment, the annihilation of humankind, and God's own self-annihilation – are postponed.

Mary becomes Mitterer's mouthpiece within the play, informing the audience that humankind lacks "love and gentleness" (55) and that this absence has resulted in the sorry state of the world. The preaching of Jesus could have changed the world for the better, but his message was recorded by men who committed egregious omissions, especially concerning the important role of woman. It is obvious, she maintains, that the earth, like the heavens, is ruled by men, and this is, in her opinion, the root of the problem. Mitterer also gives us hints as to how the situation might be improved. The masculine and the feminine would have to unite again, as had been the case before the time of patriarchy. The Son implores God: "We have to find each other again, father. Man, woman, child. The new, yet old Trinity. As in heaven, so too on earth. – Father!" (60). This "new, yet old Trinity," however, remains utopian. The play concludes with the postponing of all decisions. Mitterer, of course, cannot offer a solution, but rather attempts through his play to make his audience at least aware that the problem exists and furthermore to point to some of its underlying causes.

Those specific causes that Mitterer thematizes include first of all God's commandments to man. Satan becomes the organ of criticism, reproaching God for divine laws that have only led to war, brutality, and hatred of others. Throughout history Christians have tried to obey God's word, but their compliance – their very success in complying – has resulted in a society inimical to life and nature: "In fact, your followers, your immediate followers have stripped the earth bare! The rest of humanity was permitted to croak from starvation! But not only that. They have poisoned air, water, and earth – upon your command! Multiply and dominate the world! Isn't it true? Now they are lost" (35). Satan elaborates on a number of other divine commands that have served only to cause war again and again, for example: "You shall have no other gods before me" (36), or "An eye for an eye; a tooth for a tooth" (37).

Satan not only questions the consequences of commands found in the Old Testament. He also maintains that many of Jesus's teachings from the New Testament demand a goodness from humanity that is simply impossible to attain, and that therefore these teachings contribute to the misery of the world just as surely as do God's more brutal laws. For instance, Satan considers Jesus's words: "Love your enemy! Whoever slaps you on your right cheek, turn the other to him also," to be utterly unrealistic, and upon the Son's entreaty to "love your neighbor as you love yourself," Satan replies:

> Actually, humans do not love themselves! How then should they love their neighbor? – And why do humans not love themselves? Because you instilled in them a bad conscience. Because you, Jesus, told them: "Love your enemies!" Yet they hate their enemies! And rightfully so. That is nothing but normal. Even you, oh Lord and God, even you speak on your stone tablets continually of hatred toward your enemies! That is normal! Humans are like you, God! Your image! And for that you want to punish them? (38)[10]

In the final third of the play, the Mother of God appears as the Madonna of Lourdes and reveals another important reason for the desperate present state of mankind. She asks God to recall what had been there before him (51). He replies with irritation that there was nothing before him. When the Mother of God mentions that God had done away with all that existed before him out of jealousy, the Ghost tries to come to God's aide by asserting: "In the beginning was the Word and the Word is God. And that's that!" (52).[11] The Mother of God then points out the shortcomings of God's Word, i.e., of God's Creation.[12] She claims that God in his hunger for power has banished everything feminine from his heavenly government, thereby constructing a purely patriarchal system of power. Consequently, a similar system has remained valid on earth, one ruled by men. The Mother of God does not declare superiority for women. She admits that women are not necessarily better than men; in fact, they have been co-opted by the power structures around them. But she does maintain that if women had shared in the decision-making process, the world would be better off (63).

Some details in the play that appear at first to be somewhat arbitrary are in fact allusions to information from Mulack's work. Mitterer's Holy Ghost, for example, "wears feminine, loose, fluttering clothes, resembles, however, more a startled chicken than a dove" (11). With his effeminate looks and tendency to hover over the waters, Mitterer's Holy Ghost resembles descriptions by Mulack. She states repeatedly that the Holy Spirit who hovered over the primordial waters was feminine in pre-Christian times:

> Educated in Judeo-Christian faith, one is brought up with the idea that this world was created by a masculine spirit in solo initiative out of nothingness. Through the word of God, through his command so to speak, this world came forth. Thus we can read it on the first page of the Bible. This illustration is not so clear, however, because before the divine word is spoken, we learn of a feminine power, of Ruah, the holy feminine spirit, who hovers over the waters. The waters – or original depths – and Ruah appear to be something like fundamental conditions of the creation. The primordial waters or Tehom, as they are called in Hebrew, are considered in all cultures the feminine primordial image of matter and of chaos. They still contain, unorganized, all possibilities of developments into the most different forms of life. Even in the concept of "mater," mother, the idea of matter is still contained.[13]

Further on, Mulack points out that Ruah, the holy feminine spirit, is identical with an old goddess of wisdom who was known among Jews as Chochma and Scheschina. This goddess of wisdom is actually a figure who survived from the time of matriarchy to the Jewish patriarchy following it. Indeed, she was still worshipped among the early Christian communities as the goddess of wisdom, as Sophia, who remains important even in the Gospels. This argument finds literary expression in Mitterer's play: The Mother of God reveals that God the Father has killed the goddess who, in the beginning, ruled before him and then next to him. Or at least he attempted to kill her, but did not entirely succeed:

> MOTHER OF GOD [addressing God]: You have killed me. You have eradicated me. For a little while you tolerated the feminine next to you. That was him (*points to the Ghost*), when he was still permitted to be a woman.
> GHOST: I beg your pardon? What do you mean?
> MOTHER OF GOD: You once were a woman.
> GHOST (*baffled*): I was a woman?
> MOTHER OF GOD: Yes, you were the Holy Feminine Ghost, the feminine creativity of God. You were that which remained of me after his [God's] putsch. Yet not even that could he tolerate any longer. He made a man out of you, because he could only tolerate men next to himself (58).[14]

As we saw previously, Mitterer conveys this serious content in humorous form, perhaps, as mentioned above, so as to allow the audience to receive a criticism of contemporary religion it would otherwise reject.

    The above quote not only affords a good example of Mitterer's humor, it also reveals the confusion concerning family relationships within the playwright's divine house. In the play, God is the father of the Son, of the Ghost, and of Satan, or at any rate, he is addressed by all three as father. Satan addresses God as "Lord" (*Herr*, 18, 19 etc.), but also refers to him as "Father" (*Vater*, 20, 67 etc.). The Holy Ghost addresses God as "Lord" (*Herr*, 11, 12, 21 etc.), yet he also calls him "Father" (*Vater*, 24, 61 etc.). Calling God "Father" does not seem justified if the Ghost is to be considered a remnant of the original mother goddess, as the above quote states, unless the Ghost is not aware of his origin. It is even questionable whether Jesus can rightfully call God his father, for according to Mary's story she is raped and impregnated by Roman soldiers (53). The Mother of God is the mother of the Son but not of the Ghost or Satan. The relationships within the "divine" family become even more complicated as soon as earlier relationships are disclosed. The Mother of God is not only the mother of Jesus, but also "the mother of the universe, the divine grace, the womb from which everything comes forth" (60). God's attempt to kill her fails because humans need a "Mother" to whom they can pray. The Mother of God thus remains "The Secret Goddess of Christianity."[15] Mitterer's bewildering presentation of family relationships within the house of God is an essentially accurate translation of Mulack's fundamental ideas concerning creation. The humorous treatment of those ideas might allow an audience to hear and consider them. Furthermore, the chaotic portrayal of divine relationships serves to muddy that which must be pristinely clear according to the Church. In other words, the play brings confusion into the Creation story and thereby provokes question.

At other times, Mitterer renders Mulack's complicated discussion of creation in remarkably straightforward fashion, and in doing so the playwright again succeeds in making us smile. For example, the Mother of God tries to convince God that she deserves an equal place at his side, since such equality should already clearly result from the mere intrinsic facts: "Humankind consists of men and women. Here [in heaven] it was similar. Man and woman. God and Goddess. The feminine and the masculine. Do you remember, man?" (59). Her blunt down-to-earth reasoning makes its serious point in an unobtrusive and even light-hearted manner. Because her words do not offend, they might prompt acknowledgement of their undeniable logic.

The following scene might serve as yet another example of Mitterer's skill at transforming theological ideas into candid arguments that are effective on stage: God remains steadfast in his resolve to rule alone, without the feminine, forcing the Son to realize that patriarchal rule is here to stay. The Son therefore proposes not that humanity should be extinguished, but rather that the Holy Trinity should self-annihilate, a proposal which Satan also supports, for God, i.e., religion, serves in our times "at best as a pretext to settle old scores and for murder!" (64). The Son furthermore justifies his proposal by saying that humans nowadays have their own laws and no longer need divine laws, which are contained in the human laws anyway. Though not as magnificent-sounding as the divine ones, they are nonetheless "quite reasonable." "I think," he concludes, "it is indeed time, father, that humans stand on their own feet. Self-responsibly" (64f.).[16] God objects by pointing out that the death of the Divine would not include Satan, for Satan is *in* the human being. Although the Son agrees, he reiterates that God's existence is irrelevant in man's battle against evil: "Yes, that is the nature of the human being. They will hold their own against him [Satan], or not" (65). Satan, too, knows that humans will fight against him, with or without God: "Some of them at any rate. (*Grinning*): And at any rate more unfaithful ones than faithful ones" (65). With these words Satan repeats an earlier statement: "Whatever in the world has changed for the better within the last two thousand years came about largely thanks to the initiative of unbelievers, doubters, heretics" (49). In other words, Satan implies that any lessening of misery since the death of Jesus cannot be credited to the power institution of the Christian Church. Instead, if indeed there is now less evil than before the coming of Christ, this is due more to the initiative of liberally thinking so-called heretics than to that of so-called pious believers.

In his play, Mitterer was able only to incorporate a simplified selection of the complex feminist theological theses found in the works of Christa Mulack. Mary becomes the main mouth piece for those theories. She is not only the mother of Jesus, she also represents the primordial mother, the primordial goddess who brought forth the creation, and, moreover, she represents woman and her lot within human society. According to commentator Klaus Gruber,

> She [Mary] proves that the suppression of everything feminine from the heavenly government was the beginning of all evil. [She maintains] that God, on his way to autocratic rule, not only destroyed the idols, but also the feminine elements in his surroundings. The Ghost originally possessed feminine creativity. Then, since humans did not want to accept the strictly masculine rulership, Mary was built up as object of worship.[17]

To some extent, Mitterer continues in this play to elaborate upon motifs that he had already touched on in other plays. For example, the Dragon and the Hind from *Drachendurst* have certain points in common with God and the Mother of God from *Krach im Hause Gott*. Whereas the Dragon and God are responsible for evil, for greed, war, death, etc., the Hind and the Mother of God stand for good, for love and life. Similarities also exist between *Ein Jedermann* and *Krach im Hause Gott*, which was based on the prologue to that earlier play, as already mentioned. The characters of the two plays resemble each other in many ways, and both plays make use of a sort of heavenly trial. In the earlier play, however, the typically human case of Everyman is on trial, whereas in *Krach im Hause Gott* the divine family and humanity as a whole are on trial.

Despite Mitterer's efforts to render his criticism of certain aspects of Christian religion palatable through a humorous and ironical treatment, *Krach im Hause Gott* has received mixed reactions and caused considerable protest.[18] According to Robert Mitscha-Eibl, Mitterer was charged with mockery of religion.[19] Such controversy because of Mitterer's treatment of religious topics had also been aroused by earlier plays, for exmple *Die Kinder des Teufels*, *Stigma*, or *Abraham*. In order to promote discussion, Mitterer seems to favor provocation. Indeed, the play discussed here abounds with provocation: God the Father labels Jesus's sacrifice as having been "good for nothing"; the Holy Ghost and Jesus argue with one another so violently that God the Father starts cursing their rough behavior; Mary is said to have been raped by Roman soldiers; the Holy Ghost is called a "dumb piece of poultry," to name just a few examples. Such means are admittedly extreme and sometimes crude and coarse, yet it is a crudeness and an exaggeration intended to elicit questions and a reconsideration of issues and stances long assumed immutable. The play leaves us amused as well as thoughtful. We might indeed start pondering what is to be learned from this modern passion play: How can we begin to address the shortcomings in the dogma of the Christian Church so as to transform that Church into an institution not of murder and discord, but of humanity?

Notes

1. There are several statements in the Bible that demonstrate male contempt for the female word, for example: "Sit thou silent, and get thee into darkness, O daughter of the Chaldeans: for thou shalt no more be called, The lady of kingdoms" (Isa 47:5); "Let a woman learn in silence with all submission" (1 Tim. 2:11); "And I do not permit a woman to teach or to have authority over a man, but to be in silence" (1 Tim. 2:12).

2. Felix Mitterer, *Krach im Hause Gott* (Innsbruck: Haymon, 1994). All translations from German to English for this essay are mine. If the German is problematic, the original quote is provided in an endnote. All references to the German edition of the play are identified by the page number in parentheses.

3. Compare Gerlinde Ulm Sanford, "Onward or Downward? The Eternal-Feminine in Felix Mitterer's Play *Die Wilde Frau*," *Felix Mitterer: A Critical Introduction*, ed. Nicolas Meyerhofer and Karl E. Webb (Riverside, CA: Ariadne Press, 1995) 131-45.

4. " . . . nämlich das Weibliche. Wo ist die Frau? Warum gibt es nur einen Herr-Gott? Brauchen wir nicht sehr notwendig neben dem Vater eine Mutter, wenn wir schon jemanden brauchen, der über uns ist?," "Felix Mitterer zur Entstehung des Stückes," *Krach im Hause Gott* 72.

5. Christa Mulack, *Maria – die geheime Göttin im Christentum* (Stuttgart: Kreuz Verlag, 1985).

6. Christa Mulack, *Jesus der Gesalbte der Frauen* (Stuttgart: Kreuz Verlag, 1987). For further reading on feminist theology, I would like to provide the following suggestions: Maria Pilar Aquino, *Our Cry for Life: Feminist Theology from Latin America* (Maryknoll, NY: Orbis Books, 1993); Ellen Armour, *Deconstruction, Feminist Theology and the Problem of Difference* (Chicago: University of Chicago Press, 1999); Karen Baker-Fletcher, *Sisters of Dust, Sisters of Spirit: Womanist Wordings on God and Creation* (Minneapolis: Fortress Press, 1998); Mieke Bal, *Lethal Love: Feminist Literary Readings of Biblical Love Stories* (Bloomington: Indiana UP, 1987); Rebecca Chop and Shiela G. Davaney, eds., *Horizons in Feminist Theology: Identity, Tradition, Norms* (Minneapolis: Fortress Press, 1997); Carol Christ and Judith Plaskow, eds., *Womanspirit Rising: A Feminist Reader in Religion* (San Francisco: HarperSanFrancisco, 1992); Mary Daly, *Gyn/Ecology: The Metaethics of Radical Feminism* (Boston: Beacon Press, 1990); Elisabeth Schuessler Fiorenza, *In Memory of Her: A Feminist Theological Reconstruction of Christian Origins* (New York: Crossroad, 1983); Elisabeth Schuessler Fiorenza and M. Shawn Copeland, eds., *Feminist Theology in Different Contexts* (London: SCM Press; Maryknoll, NY: Orbis Books, 1996); Mary McClintock Fulkerson, *Changing the Subject: Women's Discourses and Feminist Theology* (Minneapolis: Fortress Press, 1994); Rita Gross, *Buddhism after Patriarchy: a Feminist History, Analysis, and Reconstruction of Buddhism* (Albany, NY: SUNY, 1993); Carter Heyward, *Touching our Strength: the Erotic as Power and the Love of God* (San Francisco: Harper & Row, 1989); Catherine Keller, *From a Broken Web: Separation, Sexism, and Self* (Boston: Beacon Press, 1986); Sally McFague, *Models of God:*

Theology for an Ecological, Nuclear Age (Philadelphia: Fortress Press, 1987); Mudflower Collective, *God's Fierce Whimsy: Christian Feminism and Theological Education* (New York: Pilgrim Press, 1985); Mercy Amba Oduyoye, *Daughters of Anowa: African Women and Patriarchy* (Maryknoll, NY: Orbis Books, 1995); Mercy Amba Oduyoye and Musimbi R. A. Kanyoro, *Will to Arise: Women, Tradition, and the Church in Africa* (Maryknoll, NY: Orbis Books, 1992); Rosemary Radford Ruether, *Sexism and God-Talk: Toward a Feminist Theology* (Boston: Beacon Press, 1983); Rosemary Radford Ruether, *Womenchurch: Theology and Practice of Feminist Liturgical Communities* (San Francisco: Harper & Row, 1985); Phyllis Trible, *God and the Rhetoric of Sexuality* (Philadelphia: Fortress Press, 1978); Delores Williams, *Sisters in the Wilderness: The Challenge of Womanist God-talk* (Maryknoll, NY: Orbis Books, 1993). Mitterer, however, mentions only Christa Mulack's work as the source of his inspiration.

7. Compare e. g. the tabular listing in Christa Mulack, *Auf den Spuren der Göttin* (Marl: Göttert Verlag, 1993) 14.

8. "In älteren matriarchalen Schöpfungsmythen ist es die Göttin, die das Licht aus dem Dunkel ihres Schoßes gebiert. . . . [In der biblischen Genesis] wird der weibliche Gebärakt durch das männliche Wort abgelöst. Dennoch geht diesem Wort auch im Alten Testament das weibliche Geistprinzip voraus, das als Ruah über den weiblichen Urwassern oder Tehom schwebt. . . . Geist und Wasser, physikalisch ausgedrückt: Energie und Materie, sind die zwei Seiten derselben Medaille, aus der die Bausteine des Lebens hervorgehen. Der schaffende Gott ist demnach das Geschöpf dieser uranfänglich weiblichen Kräfte – mythologisch gesprochen der Sohn der Göttin." Christa Mulack, *Im Anfang war die Weisheit* (Stuttgart: Kreuz Verlag, 1988) 70.

9. Robert Mitscha-Eibl, "Mitterers *Krach im Hause Gott* vor Uraufführung," *Felix Mitterer: Materialien zu Person und Werk* (Innsbruck: Haymon Verlag, 1995) 113.

10. "Die Menschen lieben sich selbst ja nicht! Wie sollen sie da den Nächsten lieben? – Und warum lieben sich die Menschen

selbst nicht? Weil du ihnen ein schlechtes Gewissen eingeflößt hast! Weil du, Jesus, ihnen gesagt hast: 'Liebe deine Feinde!' Aber sie hassen ihre Feinde! Zurecht! Das ist ganz normal. Auch du, Herr und Gott, redest auf deinen Schrifttafeln ständig von deinem Haß auf deine Feinde! Das ist normal! Die Menschen sind wie du, Gott! Deine Ebenbilder! Und dafür willst du sie bestrafen?"

11. "Am Anfang war das Wort, und das Wort ist Gott! Schluß, aus!" This is a slightly changed version of the famous opening line of St. John's Gospel: "In the beginning was the Word, and the Word was with God, and the Word was God."

12. Pondering arguments of the Mother of God, one cannot help being reminded of Hans Arp's witty pun: *Was ist das Wort? Das große W an diesem Ort.* This pun, however, cannot be translated into English very well. Hans Arp asks: *What is the Word?* In his answer, he explains that the *Word* is *the great W in the World.* The pronunciation of the German letter *W* is identical with the word *Weh*, meaning *woe*. Both Arp and the Mother of God hint at the great misery, the great woe, in God's Creation. Hans Arp (1886-1966) was a painter, sculptor, and writer of the Dada-Movement.

13. "Wer im jüdisch-christlichen Glauben erzogen wurde, ist mit dem Gedanken groß geworden, daß diese Welt von einem männlichen Geist im Alleingang aus dem Nichts erschaffen wurde. Durch das Wort Gottes, durch seinen Befehl sozusagen, entstand diese Welt. So können wir es auf der ersten Seite der Bibel nachlesen. Doch so ganz bestimmt ist dieses Bild nicht, denn bevor das göttliche Wort gesprochen wird, erfahren wir von einer weiblichen Kraft, von der Ruah, der heiligen Geistin, die über den Wassern schwebt. Die Wasser oder Urtiefen und die Ruah scheinen so etwas wie Grundgegebenheiten der Schöpfung zu sein. Die Urwasser oder Tehom, wie sie im Hebräischen heißen, gelten in allen Kulturen als das weibliche Urbild der Materie und des Chaos, in dem ungeordnet noch alle Möglichkeiten der Entwicklung unterschiedlichster Lebensformen enthalten sind. So ist auch in dem Begriff 'mater' oder Mutter noch die Vorstellung von

Materie enthalten." Christa Mulack, *Im Anfang war die Weisheit* (Stuttgart: Kreuz Verlag, 1988) 69.

14. "MUTTERGOTTES [zu Gott]: Du hast mich getötet. Du hast mich ausgetilgt. Eine Zeitlang hast du noch Weiblichkeit geduldet neben dir. Das war er *(deutet auf den Geist)*, als er noch Frau sein durfte. GEIST: Wie bitte? Was soll denn das heißen? MUTTERGOTTES: Du warst einmal eine Frau. GEIST *(verblüfft)*: Ich war eine Frau? MUTTERGOTTES: Ja. Die Heilige Geistin warst du, die weibliche Schöpfungskraft Gottes. Das, was von mir übrig blieb, nach seinem [Gottes] Putsch. Aber selbst das konnte er nicht mehr dulden. Er hat einen Mann aus dir gemacht, weil er nur Männer um sich ertragen konnte."

15. *Die geheime Göttin des Christentums.* Compare the book by Christa Mulack cited above.

16. "Ich denke, es wird wirklich Zeit, Vater, daß die Menschen auf eigenen Füßen stehen. Selbstverantwortlich."

17. Klaus Gruber, "Ein Mysterienspiel für Bregenz," *Münchner Merkur* 4 August 1994: Kulturteil.

18. Compare e. g. Martin Larcher's and Robert Mitscha-Eibl's remarks as quoted in *Felix Mitterer: Materialien*, 113 and 114.

19. *Felix Mitterer: Materialien* 113.

The Issue of Male Violence in Dramatic Works of the Two Austrian Republics: Veza Canetti and Felix Mitterer

Dagmar C. G. Lorenz

Violence against women and members of groups perceived as socially weak, inferior, and defenseless is a common motif in the literature of all ages. The representation of the perpetrators has varied over time, but not so the fascination with crime and the criminal. Writers have tended to endow the criminal with an aura of mystery and an air of the forbidden. Celebrating the offender, they disposed of the victims in a more or less casual manner. Shakespeare's Richard III, Wedekind's Jack the Ripper, Brecht's Baal and Mack the Knife are among the famous criminal characters who continue to be associated with danger and sexual prowess while their serial victims leave hardly any impression at all. The criminals are often configured as rebels who embrace a lifestyle seemingly above the law and in defiance of social norms. Relatively few authors have attempted to debunk the myth of the larger-than-life male criminal; he has persisted, be it as a means to derive vicarious pleasure or as a vehicle for social criticism. Literature and film would not be the same without demonic and demonized serial killers, rapists, gangsters, mobsters, mercenaries, and Nazis.

This article compares two dramas, *Der Oger (The Ogre)* written by Veza Canetti[1] and *Die Wilde Frau* (The Wild Woman) by Felix Mitterer.[2] Both dramas thematize the representation of male criminality and/or brutality; both trace the abuse of a woman in the isolation of a male-dominated private sphere. The comparison reveals the radicalization of gender discourse in the twentieth century, a century overshadowed by war and genocide. *Der Oger* was written after World War I, *Die Wilde Frau* after Word War II. At the same time, the article explores how and why these two dramatists differ from popular contemporary castings of the male criminal and his female victim.

Formation of the Criminal Image during the Twentieth Century

In the 1920s, under the influence of psychoanalysis, the popular image of the criminal underwent a transformation from a villain to a mentally sick individual, as in Fritz Lang's film *M*,[3] while women and children continued to be represented as the main targets of male violence. In an attempt to understand the criminal mind, the perpetrator's milieu was closely examined as an important factor in the shaping of the criminal mind. However, the increasingly rational and analytic approach to crime in the interwar era gave way to more irrational views after World War II and the Holocaust. These two events had a decisive impact on the assessment and representation of violence. In their theory of the detective novel, Pierre Boileau und Thomas Narcejac characterize hatred as the paradigmatic "new literary impulse" in the years after 1945. They maintain that the genocide transformed an entire continent into a slaughterhouse and created a drama of a horrifying innocence and a sphere beyond reason and morality, beyond good and evil.[4]

In post-WWII public discourse, Nazi perpetrators and common violent criminals were demonized until the mid-1960s when confrontation with desk murderers such as Adolf Eichmann called for a reassessment of crime and the violent offender. The seemingly insignificant defendants at the Nuremberg Trial and the man in the glass booth before the Israeli court undermined the concept of mad serial killers and monstrous villains. Hannah Arendt's study *Eichmann in Jerusalem* (1964) called into question the supposedly monstrous qualities ascribed to men like Eichmann, thus provoking a far-reaching controversy.[5] Arendt applied the phrase of the "banality of evil" to Eichmann after closely observing his pedantic daily routines and his unimpressive exterior that epitomized the secondary virtues of Western man. Her critics, focusing on the abhorrent crimes engineered by Eichmann, were outraged at the notion that he might be nothing more than an ordinary man and an ambitious, efficient manager.[6]

Arendt's portrayal of Eichmann differs markedly from the representation of German war criminals and KZ personnel by the entertainment industry and, with a few exceptions, by mainstream historiography.[7] It is the cliché of the criminal psychopath that prevailed in subsequent decades, influencing the way violent crime was conceived. Focusing on the monstrosity of individual acts, the criminal was pathologized and assigned a deviant status to match his outrageous and morally repulsive deeds. This pattern of binary oppositions can be observed in the East and West alike. Sheriffs and outlaws fought the same battle of good versus evil in traditional American westerns as did fascists and anti-fascists, uncivilized SS-men and honorable socialist resistance fighters, in GDR literature. The perpetrator was consistently dehumanized and the public assured of their own normalcy.

Portrayal of the Male Criminal in Canetti and Mitterer

The two dramas under investigation here are exceptions to the common portrayal of male criminal and female victim in a number of important ways. First, in both dramas, the woman's struggle against violence is successful, thereby disassociating female gender and victimhood. Canetti de-victimizes her female protagonist by emphasizing Draga's point of view throughout different phases of her life. The protagonist is shown as a carefree girl, as a wife and young mother in a difficult marriage, as the victim of extortion and battery, and finally as a divorced woman in command of her inheritance and single head of her household, a woman free to live and love again. In Mitterer's case, the male point of view prevails. His female protagonist serves as a medium to explore male attitudes toward women, sexuality, and ethnic difference. Instead of tracing character development over time, Mitterer observes the unities of time and place. The generational differences between the male characters establish a wider historical spectrum and insight into the male psyche at different phases. As far as the character of the woman is concerned, no information whatever is provided about her background, her intentions, her feelings and desires, and her future. An almost mythical being, she has a history of her own.

Both authors portray gender relations as problematic, and both point to the impact of recent war on those relations. Canetti, who had Socialist leanings and spent her formative years in the interwar period of "Red Vienna," sets her drama in a multicultural Viennese neighborhood. In the aftermath of the war, Vienna has become a center for immigrants and refugees. The first act of *The Ogre* is preceded by the following notation: "In the Prelude: A town in Bosnia at the time of the monarchy. Nine years later: After the collapse of the former capital. The former capital of the monarchy is Vienna." In other words, the war signifies a divide between the traditional patriarchy in which Canetti's protagonist Draga was socialized and the radically misogynistic situation in which she finds herself after 1918. Together with her despotic husband, Draga lives in the anonymity and isolation of a Viennese apartment house.

Similarly, the cabin in *Die Wilde Frau* represents a discreet male dominated sphere. Categories of biology and race are implied in references to the dark complexion and lack of language on the part of Mitterer's female protagonist, and they are linked to gender-coded behavior in such a way as to call to mind Nazi discourse on gender and race. The different ages of Mitterer's male characters signify the mentalities of different generations, as discussed by Gerlinde Ulm Sanford, and allude to the larger historical context.[8] The oldest logger, 70-year-old Hias, was born prior to World War I. His speech, his folksy, partly obscene, partly corny clichés and vulgar jokes reveal the mentality of a transitional period. Hias articulates misogynistic viewpoints freely among the other males, but acts politely, almost gallantly, toward the woman. His awkward way of dealing with the opposite sex calls to mind the double standard of the fin de siècle. Hias's physical age and his attitudes prevent him from acting on his desires, but by voicing misogynistic and racist opinions he encourages the younger men in their aggressive pursuit of the woman. Jogg, aged 45, was a child at the end of World War II. He is too young to have understood and embraced National Socialism. A descendant of the Nazi generation, he has internalized fascist and authoritarian behavior patterns nonetheless. Lex, age thirty-five, was born before the founding of the Second Republic and experienced the 1960s as an adolescent. During this time of historical revision and rebellion in most of Europe, the Nazi past continued to be repressed in Austria, which clung to the myth that it was the first victim of National Socialism, thereby exonerating itself from responsibility for the Holocaust. Lex's personal attitudes reflect the mindset of an unrepenting violent offender.

Both Canetti and Mitterer de-glamorize the perpetrators and their acts without invalidating them as human beings. Rather than casting the perpetrators as monsters, Canetti and Mitterer make social dynamics transparent to reveal the role of those dynamics in the making of the criminal. In addition, the two writers link cruelty with common unheroic qualities such as greed, selfishness, and narrow-mindedness to "normalize" the criminal and to motivate his actions. By revealing that certain qualities make the violent male successful among his peers, they show that transgressions against the moral code are in effect socially validated and rewarded. Furthermore, Canetti as well as Mitterer are concerned with the connection between lack of education and social standing on the one hand and violent behavior on the other. Their perpetrators come across as prisoners of their own mentality, lacking both the motivation and the wherewithal to modify their behavior.

Canetti and Mitterer examine the interplay between societal and personal factors. To this end they carefully construct their protagonists' environment. In Canetti's drama, brutality arises within a nuclear family that exists in isolation in a capitalist urban environment. In Mitterer's drama, it is the machismo cultivated by a team of loggers far removed from civilization that breeds violence. Both playwrights configure the individual characters and their milieu in such a way as to suggest that propensity toward dominance and brutality is a common human trait. Male proclivity toward brutality is associated with the conditions under which men are socialized and expected to live. Violence is shown to arise in settings that encourage aggressive and irresponsible behavior: there is no agency in either Canetti's petty bourgeois apartment nor Mitterer's cabin that would hold the dominant males accountable. They are the owners of the household goods and the means of production. Females are financially and socially disenfranchised from their group. Canetti's and Mitterer's dramas are microcosms reflecting a society where violence is accepted as an integral part of everyday culture. In terms of their mentality, the perpetrators are anything but deviants; they are members of the mainstream.

Literature of the First and Second Republics

The First Republic of Austria was overshadowed by the trauma of war, the collective loss of identity, and the memory of male-defined violence – committed, suffered, and tolerated. The image of the traumatized soldier returning from war only to find his old world dismantled is a common theme in post-World War I literature, both fictional and autobiographic. In fact, Adolf Hitler's *Mein Kampf* can be categorized within the latter group. In addition to such posttraumatic shock and depression, the writings of conservative veterans reveal an unprecedented polarization between men and women in terms of life experiences and gender role expectations; hence the impression that these men have come home to a hostile society.[9]

These views are incongruous with the aspirations of more progressive segments of the new republic, namely the hope to achieve democracy and, for women, equality. The newly-established democratic structures, including women's suffrage and social equity for the working class, put an end to the sense of stagnation among formerly underprivileged groups. Many women writers and members of minorities, among them Veza Canetti, subscribed to the social reforms propounded by the Social Democrats. They envisioned a future society that would provide modern men and women with the basis for partnership and mutual respect. At the same time, Canetti was aware of the increasing rightwing radicalism that threatened the new republic and herself as a Jewish woman, and she was cognizant of the undefeated conservatism in the rural areas of what used to be the Habsburg Empire.

The experience of the lost war with its unprecedented carnage had created new gender barriers between veterans who had taken part in battle and women who had supported their efforts far away from the theaters of war. In addition, the collapse of the Austrian and German empires in 1918 was accompanied by a de-glamorization of the military male; women and young civilians had to cope with the presence of de-socialized veterans prone to violence within their families and the public sphere. Veterans met with ambivalent responses – pity for the invalid and shell-shocked, but also apprehension of men who continued on their path of aggression as members of militias, freicorps, and the new right-wing extremist parties. In certain sectors of Austrian society, there was also admiration for these same unrehabilitated killers.

On the other hand, the number of pacifists opposing all forms of militarism had grown significantly toward the end of the war. Karl Kraus's *Die letzten Tage der Menschheit* (*The Last Days of Mankind*) issued a radical indictment of those participating in, benefiting from, and supporting war.[10] Veza Canetti was closely associated with Kraus and his circles. Her views can also be compared with those of other pacifists, for example the German-born Claire Goll who identified patriarchal social structures as the root cause of war. In her collection of prose texts titled *Der gläserne Garten* (The Glass Garden), Goll analyzed the military male from a feminist point of view and revealed not only the disastrous impact soldiers and officers have on the civilian environment, but also the complicity of women supporting militarism by nurturing the veterans to whom they are related.[11]

Among works of the interwar period, Ödön von Horváth's *Geschichten aus dem Wiener Wald* (1919/30, *Tales from the Vienna Woods*) is one of the most pessimistic texts. There seems to be no escape from the pre-fascist behavior and violence in the lower-middle class Viennese family, the setting of Horváth's play.[12] In contrast, most of the progressive authors of the First Republic portrayed the disorientation after the demise of the Empire as temporary and pointed to a better future ahead. Veza Canetti's *The Ogre*, conceived, ironically, on the eve of the *coup d'état* that put an end to the young Austrian democracy, suggests that the chaos engendered by the breakdown of the old patriarchal and imperial order was a painful but necessary process of transition. The disintegration of the patriarchal hierarchy into a male-dominated Social Darwinist jungle seems a precondition for forging a society that will guarantee women and children life, liberty, and the pursuit of happiness. The loss of traditional values viewed as a tragedy by Hermann Broch and Elias Canetti is the first step toward change in Veza Canetti's drama.

The Ogre traces the transformation of a woman enslaved in an abusive marriage into a free agent. The husband and mortal enemy of Canetti's protagonist, the businessman Iger, lacks the erotic appeal and charisma attributed to the most notorious literary perpetrators. Thus the reader's attention is diverted away from the perpetrator and the victim comes into focus. The drama revolves around the victim's struggle to maintain her dignity and save her and her children's lives until she finally escapes the stranglehold of her husband.

There exist discursive affinities between the literature of the First and Second Republics. However, the tenor of works dealing with the Nazi legacy after 1945 and "the murderers among us" was more strident and at the same time less self-assured than the socially critical literature of the inter-war period, although Austrian authors tended to place less trust in the effectiveness and potential of didactic writing than, for example, Bertolt Brecht. Many post-1945 writers, among them Elfriede Jelinek, revealed how the legacy of World War II entered Austrian living rooms and transformed the private sphere, bringing terror and abuse to women and children.[13] Unlike most interwar writers, Jelinek refrains from speculating as to how militarism and aggression might be remedied. In her works, gender and class imbalance appears to be too great for peaceful coexistence between men and women. Entrenched in their roles, Jelinek's characters seem impervious to the measures contemplated by Canetti and Goll: to curb male violence by withdrawing emotional support and social validation for aggressive behavior. Rather than envisioning change, Jelinek explores the polarization of male and female behavior and reveals ignorance and political indifference created by today's popular culture. In Jelinek's writing the systematic "moronization of the masses" discussed by Herbert Marcuse appears as a *fait accompli*.[14]

In contemporary Austrian literature, a work thematizing the

liberation of a woman and her triumph over male oppression would be hard to find, even among the production of feminists and social critics. Jelinek, for instance, foregrounds the institutions of modern society, especially the media, as instruments of disinformation. Marlene Streeruwitz makes the economical, social, and psychological mechanisms that keep women in their place apparent – her protagonists never reach their full potential. Peter Turrini, by highlighting the pervasive primitivism and brutality among the underprivileged, reveals the unbridgeable gap between the educated and uneducated, the rich and the poor. Felix Mitterer configures violence and domination as part of the human, or more specifically, the male psyche. His works suggest that the atavistic pack instinct, which places high-status males above low-status males and men in general over women and children, is an innate trait that civilization has failed to curb. Quite to the contrary, postwar society as it evolved from fascism into a free market economy produced an escalation of these tendencies by fostering competition and the immediate gratification of desires. In *Die Wilde Frau* Mitterer exposes the radical imbalance of power between men and women and the devaluation of behaviors and activities considered feminine.

The five loggers dominate the action of Mitterer's drama. The marginalization of the female and the elusive "feminine" is underscored by the fact that the female protagonist is a stranger without a voice or space of her own. In contrast to the males, she remains nameless. Alone and seemingly defenseless, she initially does not fight against the abuse to which the men submit her. Yet, similar to some of the female characters in Veza Canetti's novel *Die gelbe Straße (The Yellow Street)* and Draga Iger toward the end of *The Ogre*, the Wild Woman practices non-cooperation and passive resistance, and at times makes futile appeals to one or the other male to help her.[15] The Wild Woman's survival strategies call to mind the reactions of women in actual abusive situations.[16] For example, her plight resembles the ordeal of the Southern female slave as described in Harriet A. Jacobs's memoir:

> If God has bestowed beauty upon her, it will prove

her greatest curse. That which commands admiration in the white woman only hastens the degradation of the female slave. I know that some are too much brutalized by slavery to feel the humiliation of their position; but many slaves feel it most acutely, and shrink from the memory."[17]

While in most of his works Mitterer exposes the power imbalance between men and women in a historical context, the setting of the *Die Wilde Frau* is seemingly timeless.

By establishing a connection between his protagonist and the legendary Alpine "Wild People," Mitterer creates a mysterious and supernatural female character, whereas the males, with the exception of the youngest who is said to be a foundling of obscure origin, are unquestionably human. As Claudia Schmölders notes, Mitterer's protagonist can be considered a particular variant of the legendary Alpine Wild Woman, namely the Wild Cook, who performs domestic tasks and achieves considerable power over human males by controlling their food and living quarters.[18] As in folk tradition, Mitterer's loggers are also unaware of the woman's strength. Signs of her difference pervade the play, but they occur in the men's absence who accordingly remain oblivious to the risk they take by provoking her. The Wild Woman's arrival is accompanied by strange sounds and she does not seem subject to the laws of physics. Moreover, she does not seem to care about social convention and morality – apparently she attaches little or no significance to sexuality. She objects to Lex's advances because he makes demands and beats her rather than asking for her favors, but she is also unimpressed by Much's and Lex's promises to marry her (51, 56, 62). Because of her disinterest in what the males value most, namely sex and the marital commitment to a female, the men begin to regard her as a whore (20, 67).

The association of the woman with the legendary Wild Women makes it possible to interpret her as an exponent of nature as well. Thus Mitterer's play takes on an ecological dimension. The exploitation of the woman, the slaying of the deer, and the logging profession all signify the ruthlessness with which men subjugate and destroy nature. The violent ending implies that there will be dire consequences of man's aggressive and, at the same time, suicidal practices.

Only for the seventeen-year-old Wendl does an armistice with the opposite sex, if not a reconciliation across gender-lines, appear possible. Only Wendl shows no aggression toward the foreign-looking woman, and he is the sole logger to survive. This possibility is predicated on his own inferior status within the patriarchal society. He is suspected of being a foreigner or even an alien, and in the absence of a "real" woman, he has to perform the traditional female chores. Through Wendl the drama reveals that gender roles are socially constructed and could, provided the right circumstances, be deconstructed and reformed. The same is true for Canetti's work. Yet in Mitterer the thoroughly entrenched male privileges and their psychological consequences make such a change unlikely. Each one of Mitterer's loggers, with the possible exception of Hias, who dies a natural death, and the boy, too young to have internalized the dominant culture, engages in aggressive behavior against the woman and thus precipitates his own demise.

The receiver and transmitter of the unacknowledged Nazi legacy, the felon Lex, displays behavior patterns that have been identified as characteristic of authoritarian personalities and protofascist psychopaths. For example, he desires to be the exclusive "owner" of the woman and physically assaults her when he is incapable of consummating the sexual act. In fact, the claims Lex makes on the woman derive from battery rather than intimacy. Seemingly unable to experience sexual pleasure and release, Lex is the most volatile and brutal of the men. The same fact of impotence that causes old Hias to become affectionate, prompts Lex to turn violent. His sexual fantasies, even more so than those of the other men, are driven by images of rape and bondage.

Much, five years Lex's junior, seems less complex-ridden and more straightforward than the older men. A child of the post-sexual-liberation generation, he shows fewer inhibitions than the others. He is more aware of his desires and ready and able to act upon them. However, the lack of sexual inhibition makes him no less prone to violence. As scene 18 reveals, which shows the men of the middle generations killing one another, Much is equally as capable of murder as Jogg and Lex. Thus Mitterer debunks notions held by anti-fascist theorists such as Wilhelm Reich and younger authors of the 1960s according to which reduced repression leads to a decrease in violent behavior.

Wendl, age seventeen, is the furthest removed from the war and postwar era. He represents the new, gentler male of the mid-70s. Although his survival leaves room for a limited optimism, the element of hope is far more cautiously introduced than in Canetti's drama. Whereas in *The Ogre* a union between Draga and the Doctor, a modern man and member of the younger generation, is forming as the drama ends, there is no such happy ending in sight in Mitterer. Nothing spells happiness and partnership between men and women. Canetti's protagonist Draga is surrounded by loving friends as the final curtain falls, but the orphan Wendl in *Die Wilde Frau* is the sole male survivor of a massacre, a boy with no place to go and no one to keep him company as the strange woman fades into the night.

Radicalization of the Gender Discourse

The different endings of the two dramas discussed here reveal different perspectives on future gender relations and social change, a radicalization of the gender discourse over time. Canetti's rural patriarchy is characterized by several fundamentally different men who embody a range of possible interactions with women: Stjepo Pavlovitsch, Draga's tyrannical but not ill-intentioned father; his steward Bogdan Stoitsch, a fair-minded older man protective of women; and the Igers, father and son, who are misers and ruthless exploiters. Clearly, the abuse of women does not seem to be as firmly established as in Mitterer's literary universe where misogyny is a given. In Mitterer's *Wilde Frau*, even the behavior of the youngest male can be read in keeping with his environment's standards, as a reflection of Wendl's immaturity and position as a low-status male. Mitterer's drama suggests that basic paradigms have remained constant over several generations, while others have become radicalized. The analysis of men of different age groups reveals a steady increase in aggression.

Canetti, on the other hand, depicts different mentalities and conduct among men and women of several generations to show a broader spectrum of mentalities. The potential for communication and collaboration between the sexes seems particularly strong among younger people who embrace a modern lifestyle according to which women have the freedom to chose a partner and the right to own property. In such a society it is possible for a woman to divorce an abusive husband without losing custody over her children. Yet, like Mitterer, Canetti raises the issue of transmitting the paradigms of abuse and oppression from one generation to the next. Draga states: "I cursed my children ... I wished them dead. And I love them so much. It went through my head that I did not want it. One time the little girl tried to hit me. 'If she turns out like her father she had better die.' That's what I thought. – *In horror...*" (89). Beyond the categories of class and personality both authors introduce the notion of intergenerational continuity, a hard-to-break chain of behavioral transmission that Wilhelm Reich articulated in conjunction with National Socialism. In *The Mass Psychology of Fascism*, he maintains that new sexual and economic practices might eventually modify the practices of later generations, but that no change is to be expected in the National Socialists and their children.[19]

Canetti accentuates the uniqueness of the individual and, cognizant of the constructedness of gender roles and their interconnection with political and legal institutions, questions the sanctity of the so-called private sphere. Precisely because the private sphere is insulated from the public sector and societal control, women and children, disadvantaged under the law and outsiders to the dominant power structures, occupy the status of prisoners or slaves. Women who have a liberal husband may take a lover as does Mrs. Schwab (49); less fortunate ones like Draga are subject to abuse and mental cruelty. Men, on the other hand, are at liberty to act upon their desires because legally and economically they have the upper hand. Thus, upon closer look the social space said to guarantee the greatest degree of personal freedom confines women while affording men the opportunity to dominate their wives and children.

In *The Ogre* it is in the privacy of the home where the most blatant transgressions against human and individual rights take place.

In keeping with Friedrich Engels's view that in the family the husband occupies the role of the capitalist and the wife that of the proletariat, Canetti illustrates that the autonomy of the family is in fact the autonomy of men to dominate women and children. The situation is further aggravated by the Iger family's relocation to Vienna. The big city provides Mr. Iger with the anonymity necessary to conduct his shady business deals and sexual exploits, and he is free to torment his wife and children by withholding the barest necessities from them. When Draga tries to assert her rights by holding on to her inheritance, Iger resorts to physical cruelty, particularly against the children, in order to terrorize the mother and force her to relinquish her property. Yet, Canetti places Iger's behavior into a larger context. His misogyny derives from a tradition of abuse in his family, and it corresponds to his disregard of his business partners and contempt for the law.

In *Die Wilde Frau* children are not an issue, at least not in the case of the woman held captive by the loggers and used as a maid and sex slave. While Jogg does attempt to prevent an unwanted pregnancy, Lex states: "You must be kidding. You don't suppose I would jump off during the best part of the ride?"(38) In the culture of the loggers, male sexuality serves primarily as an expression of power and virility. The feelings and desires of the woman remain unexplored – there is no opportunity for her to express them. While threatened by her husband in every aspect of her existence, Canetti's Draga does manage to articulate her suffering as mother and abused wife through gestures, words, tears, and finally through her temporary insanity. Exploited, confined, and oppressed, she has nonetheless an infinitely more varied range of self-expression at her disposal than Mitterer's Wild Woman. As wife and mother she occupies a legitimate social space, and as a member of her husband's culture she speaks his language. In Mitterer there is no social space for women and children.

Situated within the larger social arena, Canetti's drama reveals networks of relationships. Though unsympathetic to Draga's plight, there are other women in her environment. Iger may be a brilliant role player and a hypocrite who knows to keep up appearances, but his activities cannot go unchecked indefinitely. Other people become aware of his transgressions. In contrast, the men in *Die Wilde Frau*, marginal in terms of the larger society and holed up in a remote hut, are free to act without restraint. The claustrophobic setting of the play, complete with S & M accoutrements such as ropes, chains, and a dead animal, evokes the setting of pornographic novels and films. Mitterer's portrayal of the instrumentalization of the female reflects the increasing fragmentation of postmodern society and the kind of anarchy fostered by the lack of general norms in a mass society. In *Die Wilde Frau* males operate as co-conspirators within a system of unquestioned domination.

Despite a certain optimism, Canetti problematizes the social conditions in the First Republic. Even with suffrage achieved after the demise of the monarchy, average women remained excluded from the public sphere and the political arena. *The Ogre* reveals that housewives and mothers lack the modicum of legal protection enjoyed even by male criminals. The private sphere appears as a highly politicized space constructed to keep men unaccountable and to prevent women from acting in solidarity with one another.[20] Nonetheless, Canetti's drama does suggest that the gratuitous violence against women and children can be stopped by intruding into the private sphere and exploding the nuclear family.

Die Wilde Frau, on the other hand, focuses on the exploitation and abuse of woman as resulting from ingrained social practices, perhaps even from gender-specific traits – hence the test-tube-like atmosphere, the representation of different generations of males, and the presence of only one female character. In this setting the interaction of the males with the strange woman appears like a test case designed to reveal paradigms of male desire and competition. Hias's constant denigration of women, for example, reflects the need to dominate and control the other, if not physically then at least verbally, and to confirm his status as a male. Even the boy Wendl, who admires the stranger from afar, is excited by the other men's sexual advances, and he masturbates when they have intercourse with her (38). In a certain sense even the boy takes advantage of the situation.

The spectrum represented by Mitterer's characters is complex enough to allow conclusions about the society to which the men belong. Their activities such as logging and poaching, their bellicose behavior toward one another, and their mercenary attitude toward a lonely, possibly foreign woman suggest an underlying system of values according to which women and nature are commodities for male consumption. The rank order the men have established among themselves, which is based on dominance and the perpetual challenge to the individual's status, calls to mind a free market society. In the presence of a rare, highly coveted good such as the body of the strange woman, this society is apt to transform itself into a Social Darwinist jungle. Ironically though, in the end the loggers succumb to the very structures they have designed, while the overtly weak ones, the boy and the woman, prevail.

As mentioned earlier, Mitterer introduces folk legends as a device to foreground the difference between the loggers and the woman. Veza Canetti's strategy to convey the otherness of women consists of the discussion of gender-specific interests. Draga and her sister Milka enjoy finery for its own sake, whereas the men use gifts of gold and silk as the exchange value for the woman herself (14, 17). The women are enticed by the aesthetic pleasure they derive from the objects, while the men treat women and jewelry as objects of trade. After her marriage to Iger, Draga is focused exclusively on her children, disregarding her husband's cruelty as much as possible (87). For him the children represent yet another commodity. Iger's ambitions are purely materialistic: he uses his family to establish business connections but denies them their every wish. Financial and social concerns are closely connected in Canetti and have a direct bearing on gender configurations.

There are parallels between *Die Wilde Frau* and Mitterer's other plays and works, many of which reveal the author's awareness of the links between misogyny, xenophobia, anti-Semitism, National Socialism, and fascism. In particular, Mitterer's historical drama on the witch trials in seventeenth century Salzburg titled *Die Kinder des Teufels* (Children of the Devil) evinces similarities with *Die Wilde Frau*. Written with an eye on Austria's fascist past, it places cruelty and abusiveness against women within the context of mass hysteria and irrationalism.[21] In both dramas, Mitterer uses female characters to expose the corruption of male-dominated systems. Like the Wild

Woman, Magdalena Pichlerin in *Die Kinder des Teufels* is presented as a strong female figure who survives the male characters and is the last one to be executed. This pattern is repeated in the drama *Stigma* and the short story "Christines Schoß" (Christina's Womb), a narrative about a woman who is physically destroyed by the medical establishment.[22] In all these works the non-traditional behavior of women results from the abuse they suffer at the hands of men. Christine, for example, lives with a woman friend after her divorce. The young beggars of *Die Kinder des Teufels*, abandoned and abused children, turn to a cult figure for salvation.[23]

The protagonist of *Die Wilde Frau* turns out to be such a cult figure. Wendl associates her with the black madonna to whom he prays and attributes supernatural powers to her. Indeed, the Wild Woman possesses powers that enable her to destroy the men who mistreat her. In an ending reminiscent of the *deus ex machina* in the tradition of Raimund and Nestroy, the Wild Woman liberates herself and takes revenge. The fairy tale ending, rather than being hopeful, drives home the point that an average woman would have succumbed to the men's violence. Strong female figures such as the Wild Woman are cast by Mitterer as imaginary alternative forces. They symbolize society's repressed potential.

Contrary to Mitterer, Canetti foregrounds the oppression of women in economic terms. Economics and civil rights, portrayed as inextricably linked, determine mobility and status. Constructing male and female characters as part of the overall social system allows Canetti to develop a modestly utopian view and to forge an ideological framework that is both feminist and socialist. Despite Elias Canetti's assertion that his wife's works lacked the radicalism of modern feminism, a closer look at Veza Canetti's texts indicates quite the opposite.[24] The nuclear family, marriage, and patriarchy come under severe attack in *The Ogre*. Female subservience is not portrayed as a function of gender but rather of money. Being in control of her own resources enables Draga to escape from her ruinous marriage, raise her children, and have a second chance at love.

The Ogre is a critique of the patriarchal culture of rural Bosnia as well as of the inequality in the new republic. There is, however, greater potential for emancipatory change in the big city. Aided by enlightened well-meaning (male) friends not bound by tradition, Draga makes the transition into modern society. In a line reminiscent of the ending of Goethe's *Faust I*, her sister Milka comments: "Sister, you are saved" (98). Woman's liberation and the end of abuse are dependent upon the destruction of male privilege. The crumbling of the patriarchal institutions after World War I represents an opportunity for women to assert themselves and contribute to shaping a society where they have full participation.

In contrast to Canetti's Draga who has both male and female allies, Mitterer's protagonist stands alone. His drama lacks Canetti's confidence that there will be a consensus according to which women will enjoy equal rights and protection. On the other hand, Mitterer's Wild Woman appears more worldly and mature than Canetti's Draga. She knows her wishes and boundaries; hence her refusal to go with Lex or to prepare the meat of the deer he has hunted. Whereas Draga comes across as suggestible to the point that she accepts an unwanted man as her husband, the Wild Woman projects a security within herself. The self-reliance of civil and women's rights activists, i.e., the awareness that in the cause of liberation there are no well-meaning allies, is integrated into Mitterer's character. These are lessons learned from the Civil Rights era and the women's movements. The Wild Woman's passive resistance, for example, calls to mind strategies employed in India's anti-colonialist freedom struggle. In short, Mitterer's configuration of gender, power, ethnicity, and sexuality presupposes the experience of the post-World War II era. His drama is informed by the theoretical discourse of the 1960s, 70s, and 80s.

In *Die Wilde Frau* liberation from oppression and exploitation is effected by the oppressed and exploited woman – she has no other recourse. At the same time, it becomes apparent that nothing short of supernatural powers and an unshakable inner autonomy are required to prevail against the violence of a dominant predatory male mentality. It takes a Wild Woman to effect complete detachment from the gender role expectations superimposed on women. The best that can be hoped for under such extreme conditions is the disintegration of the male hierarchies. Harmony or collaboration between males and females is precluded by the extreme polarization between the sexes and the vastly different ways male and female characters deal with their sexuality. Mature males define themselves through their heterosexuality, but the Wild Woman is indifferent to the manifestations of male sexuality. Her behavior is determined by the threat of violence and coercion, both of which she quietly resists but fails to elude; she is beaten repeatedly by Lex. Her reactions indicate that she views human males as aliens and enemies whose non-violent sexual advances she tolerates without pleasure and whose brutality she abhors.

In *The Ogre* money takes priority over sexuality. Marriage is a financial arrangement between wealthy men whose interests differ from those of the women in every way imaginable. Draga displays romantic but no sexual interests, as is apparent from her encounter with the young student, and Iger pursues his sexual desires outside the marriage. After Draga has become a mother, all her thoughts and worries revolve around her children. However, despite the opposition between the older men's materialism and the relationship-centered outlook of the women, the divide between Canetti's male and female characters is caused by conditioning and conventions rather than a fundamentally different psychology. Young Iger is the only character who comes across as truly and solely destructive.[25] Other male characters such as Dr. Schwab and Bogdan Stoitsch demonstrate that there can be love and loyalty between men and women.

The Ogre is a reflection of the changing position of women in inter-war Austria. Gender problems, in particular women's coming-of-age and assuming their place in society, are key issues on which the future of the young republic depends. Canetti's protagonist Draga overcomes her socialization in a traditional patriarchy and her plight in an oppressive marriage. In the final scene she appears ready to meet the challenges of modern society. However, history has proven Canetti's optimism based on a dynamic model of gender and society to be overly optimistic. Under National Socialism the fledgling women's movement was shattered and the battle for workers' rights came to naught as the Left was destroyed by right-wing extremism. The veterans and war lords of World War I established a social order to their liking, one that marginalized and instrumentalized women. *Die*

Wilde Frau, written upon the background of Nazi history and its continued legacy in Austria, conveys a sense of irreparably damaged gender relations coupled with intractable xenophobia. Mitterer's collection of Austrian men disenfranchises woman and reduces her to her sexual functions and traditional gender role. To a large extent this process echoes the insights of feminist writer Marlene Streeruwitz, who calls on women to refuse making images of themselves available because of the commodification of women by the porno industry.[26] Streeruwitz describes woman as a "tolerated collaborator" in the network of marketing concepts, as a minority, tolerated in a nationalist sense. If woman were indeed to have equal rights, Streeruwitz explains, she would have everything that is an equal participant's due: work, respect, dignity.[27] The role Mitterer's woman protagonist plays in the minds of his male characters and the place she occupies in their cabin – a cot accessible to everyone who wishes to take advantage of her – expresses the dilemma stated in Streeruwitz's essay, an impasse with no solution in sight.

Notes

1. Veza Canetti, *Der Oger*, ed. Elias Canetti (Munich: Hanser, 1990). Translated by Richard Dixon as *The Ogre* in *Anthology of Contemporary Austrian Folk Plays*, ed. Donald Daviau (Riverside, CA: Ariadne Press, 1993). Translations of original quotes in this article are my own and based on the 1990 edition.

2. Felix Mitterer, *Die Wilde Frau* (Munich: Friedl Brehm Verlag, 1986). Translations of original quotes are my own.

3. *M*, dir. Fritz Lang, DVD, Voyager Films, 1998 (Original: 1931).

4. Pierre Boileau and Thomas Narcejac, *Der Detektivroman* (Berlin and Neuwied: Luchterhand, 1964) 134-35.

5. Hannah Arendt, *Eichmann in Jerusalem* (Munich: Piper, 1964).

6. See Dagmar C. G. Lorenz, *Verfolgung bis zum Massenmord* (New York: Lang, 1992) 29.

7. See for example Christopher R. Browning, *Ordinary Men: Reserve Police Battalion 101 and the Final Solution in Poland* (New York: HarperCollins, 1992).

8. Gerlinde Ulm Sanford, "Onward or Downward? The Eternal-Feminine in Felix Mitterer's Play *Die Wilde Frau*." *Felix Mitterer. A Critical Introduction*, ed. Nicholas J. Meyerhofer and Karl E. Webb (Riverside, CA: Ariadne Press, 1995) 131-45.

9. Characterizing polarity and antithesis as typical Austrian epistemological patterns, Lorna Martens writes that in Austria the interest in dualities "is present to a more intense and obsessive degree." Lorna Martens, *Shadow Lines. Austrian Literature from Freud to Kafka* (Lincoln: University of Nebraska Press, 1996) 11. According to Martens, the stagnation is articulated and deplored in the retrospective texts of conservative authors who thematize the "seemingly unshakable order" of the era of Emperor Franz Joseph (5).

10. Karl Kraus, *Die letzten Tage der Menschheit* (Vienna: Verlag "Die Fackel," 1918/19).

11. Claire Goll, *Der gläserne Garten*, ed. Barbara Glauert-Hesse (Berlin: Argon, 1989).

12. Ödön von Horváth, *Geschichten aus dem Wiener Wald* (Frankfurt/M.: Suhrkamp, 1977).

13. See for example Elfriede Jelinek, *Die Ausgesperrten* (Hamburg: Rowohlt, 1985).

14. Herbert Marcuse, "Repressive Tolerance," *A Critique of Pure Tolerance* (Boston: Beacon, 1965) 81-118.

15. Veza Canetti, *Die gelbe Straße* (Munich: Hanser, 1990). The drama *The Ogre* is a variation of a central episode in *Die gelbe Straße*; however, with a tragic ending. See Dagmar C. G. Lorenz, "The Motif of the Wild Woman in Felix Mitterer, Rahel Hutmacher, and Adalbert Stifter," *Felix Mitterer. A Critical Introduction* 161-77.

16. See Todd C. Hanlin, "'Sie ist keine Jungfrau mehr!' Sexuality and Religiosity in Felix Mitterer's *Stigma*," *Felix Mitterer. A Critical Introduction* 57-67.

17. Harriet A. Jacobs, "Incidents in the Life of a Slave Girl: Written by Herself," *Early African-American Classics*, ed. Anthony Appiah (New York: Bantam Book, 1990) 111-316; here 132.
18. *Die wilde Frau*, ed. Claudia Schmölders (Cologne: Eugen Diederichs, 1983) 67.
19. Wilhelm Reich, *The Mass Psychology of Fascism*, trans. Vincent R. Carfagno (New York: Farrar, Straus and Giroux, 1970). First published in 1933.
20. Compare Simone de Beauvoir, *Das andere Geschlecht* (Hamburg: Rowohlt, 1951) 12.
21. Felix Mitterer, *Die Kinder des Teufels. Ein Theaterstück und sein historischer Hintergrund: Mit Beiträgen von Heinz Nagl, Norbert Schindler, Meinrad Pizzinini* (Innsbruck: Haymon, 1989).
22. Felix Mitterer, "Christines Schoß," *An den Rand des Dorfes* (Vienna, Munich: Jugend und Volk, 1981) 115-22.
23. Norbert Schindler, "Die Entstehung der Unbarmherzigkeit. Zur Kultur und Lebensweise der Salzburger Bettler am Ende des 17. Jahrhunderts," *Kinder des Teufels* 134-45. The victims of the Zauberer-Jackl-Prozesse (1675-1690) were almost exclusively beggars and traveling comedians.
24. Elias Canetti, "Veza," *Die gelbe Straße* 6-7. Elias Canetti writes that his wife's convictions were close to those held by militant feminists but that she already held them in the interwar period. At the same time, she was not militant, duplicating the male-defined ambition to dominate. He maintains that Veza Canetti had high aspirations for women because she was convinced of their human potential.
25. He torments his wife and children deliberately and mercilessly, as Draga describes: "He has beaten the children, the *little* children! With his cane! With the shovel! With the knife! Save me from him!" (96).
26. Marlene Streeruwitz, *Und. Überhaupt. Stop* (Vienna: edition selene, 2000) 65-69. "Über die Geschlechtsorgane sind wir Frauen öffentlich. Über die Geschlechtsorgane ist das Bild der Frau öffentlich und meint immer die Geschlechtsorgane ... Pornographischer Pathos

hält die Erinnerung an die zu benützenden Geschlechtsorgane der Frau aufrecht. Der Playboy und Hustler Folger mit den Playmates des Monats. Jedes Pin up. Jeder Pirelli Kalendar. Die nicht anwesenden Geschlechtsorgane sind in der Darstellung anwesend."

27. Streeruwitz 79. "Die Frau ist heute eine weiterhin geduldete Mitspielerin im Geflecht der Marketingkonzepte. Eine im nationalistischen Sinn geduldete Minderheit. Toleriert. Wäre die Frau gleichberechtigt, hätte sie alles, was die teilnehmende Person ausmacht. Arbeit. Achtung. Würde."

Body, Voice, and Text in Elisabeth Reichart's Dramatic Monologue *Sakkorausch*

Laura Ovenden

Having established herself as a fictional prose writer, increasingly Elisabeth Reichart is venturing into the realms of drama. At one point in 1999, two productions of her work were simultaneously on the Austrian stage: a dramatization of her novel *Februarschatten* (1984, *February Shadows*, 1989) and a satire *Afrika*. In 2000, a German production of *Sakkorausch* (1994, *Foreign*, 2000) was on offer and Reichart's first play for children was planned.[1] In addition to these productions for the theater, Reichart has had two radio plays produced by Austrian State Radio: *Foreign* was transmitted in November 1995 and *Furien* (Furies) in March 1999.[2] The focus here is on the first text Reichart wrote for the theater: the dramatic monologue *Foreign*. The play revolves around an historical figure, the nineteenth-century Austrian philosopher Helene von Druskowitz, and raises questions concerning female subjectivity.[3] The aim of this article is, on the one hand, to explore the ways in which Reichart expresses this concept in terms of body, voice, and text in her own works and, on the other hand, to consider how these aspects have been treated on stage, i.e., to explore the theatrical realization of female subjectivity as presented by the author.

From her earliest texts, Reichart has made use of the modernist technique of the interior monologue, and an important reason for her use of this form relates to her key motivation for writing: to explore events, subjects or people repressed, tabooed or forgotten by society.[4] Thus in the novel *Komm über den See* (1988, Come Across the Lake) and the radio play *Furien*, the people to whom she lends a voice are the Austrian women involved in the resistance during the Second World War. In her most recent novel *Das vergessene Lächeln der Amaterasu* (1998, The Forgotten Smile of Amaterasu), the life and work of the long-neglected Italian Renaissance painter Artemisia Gentileschi runs as a leitmotif through the text.[5] Towards the end of this novel, when the text takes the form of a monologue and the references to Gentileschi become more frequent, the narrator addresses the artist directly and pays tribute to her by listing all her lost paintings. In such passages the narrator finds her own voice and Gentileschi's missing works are, at least within the monologue, redeemed from oblivion. This revoicing of historical figures through fictional ones is also informed by Reichart's historical and political awareness. She allows figures to speak who were not given recognition during their lifetime and, through their often anachronistic presence in her fictional texts, she creates links between the past, present, and future and contributes to contemporary political and feminist debate. This usually involves exposing the connections between patriarchy and fascism and the related issue of the potential violence inherent in language, a violence that can and has taken the form of suppression of the female voice.

Reichart's first work *February Shadows* focuses on such a suppressed voice. The recent dramatization of this novel highlighted the relationship between body, voice, and text. For this reason I shall now briefly discuss the text and how it was staged before turning to the main subject, *Foreign*. In contrast to the articulate narrator of *Foreign* who prophesies the horrors of the World Wars, the protagonist of *February Shadows* is inarticulate and forced to remember the past. Despite such an obvious difference, both texts explore notions of the female subject and in both texts the effects of war and the self-perpetuating nature of violence are constantly felt. In addition, the process of dramatizing the novel made manifest the parallels between *February Shadows* and *Foreign*, for in both the female voice is suppressed, the body subjugated, and writing offered as a potential, if fragile, mode of expression.

February Shadows, now in its sixth edition, was Reichart's hugely successful debut novel. The dramatic adaptation of the text was written by Brigitte Heusinger and Kai-Oliver Sass and premiered in Linz, Upper Austria, in October 1999. The historical event underlying the fictional text *February Shadows* is the massacre of escapees from the concentration camp at Mauthausen in February 1945.[6] The middle-aged protagonist Hilde witnessed this atrocity as a child and has repressed all memories of it ever since. The death of her husband, Anton, at the beginning of the novel marks the beginning of a long and painful *Erinnerungsarbeit* (labor of recollection). The repression of her individual voice is intimately connected to an event which had long been a taboo subject in Austria's recent past. At the same time, it is implied that as long as her husband was alive, articulation was impossible, suggesting that within a traditional marriage, a woman is not given access to speech: "It was hard to modulate one's own voice to his voice. A man who spoke so softly. Who does not like loud words. Hilde had only ever heard loud words. I practiced speaking softly."[7] Moreover, as her sister-in-law used to remind her, she did not deserve that right: "Without Anton you are nobody" (14). This lack of self-esteem also contributes to Hilde's many years of silence. Consequently, the female voice is muted by the combined forces of fascism and patriarchy.

In tracing Hilde's painful acquisition of a voice, Reichart links the historical situation of postwar Austria with that of women's subjectivity. The effects of the collective and personal process of witnessing, forgetting, and unwillingly remembering are explored in Hilde's gradual articulation. The effect of the long-term repression on Hilde's language is conveyed by the switching between first and third-person narration (as demonstrated in the first of the quotations above) and the short, disjointed sentences she produces.

Hilde's breathless and staccato stutterings, which are held together not by logic but by free association, proved particularly problematical on stage. This contradicted the expectations of the production team which had assumed that the close relationship between voice and text in the monologue form would ease the process of dramatization.⁸ However, according to Heusinger, the "fragmented, associative sentences" of Reichart's text, used by the author to retrace the gradual and unwilling resurfacing of fragments of memory, run the danger on stage of conferring an impression of insanity and thereby preventing audience identification.⁹ The dramatization employed several strategies to avoid this misinterpretation, which included giving Erika a larger role, providing more of a narrative thread at the beginning, and offering a pre-performance introduction to the text.¹⁰

In the novel, the regime of silence is enforced by physical abuse from a tyrannical father, as Hilde's repressed memory of the traumatic incident reveals. It is only her revulsion at the thought of having to dance with another woman at a pensioners' gathering that brings the memory to the surface:

> When the father had stopped kicking them, when they were both covered in bruises, when she crept into bed with the mother, yes crept, since she could not walk because of the pain, the mother comforted her, comforted her by simply allowing Hilde to cuddle up to her warm soft skin, so that her skin burned less, he stumbled into the bedroom after another liter of hard cider and shouted them apart. Had ripped them apart. Had shouted words at them which Hilde had since forgotten. Which continued to hurt her. As if the sound had penetrated her body. Never left her body again. And then she knew only that she had never touched the mother's body again, and never crept under the blanket to her again. (51-52)

As the quotation suggests, the physical abuse not only disturbed the relationship between Hilde and her mother, but also alienates Hilde from her own body. The image is of Hilde's body being scarred by abusive language. This stigma is then passed on to the next generation, as it becomes clear that Hilde's relationship to her own daughter has also been affected by the trauma of the past.

Hilde's disturbed relationship to her own body has political significance, too, for it represents the consequence of reifying women in patriarchal society; the father's assumed right to possess and abuse his wife and children is a key example of the unequal status of the sexes in patriarchal societies, which feminists have highlighted and criticized. On stage this reification of the female must be conveyed by the actor's estranged relationship to her body. In the dramatization it was effectively conveyed by Hilde's mechanical, puppet-like movements and the way she physically repelled Erika's signs of physical affection.

Hilde's initial puppet-like movements on stage have an additional function. In Reichart's text, Erika is writing a book about her mother, and the movements of the actor can suggest that Hilde is literally coming to life through the writing process. With this use of the female body on stage, the dramatization managed to convey the self-referentiality of the novel, which is a text about the genesis of a text. Only through her daughter's act of writing does Hilde manage to regain some sense of her own subjectivity. On stage this was conveyed by Erika frequently speaking for the mother at the beginning of the play as she quotes from her book. Gradually, however, the process is reversed. The object becomes subject and Hilde slowly attains the sovereignty she has by the end of the novel.[11] Finally, both texts (Reichart's and Erika's) can be seen as attempts to understand the generation who experienced the war, as a type of personal and political *Vergangenheitsbewältigung* (coming to terms with the past). The difficulty of such an attempt on both levels is apparent in the highly ambivalent ending of the novel.

As I have suggested above, the form of the monologue, which dominates *February Shadows*, is an effective vehicle for problematizing the articulation of the female protagonist. Language remains the focus of this literary form as retreating into silence would result in the literal disappearance of the first-person narrator.[12] The associative style of the monologue can create the impression however of insanity, which would be inappropriate for *February Shadows* and was therefore carefully avoided in the stage production. In *Foreign* the associative, fragmented sentences can also create the impression of insanity but, as we will see and in contrast to *February Shadows*, this perception is not discouraged. It is, however, then subjected to critical scrutiny within the monologue itself.

Reichart was commissioned to write the dramatic text *Foreign* for the 1994 *Wiener Festwochen* (the Vienna Festival) and she took as her subject the real Helene von Druskowitz.[13] In Reichart's text, she frequently quotes from Druskowitz's *Pessimistische Kardinalsätze* (1905, Pessimistic Axioms); in fact, she lists Druskowitz as her "co-author."[14] As this approach makes clear, Reichart is revoicing a female precursor. In a stage production, however, body, voice, and text are combined, for Druskowitz is not only revoiced but reincarnated, and at the same time Reichart incorporates into her own text unmarked but verbatim passages from Druskowitz's writings.

In Helene von Druskowitz (1856-1918) we have a woman whose body was confined, whose voice was, if not actually repressed, then allowed at the least to descend into silence, and many of whose texts have disappeared. Druskowitz was the first Austrian woman to receive a doctorate in Zurich in 1878 and she published a considerable number of philosophical and literary texts. In 1891, at the age of thirty-five she was committed to a psychiatric hospital and she remained incarcerated until her death. Her lack of physical freedom during this period did not, however, prevent her from publishing further. Her ironic and polemical manifesto *Pessimistische Kardinalsätze*, which can be seen as a call for radical separatist feminism, appeared after she had spent fourteen years of her life in an asylum. There, it seems, Druskowitz led the life of an active, if lonely, feminist writer. In her asylum medical notes, we are told that of the various forms of medication given to her she preferred paraldehyde because it reminded her of schnapps, that she smoked a pipe, composed poems in praise of alcohol, wrote illegible plays, sent androphobic satires to feminist periodicals, hallucinated and talked to herself at night.[15] Despite the fact that the reports also note that she was harmless, good-natured, and civil to her wardens, her unorthodox behavior was certainly a threat to the social order of patriarchal society and therefore reason enough to keep her incarcerated.

In his classic work *Madness and Civilization: A History of Insanity in the Age of Reason*, Michel Foucault presents reason and madness not as universally objective categories but as the outcome of historical processes. He shows how attitudes and "discursive practices" concerning the mad have evolved, how in different periods insane people have been tolerated or even valued by society and allowed to wander freely, while in later periods they have been excluded, confined, and reduced to silence. Not until the nineteenth century, however, was madness medicalized as mental illness and the asylum assigned a therapeutic rather than punitive role. Although Foucault does not address women specifically, his study is useful for feminists for it shows how discursive regimes have changed over the centuries with the intention of controlling and confining people. This understanding of discourse is important for feminist historians who have demonstrated that in the nineteenth century "a close association between femininity and pathology became firmly established within the scientific, literary and popular discourse."[16]

Such a discourse suggests that the incarceration of Helene von Druskowitz may have had less to do with providing therapeutic treatment and more with controlling a dissenting, angry female voice. The literary study, *The Madwoman in the Attic*, investigates the life-threatening effect of the dominant, patriarchal discourse upon women writers of the period:

> If contemporary women do now attempt the pen with energy and authority, they are able to do so only because their eighteenth and nineteenth-century foremothers struggled in isolation that felt like illness, alienation that felt like madness, obscurity that felt like paralysis, to overcome the

anxiety of authorship that was endemic to their literary subculture."[17]

The description offered here by Gilbert and Gubar poignantly depicts Druskowitz's own alienated situation in the asylum.

At the beginning of *Foreign*, Reichart dramatizes the dominant, patriarchal discourses of the female body by putting an incarcerated woman on stage. Furthermore, her subject is a woman whose body was in the hands of male doctors who attempted to control it with drugs. Reichart does not, however, simply dramatize this subjection of the female body by medical discourse. She has a voice rise above the subjected body, a voice which remains both self-conscious and ironic. The repetition of the self-assured "I" at the beginning of the text is the first indication that Druskowitz is confident of her own abilities and sense of self. It is also expressive of the anger and stubborn resistance which Reichart admires in Druskowitz and gives literary form.[18] Her voice can be heard throughout the monologue, and it indicates that Druskowitz sees through her incarceration and the attempts to supposedly heal her body and mind: "For twenty-three years they have been trying in vain to drive me crazy with all available means. Paraldehyde daily. Supposedly to cure me. But the doctors themselves are the affliction. So afflicted are they that they would have to drink it in liters to be cured" (116). Through the irony and self-assurance of her words, Druskowitz subverts the discourse of those responsible for her incarceration – "these ignorant bunglers" (109) – and she does so frequently with humorous superiority.[19]

In the first production of *Foreign* for the Vienna Festival, in which the significance of the relationship between body and voice was emphasized in the subtitle *Eine Installation für Körper und Stimme* (An Installation for Body and Voice), a dancer performed alongside the narrator, thereby presenting in visual form the disparity between her female body and her provocative sentences. The combination of a female dancer and a female speaker symbolized the ambiguous and divided life of Druskowitz. The dancer was counterpointed against video screens which projected the "talking head" of the narrator. With this contrast of physical human movement and static machinery, the violent separation of voice and body was given a powerful image. The image of a female dancer also conveyed the historical Druskowitz's tenacity and the forces of resistance in her: the incarcerated body still insisted on expression even if in the form of the disembodied voice. The dancing female is, however, an ambiguous sign. On the one hand she can symbolize freedom of expression and the female in charge of her own body, while on the other the display of the body as commodity can be interpreted as a form of objectification of the female. If the image of the female dancer is viewed positively, the reification is reversed in the sense that the dancer is in control of her body and can be seen as subject rather than object. With this complex of associations the public performance of *Foreign* in Vienna drew attention to, re-enacted, and reversed those painful processes concerned with female subjectivity and the reification of the female.

Related closely to these dominant discourses of the nineteenth century is Reichart's choice of "Sakkorausch" from the long list of pseudonyms Helene von Druskowitz adopted during her literary career.[20] The pseudonym can be seen as a key to the text and any successful performance of it, because it relates closely to issues of female subjectivity. Literally, the name is a combination of the German words for "jacket" and "exhilaration" or "intoxication." The term *Sakko*, which usually refers to a loose-fitting jacket for men, could allude to the nineteenth-century convention of women writers adopting male pseudonyms in order to hide their gender from readers and public. In the Stuttgart production, this convention and its impact upon the female body and mind was visualized in Druskowitz's costume, consisting of a series of men's gray suit-jackets strung together to form a train that encumbered her as she walked. During the course of the play she gradually dismantles the guise, indicating that it is only a screen and that in fact she is dissecting patriarchal discourse.

In addition, the term *Sakko* suggests that Druskowitz is performing masculinity, i.e., usurping the role of a man, an interpretation strengthened by the real Druskowitz's pipe-smoking and predilection for alcohol. My use of the term "performing" refers to Judith Butler's study *Gender Trouble* (1990) where, drawing on Foucault, she analyzes the way in which we construct categories to understand sex, gender, and desire. Joseph Bristow explains:

> Butler uses the word performative to describe how the body provides a surface upon which various acts and gestures accrue gendered meanings. What she calls "corporeal signification" reveals that gender does not appeal to an ontological essence granted by nature. Rather the widespread belief that there is indeed a core gender identity actually depends on performative acts that give the illusion of naturalness.[21]

Through performative acts, we learn to become women or men, feminine or masculine. Elsewhere in *Foreign* the narrator refers to such social conditioning: "I played the good girl far too long" (124). The female masculinity which the real Druskowitz displayed in the asylum could, therefore, be an example of the crossing of accepted gender roles. Such behavior was and still is often seen as a distinct challenge to the social order. Although not referred to directly by Reichart, most biographical essays also mention the lesbian love affair described by the author herself during internment in the asylum. There is little material to substantiate Druskowitz's statement, but admitting what would certainly have been termed sexual deviancy at the time probably contributed to her being labeled insane.

The *Rausch* of the pseudonym seems to refer to Nietzsche's dionysian principle of intoxication, as introduced in *The Birth of Tragedy*. It is a principle associated with the aesthetic disposition: in this state of ecstasy, the genius, assumed to be male, is provided with prophetic inspiration for his work.[22] Here again Reichart's Druskowitz usurps the role of the male genius in her desire to be inebriated: "Drinking lends wings to my mind, lightens my thoughts. Alcohol loosens one's dependence on matter" (111).

Reichart does not, however, leave it at a performance of genius; she calls into question the whole concept of genius by thematizing not only the performance of genius but also the discourse of the performance of genius. Just as the earlier novel *February Shadows* was self-consciously about the process of writing, the novel *Foreign* presents the performance of the performance of genius, and this performance is then performed on stage.

For a late-twentieth-century audience a woman performing genius inevitably calls to mind the image of the madwoman in the attic, and Reichart plays with this association. For example, in the sixth line of the monologue the figure of Druskowitz asserts self-consciously: "My sentences prove my insanity" (105). The audience has to decide, therefore, whether the words that follow are informed by the clarity and/or irony of this sentence. Here and elsewhere the narrator is playing up the role of the patient. In other words, she assumes the position she has been forced into by others and performs it in an exaggerated way. This performative irony is one way in which Reichart subverts the assumption of madness.

The self-conscious performance of insanity is further supported and enhanced through the form of the interior monologue. In *Foreign*, the sentences of the text are held together by associative logic. The predominance of free association could be a sign of Druskowitz's insanity on the one hand or simply her loneliness on the other. After all, the incarcerated female philosopher Druskowitz had no one with whom to share her ideas. The disjunctive style serves to remind us that this monologue is a frustrated dialogue. Again Reichart's text calls into question the automatic assumption of madness, leaving the reader or audience to decide.

The opening of *Foreign* thematizes the relationship between body, voice, and text, a relationship that characterizes the entire novel. It begins with a spatial image: Druskowitz is stationary and looking out through a window. Although she is imprisoned, the emphasis is on a sense of movement, of falling: "The setting sun. / One of the countless sunsets that I saw through this window, that I will see. / I'm falling into its descent. / I'm descending, down. / Above me my sentences, my names" (105). This sense of downward movement is counterbalanced in the second section, this time in the flying mentioned in the seemingly random snatch of folksong.[23] The fear of disappearing or dying and the desire of the incarcerated body to be free are both expressed in these acts of falling and flying. Furthermore, flying and falling can be understood as the dramatic realization of the states of mind which in their extreme form of patriarchal, medical discourse are known as mania and depression. Hence the acts of falling and flying run as a leitmotif throughout the monologue, concluding with "FLY, Your Highness, FLY" at the very end (128).

The German word *Untergang*, translated above as "descent," evokes a number of related associations, including decline, the act of going under, death, or disappearing into darkness.[24] The opening of the monologue thereby hints at a connection between the subjection of the female body and the discourse of war, a parallel which in Druskowitz's work *Pessimistische Kardinalsätze* ultimately leads to the end of the world. Only later, however, does this connection become clear as we discover that the monologue is set at the outbreak of the First World War, and only later does the narrator make anachronistic reference to the Second World War. In the Stuttgart production of *Foreign*, in contrast, these parallels were made blatant from the first scene. The play opened with the actor lying on the floor entombed, as if in a coffin, in her elaborate patchwork of jackets, including military uniforms, with the sunset casting a shadow over her. This opening scene thus emphasized the connection between the three *Untergänge* of the sun, the world, and Helene von Druskowitz. In light of this, then, the narrator's descriptions of her male tormentors, though sometimes funny, are never harmless, for she sees a destructive conjunction between men and their bodies that culminates in the brutality and destruction of war. The narrator's sober prophetic vision – "I see them erecting stones. / Grave stones. / But they just chisel in names. / The earth remains free of bones. They even make up a name for it: / war memorial" (119) – reminds the reader of the drastic destruction wrought on the bodies of men in their millions during

World War One. Thus Reichart problematizes the representation of the male body in terms of the historical continuum of war.

Despite its emphasis on the single female voice, *Foreign* is in various ways a multivoiced text. Anachronistic passages which seem to allude to the Second World War – "long after I am gone that other dying will begin, / no one will believe that it started with my dying" (123) – can be understood as projected voices offering futile prophecies. Other examples of anachronism highlight the acts of witnessing and remembering, such as the use of the first person in the second line of the monologue – "I saw ... I will see" – and link past and future tenses in a manner similar to *February Shadows*. The third section of the beginning of *Foreign* provides an example of anachronism that can be related to Austria's recent past. Rather than suggesting the hallucinations of the mentally disturbed, the personified image of sentences bearing witness against the writer calls to mind the book burning of the Thirties and the violent intentions behind such censorship implied in the line: "Step right up! Witness away! And step on it!" (105). All these examples link the omnipresence of war with the suppression of the female voice through incarceration, repressed memories, and a lack of freedom of speech. The perpetuation of this suppression of the female voice is conveyed in the linking of tenses.

The monologue also contains a variety of voices that can be related to the position of women in the nineteenth century. Marie von Ebner Eschenbach's patronizing advice to Druskowitz reflects dominant thinking of the time: "'My child, what do you intend to live on? ... You are mad to reject this marriage proposal again'" (114). The feminine literary voice of Elizabeth Barrett Browning is audible in her poem "My Doves," and the strident radical voice of Helene von Druskowitz is heard in the radical feminist proposals from her *Pessimistische Kardinalsätze* which pepper the monologue. In addition to this stridency, the text provides many opportunities for the voice of the monologist to express madness, anger, resignation, and weariness. The variety of voices can be differentiated in performance and the rich acoustic qualities in the text, produced by the alliteration and the wordplays, can be drawn out.

Juxtaposed to these voices from the past is a contemporary voice that serves to refute positions and attitudes from the past by revealing where these positions or attitudes have in the meantime led. For example, the destruction inherent in the dominant male discourse is shown to result inevitably in war with the following reference to the grim legacy of the First World War and fascism: "With pus from wounds that will not heal they will feed their children and their children's children, and thereby nurture the next war, with all the care they can muster" (119). The disillusioned description of the achievements of female emancipation is also clearly written from a contemporary perspective, and again the gap in time functions to highlight the falsity of a hope still prevalent today: "He will offer the woman some few morsels and persuade her that these crumbs are half the power" (116).

Again anachronism is used to devastating effect when the birdlike language associated with the poet "Elizabeth" is implicitly contrasted with appalling neologisms reminiscent of the Third Reich – *"Maulschande"* and *"Blutschaum"* translated here as "mixed mouths" and "mongrel blood" (126). The narrator suggests that the cacophony of vile expressions drowns out any other language, while her reference to "pitiful, empty phrases" (126) seems to imply that contemporary language is equally suspect. The author herself describes present-day speech as *Gerede*, or meaningless blather.[25] In an article written before *Foreign* was published, but equally applicable to it, Konstanze Fliedl describes the dilemma of Reichart's protagonists as follows: "Reichart's young heroines will rebel against exclusion from the dominant discourse – only to find themselves faced with the problem that the language they are fighting for is at the same time irredeemably compromised, that there are no longer any untainted words."[26]

The tenuousness of the female voice is represented in the figure of Elizabeth, who silently feeds the birds in the asylum grounds. This woman seems to be either a figment of the narrator's imagination or another asylum inmate whom she associates with her favorite English poet, Elizabeth Barrett Browning.[27] Druskowitz tries to coax Elizabeth out of her silence: "I will read your poems aloud to you. / I always carry them with me. / I feel them in the palm of my hand, which reaches into thin air. / Force of habit" (106). However, Elizabeth, who is mistreated by the guards and dies during the monologue, cannot live the type of feminism embodied by Druskowitz's radical separatism. In the monologue, the figure of Elizabeth seems to represent the broken, silent madwoman Druskowitz refuses to become. Although inspired by her poems, the narrator has in Elizabeth a warning of what could happen if she gives up speaking or writing. Silence would soon result in death.

Indeed, it is only after Elizabeth's death that her poem, "My Doves," returns fully to Druskowitz's memory: "Her life in exchange for a poem" (127). This is one of several examples in the monologue where the role of text is highlighted. Here the poem is transformed into voice since the incarcerated Druskowitz does not have access to the written text. Consequently, through the relationship depicted between the two figures and the poem, Reichart underlines the tenuousness of remembering. The scene demonstrates how *Erinnerungsarbeit* (the labor of recollection) is not about finding something lost in the past, but about reconstructing memory at a specific point in time with remembered fragments. As a result, the monologue presents not only the experience of an individual remembering, but comments on the socio-political aspect of the labor of recollection.[28]

Such remembered fragments can of course take the form of texts or memories. As a qualified historian who collected fragile written evidence in the form of political *Flugblätter* (leaflets) and interviewed Austrian resistance fighters for her doctoral thesis, Reichart is acutely aware of the varying degrees of importance attached to written as opposed to spoken accounts of events. Within the field of historiography written texts are often considered more important and reliable than witness accounts, and it is also important to note that it is more likely that women's voices are heard in oral history projects than in traditional histories. Consequently, if we focus on *Foreign* as a piece of writing rather than as a monologue, its significance as written evidence documenting the past and the irony of the reader reading a document of the lost voice of Helene von Druskowitz are foregrounded. Quotations from the *Pessimistische Kardinalsätze* also remind us of all the other lost texts by Druskowitz, above all her many plays, while the presence of the monologue *Foreign* underlines the fact that some voices are allowed to remain in the form of texts, while others are lost.

The receptacle for such written texts in Reichart's monologue is the battered leather handbag to which Druskowitz refers repeatedly. It is the central leitmotif that holds the highly associative text together.[29] Druskowitz provides detailed physical descriptions of it that enable the reader to form a mental picture. On occasion, the reader is even told of the handbag's practical purpose: to keep safe the narrator's plays, manifesto, and perfume as well as Elizabeth's poems and birdseed. The illusion of its physical presence is, however, soon dispelled as the theme of its absence establishes itself. The significance of the handbag lies in the fact that it is not there, that it has been stolen.

This leitmotif connects all three aspects of body, voice, and text. It can be seen as a multilayered metaphor for female subjectivity. The mother of the narrator is described as the source of the handbag: "The only present from my mother" (107), suggesting that the bag can be seen as a metonym for the female body. This interpretation is reinforced by the fact that without her bag Druskowitz feels naked: "As if they had skinned me. / No skin. No bag" (107). The obvious Freudian symbolism of the handbag as womb is reinforced by the fact that Elizabeth keeps her birdseed in it. The bag is also associated with female sexuality; it is the site of repressed desires and has a "voracious" appetite (108): "I want to go to Africa, the leather whispered to me, as I tried to fall asleep upon it. / The leather sought after its body; I sought sleep. Nevertheless we never reached Africa" (106). The narrator's feelings for the bag oscillate between yearning and hatred, suggesting that women's views of their bodies are also complex and influenced by both psychological and social factors.

Finally, the bag is associated with the female voice and the stealing of it is seen as an attempt to silence the narrator: "They stole my bag from me on purpose because of the imminent outbreak of war. / I protest against this expropriation of my mind" (113). It is the locus of the central text for *Foreign*, Druskowitz's radical manifesto. In the monologue, the narrator is concerned that the contents of her handbag, especially her manifesto, may be incriminating: "That is why they stole my bag! To use it as testimony against me!" (120). However, towards the end of *Foreign* the narrator seems to have reconciled herself with the disappearance of the bag: "I no longer need my bag. Elizabeth will never again miss her bird food. It will rot in the bag. The rot will spread to my works. It will all just rot away. / Only my manifesto must be saved. I must memorize it" (127). The suggestion is that by memorizing her manifesto the narrator can overcome the fragility of the written text. The spoken word, oral history, seems to have the last word on this occasion.

In her creation of the leitmotif of the handbag, Reichart has managed to link the specific situation of Druskowitz with wider issues concerning female subjectivity. She has taken a traditional symbol of femininity and reinvested it with contradictory meanings in order to portray the complexity of the relationship between the female body, the female voice, and the woman-authored text. In addition, she has highlighted the position of the female subject in the past, the present, and the future, and she has underlined the precariousness of this voice.

In both *February Shadows* and *Foreign*, Reichart's literary exploration of female subjectivity is complex and intertwined. In her linking and thematizing of the three aspects of body, voice, and text, she gives concrete form to this often abstract concept. This is particularly striking when she gives examples of the effects of patriarchy and fascism on the female body and voice. In my analysis of *Foreign* I demonstrated that this exploration of female subjectivity works on many levels, from the form of the monologue and the allusions in the title, to the intertwining of body, voice, and text in the opening passage. In her creation of the handbag, Reichart provides an important thread through the associative text, a leitmotif which, however, broadens and complicates the issues of female subjectivity even further. Any successful theatrical realization of this monologue needs to draw out these various levels in the text and keep the levels of fantasy and reality fluid in order to make the audience ask why the actor appears insane. If a dramatic production explores the nexus of body, voice, and text and manages thereby to avoid a reductive interpretation of the text, it will do justice to a fascinating historical figure and a fascinating dramatic text.[30]

Notes

1. *Februarschatten* premiered 9 October 1999 in the *Kammerspiele Landestheater*, Linz, directed by Brigitte Heusinger. *Afrika: Eine Einbildung* premiered 8 November 1999 at the *Theater Drachengasse*, Vienna, directed by Christine Wipplinger. *Sakkorausch: Eine Installation für Körper und Stimme* premiered at the *Wiener Festwochen* on 26 May 1994 and was directed by Martina Winkel and Airan Berg. *Sakkorausch: Ein Monolog* premiered 1 July 2000 in the *Theater Rampe*, Stuttgart, directed by Eva Hoesmann. *Inselfeier: Eine Farce* premiered 12 December 1996 in Salzburg at the Mozarteum, directed by Bernd Jeschek.

2. *Sakkorausch* broadcast on 14 November 1995 and *Furien* on 9 March 1999, both by ORF (Austrian Broadcasting Corporation).

3. For an overview of feminist theoretical positions on female subjectivity, see the introductory chapter of Stephanie Bird's *Recasting Historical Women: Female Identity in German Biographical Fiction* (Oxford: Berg, 1998) 1-25.

4. See Laura Ovenden, "Writing in the Margins: Elisabeth Reichart's 'Auseinandersetzung mit Tabubereichen oder mit Verschwiegenem,'" *Literature, Markets and Media in Germany and Austria*, ed. A. Williams, S. Parkes, and J. Preece (Bern: Lang, 2000) 99-114.

5. Artemisia Gentileschi was "rediscovered" several years ago and is now a subject of much feminist art history; Helene von

Druskowitz is, as a result of the *Pessimistische Kardinalsätze* which were reissued by a small feminist publishing house in 1988, no longer unknown within feminist circles. However, outside of feminist research both are still relatively unknown. Reichart, *Komm über den See* (Frankfurt/M.: Fischer, 1988), *Das vergessene Lächeln der Amaterasu* (Berlin: Aufbau, 1998).

6. On 2 February 1945 around 500 of the 570 prisoners of war held in the concentration camp Mauthausen in Upper Austria escaped. The National Socialists with the help of the local inhabitants, who until that point considered themselves apolitical, hunted down and murdered the majority of the men, mainly Soviet officers, as they hid in the surrounding countryside. Only seventeen of the escapees are known to have survived. This massacre was rarely discussed during the immediate postwar years and referred to as "The Rabbit Hunt of the Mill District."

7. *February Shadows*, trans. Donna L. Hoffmeister (Riverside, CA: Ariadne Press, 1989) 15. Subsequent references to this translation are cited in my text with page number.

8. Brigitte Heusinger, "Annäherung an *Februarschatten*," original contribution for the Linz *Landestheater* program, 1999/ 2000, No. 6, 6. Translation mine.

9. Heusinger explains: "For the author, it was important that at the moment of Anton's death, chinks appear in the armor of Hilde's repression and diffuse fragments of memory are forced to the surface. For the stage version, however, this would have meant our having to establish the character of Hilde by means of fragmented, associative sentences, which work well when written but which on stage would make her appear crazier than she is and thus hinder the creation of a theatrical character with whom one can also identify." Heusinger 9-10. Translation mine.

10. I would like to thank Brigitte Heusinger for kindly providing me with a copy of the stage script.

11. In her afterword to the second edition of *February Shadows* Christa Wolf writes: "The author does not want to do to her pro-

tagonist what was done to her during her whole life. She does not want to make an object out of her." Wolf, "Nachwort: 'Struktur von Erinnerung,'" Reichart, *Februarschatten: Roman* (Berlin/GDR: Aufbau, 1985); new edition (Berlin: Aufbau Taschenbuch, 1997) 118; *February Shadows* 144.

12. This is precisely what happens in Reichart's story *Fotze*, which was published in 1993 and ends with the first-person narrator descending into silence. Reichart, *Fotze* (Salzburg: Otto Müller, 1993).

13. *Sakkorausch*, Vienna production. See Roland Koberg "Weltreise ohne Ziel," *Falter* 27 May-2 June 1994: 18.

14. *Foreign*, trans. Linda C. DeMeritt, *La Valse and Foreign by Elisabeth Reichart* (New York: SUNY, 2000) 99-136. Subsequent references to this translation are cited in my text with page number.

15. See Hinrike Gronewold, "Die geistige Amazone," *WahnsinnsFrauen*, ed. Sibylle Duda and Luise Pusch (Frankfurt/M.: Suhrkamp, 1992) 96-122; and Ursula Kubes-Hofmann, "Berichte über zwei 'Entartete,'" *Die Frauen Wiens*, ed. Eva Geber, Sonja Rotter, and Marietta Schneider (Vienna: AUF-ed, Der Apfel, 1992) 126-40.

16. Jane Ussher, *Women's Madness: Misogyny or Mental Illness?* (London: Harvester Wheatsheaf, 1991) 64.

17. Sandra M. Gilbert and Susan Gubar, *The Madwoman in the Attic* (New Haven: Yale, 1979) 51.

18. See Reichart's essay "Frauentafel" (Woman's Fate) which accompanies the monologue, 131-36.

19. Interestingly, in the radio play where the voice is disembodied, the listener is made most aware of the isolation and loneliness of Druskowitz, and the fragility of the disregarded female voice is underlined.

20. Further pseudonyms included Adalbert Brunn, H. Foreign, H. Sakrosankt, Erna, and von Calagis. The English translation uses the pseudonym "Foreign" as its title.

21. Joseph Bristow, *Sexuality* (London: Routledge, 1997) 214.

22. Christine Battersby, *Gender and Genius* (London: Women's Press, 1989).

23. In one commentary on the ladybird rhyme, which has numerous foreign parallels, it is seen as a charm intended to speed the sun across the dangers of sunset, an interpretation which shows the snatch of song at the beginning of *Foreign* to be anything but random since it is the monologist's response to the setting sun. See Lina Eckenstein, *Comparative Studies in Nursery Rhymes* (London: Duckworth, 1906), specifically Chapter IX on "Custom Rhymes."

24. The German term also calls to mind the popular philosophy of history by Oswald Spengler, *Der Untergang des Abendlandes* (1918, *The Decline of the West*, 1932) in which the author captured the contemporary mood of Germany and predicted the disastrous results of the Nazi regime.

25. See Reichart's interview with Karl Müller, *Deutsche Bücher*, XXVII.2: 88-98.

26. Konstanze Fliedl, "Etymology of Violence: Elisabeth Reichart's Prose," *Contemporary German Writers, Their Aesthetics and Their Language*, ed. Arthur Williams, Stuart Parkes, and Julian Preece (Bern: Lang, 1996) 251-66; here 255.

27. See Druskowitz's laudatory essay on Elizabeth Barrett Browning in her study *Drei englische Dichterinnen* (Berlin, 1885).

28. In this sense Reichart's work is reminiscent of Christa Wolf's. See Ortrud Gutjahr, "'Erinnerte Zukunft': Gedächtnisrekonstruktion und Subjektkonstitution im Werk Christa Wolfs," *Erinnerte Zukunft. Studien zum Werk Christa Wolfs*, ed. Wolfram Mauser (Würzburg: Königshausen & Neumann, 1985) 53-80.

29. For a discussion of the role of metaphor and metonymy in associative, modernist texts such as *Foreign*, see David Lodge, *The Modes of Modern Writing: Metaphor, Metonymy, and the Typology of Modern Literature* (Ithaca, NY: Cornell UP, 1977) 73-124.

30. I would like to thank Robert Gillett for his helpful comments on an earlier draft of this article.

Staging Superficiality: Elfriede Jelinek's *Ein Sportstück*

Linda C. DeMeritt

Elfriede Jelinek's numerous plays over the past twenty years have elicited a variety of responses from critics and audiences: outrage, vociferous rejection, scandal, laudatory applause, pointed silence – but seldom indifference. Even while she was earning accolades and her plays were proclaimed best of the year in Germany, the most important theaters in Austria periodically refused to premiere or produce her work. Even as her reputation as one of the most important new literary voices not only in the German-speaking world, but indeed internationally became indisputable, she was reviled on political posters in her homeland. And then, on 23 January 1998, Einar Schleef's production of Jelinek's *Ein Sportstück* (1998, A SportsPlay) premiered at Vienna's national theater, the *Burgtheater*, and was greeted with fifty-five minutes of standing ovation. Critics have also for the most part praised both text and performance. With this success, Austria's foremost *Nestbeschmutzer* seemingly moved into the mainstream.

Some of the controversy surrounding Jelinek, especially in her own homeland, most certainly has to do with the themes the author addresses, specifically with her portrayal of virulent fascism, xenophobia, and misogyny in contemporary Austrian society. The vehement response her work elicits can perhaps serve as an indicator of the pertinence of her social critique. The playwright's dramatic techniques, however, are equally provocative. Jelinek has stated repeatedly that she writes against the theater and its stated repeatedly that she writes against the theater and its conventions. Her rejection of traditional theater is most evident in the superficiality of her plays, or to use the author's own words, in the intended "shallowness" of her theater. Jelinek's dramatic language recalls her recent prose works, and its density and high level of abstraction are challenging to realize on stage. According to Corina Caduff, the playwright "disembodies" her actors. In other words, the actor's body is not accessible in either a metaphorical or physical sense, and this absence of corporeality is one reason for the less than enthusiastic response to some of her earlier dramas.[1] The depthlessness of her drama as a whole – the absence of action, of dialogue, and of psychologically motivated characters – renders Jelinek's dramatic work "undramatic"; her concept of the theater is antithetical to conventional assumptions about theatricality.

The text of *Ein Sportstück* provides an opportunity to explore several questions that are of significance to Jelinek's theater pieces in general, for it epitomizes the lack of depth that typifies all of her works, both dramatic and prose. Such "shallowness" can and has been termed postmodern, but Jelinek's aesthetics are always engaged, just as her linguistic experimentation is consistently motivated by a political purpose. Schleef's production of the play poses broader questions concerning the relationship between playwright and director and, in addition, raises concerns as to the realization of Jelinek's "shallowness" on stage. Here the issue is whether the staging, like the text, is able to ground its superficiality within the seriousness of societal critique.

Jelinek's Plays: An Overview

Jelinek's first drama, *Was geschah, nachdem Nora ihren Mann verlassen hatte, oder, Stützen der Gesellschaften* (1979; *What Happened after Nora Left Her Husband, or Pillars of Society*, 1994), premiered in October 1979 as part of the experimental *steirischer herbst* in Graz with Kurt Josef Schildknecht as director. As Allyson Fiddler has pointed out, the author's theatrical debut has been unjustifiably dismissed or neglected by critics, for it anticipates later dramas both formally and thematically.² The play makes extensive use of citation and parody, most obviously through its intertextual references to Ibsen. Furthermore, it presents the question of a woman's right to self-determination and liberation within the context of a patriarchy connected to fascism as well as within the confines of a materialism based on the marketing and control of people as commodities.

In her second drama, *Clara S. Musikalische Tragödie* (1981, Clara S. Musical Tragedy), Jelinek again utilizes the aesthetic technique of montage, incorporating unmarked historical texts into her own and commenting upon those texts through juxtaposition. The drama portrays the powerlessness and isolation of female artists within a society determined by capitalist structures, and it questions the possibility of authenticity or artistic originality, thereby thematizing the very issue posed formally through the montage technique. *Clara S.*, which was scheduled to premiere at the *steirischer herbst* in 1981, was cancelled under a cloud of scandal. The premiere of the play one year later at the *Schauspielhaus* in Bonn under the direction of Hans Hollmann marks the beginning for Jelinek of a decade-long hiatus from the Austrian stage.

In 1985, Horst Zankl directed the premiere of *Burgtheater. Posse mit Gesang* at the *Werkstatttheater* in Bonn. This drama highlights the theme of everyday fascism already present in Jelinek's two earlier plays, showing the reflection and perpetuation of fascist thought in language. The historical subtext is the speech of the *Burgtheater* itself, as represented particularly through Paula Wessely and Attila Hörbiger. It illustrates the continuity between propaganda under Hitler and the *Heimatfilm* of the fifties, and in doing so prompted yet another scandal in Austria. The *feuilletons* accused Jelinek of character defamation, even of "murdering" Wessely,³ and Jelinek responded by stipulating the *Burgtheater* as the only theater in Austria that would ever be allowed to stage the piece. The scandal is of interest because it derives from a misunderstanding characteristic of Jelinek's reception, namely that her dramas are realistic and historically accurate, that they are about people rather than language, real-life figures as opposed to "figures of speech."[4]

In 1987, Hollmann directed the third of the Bonn premieres, *Krankheit oder Moderne Frauen* (1987, Malady or Modern Women), which depicts the impossibility or non-existence of the existence of woman as expressed through the metaphor of the lesbian vampire. One year later, Hans Hoffer directed the premiere of *Wolken. Heim* (1988, Cloud.Cuckoo.Land.), Jelinek's investigation of German nationalism and its origins within philosophical idealism and her most radical realization thus far of the attempt "to let language coax forth and criticize its own ideological potential."[5] It consists almost exclusively of quotations, sometimes rendered accurately, sometimes distorted, and all spoken in one long monologue by an all-encompassing "we" that stamps out dialogue, difference, and otherness.

It was the Viennese *Volkstheater* under the direction of Emmy Werner that brought Jelinek's plays back to the Austrian stage, beginning with *Krankheit* in 1990. The success of this and subsequent plays enabled the playwright's breakthrough in her own homeland, and in 1992 the *Akademietheater*, smaller sister to the *Burgtheater*, offered the world premiere of Jelinek's next drama, *Totenauberg* (1991, *Death/Valley/Summit*, 1996), directed by Manfred Karge. This play, which portrays past and present fascism in such discourses as sports, the ecology movement, tourism, and racism, was named play of the year by the German periodical *Theater heute*. Claus Peymann himself, head of the *Burgtheater*, directed the premiere of Jelinek's next play, *Raststätte oder Sie machens alle* (1993, Truck Stop or Everyone's Doing It), again in the *Akademietheater*. Although Jelinek apparently returns to a more traditional form for this drama, using scenes, dialogue, and even characters with names, her text is nonetheless highly artificial and exaggerated, a biting satire of capitalism's triumph over socialism culminating in a market free-for-all of buying and selling. Hyped as a scandalously pornographic farce that would force director and playwright to leave the country,[6] Peymann's staging was in fact tame, reducing the scenes of wild debauchery to a realistic portrayal with a clear moralistic message rather than allowing his imagination the free and ambivalent rein of parody.[7]

The scathing reviews of this play, in addition to the numerous scandals and negative publicity that had embroiled Jelinek since her literary debut, prompted what the author termed an "inner emigration."[8] She refused all interviews and the world premiere of her next play, *Stecken, Stab und Stangl: Eine Handarbeit* (1997, Stick, Staff, and Pole: A Needlework), directed by Thirza Bruncken, took place not in Vienna but in Hamburg. Yet, the play foregrounds an Austrian event – the brutally xenophobic murder of four Romany gypsies in Oberwart, Burgenland – and it decries the further brutalization of the event through a media monopolized by the political right. The title encapsulates the multilayered and ambiguous linguistic surfaces of the text: *Stecken* and *Stab* refer to the Bible; *Staberl* is the name of a columnist for the *Kronen-Zeitung*, one of Austria's more reactionary newspapers; and *Stangl* refers to Franz Stangl, commandant of the Treblinka concentration camp.

The world premiere of *Ein Sportstück* at the *Burgtheater* thus represents the end of Jelinek's (short) period of inner emigration. More importantly, the text epitomizes the triviality, "shallowness," or superficiality in both theme and form characteristic of Jelinek's entire dramatic production, while at the same time being uncompromisingly critical. Finally, the production by Schleef serves as one example of staging that did indeed become a popular success, thereby vaulting the playwright into the position of "house author" at Austria's national theater.[9]

Jelinek's "Shallowness"

According to Linda Hutcheon in her classic work *The Politics of Postmodernism*, the postmodern view is that representation is not a reflection, but rather a construction of reality. Postmodernism asks whether the "real" has ever existed outside our social or cultural interpretations of it. We can no longer assume that the representation provides a transparent window or immediate access to the referent. Rather, "it ... now self-consciously acknowledges its existence as representation – that is, as interpreting (indeed as creating) its referent."[10] How do we know our world, how do we know our history, but through the creation of ideologies, of narratives, of pictures which impose a certain logic and hierarchy upon that world and history? Postmodernism acknowledges its dependence upon such narratives – its complicity – while simultaneously rendering this complicity overt. This is the paradox of postmodernism: its simultaneous reliance upon and questioning of representation. Postmodern texts use and abuse specific forms of representation as well as more general representational conventions in an attempt to de-naturalize them.[11]

In an early essay titled "Die endlose Unschuldigkeit" (Endless Innocence), Jelinek describes the "innocence" of the masses as ignorance concerning their manipulation by mass media representations of reality. The pictures and myths of contemporary society have become so pervasive that they ooze a "slime of naturalness" that preempts change, resulting in endless repetition.[12] We take mass media representations of reality for granted, oblivious to their manipulative force, accepting without question the dominant ideology and thereby ensuring its perpetuation. The title of another essay reads as a description of the desired effect of her literature upon that sense of naturalness: "Ich schlage sozusagen mit der Axt drein" (I smash into it with an axe, as it were).[13]

Marlies Janz identifies the destruction of myth or ideology, the de-naturalization of representation, as the constant underlying all of Jelinek's literary production.[14] The dominant societal ideology that Jelinek challenges remains throughout all of her works that of capitalism, and to ignore the Marxist feminist content of her works is to misunderstand them. The author consistently "portray[s] the oppression of men and women by a capitalism that values human beings only as exchangeable commodities, and then the further oppression of women by a sexism that automatically assigns to them less value than to men."[15] Jelinek's challenge, however, remains negative – a negativity criticized at time by Marxists and feminists alike – for to posit an alternative would be only to reinstate the representations of authority.

The primary tool of destruction utilized by Jelinek is that of "shallowness," or superficiality. In an important theoretical essay titled "Ich möchte seicht sein" (I want to be shallow), the author attacks the traditional theater where actors stand on stage and imitate life, where the director as God pulls invisible strings so as to represent something besides exactly what is on stage, namely actors: "I don't want to play, and I don't want to see others play, either. I also don't want to get others to play. People shouldn't say things and pretend they are living. I don't want to see that false unity reflected in the faces of actors: the unity of life."[16] Her figures, whether on stage or in the pages of her prose, are not meant to depict some deeper meaning; they do not refer to anything except themselves. For Jelinek, this something deeper does not exist, and to fake it is to manipulate the audience with one further picture or ideology. Instead, she advocates a flat theater, like a roll of randomly shot film; it should be non-representational, like a fashion show in which the clothes themselves, not the models, comprise the content.[17] Jelinek's theater is non-theatrical: "I don't want theater. I want a different theater."[18]

"Shallowness" implies the hollowing out or so-called "death" of the humanistic subject. As has been pointed out by numerous critics, Jelinek's characters, with the possible exception of Erika from *Die Klavierspielerin* (*The Piano Player*), lack psychological depth, feelings, and moral convictions. They reflect the impossibility of individuality, identity, and self-determination in contemporary society, devoid of a personal history or background that could be told within the ordered and ordering confines of coherent narrative. They become interchangeable carriers of language, with neither dialogue nor communication possible, resulting in the blocks of monologue typical of Jelinek's dramas, especially in the 1990s.

This spoken text always parodies one or several sub-texts, and critics situate the author within the satiric Austrian/Jewish tradition of a Karl Kraus or Elias Canetti. However, as John Pizer points out, whereas Krausian citation still has a destructive/redemptive dialectic, for Jelinek the original, authentic, and pure is irrevocably gone; there is only reproduction, imitation, and repetition.[19] There is no longer a meaningful hierarchy to assign priorities; everything is equally important – or unimportant – and simultaneous. Everything has become a surface picture, second-hand reality, a giant TV screen, and Jelinek has said that her figures should themselves speak as if they were on television: "It is not first-hand speech, just like there is no first-hand nature, but rather second-hand speech, speech in a second-hand nature."[20]

Jelinek takes our language, representations, and ideologies at face value and makes them speak for themselves: "Both the matter at hand and its meaning are communicated in the same breath."[21] The urge to see language as a transparency to a hidden reality is consistently thwarted; instead, her figures provide their own interpretation and essayistic commentary up front: "They are their own message."[22] The author's destructive impulse goes beyond the myth of subjectivity, gender relations, and capitalism to attack the interpretive stance itself. According to Dagmar von Hoff, "Jelinek reflects the interpreter back into her texts at the moment when he or she must determine that the dramatic figure itself already incorporates the interpretive horizon."[23] Language means nothing more than what it says; there is no significance or depth under the surface. In a sense, everything has become representation, but by thematizing the superficiality the author works to de-naturalize the surface.

Critics have struggled with the combination of Jelinek's "shallowness," which has been called postmodern, and her political engagement. Allyson Fiddler, for example, writes that "while many of Jelinek's literary techniques may be termed postmodernist, the Marxist and feminist critique presented in her work seems to form an unhappy alliance with postmodernism."[24] For Hutcheon, on the other hand, and she admits that here she differs from most critics, postmodern intertextuality can be political. Self-reflexivity, though not tied to a specific course of action, can be a challenge to authority.[25] Using Hutcheon's terms, then, we can say that Jelinek simultaneously uses and abuses contemporary representations. The author inscribes within her texts the dominant ideology, but the self-consciousness or "shallowness" of the inscription undermines the authority of that ideology; by drawing attention to its own artifice, we can recognize that it is culturally constructed.

Ein Sportstück: The Text[26]

Jelinek's *Sportstück* criticizes mass phenomena and behavior as typified in sports today. The author conceives of sports not as the romanticized, solitary attempt to push the limits of one's own abilities, but as a public spectacle broadcast to the masses through TV. The ritual of the sporting event has been the subject of earlier Jelinek works, most notably of *Death/Valley/Summit* where it appears in the form of the skier/tourist, and it signals variously the tourist industry, Austrian nationalism, and obsession with the body, health, and youth. Jelinek deplores the high status of sports in Austria, where a Jörg Haider wins votes on the basis of his youthful jogging form and citizenship is granted immediately to the latest super athlete, but denied to political refugees. She perceives a continuum between the masses who turned out for Hitler and the masses who mobilized behind skier Schranz when he was disqualified from the Olympics. In her words: "History is repeated as farce."[27]

Jelinek's play attempts to debunk the myth, or "innocence," of sports by showing the aggression, hostility, and blind obedience inherent in the team mentality, which is depicted as being overtly racist, anti-Semitic, and sexist. Belonging to a group implies exclusion of others; adulation of strength and body implies scorn of weakness and the mind. Team sports encourage the same type of brutality and nationalism necessary for the waging of war, and Jelinek's play draws parallels between abusive interpersonal relationships, bellicose factions in Yugoslavia, fascism, and above all capitalism. For Jelinek, the war driving all other wars is an economic one, and it is the rules of supply and demand that determine all forms of being including sports. *Ein Sportstück* is about the production, marketing, and sale of the human body and emotion. In her stage directions, Jelinek stipulates the commercialization of her own figures and production: the chorus is to wear identical name-brand sports shoes, the entire cast should be clothed in sports garb so as to attract sponsors, and the leader of the chorus should be linked to current sporting events which are to be broadcast to the audience throughout the entire performance (7).

Jelinek's play consists not of dialogue between characters interested in communicating with each other, but rather long monologues and language blocks, citations arranged side by side in a montage without regard as to whether the "high" literature of such respected authors as Kleist and Hofmannsthal or "low-brow" TV soaps and scandal pages are cited. This dramatic practice serves to render everything equally significant, or insignificant, and moreover demonstrates the impossibility of authenticity or originality. Reality is mere repetition, nothing more than a copy, like TV where the same stories are told again and again and the audience enjoys the option of saving and replaying them endlessly. Jelinek's play is structured on the principle of juxtaposition. Throughout *Ein Sportstück* she establishes comparisons that jar in their apparent incongruity and yet are in fact enabled by identical factors. For example, Hector mentions swimming, the Gulf War, jogging, and the Trojan War all in the same breath as plausible reasons one might want to venture outside, obviously equating sports and war, and Achilles compares a passion for life with lustful desires to renew one's parking permit, obviously equating life and societal commercialization (124-25). These two characters in and of themselves, who pit their strength and might against one another on the tennis court rather than the battlefield, repeat the sports / battle / murder / commercialization equation one more time.

Jelinek hollows out or trivializes her dramatis personae, leaving only surfaces of spoken words behind. Her figures, although they at times allude to real-life people, refuse to assume and act out a unique identity that comes to life on stage. Reduced as they are to mere voices, they are difficult to distinguish, a confusion which is enhanced further through the utilization of generic character names: The Woman, Man, Victim, or A Young Woman. With the exception of Elfi Elektra's words, all speeches, including those of the women, are to be spoken by male voices, with the actors on stage merely mouthing the words (17). Such radical severance of the text from the body literally and visually represents both the abstract undifferentiation of contemporary discourse and its domination by patriarchy. The extensive use of a chorus, the play's most important voice according to the stage directions, foregrounds the disappearance of the subject and the lack of individuality within this discourse.

The play is devoid of all action except one: the figures slowly kick and beat a man to death. Even the act of dying, however, is not profound or tragic, but rather incidental and trivialized. The victim periodically gets up and sees to various menial chores or engages in everyday activities, such as sweeping or reading. He comments upon his own demise, analyses his fatal mistake, and chats with his tormenters. He observes his death, distanced, as if watching a television show. Jelinek's "shallowness" strips the traditional theater of dramatic dialogue, action, and even of its dramatis personae, leaving nothing in its wake but television and marketing. All of life and death has become one huge spectacle, a show that conceals nothing behind it.

Jelinek's drama becomes a type of surface screen where the figures say up front what they are and interpret themselves as well as the play. Her actors do not act, but talk, and what they say is undisguised authorial interpretation of her own play's meaning. The best example of this self-referentiality can be found in two passages that frame the entire drama. At its beginning, Elfie Elektra, Jelinek's alter ego, laments that no one has a sense for the depths any longer, with the exception of deep-sea divers (13). At the end, that same diver emerges to complain that his sister, Elfie Elektra from Bregenz, constantly tries to uncover depth where there is only surface (168). Thus the figures play with the theme of literary "shallowness," voicing the predilection of author and reader alike to look beneath the surface for a meaning and significance that are simply not there. Furthermore, that theme is positioned in the context of capitalism with the descriptive "from Bregenz," which recalls the name of a well-known Austrian manufacturer of electrical appliances and links the production and consumption of literature to market structures in general. This framework opposing writer and athlete, discussing depth and "shallowness," within the over-arching context of commercialization, thus self-consciously suggests the play's own interpretive outline.

Jelinek uses all of her figures to foreground and comment upon certain societal myths. The female characters bring to the surface the image of woman as creator in the sense of both life-giver and artist, and then they negate that myth by taking rather than giving life, by creating death, or at best, nothingness. The mother sends her sons into sports as preparation for future wars; the Amazon queen Penthesilea kills and is killed on the battlefield; and The Old Woman, a reference to the widow Elfriede Blauensteiner, kills several husbands for their inheritance. On Jelinek's stage, the murders are not shown or acted, but rather narrated by the murderer herself, who then also provides a self-interpretation. The Old Woman, for example, tells the audience that her concrete contribution to a materialist society is the production of death: "I kill. That is the service that I produce" (76). She insists that she is a contributing member of the service industry, as are the artists Elfie Elektra and The Author, both of whom allude to Jelinek herself. Their product is to constantly criticize, find fault, and engage in political causes, although they admit that the object of their criticism and engagement remains unknown (19). Their words are always the same and the values they propound are plagiarized from the newspapers. Societal images of the original muse or the mother-figure are cited and then destroyed through self-conscious parody.

The male figures can be roughly divided into athletes and warriors, whereby the two groupings continually fuse and overlap. Andi, a reference to the Austrian bodybuilder Andi Muenzer who died from steroid abuse, literally embodies the primacy of surface over inner depth. He complains that though his muscles are still in tact, his liver and kidneys have had it (97). The chorus makes explicit the commonality between female and male groups by stating that the human body, be it that of the athlete, woman, or warrior, is manufactured for quick consumption in a throw-away society (26). Here Andi rises from the dead to worship the god

Arni, a direct reference to Arnold Schwarzenegger. Bodybuilding has become society's new religion. The inner soul has disappeared; there are no values except those of consumerism (157); and feelings are elicited solely through television. Jelinek's figures say they have deep yearnings, but for shoes (170).

To make language reveal its own ideology, Jelinek plays with individual letters, syllables, words, phrases, and sentences. She uses alliteration, rhyme, and repetition freely, the sound and rhythm of the language determining its flow. The text moves forward associatively, one word at any time triggering unexpected connections on the basis of semantic ambiguity. Hektor and Achilles, whose battle transpires on the tennis court, state: "We will not return them because they have been beaten enough" (134), referring not only to tennis balls, but also to human beings, who are then further likened to unwanted goods from a supermarket. Metathesis, where sounds in a word or between words are transposed, is a favorite tool of the author to expose a meaning or subtext. For example, by switching just a few letters in German, "Liebesbeziehung" (love relationship) becomes "Leibeserziehung" (education of the body) (22), indicating the transformation of interpersonal love into physical training. Jelinek's text juxtaposes the most profound with the most trivial, and abstract concepts are made into something concrete: human emotions and interactions are compared repeatedly to clothing and fashion. Values in general are instrumentalized or, as in the following example, commercialized: "... the latest conscience model isn't even on the market yet. Perhaps we should have bought the old one – before this poor indefinite article is out-of-print for good" (161). The proliferation of word plays in this short passage is typical for the drama as a whole. "Shallowness" constitutes both content and form of Jelinek's play. It permeates every level of the text, from its structure to its portrayal of character and action to its language.

Ein Sportstück: The Performance

The premiere of *Ein Sportstück* was remarkable for various reasons: First, it lasted five hours, and this was the so-called short version. The long version – seven hours! – premiered in March. Second, it was labeled a "work in progress," which meant that it had never been rehearsed from beginning to end. Third, the audience was asked to appear in sports attire so that a prize could be awarded for the best outfit. Finally, but this is perhaps not so remarkable for a Jelinek play, it caused a scandal. At 10:40 p.m., ten minutes before the play had to end according to union contracts, the director, on his knees and with the support of the cast, begged the head of the *Burgtheater,* Claus Peymann, to allow the play to continue. Peymann agreed, assuming the additional costs himself, but only on condition that from now on the play would conclude before 11:00 p.m.

Although reviews of the staging have in general been positive, one wonders whether Jelinek's play has in fact been premiered. Her text begins with the words: "The author doesn't provide many stage directions. She has learned that in the meantime. Do what you want. The only thing that I insist on is: a Greek chorus ..." (7). Jelinek chose Einar Schleef as director based on his reputation for staging choruses. She has stated that he is a genius and gave him free rein in staging the play. Schleef adds and subtracts at will from the original text, as if to say that he, like Jelinek, doubts the existence of authenticity, and that he, like Jelinek, will undermine all forms of authority, including that of the author. His staging is in many ways "shallow," trivial, and artificial; however, what is lacking at times is the self-reflexive distancing of the text, which in turn forms its political and critical content.

Schleef undermines the notion of psychologically motivated characters, and his negation of realist conventions throughout the performance is consistent with Jelinek's text. There is no dialogue or communication, but rather blocks of text spoken by various figures whose lack of individuality is best illustrated by the dominance of the chorus. These blocks of speech, as in Jelinek's text, are quotes, although Schleef at times uses different citations than Jelinek. Often the meaning of the words becomes incidental; what is being said is not as important as how it is said. Schleef adds innumerable musical texts, such as Gregorian chants and a bawdy song from Mozart, which transform Jelinek's theater of words into a theater where words and music unite. Jelinek's already strongly rhythmical text is enhanced even further through song, chanting, humming, drill whistles, stamping of feet, and, above all, repetition. Artificiality marks the entire stage, with actors appearing in outlandish costumes and walking on stilts; the predominant colors are black and white, resulting in strong contrasts and symmetry.

Action is limited to the presentation of speech, which most frequently makes explicit the connection between the sports mentality and war. It is impossible to recapitulate plot, for there exists no development or progression, but rather stasis and scenic montage. The most stunning and memorable scenes involve the chorus chanting text accompanied by gymnastic exercises or drills. For example, dressed in black monk's robes, the chorus half sings and half speaks Jelinek's text about war, sports, politics, clothing, and body, while intermittently and on command running to the front and then back of the stage. Cued by a conductor standing in the balcony, approximately fifty voices in unison hurl words at the audience, but the naturalism of speech is subverted. They break sentences, elongate syllables, repeat sounds or words or sentences, add crescendos and diminuendos, manipulate tones, and fall into double time. Later, in a grueling twenty-five-minute aerobic workout, a forty-two-member chorus chants text describing the brutality and aggression of mass behavior in a type of rap song and dance. Again the meaning or content of the words is embodied in the action or form of the chorus, whose rhythmic and repetitive movements consist of kicking, beating, and punching an imaginary victim. Thus, similar to Jelinek, Schleef both presents mass behavior and comments upon that behavior.

There is, however, a danger in Schleef's staging. He illustrates the behavior of the masses through sports, but that very same behavior is fostered in the audience. Whereas Jelinek's text creates enough distance to criticize the blind obedience and passion inherent in sports, the strong rhythm, repetition, and stylization of Schleef's staging mesmerize the audience at times. This is particularly true of the aerobics scene discussed above which is apt to elicit aggressive and even sexual feelings, but very little thought on the part of an audience. The self-reflective commentary gets lost in the sheer frenzied physical energy of the performance. Simply put, the audience does not care if it understands the words, but without the words the discrepancy, or distance, that provokes criticism disappears. Similarly, the long version of Schleef's production incorporates extensive film clips taken from within the *Burgtheater* itself, the most memorable following a naked man running endlessly up and down narrow stairways in a pack of very large dogs. Such scenes strengthen the artificiality and self-consciousness of the performance, but again they provoke at times not thought or criticism, but merely a voyeuristic admiration for the man's stamina and the dogs' patience.

In some ways, then, the performance affirms the very mass phenomena criticized in the text; Schleef's staging replicates it, but without distancing the audience.[28] In fact, the very length of the performance engenders the type of group mentality attacked by the author. Similar to sports, the audience has a challenge to meet, an adversary, in this case perhaps the incomprehensibility of the performance or even time itself, and fortification is provided in the form of a sack lunch and two intermissions. United in its attempt to meet the challenge, the audience excludes those lacking the requisite understanding or dedication to the theater, and it can be carried away by the dynamics and spectacle of the theatrical happening.

Conclusion

A tension exists between what is achieved through the text on the mental stage of the reader and what can be achieved on an actual stage before an audience. The balance in Jelinek's text between formal experimentation and Marxist feminist critique becomes lopsided on stage. In many ways, Schleef follows the text and makes his performance "shallow," but the subordination of the word to an overpowering picture of sight and sound at times effaces self-reflexivity. Jelinek's "shallowness" is rendered merely trivial, and the subversive ends of the drama itself are not fully realized.

Ein Sportstück represents in radical form the author's continuing attempt to subvert the assumed naturalness of representation by forcing surface to *re-present* itself as depth, which is to say, by turning depth inside out to reveal it to be nothing more than exactly what is said on the surface. The political dimension of Jelinek's superficiality lies in the recognition of the constructedness of cultural discourses. By foregrounding its own artifice, her theater questions the assumption of naturalness and thereby thwarts its endless perpetuation. Jelinek offers no solution or alternative, but her deconstructive dramaturgy brings to the surface the power structures and interests that lie behind our supposedly innocuous myths.

Notes

1. In her interesting and insightful article, Caduff explores why the plays of another experimental and controversial Austrian playwright, Werner Schwab, were generally embraced in the early 1990s whereas those of Jelinek met with rejection, and traces the difference in reception back to the playwrights' differing treatments of body: "Kreuzpunkt Körper: Die Inszenierungen des Leibes in Text und Theater: Zu den Theaterstücken von Elfriede Jelinek und Werner Schwab," *Das Geschlecht der Künste*, ed. Corina Caduff and Sigrid Weigel (Cologne, Weimar, Vienna: Böhlau, 1996) 154-74.

2. Allyson Fiddler, "Jelinek's Ibsen: 'Noras' Past and Present," *Theatre and Performance in Austria: From Mozart to Jelinek*, ed. Ritchie Robertson and Edward Timms (Edinburgh: Edinburgh UP, 1993) 126.

3. See for example Michael Jeanée, "Miese Hetzjagd!," *Kronen-Zeitung* 1 December 1986: 18-19.

4. I owe this formulation to Jutta Landa, who first used it in the 1998 MLA talk that is the basis of her article included here.

5. Marlies Janz, *Elfriede Jelinek* (Stuttgart: Metzler, 1995): "der Sprache selbst ihr ideologiekritisches Potential zu entlocken ..." (123).

6. See for example the cover story in *Profil*, 31 October 1994.

7. Armgard Seegers, "Partitur für den Seitensprung: Elfriede Jelinek im Gespräch," *Hamburger Abendblatt* 21 January 1995.

8. Jelinek mentions as reasons for her inner emigration the general hatred directed toward her and the lack of protest against defamatory FPÖ election posters. See for example Stefanie Carp, "'Ich bin im Grunde ständig tobsüchtig über die Verharmlosung:' Ein Gespräch mit Elfriede Jelinek," Program for *Stecken, Stab und Stangl, Deutsches Schauspielhaus*, Hamburg, 12 April 1996, 16-17, or Gisela Bartens, "'Das ist meine Lebenskatastrophe:' Elfriede Jelinek im KLEINE-Exklusivinterview," *Kleine Zeitung* [Graz] 18 December 1994: 58-59.

9. This overview does not include a number of shorter Jelinek plays, for example *Präsident Abendwind. Ein Dramolett (President Evening Breeze)* which premiered in 1987 in Berlin, or the more recent *er nicht als er (zu, mit Robert Walser)* (he not as he [about, with Robert Walser]) which premiered in 1998 at the *Salzburger Festspiele*.

10. Linda Hutcheon, *The Politics of Postmodernism* (London; New York: Routledge, 1989) 34.

11. Hutcheon 8.

12. Elfriede Jelinek, "Die endlose Unschuldigkeit," *Die endlose Unschuldigkeit: Prosa - Hörspiel - Essay* (Schwifting: Schwiftinger Galerie-Verlag, 1980) 56.

13. Elfriede Jelinek, "'Ich schlage sozusagen mit der Axt drein,'" *TheaterZeitSchrift* 7 (1984): 14-16.

14. Janz VII-VIII.

15. Linda C. DeMeritt, "A 'Healthier Marriage': Elfriede Jelinek's Marxist Feminism in *Die Klavierspielerin* and *Lust*," *Elfriede Jelinek: Framed by Language*, ed. Jorun B. Johns and Katherine Arens (Riverside, CA: Ariadne Press, 1994) 110.

16. Elfriede Jelinek, "Ich möchte seicht sein," *Gegen den schönen Schein*, ed. Christa Gürtler (Frankfurt/M.: Neue Kritik, 1990) 157. Translation by Jorn Bramann as it appears on Jelinek's homepage.

17. Jelinek, "Ich möchte seicht sein" 158.

18. Anke Roeder, "'Ich will kein Theater. Ich will ein anderes Theater': Gespräch mit Elfriede Jelinek," *Autorinnen: Herausforderungen an das Theater*, ed. Anke Roeder (Frankfurt/M.: Suhrkamp, 1989) 141. My translation.

19. John Pizer, "Modern vs. Postmodern Satire: Karl Kraus and Elfriede Jelinek," *Monatshefte* 86.4 (1994): 502-03.

20. Kathrin Tiedemann, "'Wenn ich total heiter bin, werde ich am schrecklichsten sein': Elfriede Jelinek im Gespräch mit Kathrin Tiedemann," *Theaterheft: Bremer Theater Schauspielhaus* 12 November 1994: 21.

21. Janz 8.

22. Elfriede Jelinek, "Sinn egal. Körper zwecklos," *Theaterschrift* 11 (February 1997): 24.

23. Dagmar von Hoff, "Stücke für das Theater: Überlegungen zu Elfriede Jelineks Methode der Destruktion," *Gegen den schönen Schein* 112. My translation.

24. Allyson Fiddler, "There Goes That Word Again, or Elfriede Jelinek and Postmodernism," *Elfriede Jelinek: Framed by Language* 130.

25. Hutcheon 8.

26. Elfriede Jelinek, *Ein Sportstück* (Reinbek bei Hamburg: Rowohlt, 1998). Future references to the play will be indicated in the article itself with the page number in parentheses. My translations.

27. Dagmar Kaindl, "'Eine Vorbereitung auf den Krieg': Jelinek über den Sport," *News* [Vienna] 8 January 1998: 122.

28. While most critics were enthusiastic about Schleef's production, two reviewers express some uneasiness and question whether the performance did not in fact affirm precisely what Jelinek meant to attack. See Sigrid Löffler, "Um die Ecke gedacht," *Die Zeit* [Hamburg] 29 January 1998: 51-52; Karin Kathrein, "Ein Happpening nahe am Absturz," *Kurier* [Vienna] 25 January 1998: 29.

Figure and Speech
on Vienna's Major Stages in the Nineties

Jutta Landa

> Oh yes, yes, I allow my words to run along unfettered.
> Even the shabbiest word has learned how to salute.
> I cordially thank it.
> (Elfriede Jelinek)[1]

> Language drags the person behind –
> like tin cans tied to a dog's tail.
> (Werner Schwab)[2]

Figures of Speech

Competing with such proliferating cultural forms as film, photography, rock concerts, or MTV, drama has steadily been losing ground with audiences in most major cities in the world.[3] Not so in pre-millennium Vienna, where (to use an expression by the ex-director of the *Burgtheater*, Claus Peymann) a stage-crazed Viennese audience continued to indulge its *Theaterknall*.[4] However, this Viennese infatuation with the stage is all too often marred by conflict and strife, as witnessed by the unloading of a pile of manure at the *Burgtheater* to protest the premiere of Thomas Bernhard's play *Heldenplatz* in 1988. Conservative forces, insisting on the civilizing and moral powers of canonical drama, clash with those theater makers or spectators who are in search of a contemporary, more volatile articulation. (Ironically, in the manure incident, cultural righteousness managed to stage its very own scatological installation). This ongoing battle was epitomized by the controversies surrounding the tenure of Claus Peymann, whose strategy was to bring to the prestigious Viennese *Burgtheater* contemporary plays by Austria's literary renegades and alleged *Nestbeschmutzer* (someone who befouls his/her own nest) Thomas Bernhard (1931-1988), Elfriede Jelinek (1946-), Peter Handke (1942-), Peter Turrini (1944-), and Werner Schwab (1958-1994). Watching or reading these plays, one cannot help wondering why they were considered by many critics, politicians, and theatergoers as scandalous. Although they do contain some sex and violence, the average theatergoer should be all but jaded by the ongoing parade of nudity and graphic brutality on television or film. Also, most of the plays are not mere postmodernist installations, but maintain a recognizable dramatic structure and more or less articulated speech. Nevertheless the plays were largely considered disturbing, tasteless, and anarchical. In an attempt to analyze their potential for irritation, I claim that the real provocation of the plays, aside from their trespassing into the tradition-bound environment of Vienna's premier theaters, lies first and foremost in their handling of language. The plays privilege dramatic speech over figures to the extent that the dramatic characters are literally reduced to figures of speech, to mere "speechmachines" navigating a shifting territory of textual planes.[5]

The theater landscape in Vienna to this day is dominated by its triad of major stages: first in line is the *Burgtheater* with its affiliated experimental stages such as *Lusterboden* or *Vestibule* and its "reserve theater" called *Kasino am Schwarzenbergplatz*, as well as its "rehearsal stage" at the Arsenal. The second major stage is the *Akademietheater*, which is really the smaller house of the *Burgtheater*. All of these were under the directorship of German-born Claus Peymann from 1986 to 1999. The third leg in the triad is the *Volkstheater* under the present directorship of Emmy Richter, a union-owned theater that fluctuates between tradition and innovation in order to fill a house of 300 seats, over-sized for today's standards. Next among the Viennese theaters vying for audience attention and financial subsidies is the *Theater in der Josefstadt*, which offers nostalgic, elegant *Salontheater* á la Chekhov. The *Theater an der Wien* primarily features musicals and opera. An avant-garde theatrical concept is offered by the *Schauspielhaus*, which specializes in premieres of comparatively unknown authors. Vienna's theatrical spectrum also includes a sprawling array of so-called "cellar theaters" and experimental stages and initiatives, as well as independent groups who rent theaters (and occasionally a hearse factory[6]) for their daring and innovative (lay) productions.

One can deplore with the independent "theater maker" Robert Quitta that the public debate on theater in Vienna stubbornly "revolves around the major stages *Burgtheater, Volkstheater* and *Josefstadt*,"[7] but since these institutions flag cultural dominance and official representation, they are still prime indicators as to the significance of a given play. Especially a premiere or production in the *Burgtheater* constitutes an *a priori* affirmation of the play so honored, a validation that might even overrule negative reviews by theater critics and pull in audiences on the theater's reputation alone. The following plays by contemporary authors were staged at major theaters, in particular the *Burgtheater*, during the 1990s: Peter Turrini's *Tod und Teufel* (Death and the Devil), *Alpenglühen* (*Alpine Glow*), and *Schlacht um Wien* (*The Battle for Vienna*) were premiered in 1990, 1993, and 1995 respectively at the *Burgtheater*; and his latest plays *Endlich Schluß* (*Enough*)[8] and *Die Liebe in Madagaskar* (Love in Madagascar) opened at the *Akademietheater* in 1997 and 1998. Elfriede Jelinek's *Wolken. Heim* (Cloud. Cuckoo. Land) and her early *Was geschah, nachdem Nora ihren Mann verlassen hatte oder Stützen der Gesellschaften* (*What Happened after Nora Left Her Husband, or Pillars of Society*) were performed at the *Volkstheater* in the years 1993 and 1992 respectively, while her *Raststätte* (Truck Stop) was premiered in a 1994 production by Claus Peymann at the *Burgtheater*, as was her *Sportstück* (SportsPlay) in a seven-hour production that enjoyed unprecedented audience success by Einar Schleef in 1998. In the case of Werner Schwab, the *Volkstheater* was the first big Viennese stage to perform his plays *Volksvernichtung* (*People-Annihilation*) and *Offene Gruben Offene Fenster: Ein Fall von*

Ersprechen (Open Ditches, Open Windows: A Case of A-Speaking), both in 1992, although they had premiered elsewhere. The *Burgtheater* hesitated on Schwab; only after his death did his *Präsidentinnen* (*First Ladies*) find its way to the *Kasino am Schwarzenbergplatz* from where it was immediately transferred to the bigger and more prestigious *Akademietheater*. The first Thomas Bernhard ever at the *Burgtheater* was Peymann's opening production of *Der Theatermacher* (*Histrionics*) in September 1986 with its significant first lines: "What, here in this musty atmosphere?"[9] It was followed by *Heldenplatz* in November 1988, which caused a storm of controversy but played very successfully to the audience. Peter Handke was also premiered at the *Burgtheater*'s *Lusterboden* with his *Spiel vom Fragen* (*The Art of Asking*) in 1990, his *Die Stunde da wir nichts voneinander wußten* (*The Hour We Knew Nothing of Each Other*) in 1992, and his *Zurüstungen für die Unsterblichkeit* (Preparations for Immortality) – a Peymann production – in 1997. Handke's highly controversial play *Die Fahrt im Einbaum, oder, Das Stück zum Film vom Krieg* (The Trip with the Outrigger or the Play for the Film about the War) became Peymann's farewell production at the *Burgtheater* in June 1999.

Why did these plays by authors who were perceived as scandal-prone find entry into Vienna's most prestigious theater? There is no doubt that Claus Peymann, imported from Bochum and managing and artistic director of the Viennese *Burgtheater* for thirteen years, played a crucial role in this revolution. Peymann's overbearing style, his refusal to mollify the tenured stars of the *Burgtheater* ensemble, and his emphasis on extravagant, over-rehearsed *Regietheater* ("director's theater") went hand in hand with his devotion to contemporary authors. This almost maniacal love,[10] combined with his unabashed criticism of Austrian institutions, embroiled Peymann in a chain of provocations, accusations, and counter-accusations. In many ways the director himself became a spectacle who transported the drama of his directorship off-stage, into the public arena of the mass media.[11]

Peymann's attempt to do away with what he derogatorily labeled a "theater for princesses" and to reinvent the *Burgtheater* as a venue for the "departure into a new political interrogation of meaning"[12] catapulted plays into the limelight whose contemporariness extended beyond social and political issues into an investigation of language. In Peymann's terms, the task of drama was to "keep language awake."[13] Plays such as Jelinek's *Totenauberg* (*Death/Valley/Summit, 1996*), Handke's *Art of Asking*, Schwab's *Offene Gruben Offene Fenster: Ein Fall von Ersprechen*, and even Turrini's *Battle for Vienna* sport a cast that has transmuted into interchangeable language-emitting "artificial constructs."[14] Realistic, psychological character coding is discarded in favor of a droning rhetoric. The interchangeability of these speech machines is evidenced in their generic labeling: thus Jelinek's *Sportstück* features prototypes such as Woman, Old Woman, Victim, the super athlete Andi, and the Authoress; her *Death/Valley/Summit* sports The Old Man, The Middle-Aged Woman, Local Peasants, and Cheerleaders. In Turrini's *Battle for Vienna* the list of characters includes The Old Man, The Rustic Peasant, The Monk Choir, and The Man in Leisure Clothes. Importantly, this generic labeling is devoid of signification. Plays have transmuted into a collection of monologues severed from the characters who soliloquize. Jelinek's *Sportstück* is "a play comprised of great monologues – prose passages of a reading performance by the individual reader."[15] In her play of 1998 titled *er nicht als er* (he not as he),[16] the cast is an anonymous collective, simply: "Several people, but quite good-natured with each other (perhaps lying in bathtubs as they were formerly used in lunatic asylums)." No hint is given as to who is speaking which passage of the dramatic text, which Jelinek describes in a loose-leaf insert to the book edition as an "essay, or a collection of aphorisms" and which in its typographical arrangement indeed appears as such. As Jelinek maintains in an interview from 1989, this deindividuation or lifelessness is exactly her intention: "I reject the desire that has attracted almost all writers to produce life in the theater. I want exactly the opposite: to produce lifelessness. I want to exorcise life from the theater. I don't want drama."[17]

As figures are reduced to mere speech bubbles, to articulation machines or discourse cyborgs activated for the duration of a monologue, language aggressively pushes itself into the foreground. But it is language of a different order, as Jelinek herself states in her acceptance speech of the Georg Büchner Prize:

> Two things stand opposite each other, language and its owner. Language is language; it might mean whatever it wishes to; it might want to say nothing and still speak, but whatever the speaker thinks is always fastened to an object. This will be a feast! Finally the speaker may devour his or her object. Some will cheer this speaker high, but not too high. But nothing else will be achieved, except that that which is without boundaries – thinking itself – is tied fast to language, and the speaker has strained against these fetters ever since.[18]

What is striking in this quote is its attaching of a corporeal quality to language. Significantly, this corporeality is a revolting one, often involving processes of ingestion and digestion. Language is a violent corpus, one that tears and drags the speaker behind it, deprives him or her of subjectivity, belies autonomous thought, and incarcerates figures in a language prison.

Language as an agent of assault can be found as early as 1966 in Peter Handke's *Publikumsbeschimpfung* (*Offending the Audience*, 1969). However, there is a difference between the language of assault in the 1960s and 70s and that of the 1990s. The tirades of *Offending the Audience* address the audience, thus postulating a belligerent attitude, but nevertheless a communicative interplay between spectators and actors. For the early Handke, language as a tool of aggression is turned against the audience primarily through the extrapolative and suggestive powers of the theater. In Jelinek, Schwab, and the later plays of Handke or even Turrini, speech attacks the speaker-actor him- or herself and is replete with a violent corporeality. This corporeality pushes the dramatic language of assault to new limits in that it ignores the inherent needs of any audience (such as the need to constitute meaning or to construct a plot) and renders the plays in question for all practical purposes unperformable. And yet these plays were performed all the time in the 1990s.

Elfriede Jelinek: A Dramaturgy of Lifelessness

Among the most unperformable plays that enjoyed highly successful performances in the 1990s are Elfriede Jelinek's dramas. Her figures, as Jelinek maintains in an interview, "constitute themselves out of what they say and not out of who they are. They claim something about themselves instead of living on the stage."[19] As the Jelinek scholar Marlies Janz has shown, Jelinek has pursued this dramaturgy of lifelessness from her very beginnings as a dramatist. Already in her *Nora* play the figures are disembodied voices that speak prefabricated texts. They "might wrap themselves in a costume – but none of it will make them come alive." Janz continues: "In Jelinek, the figures do not 'embody' anything (no character, no soul, no inner life). Rather, a clichéd, non-authentic, perpetually 'quoting' speech and a reified body drift next to each other."[20] Hence, Jelinek's *Sportstück* is, according to the author's loose-leaf note in the book edition: "A drama comprised of long monologues."

The German title of her play *Totenauberg* from 1991 alludes to the residence of Martin Heidegger, Todtnauberg, but the deformation of the original name conjures up visions of a concentration camp – *tot* means "dead" in German. Despite the obvious reference to the philosopher, the stage directions make it quite clear that except for a "tiny visual quote, maybe the mustache" and occasional embedded quotations, the historical figure cannot be identified by the language gruel he disgorges.[21] Nor would it illuminate meaning if an interpreter were to undertake the task of identifying Heidegger sources in the play. As Jelinek herself has stated in an interview with Eva Brenner, *Totenauberg* was her most radical play so far. Instead of dialogues one finds "textual planes set one against the other. It is written [in such a way] that it forces you to deal with the properties of language itself, to engage patterns of speech, whether a director wants to or not."[22]

Jelinek's *Wolken. Heim* is also devoid of dialogue. Instead, the play is comprised of one long monologue voiced by "we" whose individual members cannot be distinguished by their utterances. The entire text is a fabric of quotes from a variety of sources, ranging from Hölderlin, Hegel, Fichte, and Kleist to RAF letters, all of which are transformed or rather deformed into the ramblings of an obviously fascist collective subject.[23] Speech in this play is not only dissociated from character, it has deteriorated, regardless of its ideological allegiance, into historic debris, a sort of compost that fertilizes present day *Heimat* mythology. In *Wolken. Heim* Jelinek has perhaps driven her "interest in the idea, the possibility, to exhibit language and figures publicly, to unite the highest possible reality with the highest possible artificiality"[24] to its extreme.

Werner Schwab: The Language of Grunge

Werner Schwab shares with Jelinek a much touted supremacy of stage language and its simultaneous disparagement, in his case as grunge or trash. The very titles of the collections of his plays refer to this antagonistic relationship: *Fäkaliendramen* (1991, Fecal Dramas) as opposed to *Königskomödien* (1992, Royal Comedies).[25] Schwab likens dramatic utterance to body secretions; consequently theater as it existed in the early nineties appeared to him as "das LÄCHERLICHSTE und EITERÜBERFLÜSSIGSTE," which translates roughly as "something most ridiculous and pus superfluosest," whereby the odd English corresponds to the playwright's own frequent perversion of normal German syntax and word formation. Hence Schwab sets out to rescue the theater by "transforming language into pure human flesh and ... self-naturally the reverse."[26]

As Schwab emphasizes again and again, his plays originate through language alone. Probably the most radical of the playwrights discussed here, Schwab drives the corporeality of dramatic language to excess by treating it as virtual stage character or stage fixture that needs its own stage directions. Thus the stage directions in *Mein Hundemund* (My Dog Mouth) under the rubric "language" read as follows: "Language is always the body of the person who happens to act. Language drags the person behind – like tin cans tied to a dog's tail. One simply cannot do anything but language" (FD 181). In *Offene Gruben Offene Fenster* the speech directions are quite revolting: "All speaking is extremely accidental. One colors the words personally, so that all perhaps know what's what. Each word, each thought connection is actually a sounding balloon. On the other hand one regards the spoken words as fresh blood one wants to put into one's mouth after one has injured oneself" (KK 9). For Schwab, language is enmeshed in processes of ingestion and digestion, establishing itself purely as a material with revolting properties, unsuitable to convey meaning.

Speech in Schwab's plays can manifest itself as a stage figure such as the Vehicle in *Offene Gruben Offene Fenster*, which (or who) is supposed to exemplify "what language construction prevents by its nature" (KK 9). The Vehicle punctuates the dialogue between Him and Her, which spins out of control, with pantomime actions that could or could not reveal the intent behind the garbled speech patterns. Schwabian language in general appears to be an organism, mutating out of control like a tumor, resulting in untranslatable deformations and impossible *composita* such as "fataldreckig" (fataldirty: KK 115), "faltenärschig" (wrinkle-assed: KK 128), "tatlautlich" (actsoundly: KK 108), "sondermüllfühlig" (specialtrashyfeely: KK 127), and "Schweißfußnoten" (athlete's footnotes: KK 57). Signification is hardly intended. As Schwab readily admits in his play *Hochschwab*: "The words leave the objects and the chains to the objects and don't mean anything any more, don't mean anything at all any more and are entertainment" (KK 96). In fact, lack of signification is a deliberate defense strategy against the appropriation of the latest cultural fad. It refutes the cultural snob who attempts to ride the tide of success of the radical playwright, by engaging in a reading of his play. Accordingly, Schwab warns in his foreword to the program of the *Volkstheater* production of

People-Annihilation titled "Hausbeispiel und Spielgebisz," which again can be translated only roughly as "house example and play dentures": "Each halfway congruent and still exoterically justifiable hermetic little game is instructionarly appropriated 'from above,' that is from the medium itself."[27]

The corporeal nature of language in Schwab's dramas is evidenced more recently in their set-up as art installations rather than as stage plays. A case in point is the 1999 Austrian premiere of *Der Himmel mein Lieb meine sterbende Beute* (1992, Heaven My Love My Dying Loot) in the *Schauspielhaus* as "theater installation with four crates, six slime figures, three painter apprentices, and a voyeuristic audience."[28] In this adaptation the spectator is ambulant, picking his or her visits between different installations that taken in sum constitute Schwab's play. Although Schwab might not have foreseen such an interpretation, the production takes its cues from the play's quality as an ensemble of texts.

Peter Handke: Language is King

While there is a generational and certainly an aesthetic gap between the verbal grunge of Schwab's *Königsdramen* and Peter Handke's esoteric language musings in his later plays such as *Zurüstungen für die Unsterblichkeit*, labeled *Ein Königsdrama* (A Royal Drama), their common point of departure is the privileging of language over character. Starting with his long poem *Über die Dörfer* (1981, *Walk About the Villages*), Handke turned from the verbal aggression of his early plays to a more hymnal, rhapsodic tone, whose elevated pitch can however be equally off-putting. This obsession with language and a highly irritating pathos also dominates Handke's play titled *The Art of Asking*. Here, the seven figures include stock characters of the epic and the drama genre, for example Parzival and the *Mauerschauer* (a name derived from "teichoscopy," the *coup de théâtre* whereby an actor witnesses and reports events that take place off-stage). They engage in an asking game whose lofty goal is the redemption from the sheer babbling of our time. Such incessant chatter of contemporary society disguises our inability to ask the right questions.[29] The (hardly discernible) plot of the play is the quest for a cure from this "disease of asking." In Handke's typical metatheatrical fashion the objective of the play constitutes the play itself and is thoroughly discussed on stage:

> Our predecessors will have known why asking questions was not the subject matter for a drama, for if it is a subject matter, then it consists of so many disparate forms, all running in so many unacceptable directions that a consistent, purposeful form is perhaps not possible. But our awakening cannot be completely impossible and foolish, otherwise I would not be so full of desire for it. Asking goes along with walking: go ask, outside, in the open countryside ... Role in an asking drama, that I have always wanted, let me embody you. (30-31)

As the quote shows, even this recondite play ascribes corporeality to language: questions "run off in unacceptable directions" and are inextricably linked to physical movement such as "asking goes along with walking" (31) or "working as asking" (157). Especially the invocation: "Role in an asking drama, that I have always wanted, let me embody you" with its conscious play on the German phrase *eine Rolle verkörpern,* which means to play a role, or literally "to embody a role," points to the unity of verbal utterance and physical representation. At the end of the play, the figure of the Native phrases his (unsuccessful) determination to put an end to all asking in physical terms: "I am biting the head off of each question" (156)

The connection between language and body is examined and thematized in nearly all of Handke's later plays. For example, in *The Hour When We Knew Nothing of Each Other* language becomes strikingly apparent through its very absence. Throughout the entire play not a single word is spoken, while an array of people from all walks of life cross the stage in a fascinating rhythm of speechless comings and goings. Language here is reduced to its corporeal sign: gesture takes over meaning. *Zurüstungen für die Unsterblichkeit* is yet another of Handke's "unperformable" plays that Peymann tackled as a director. The critic Thomas Assheuer wrote on occasion of its premiere: "the language universe, this all-determining obsession, the great pathos of these plays cannot be ignored."[30] Words literally make up the throne on which the king resides, resulting in what Benjamin Henrichs calls "a whole Noah's Ark of insane or ridiculous sentences," simultaneously mystifying and irritating the audience which "experiences the poet and singer on at least two instruments: playing the harp or screeching on a saw ("Nervensäge")."[31] Handke's latest play, *Die Fahrt im Einbaum* in Peymann's final production at the *Burgtheater*, promised but did not deliver a huge scandal due to his well-publicized pro-Serbian stance. The fact that the scandal did not take place can be attributed to a tame production, a splendid cast, and last but not least to its "dragging dramaturgy" which degraded actors to "text reciters"[32] à la Jelinek. In this very recent review, the all too familiar phenomenon of habituation can be detected: the controversial speechmachinery of the early 1990s has been overworked to the point where it has become simply boring.

Peter Turrini: Language as Reality Mask

Yet another example, though much more confined within dramatic tradition, of speech dominating over figures can be found in Turrini's later plays *Alpine Glow* and *Battle for Vienna*. *Alpine Glow*, according to Klaus Zeyringer, "plays with perpetual transformation, with appearance and its reflection, with delusions and illusions, deception and reality masks. Sentences and roles are tried on and rejected, false confessions are made."[33] Characters "flip" into their opposites,[34] leaving the spectator wondering if the woman who visits the blind man in his solitary mountain cabin is a secretary or a prostitute. In *Battle for Vienna* the dramaturgy of multiple personalities is driven to the point where actors have complained that the "figures don't come alive."[35] This complaint is justified if one considers that Turrini is famous for his larger-than-life figures torn between their passions, desires, and absurd delusions on the one hand and their social and economic deformations on the other. After all, Turrini is the author who maintains that "the theater only takes place when human beings come out on the stage, when somebody appears. The theater is a fundamentally exterior art, thank God."[36] However, the complaint is not justified if one views *Alpine Glow* and *Battle for Vienna* as new directions taken by Turrini in his struggle to find theatrical images that are qualitatively different from sensationalist media images and yet achieve an even stronger visceral effect. Thus, Turrini's multiple figures, while still retaining their dramatic appeal, ultimately appear as language constructs that metamorphose ad lib, defying a fixed image.

Even his more recent play, *Enough*, which resorts back to believable, psychologically convincing figures, thematizes the same idle babble which, as we have seen, is attacked by his contemporaries. Thus the ultimate reason why the Man in *Enough* commits suicide is his longing for silence. Despite his attempts to soundproof his apartment, words keep on painfully intruding into his consciousness:

> And when the memory of noise and sounds began to fade away, another memory crept in: words, chunks of words, sentences and phrases, which I had spoken, read, written or heard at one point or another in my life. There was nothing thematic, logical or chronological about any of it. The words "Serbian Republic" came up with "scrambled eggs." Questions my wife had asked me years ago burst into a political speech I once wrote. Jokes I told at parties mixed with passages from the Bible. Clichés from the weather report merged with stanzas of a poem I'd learned by heart in school. And the Munich Peace Agreement, which

I had researched carefully for an article of mine, was broken up by fragments from a farewell scene. Lines from my columns mingled with my son's reproachful voice, and terms of endearment I used to use came out of the mouths of TV news anchors.[37]

A Jelinek-like pastiche of discourses reels off in the suicide's mind. This awareness of "sheer babble," even in those plays where he stays away from language experiments, puts Turrini in the close vicinity of Jelinek, Schwab, and Handke.

Corporeal Language and Cultural Protest

So far I have collected evidence for what I see as the distinctive trend in Austrian drama of the 1990s to make language autonomous, even corporeal. What remains open is an investigation into the reasons why the privileging of language has opened Vienna's major stages to these plays. First of all, acceptance finds its path via historical ties. The foregrounding of language hearkens to a Viennese tradition of language skepticism which can be traced at least as far back as Hugo von Hofmannsthal[38] and which continued with the influence of Ludwig Wittgenstein's *Tractatus Philosophicus* on the radical language experiments of the poets of the *Wiener Gruppe*. H.C. Artmann, Friedrich Achleitner, Konrad Bayer, Gerhard Rühm, and Oswald Wiener in turn became catalysts for such playwrights as Bernhard, Handke, and Turrini, partially through the mediation of the *Grazer Forum Stadtpark*. An important cultural mediator was the composer Gerhard Lampersberger who opened his house, the *Tonhof*, in Maria Saal to avant-garde writers and composers. Another line of influence stems from the early preoccupation of Ingeborg Bachmann and subsequently Elfriede Jelinek with Martin Heidegger's language philosophy. Especially Heidegger's concept of *Gerede*, i.e., idle talk or babble in which speaker and listener do not stand in any genuine personal or intimate relation to the topic at hand, is strongly reminiscent of

Jelinek's dissociative monologues. A third line of influence would be the playwright Ödön von Horváth whose famous *Bildungsjargon* (the pseudo-educated jargon of the lower classes) and signature dramaturgy of silence found their way into the postwar Viennese cabaret, and from there via Helmuth Qualtinger's *Herr Karl* (1961), the ultimate self-exposing monologue of the Austrian Nazi opportunist, to Turrini and others.

In the early 1960s, the so-called "material actions" of Günter Brus, Otto Muehl, Hermann Nitsch, and Rudolf Schwarzkogler – crude happenings performed on the human body – became a strong dramaturgical force in the early plays of Turrini, Wolfgang Bauer, and later of Schwab. From the Action Group's version of a theater of cruelty stems the stage invasion of dirt, filth, stinking slops, body fluids, as well as the empty actionism of throwing, piling up, or even trashing stage props, strategies that were extremely disturbing in Turrini's early plays. The cultural protest articulated in these regressive gestures resurfaces in the revolting physical properties ascribed to speech, especially in Schwab's and Jelinek's plays. The disgust with a postwar public language that shamelessly incorporates protest and flattens it into a discourse of affirmation was also fuelled by Theodor Adorno's and Max Horkheimer's disparagement of the culture industry. It is exactly this frustration with the promiscuity of language that Jelinek and Schwab voice, the latter by comparing language to an ownerless dog that kicks around in the dust, the former by having her characters quote and misquote ad infinitum without any relevance or reference to their own subject status. Jelinek's method of the unauthorized quote displays a language that can incorporate anything, leveling conflicting ideologies in the process, and becoming empty cant that will justify any horror.

Acceptance of the plays under discussion certainly also has to do with what Watt calls the migration of postmodern narratives and attitudes into the theater. Schwab's, Jelinek's, Handke's, and even Turrini's plays display the postmodern theater's repudiation of the "specificity of the dramatic text," its rejection of the "existence of rules and regulations governing dialogue, character, dramatic structure" and, most importantly, of "conversational dialogue from the stage as a relic of dramaturgy based on conflict and exchange." Thus characters that are literally figures of speech are indicators of postmodern "nomadic subjectivities or multiple subject positions, of chance and mutation."[39] Also, if speech takes over the figures, it simultaneously takes over the author, reducing the Author-God to a collector and arranger of speech debris whose production of meaning cannot be controlled. Conversely, in a postmodern society inundated by media-generated images, pure language, i.e., language that will not be compromised by the attempt to give life to a character, is the one distinguishing phenomenon that turns the stage into the *other* medium, where (contrary to TV for instance) the undivided attention of an audience is demanded and obtained through the very physical confinement of a closed auditorium. This of course assumes that visual hype is not reintroduced into the plays via the performance, which it often is. Yet one cannot blame a stage director for spicing up a drama whose main objective it is "to keep language awake" rather than the audience.

Furthermore, the privileging of speech over figure in Austrian drama of the 1990s has to do with the aura of the big state theaters as monuments of culture. Certainly, and without implying intent, it can be said that an elevated language which engages the lofty traditions of language critique or revelation of cultural myths promises an entry ticket to Austria's premier stages. What is more important to the authors however is that the bow before high culture often allows the piggyback transport, via language, of the revolting and the perverse, in other words the rushing invasion of low culture into the temples of art. This "defilement" has been the cause of unending opposition from conservative parties against Peymann and his opening up of the *Burgtheater* to "the likes" of Turrini and Jelinek. Speech before figure also caters, perhaps against its own intention, to the much-maligned "director's theater," a dramaturgy style that conceives of the dramatic text as a mere blueprint for the director's vision.[40] Again and again writers will complain (or resign themselves to the fact) that their plays are not appropriately realized. For example, Jelinek productions have attempted to individuate her speech machines through different clothing, voices, gestures, and facial expressions. Yet, the drawback of having one's play misinterpreted via its transformation into a performance is outweighed by the advantage that once the play arrives at a major stage, it will launch its inherent attack against the ossified structures of the very theater that will stage it.

In their call for a destruction of the dramatic code, all of the plays discussed here by implication call for a destruction of theater hierarchies and in fact of dominant societal hierarchies in general. How else but as an attack upon the institution of theater can one see the abolition of life, character, and plot? How else can one interpret the staging of a language that resembles disease and disgorgement rather than a controlled exchange of information and opinion for the purpose of communication? And of course, behind the attack against the institution stands the attack on the world stage that is Austria. No matter how hermetic the language games, distortions, and anagrams; they nevertheless voice a critique of social ills, albeit in peremptory and spotty fashion: Austria as a banana republic (a Turrini term) whose villagers will sell their folklore, morals, and landscape to hordes of tourists; Austria as a collection of skiing fans who are spellbound by sports-generated violence; Austria as an enclave for a male dominated discourse of brutality that reigns over its violated and equally violating women; Austria as a political haven, a refuge for murderous xenophobia and a virulent anti-Semitism in conjunction with a denial of the Nazi past. In the last instance, the plays attack the cultural imperialism of a small nation whose culture politics remain firmly in the hands of a government which appoints its state theater managers and university professors.[41] To maintain any measure of resistance against a state-controlled culture, language has to emulate the unspeakable functions of the human body: disgorging and eliminating, it destroys all hierarchies. Such a language will result in the irritation that the late Thomas Bernhard sees as the main function of Austrian theater. His theater maker Bruscon says:

> It is the irritation
> that matters.
> We are not here
> to grant people
> a favor
> The theater
> is not an institution that grants favors.⁴²

It is an irritation which recent political events in Austria show is absolutely necessary on the one hand, but also and paradoxically ineffectual on the other. Since I first lectured on this topic in December 1998, Austria has witnessed the rise to power of the populist Freedom Party (FPÖ) in a coalition government with the conservative People's Party (ÖVP). Under the stewardship of Jörg Haider, the FPÖ has attacked the very authors who are featured in this article as parasites who live off tax money and produce unsavory writings. Understandably, their reaction to the new coalition is one of shock and fear that the cultural climate in Austria will once again become restrictive. Peter Turrini protested in an open letter against Haider, and Elfriede Jelinek has put a performance stop on her plays. Although it seems that Klaus Bachler, who succeeded Peymann as the director of the *Burgtheater*, is continuing to encourage contemporary dramatists, nobody can say at this point whether the political caesura means a reversal of the inroads contemporary theater made in pre-millennium Austria. And for some, these inroads were never enough in the first place. Hortensia Völckers, for example, co-director of the Vienna Festival 2000, notes the absence of more innovative theatrical projects that incorporate text, film, dance, theory, and art.⁴³ Whereas the progressive "theater maker" Quitta could still claim in 1993 that "Vienna is the theater capital of the world,"⁴⁴ Völckers maintains that "this year's [1999] theater houses have long been standing elsewhere." Perhaps not, according to Eva Feitzinger of the Viennese theater agency Thomas Sessler, who is banking on the hyperverbal talent of such promising young playwrights as Dea Loher, Monika Helfer, Michaela Ronzoni, and Franzobel.⁴⁵

Apparently, Austrian theater in the new millennium continues its cycles of acceptance and repudiation, the discussion of which eminently serves to keep audience interest for Vienna's stages and performances awake.

Notes

1. This essay is an expanded and updated version of a lecture of the same title presented on 30 December 1998 at the 1998 MLA Conference in San Francisco. The quote is from Elfriede Jelinek's *er nicht als er (zu, mit Robert Walser)* (Frankfurt/M.: Suhrkamp, 1998) 31. All translations, unless otherwise indicated, are mine.

2. Werner Schwab, *Mein Hundemund, Fäkaliendramen* (Graz: Droschl, 1991) 181.

3. Stephen Watt, *Postmodern Drama: Reading the Contemporary Stage* (Ann Arbor: University of Michigan Press, 1998) 17. Watt also deplores the relative absence of drama in postmodernist critical discourse.

4. Claus Peymann, "Abrechnung [I]," *profil* 14 Dec 1998: 122.

5. Elfriede Jelinek uses the term *"Sprechmaschinen"* in her interview with Wolfgang Reiter, where she also traces this strategy back to the Theater of the Absurd. See Wolfgang Reiter, *Wiener Theatergespräche* (Vienna: Falter, 1993) 20. In a more recent article on Jelinek, Reiter uses the term *"Textflächendramatik."* See Wolfgang Reiter, "Lieben Sie Jelinek?," *profil* 6 September 1999: 176.

6. As for example the *Sparverein der Unzertrennlichen* did. Interview with Kurt Palm in *Theatergespräche* 163.

7. Interview with Robert Quitta in *Theatergespräche* 103-22.

8. This Turrini play was translated into English under the title *Enough* by Andrea Hacker and produced by Louis Fantasia in June 2000 in Los Angeles.

9. Thomas Bernhard, *Der Theatermacher* (Frankfurt/M.: Suhrkamp, 1984) 11.

10. In a recent interview, Peter Turrini states: "When I write a new play, he takes care of me, supplies me with money, and then

picks up the manuscript ecstatically and runs down the mountain with it." Jutta Landa, "The Drama Is an Exterior Art: An Interview with Peter Turrini," *"I Am Too Many People": Peter Turrini: Playwright, Poet, Essayist*, ed. Jutta Landa (Riverside, CA: Ariadne Press, 1998) 15.

11. In his numerous interviews, Claus Peymann never held back his discontent with Austria, Vienna, and the *Burgtheater* in particular. He culminated his tirades with a three-part "reckoning" which ran in Austria's magazine *profil* from 14 December 1998 to 2 January 1999. Peymann's "guest performance" at the *Burg* came to an end in the wake of the Socialist Viktor Klima's rise to Chancellor in the 1997 elections. The Department of Culture was shifted from the Ministry for Education and Culture, whose Rudolf Scholten had been sympathetic to Peymann's directorial antics, to the Chancellery directly. Subsequently Peymann did not apply for an extension of his contract, which expired in 1999.

12. Claus Peymann, "Abrechnung [III]," *profil* 12 January 1999: 92.

13. Claus Peymann, "Abrechnung [I]" 122.

14. Wendelin Schmidt-Dengler, *Bruchlinien: Vorlesungen zur österreichischen Literatur 1945 bis 1990* (Salzburg, Vienna: Residenz Verlag, 1996) 456.

15. Elfriede Jelinek, "Ein Sportstück," insert in the book edition: *Ein Sportstück* (Reinbek bei Hamburg: Rowohlt, 1998).

16. Elfriede Jelinek, *er nicht als er (zu, mit Robert Walser)* (Frankfurt/M.: Suhrkamp, 1998). My translation of the title does not render Jelinek's wordplay on the Swiss poet's name: Robert Walser.

17. Anke Roeder, "Elfriede Jelinek: 'Ich will kein Theater – Ich will ein anderes Theater,'" *Autorinnen, Herausforderung an das Theater*, ed. Anke Roeder (Frankfurt/M.: Suhrkamp, 1989) 159.

18. Elfriede Jelinek, "Was uns vorliegt. Was uns vorgelegt wurde," *Der Standard* 19 October 1998: 12.

19. Roeder 143.

20. Marlies Janz, *Elfriede Jelinek* (Stuttgart, Weimar: Metzler, 1995) 37.
21. Elfriede Jelinek, *Totenauberg. Ein Stück* (Reinbek bei Hamburg: Rowohlt, 1991) 5.
22. Eva Brenner, "Where Are the Big Topics, Where Is the Big Form?" *Elfriede Jelinek: Framed by Language*, ed. Jorun B. Johns and Katherine Arens (Riverside, CA: Ariadne Press, 1994) 20.
23. See Janz 123.
24. Theatergespräche 22.
25. Werner Schwab, *Fäkaliendramen* (Graz: Droschl, 1991). The volume contains the plays *Die Präsidentinnen*; *ÜBERGEWICHT, unwichtig: UNFORM*; *Volksvernichtung*; and *Mein Hundemund*. Schwab's *Königsdramen* (Graz: Droschl, 1992) contain *Offene Gruben offene Fenster*; *Hochschwab*; *Mesalliance, aber wir ficken uns prächtig*; *Der Himmel mein Lieb meine sterbende Beute*; and *Endlich tot endlich keine Luft mehr*. Subsequent references to *Fäkaliendramen* will be indicated in the text with FD, to *Königskomödien* with KK.
26. Werner Schwab, "Das Grauenvollste – einfach wundervoll," *Theater heute* 12 (1992): 9.
27. Werner Schwab, "Hausbeispiel und Spielgebisz," *Materialien III* (1992/93) (Vienna: Volkstheater, 1992) 6.
28. Wolfgang Reiter, "Dichters Kunst," *profil* 20 September 1999: 167.
29. Peter Handke, *Das Spiel vom Fragen* (Frankfurt/M.: Suhrkamp, 1989) 52.
30. Thomas Assheuer, "Die Ornamente der Ordnung," *Die Zeit* 7 March 1997: 13.
31. Benjamin Henrichs, "Ein Königreich für ein Kind," *Die Zeit* 21 February 1997: 14.
32. "Umstrittener Handke in Wien: Der Skandal blieb aus," *Neue Presse* 16 June 1999: 6. The anonymous article in this German newspaper based in California summarizes German media reactions to the premiere of the play.

33. Klaus Zeyringer, "Bestände, Aufnahmen: Österreichische Literatur der achtziger und beginnenden neunziger Jahre im Überblick," *Germanistische Mitteilungen = Acta Austriaca-Belgica* 2/43-44 (1996): 137.

34. See Karin Kathrein, "Die Welt ist mir abhanden gekommen: Interview with Peter Turrini," *Peter Turrini: Liebe Mörder! Von der Gegenwart, dem Theater und dem lieben Gott*, ed. Silke Hassler and Klaus Siblewski (Munich: Luchterhand, 1996) 115.

35. See the critique of the actor Traugott Buhre, quoted in H. Sichrovsky, D. Kaindl, and S. Ziegler, "Die Schlacht um Turrinis Schlacht," *NEWS* 18 May 1995: 169-70.

36. Peter Turrini, "Die Schlacht um Wien," *Peter Turrini: Liebe Mörder!* 128. See also Jutta Landa, "The Drama is an Exterior Art: An Interview with Peter Turrini," *"I Am Too Many People"* 12-29.

37. This passage has been taken with some slight modifications from Andrea Hacker's unpublished translation of the play (see footnote 8).

38. It is no coincidence that Peter Turrini, in discussing his dramaturgy for *Alpine Glow*, paraphrases the most famous sentence of Hofmannsthal's Lord Chandos letter: "Die Welt ist mir abhanden gekommen" (The world has gone astray from me). *Peter Turrini: Liebe Mörder!* 115.

39. *Watt* 37.

40. While for instance Elfriede Jelinek claims that she does not care what happens to her play in the hands of a director, she has also deplored the fact that few directors can keep up with her visions (see Reiter 16).

41. Peymann was "clandestinely" appointed by the mayor of Vienna at the time, Helmuth Zilk.

42. Bernhard, *Der Theatermacher* 124.

43. P. Schneeberger, "Wien ist nicht Paris, Interview with Hortensia Völckers," *profil* 20 December 1999: 160.

44. *Theatergespräche* 111.

45. Jutta Landa, fax interview with Eva Feitzinger, Los Angeles – Vienna, 2 May 2000. At this point I would also like to thank Eva Feitzinger for all the valuable insider information she has given me on the Austrian theater scene.

"Theater as a Form of Upscale Junkyard": Werner Schwab's Plays: Nonsense That Defies Reason or Disguised Morality?

Beate Hochholdinger-Reiterer

Out of nowhere and without warning, the plays of a young Austrian author captured the German-speaking theater scene in the early 1990s. The characters were recognizable, but the dramatic techniques irritating; the rhetoric sounded familiar but foreign at the same time, forcing the audience to surmise its meaning. On the whole, a relationship to traditional dramatic form could not be denied, and yet this playwright seemed somehow "alien" within the theater universe. How fortunate that this alien quickly evolved into a shooting star. The dull theater establishment of the departing twentieth century needed nothing more desperately than the refreshing, controversial dramaturgy of Werner Schwab.

The young author from Graz gained sudden fame with two highly acclaimed premieres and was quickly dubbed the great new hope of the German-speaking theater. He received numerous prizes and awards.[1] Theaters, greedy for new releases, bombarded Schwab with requests, and he readily complied. His plays and provocative statements created much publicity, and he was celebrated like a popstar by the media. *Zeitgeist*-magazines as well as more serious theater publications were eager to interview the dramatist who staged himself as the *enfant terrible* of Austrian theater. Since the death of Thomas Bernhard in February 1989, the position of "polarizing intellectual" had stood empty. Neither Peter

Handke, nor Peter Turrini, nor Elfriede Jelinek had been able to fill the role, much to the chagrin of a media world that has traditionally profited from the exploitation of controversy or even scandal. Hence Schwab entered the scene "as a real-life market opportunity,"[2] always stressing his persona and his work as one entity, as a *Gesamtkunstwerk*.[3] He referred to himself as "Project Schwab," for which he deduced the following formula: "Management + Legend + Text = Victory + Pleasure."[4]

In an interview from 1992, Schwab stated that "the legend was created by the German *feuilleton*, which enjoys dealing with personalities like me because they expect to receive some previously unknown cultural insight. And because they can use the term 'The blond Giant' once again. If I were only 5'2" tall, fat, balding, and bespectacled, I would lose at least one third of my success."[5] This interview, in addition to offering further examples of the provocation typical of Schwab's public statements, also and more importantly addresses the fact that it is the extraordinary interest of the German literary world – as opposed to that in Austria – that catapulted him to fame. The success of his theater career has depended on the interest of literary reviews in German newspapers, which in turn opened markets in Germany to his work: "This is the oldest story in Austria: that one has to receive justification from abroad before one can be successful within his or her own country."[6] Initial performances of Schwab's plays passed without any significant publicity in Austria.[7] It was only when producer Hans Gratzer began his second tenure at the Viennese *Schauspielhaus* on 12 January 1991 with Schwab's play *ÜBERGEWICHT; unwichtig: UNFORM (OVERWEIGHT, unimportant: MISSHAPE)* that the international press took note of the young author. Then, in the same year, on 25 November 1991, the *Kammerspiele* of Munich premiered the "radical comedy" *Volksvernichtung oder Meine Leber ist sinnlos (People-Annihilation or My Liver Is Senseless)*, and Schwab became one of the most successful dramatists in the German-speaking theater of the late twentieth century.

Werner Schwab died in Graz on 1 January 1994, not quite thirty-six years old. The police report identifies "alcohol poisoning" as the cause of death. The autopsy revealed an alcohol level of 4.1 promille. No evidence was found that Schwab had committed suicide.[8] The public had knowledge of the dramatist's excessive lifestyle; his extreme alcohol consumption as well as his obsessive writing fits and self-abuse had been reported by the media. Nevertheless, Schwab seemed to disappear with the same shocking suddenness with which he had surfaced only a few years earlier. One of the numerous eulogies noted: "A comet whose glow has died out."[9]

Immediately after Schwab's death, those plays that had not yet been performed were staged. However, since 1998, performances of his plays in the German-speaking world are noticeably less common. In addition to radio plays, prose, and essays, Schwab left behind fifteen dramas that have been published in three anthologies and one single-drama edition.[10] English translations are currently available for four of his dramas, including his two most successful ones: *Die Präsidentinnen (First Ladies)* and *People-Annihilation or My Liver Is Senseless*.[11] The two anthologies appearing during Schwab's lifetime – *Fäkaliendramen* (Fecal Dramas) and *Königskomödien* (Royal Comedies) – can be differentiated by their fundamentally different milieus. Whereas the *Fäkaliendramen* are situated in the petite bourgeoisie, the milieu of the underprivileged, the *Königskomödien* take place in a middle-class milieu and the art scene. Schwab wrote three adaptations of the classics and termed them "cover dramas," an allusion to the "cover version" term in pop music.[12] Since Schwab, according to his own statements, typically worked on several plays simultaneously, one cannot establish an accurate chronology for the creation of his dramatic works.

"Tales and Fate are of no interest to me."[13]

Though Schwab altered settings and characters from one drama to the next, he nevertheless remained true to a majority of his themes. The unmasking of the petit-bourgeois family as a hellhole and the exposure of the family ideal as a modern form of serfdom are two themes that find repeated expression. In Schwab's stage world, the phrase "own flesh and blood" is transformed into "children in bondage," and the words reflect the reality he portrays.[14] His dramas present sado-masochistic mother-child relationships, from which the sons fail to free themselves even during adulthood.

> Mrs. Wurm (straightening up like a rod): I am your mother. I brought the gift of life into your body. Because I brought you into the world you did not have to remain in hell where everything has to wait for life. Everything must exist, and I damn you down into all the painful pains where your constantly re-growing sex will be cut off again and again. You will not tear down anything but yourself. You will accompany the dried-up plates into the cupboard, and the garbage can will show you who you are once you have to give it over to the big mass garbage can. (Herbert walks anxiously into the kitchenette and starts to dry dishes vigorously. Mrs. Wurm stands next to him, watching.) (*People-Annihilation*, 249-50)

The brutality of the dominating mother figures (all of them practicing Catholics) corresponds to an equally violent Catholicism in Schwab's plays. According to Elisabeth Krenn, "Schwab does not forego any opportunity to attack and expose the Catholic Church, which he views as an institution of structural violence, of domination and oppression."[15] Liberation attempts seem doomed to failure. The sons respond to their suffering by verbalizing violence and murderous fantasies:

> Herrmann: … But before the old rotting Mom will die out of little Herrmann, little Herrmann will be nice to his Mami one more time. The clever Herrmann will cleverly bore a fresh hole into the head of his Mom and then put his lu-lu

into the Mom-head because he loves his Mom so much, that's what little Herrmann will do. A fresh hole Herrmann bores for himself because the old hole is gruesome to Herrmann, that's the hole he came out of, little cripple Herrmann. ... Yes no, what doesn't she like if one finally is nice to her, the Mom? Uncle stepfather also was nice like that to little Herrmann, oh how he pressed little cripple Herrmann to his throat and stuck the big uncle lulu into the child's mouth and uncle stepfather also said that this is so very nice that one cannot talk about it to anyone. Let the children come to me, is what uncle stepfather said, because he knew his way with his authentic Catholic belief. (*People-Annihilation*, 252)

The above passage is typical of Schwab in its portrayal of pathologically dependent relationships within the petit-bourgeois family. Its depiction of the abuse of children in the family environment is also a constant in Schwab's theater universe and constitutes one of his most important taboo topics. While Herrmann Wurm attempts to master his traumatic childhood experiences through fantasies obsessed with violence, the aggression exhibited by Laura, Greta's daughter in *First Ladies*, is directed towards herself. After she had been abused by her father with the knowledge of her mother, Laura emigrated to Australia, "but before she went she had everything taken out, just like a dressed chicken, the ovaries and God knows what, all the things you need for grandchildren" (*First Ladies*, 8). Another character, Erna, wishes for grandchildren, but her hope also remains unfulfilled since her son abstains from engaging in intercourse so as to spite her. "Erna: ... And he could so easily have an intercourse, the way things are today. Nowadays people are having an intercourse all the time, but he deliberately doesn't have an intercourse, because an intercourse like that can set off a real pregnancy and at the end of the day that might possibly add up to a little grandchild" (*First Ladies*, 7).

Numerous dialogues in Schwab's work center on the significance of producing offspring, be it children or grandchildren. These conversations, often ideologically garnished, reflect the parents' and grandparents' egotism and claim of ownership motivated by their need for the continuation of the family. In *OVERWEIGHT, unimportant: MISSHAPE*, Piggy is convinced that "our progeny will carry on spreading us into all the futures" (*OVERWEIGHT*, 67), a concept which – considering the course of events of the play – can only be interpreted as a dangerous threat. Such a threat finds immediate embodiment as Piggy himself is revealed to be a pederast and perverted Christian. Schwab's play is subtitled *A European Supper*. The symbolic consumption of the Body of Christ, the highpoint of a Catholic Mass, is rendered real on stage as the Beautiful Couple falls victim to the collective cannibalism of the inn's guests.

OVERWEIGHT, unimportant: MISSHAPE can also be interpreted as thematizing Austria's National Socialist past. It is "a play about a special kind of inheritance, the proof of belonging to a strong breed. *Natural Born Killers* made in Austria."[16] In Schwab's plays the generation that experienced and survived the Nazi terror regime encounters the next generation which, according to the author, unconsciously perpetuates the Nazi legacy. By allowing his characters to blurt out fascist rhetoric or to deliver flowery but empty speeches about "the final victory of human reason" (*OVERWEIGHT*, 58), Schwab ties xenophobic sentiments of current-day Austria to its Nazi past.

> Mister Haider: Furthermore, we are not really a truthfully real family. A garden is our substitute child. My wife has sealed ovaries from providence. The couple we are describing will never have screaming children. My wife is as sterile as a used-up eraser. For every one of our unborn children two foreign quarter-beings create an eighth of a being, which will have to exist as an inferior Austrian. Until now, as the town-councilor of our

community, I have been able to impede the entire foreign world.[17]

Schwab's radical exposure of the family as an ideologically questionable and structurally violent institution is developed primarily in reflection of Nazi history and the Catholic clerical traditions in Austria. Thus the ideology of the family as the core of the state loses all positive connotations in his works, as stated by Mrs. Kovacic, a character from *People-Annihilation*: "An authentic state is a big-bodied family where everything finds itself together of its own accord, and a real cutthroat family must be able to stick together" (27). It is precisely those characters who claim to embody the ideal family image that are most consistently exposed by Schwab as possessing highly suspect value systems. Their questionable consciences are revealed through their own actions, their interrelationships, and most obviously by their language use.[18] When the father catches his son masturbating in *Antiklimax* (Anti-Climax), he rejects the son's suggestion to join him with the following words: "Never. What the likes of you is erecting here will be wasted away by a government, drop for drop. But I am the *Volk*, and the *Volk* does not touch itself indecently. No, never. The *Volk* does not masturbate, it impregnates."[19]

Schwab implies with repeated vehemence a connection between the family on the one hand and society or the state in general on the other, between the family home or neighborhood inn and the collective living room or beer tent of the nation, and the connection is underlined on the linguistic level through his use of Nazi vocabulary. Such parallels of course lend themselves to broader political interpretations.[20] The characters' empty statements about being rooted in a common way of life also demonstrate explicitly that Schwab's plays do not deal with the fate of individuals. Rather, the author presents cross-sections of what is frequently and popularly termed the "Austrian Soul."[21]

> Mr. Kovacic: Nothing is ever dreary in solidarity, no end of togetherness luxuriates there. Community is the sense of life.
>
> Mrs. Kovacic: A family is the best example of such an example.
>
> Mr. Kovacic: Where there is a family there are no unkissed people. Where there is a family there is an economy, and where an economy marches up, a state climbs up and where a state is at home there life returns into an orderliness.
> (*People-Annihilation*, 265)

At the beginning of his career, Schwab was suspected by some reviewers of flirting with right-wing thought. Such misinterpretation is perhaps understandable considering the difficulty and even inaccessibility of much of his dramatic oeuvre; many critics simply did not recognize or understand his artistic principle of the "transforming montage." However, Schwab's dramas are in fact an attempt to deal with Austria's unresolved past.[22] And it is above all the *language* of the past that has not been overcome. Since the characters "do not speak but are spoken for,"[23] they unconsciously emit obscenities as well as Nazi and fascist ideologies without thinking and without filtering them – and without suffering any consequences for them. In *First Ladies*, Greta, a former Nazi sympathizer and accomplice in knowing of her daughter's abuse at their hands, states: "You have to take words the way they come out" (28).

In November 1991, shortly before the premiere of *People-Annihilation or My Liver Is Senseless*, the author issued the following response to a question concerning the social criticism in his work:

> But I claim that the theater is not responsible for direct social criticism, because it is always bad theater when one intends to do that. In my works this kind of material is presented as scrap metal, with a scrapped half-life of time ... I do not care

> about the topic, irrespective if it is the revised edition of a Donald Duck story or hostility towards foreigners. For me, it is all linguistic material that has lost its societal relevance and hangs around like scrap metal in a junkyard. Scrap with which I play. Theater as a form of upscale junkyard.[24]

Schwab's relationship with the public can be regarded as a witty and permanent *game* that he has played with the media, a game marked by a proliferation of supposedly revealing self-commentary. The dramatist has not shied away from offering his own interpretations, but such authorial comments must of course be taken as part of an intentional marketing strategy. Indeed, from the beginning Schwab created the image of a politically incorrect and barely schooled literary *enfant terrible*, and he continued to cultivate this image in every subsequent interview. According to critic Helmut Schödel, "Schwab invented a double to fit the nightmarish image. He brought out the dark sides of his personality and sold his shadow as the author Werner Schwab: With long strides in pilot boots, with flying trenchcoat and a blond strand of hair, the bad city cowboy conquered our snug little theater scene."[25] Provocation was demanded at any price, which is why Schwab's statements concerning his own work can only be evaluated vis-à-vis his projected image. In my opinion, Schwab's self-stylization has obstructed the critical response to his works. Above all, his supposed disinterest in social themes, his refusal to take a moral stand, and his staged cynicism have persistently determined the interpretation of his texts.[26]

However, Schwab's greatest achievement lies precisely in his ability to discover and reveal – through montage and the overt alienation of his linguistic material – new relationships of meaning in the "linguistic scrap metal." This achievement stands in opposition to the part of his image which denounces that very same artistic procedure and is directed instead at pleasing a media world interested solely in quotable quotes and placard labels such as "Scrap metal with a scrapped half-life of time." The casualness with which themes are adopted or dropped in one play, only to reappear under different circumstances in another, is programmatic for Schwab and it serves to challenge the audience to peer behind his "word scenes." Within a single play one can identify many "sub-relationships."[27] However, they will reveal their complexities and cleverness only when one recognizes the links between the texts and actively participates in the reconstruction of the whole.[28]

"How vilely language elucidates, defends, and destroys itself."[29]

By far the most significant sign of Schwab's work is his artistic language, created and recreated in every text. Its uniqueness has stood at the center of popular and scholarly attention from the very beginning.[30] It became immediately apparent that Schwab's style was "well-designed, repetitive, yet not easily imitated, and recognizable": simply put – "a trademark."[31] On the occasion of Schwab's recognition as Young Dramatist of the Year in 1991, Peter von Becker described the author's dramatic prose with these words:

> Schwab combines slang and officialese, waste paper and waste words, fantasies of sex and violence, malice and a longing for life or even love to create an artificial, exaggerated (and sometimes overloaded) realism. The many monstrous words obtain a truly urgent and monstrous physicality. Each character is also a language body, demolished and obscene, which provokes and irritates the reader, audience, public with its naked "misshape." Sentences break out in leprosy; bodies become cripples. Damaged, deformed life takes its toll as it speaks.[32]

With every new drama the specific idiom was perfected, but occasionally driven to the limits of comprehensibility.[33] Each drama provides instructions for the director, for stage setup, and for individual characters, as well as details on the language to be utilized: "The language the first ladies generate is what they are themselves. To generate (clarify) oneself is hard work, which means that basically everything is resistance. That should appear in the play as effort" (*First Ladies*, 2). As has already become evident, the characters are not masters over their own language: "Language drags the person behind – like tin cans tied to a dog's tail."[34] Schwab's artistic language at its best can be recognized as a further extension of Austria's critical prose tradition reaching from Johann Nestroy to Elfriede Jelinek, though a detailed analysis would undoubtedly highlight existing differences.

Schwab's dramatic prose is not marked by any form of dialect. However, structures of Austrian colloquial speech (for example, the use of the indefinite article with abstract terms as well as definite articles with names) have been transported into High German and then combined with a bureaucratic officialese consisting of "nominalizations and verbal phrases."[35] Intensive use of neologisms, the reversal of subject and object, and a preference for the passive voice all serve to underscore the I-lessness, i.e., the lack of a sense of self, suffered by the characters, and such characteristics contribute to the uniqueness of Schwab's language. Signature traits of Schwab's style also include incorrect usage of prepositions and particles, as well as proliferation of such within a word or sentence construction. Finally, a large part of the humor underlying Schwab's work derives from the invention of unexpected and irritating metaphors drawn from frequently outrageous or provocative areas: "The semantic fields from which the majority of Schwab's metaphors emanate can roughly be apportioned to the spheres of the *human body, animals, feces, language, nature, religion, and nourishment.*"[36] Schwab's primary intent is to "create semantic confusion."[37] Scholar Elisabeth Krenn adds as an additional motivating force behind Schwab's idiosyncratic and highly creative language the playwright's "childlike joy of playing with words." Krenn continues:

> Just as he created sculptures with decaying material in a process of dismantling and constructing something new, he destroyed language to reconstruct it anew, but according to his strict rules: upon the destructive act of demolition follows the constructive act of recreation. ... His plastic and logical language, which sounds so broken, is the equivalent of the broken characters in his works.[38]

The tight mesh of body and language in Schwab's dramas, identified initially by the *feuilletons* as being significant, has become a popular topic for scholarly analyses of Schwab's theater texts as well.[39] In Schwab's theater it is a small step from the internal world of the characters to the insides of their body. "Bile and phlegm, tongues, sperm, holes, and flesh become dialogue-metaphors for conditions that are of the outside world as well as of the soul. By writing 'the skin off the body' of his characters, Schwab renders inwardness figural in a literal sense."[40] It is precisely this grotesque and even lascivious language, its negation of every norm and convention, which constitutes the extreme theatricality of Schwab's works, and it is this theatricality which has made them in turn so immensely popular. The author's "hope to save the theater" lies in his ability "to transform language into pure human flesh ... and of course vice versa as well."[41]

Attempts to situate such drama within literary tradition identified Franz Xaver Kroetz's and Heinz R. Unger's critical folk play (*Volksstück*) early on. Of course, in line with his "bad cowboy" image, Schwab resisted such associations: "I wanted to write something totally foreign to me, so why not a type of folk play. But I am not at all interested in its social dimension."[42] One cannot deny the presence of diverse artistic influences upon Schwab's dramas. Three traditional paths suggested by Dieter Hornig appear particularly plausible to me:

> The first of these traditional paths accords with Alfred Jarry. Artaud's "Theater of Brutality" – the

> Artaud-biography by Elena Kapralik ... was Schwab's Bible – up to Beckett and Thomas Bernhard. ... Another path lies within the Austrian tradition. It is a path that reaches from the *Fastnachtspiele*, the *Volkstheater* and the *Hanswurst* of the eighteenth century through Nestroy to Karl Kraus, Canetti, Horváth, and the scenic texts of the *Wiener Gruppe*. A tradition of orality, of farce and the grotesque, of the "radical comedies," to use one of Schwab's terms, in which the entire uncensored body is put to use once again...[43]

As the third path Hornig identifies "that tradition of painting which reduces the body to its material substance, to the tortured, flayed body as seen in the apocalyptic pictures by Bosch, or to its cadaver, painting as anatomy as in the pictures of Leonardo, then Goya, and finally Francis Bacon. Within the Viennese context, which was well known to Schwab, one can point to the drawings of Alfred Hrdlicka and Alfred Frohner."[44] This third, non-literary line is lent further weight when one considers the fact that Schwab studied sculpture in Vienna before turning to writing.

Schwab's works contain numerous references to various artistic traditions. However, while the fact of intertextuality is irrefutable, disagreement exists concerning the intention and meaning of such literary quotation and indeed of his theater in general. Julian Preece elucidates the playwright's impressive technical and reflective ability by means of content analyses that extend beyond individual works, and always in consideration of the genre's theoretical context and the realization of the texts on stage:

> Schwab becomes a master of styles and genres, an adept technician of plot and structure. The impression of sameness is engendered merely by his language; here the variations are subtle. His rootedness in the theatre is explicit, too, in the manner that all his plays are, in one way or

another, highly self-conscious works of art, which draw attention constantly to their own artifice and artificiality; to their status as performances.[45]

Günther A. Höfler arrives at a contrasting conclusion when he determines the main attributes of Schwab's works to be the "impermeability for coherent interpretations and intensity."[46] Where Preece regards Schwab's treatment of drama traditions and theater conventions as reflective and meaningful, Höfler emphasizes the inability to classify Schwab's approach. According to Höfler, Schwab's texts establish their appeal by making use of formal signals that trigger pre-existing expectations which are not, however, realized.

> The montage technique of placing diverse structural models with signals ending nowhere side by side with an episodic abundance creates inconsistency and thwarts any attempt to recognize a story line. The arrangement of formal clichés, topoi, popular genres, and other elements develops into a patchwork that can no longer be considered a folk play (*Volksstück*). On the contrary, it lays the foundation for a shock-oriented Performance event that informs about nothing and poses no questions and which no longer permits any logical form of interpretation. Consequently, the theater code gravitates toward dissolution. The suspense between story and plot, constitutive of any conventional play, is entirely lacking: where there is no story, the plot itself becomes arbitrary.[47]

Such an interpretation raises a question concerning the popular appeal of Schwab's plays: How can a play that dissolves the theater code enjoy such indisputable success? Sooner or later those scholars who stress the lack of psychological depth, the stiffness, and the absence of locality in Schwab's stage figures must confront the question concerning the causes for the overwhelming public success of Schwab productions.[48] Is it enough, to use Höfler's words, that a play portrays nothing but "the act of its own realization?" It "does not provoke thought, rather it evokes laughter – at least that."[49]

A reading of Schwab's dramas that focuses on issues of staging and theatricality reveals that these plays are in fact eminently functional for the conventional theater. Thus, even though Höfler's observation of "episodic abundance" is correct, one simply cannot speak of a dissolution of story. Schwab's plays consist of basic plots that are relatively easy to summarize: In *First Ladies* three women watch the telecast of a papal sermon and enjoy an improvised little celebration over the next few hours during which they reveal their personal biographies and secret aspirations. In *OVERWEIGHT, unimportant: MISSHAPE* representatives of various social classes rendezvous in a local inn; a Beautiful Couple that is also present falls victim to murder followed by cannibalism. *People-Annihilation or My Liver Is Senseless* features a landlady who invites her tenants to a birthday party in order to poison them during dinner. And in *MESALLIANCE aber wir ficken uns prächtig* (MESALLIANCE, but We Do Fuck Splendidly) plans are made for the approaching birthday party of the twins Johannes and Johanna that is to include the entire neighborhood. While the party is in progress the incestuous twins are caught by their parents in intimate embrace in the bathroom.

These basic plots are developed using mainly conventional dramatic techniques. Direct and indirect character traits are portrayed through dialogue; time and location barriers are overcome through the use of teichoscopic techniques. For example, in *First Ladies* the three main figures together imagine a folk festival in which each woman freely fantasizes about her individual aspirations for joy. The plays exhibit expositions, culminating climaxes, and multiple endings within a single play. This principle of "soft" or "retracted" endings, whose purpose is to present not one story but a conglomerate of stories, constitutes together with his artistic language the uniqueness of Schwab's dramatic innovation. According to Schwab, a play should follow the principle of a mathematic equation, "which cancels itself out at the end. It has to be readable from the beginning and from the end as an equation. Otherwise, it is not a good play."[50] In one of his earliest interviews, conducted in November 1990 during rehearsals for the premiere of *OVERWEIGHT, unimportant: MISSHAPE*, Schwab states that he undoubtedly uses "traditional structures" and continues: "I am thirty-two years old and have seen just one play all my life. ... As far as dramaturgy is concerned, you either know how to do it or you don't."[51]

The recognition of basic traditional dramatic structures by the audience was certainly a key contributor to Schwab's success. The multitude of conflicting analyses of Schwab's work is driven, in my opinion, to a large extent by precisely this discussion concerning innovation: Has Schwab, this supposedly so innovative dramatist, in fact created anything new? According to Austrian journalist Sigrid Löffler, an affirmed Schwab opponent, the playwright has introduced only "two special innovations": first, the "trick with the retracted ending," and second, an artistic language which she calls his "special idiom as bully. ... Two such innovations are evidently sufficient to position the newcomer Schwab overnight in the theater world – as long as one gives his image a bit of a boost. He thrives on being a lout."[52]

Schwab employs traditional dramatic techniques, but gradually changes them. Hence, the last act of the radical comedy *OVERWEIGHT, unimportant: MISSHAPE* – in which the Beautiful Couple that had previously been murdered and consumed is resurrected – can be interpreted as a reclaimed exposition. Whereas the couple is mute at the beginning of the play, they engage at the end in complacent and arrogant conversation. In a strict reading that emphasizes chronology, the motivation for the collective murder appears to be revenge. However, if we ignore the logic of cause and effect such retracted endings can be interpreted as attempts at radical subjectivity and fragmentation of perspective. Schwab comments: "Because only through exaggeration can you explain something. If you try to remain as objective as possible, you can't communicate anything at all. But from the very beginning, and especially in the endings, I greatly tempered this, which then prompted more than one critic to have the effrontery as well as stupidity to accuse me of cowardice."[53] A further example is offered by MESALLIANCE *aber wir ficken uns prächtig*. The final act brings to a close the basic plot – namely, the ending of the previous act with the discovery of the incestuous relationship of the twins – but in three different versions. And the reason for such fracturing and proliferation of perspective is, according to Schwab, that it is "much harder, more gruesome and more disillusioning when a firm continuum falls apart into nothingness."[54]

Most scholars and feuilletonists agree that Schwab's depiction of character is marked by a lack of psychological depth. The stage directions quoted earlier in this article support such an argument in their emphasis on language as opposed to character. According to Günther Höfler, the dramatic figures do not possess or determine language and they cannot express themselves through language; rather, language speaks itself and thereby attains its own physical dimension. The lack of a dramatic sub-text causes the "characters and the actual horror to appear strangely hollow and flat. Since everything is said, and the signifier tends to merge with the signified, no reference to a hidden meaning or image can be detected – and with that, there is no desire to comprehend the text. This is one of the causes for boredom when one reads these dramas."[55] Considering his figures' purported shallowness or indeterminate contours, one must again ask why so many actresses and actors applaud the "incredible physicality"[56] of Schwab's characters, why they see in his dramas such a richness of possible roles. I believe it is precisely the combination of a conventional, but somehow altered dramaturgy with the artificiality of Schwab's language that renders these plays enjoyable for actors and public alike.[57] Just as it is possible to reconstruct basic plots from Schwab's plays, so too do his characters take on concrete form and plasticity through their actions and dialogue. Though they eschew solutions and simplifications, these dramas do unfold at least elements of the characters' life stories on stage. In short, Schwab's works function on the conventional stage primarily because they follow conventional structures and patterns. By placing too much emphasis on his irritating language, his retracted endings, and the portrayal of violence and destruction, in conjunction with the public's desire for something "new," Schwab's critics have deflected attention from the dramatist's very real artistic talent. A "genius" was needed to define a new dramatic form at the end of the twentieth century, and thus the media promoted Schwab as such.[58]

"Writing is never fun, writing is always deadly."[59]

Critiques of Schwab's dramas as texts, as opposed to stage productions, consistently mention boredom and intellectual strain on the part of the reader.[60] However, on stage the boredom is somehow overcome. According to Michael Merschmeier:

> the highly artificial nature of the language changes into a strange realism as soon as it no longer exists on paper but is actually spoken out loud. This produces an uncanny, frightening outcry against the world of organized syntax, of distinct rules and true words and values. Schwab's language is full of smutty, frenzied tragi-comedy.[61]

In other words, precisely because the characters are at the mercy of the words they utter, and because objects and subjects in Schwab's artistic language have reversed themselves, the *embodiment* of the roles by actors and actresses seems to be so successful. It is as if Schwab's texts, in which the body disintegrates into individual fragments and ingredients, depend to an extreme extent on the bodies of the actors and actresses. "Schwab's body texts – as compared with Jelinek's texts – have the advantage that they can be applied onto the actor's body and hence gain physicality. In this way Schwab apparently is able to return the body, threatened by annihilation, to the stage."[62]

Violence and destruction are determining elements both as content and form, whereby verbal and physical violence are of equal significance in the texts. On the verbal level, standard High German is shattered and replaced by the Schwab "idiom," and this corresponds on the physical level to the violent outbreaks and killings portrayed on stage.

> People never hide their thoughts or motives because they say everything out loud. This makes Frau Grollfeuer's racist attacks on the Kovacic family, or the accusations of adultery in *MESALLIANCE* all the more brutal for their unclothed aggression and directness. Although no one would usually express such abuse directly and, when it is expressed, it is in any case not usually meant literally, the remarks are simply the literal articulation of metaphorical insults. In this sense there is often no dramatic 'subtext' to the dialogue. When someone says: 'I could murder you,' or words to that effect, he means the threat and is probably about to carry it out. As a result of the latent violence of spoken thoughts, the violent scenes in Schwab's plays, which inevitably attract much attention, are in no way gratuitous or divorced from the dramatic action.[63]

The uninhibited speech flow of the characters functions to overcome the missing dramatic subtext. The characters' inner depths and motivation are not hidden between the lines or in unspoken words; the words themselves speak more than clearly for themselves and for their speakers. The multitude of interpretations that are possible for the text do not arise from what is *not* said but rather from what *is* said, from that which explicitly flows forth from the characters, and this also explains why actors and actresses often refer to the plasticity of their roles. Where language becomes the body of the character, only the "bodying forth"[64] of language, i.e., only the on-stage realization can project the meaning or sense demanded by an audience. This reminds us of Thomas Bernhard's plays where a successful staging produced a so-called grammar for accessing the texts and also demonstrated the author's mastery of dramaturgy. Similarly, the eminent theatricality and tragicomic qualities of Schwab's plays first became apparent through their successful staging.

Perhaps paradoxically, scholars reconstruct an order and sense for Schwab's oeuvre of deconstruction, whereby their critical analysis and attribution of meaning mitigate the many layers of performed violence. In contrast, the undeniable elements of playful chance in his works seem to create problems. It is possible to unravel the many playfully self-referential comments in his work. The playwright endows characters from different dramas performing different functions with the same name (for example Herrmann or Mariedl) and names public figures on the basis of various roles, behaviors, or political convictions (for example Herr Haider). He incorporates misleading biographical traits (for example Herrmann Wurm as the dramatist's alter ego) and varied literary traditions. It is also possible to explore the deconstruction and reconstruction of language within the context of literary play. However, there is a danger in concentrating exclusively on the decoding and determination of meaning. Exploration must strive to describe the Schwab idiom and not categorize or even standardize it according to linguistic criteria.

Schwab's irritating texts yield diametrically opposing interpretations precisely because of the playful sense of randomness presented on the surface of his plays. It is not possible within the context of a single play to comprehend any of the themes satisfactorily. Furthermore, the genre classifications defy comprehension, leaving the audience to take them as a joke of the author. Finally, the artistic language is inconsistent, frequently ambiguous, and accordingly all too easily dismissed as pure nonsense. Only in the context of Schwab's entire oeuvre, the significance of which has certainly not yet been fully recognized, can we attempt to construct meaningful connections and relationships. The openness of the texts grants a certain freedom of interpretation to scholars, actors, and actresses. The determination of meaning must after all remain fragmentary.

Any attempt to interpret Schwab's oeuvre solely on the basis of his public image will yield nothing more than the label of "nonsense-drama."[65] An alternative and more productive method is to accept the image as part of the general game, to reject his programmatic refusals to reveal meaning, and to confront the destruction by searching for sub-relationships. In this way, an understanding of Schwab's oeuvre might be facilitated. But only provisionally of course, only for the time being, for in the words of the playwright: "Writing a play? That's nothing more than making a crude remark."[66]

Translated by Mark Ampaw and Linda C. DeMeritt

Notes

1. In March of 1991, Schwab received the *Forum Stadtpark-Literaturförderungspreis* in Graz. In May of the same year the premiere of *ÜBERGEWICHT, unwichtig: UNFORM* was invited to the theater festival in Mülheim, and Schwab was proclaimed to be representative of a new generation of dramatists. In October of 1991, the journal *Theater heute* selected him as Young Dramatist of the Year and promoted him to Dramatist of the Year the very next season. Schwab also received the Mülheim Award for Drama in 1992.

2. Michael Merschmeier, "'Alles Tote bin ich.' Über den Dramatiker Werner Schwab – und Aspekte des Theatermarkts," *Theater heute* 2 (1994): 1.

3. See for example Sigrid Löffler, "Monstren, Gefühle und sieben Gerüchte," *Süddeutsche Zeitung* 5 October 1993: 13: "The Germanic Hun – two meters tall, with square jaw and blond hair, born in 1958 – has been declared the new hit of the year. And all thanks to the right design and appropriate ideological style of his

public appearances: Baudrillard or Derrida at the tip of his tongue and preferably in black leather, one strand of hair falling over an eye."

4. "Koberg am Apparat: Herr Schwab, was ist eine Karriere?" *Falter* 3 April 1992: 28.

5. "Koberg am Apparat" 28.

6. Elisabeth Loibl, "Philosoph & Popstar," *Basta* [Vienna] 11 (November 1992): 140.

7. *Das Lebendige ist das Leblose und die Musik* premiered in a discotheque in Graz on 22 April 1989, directed by Werner Schwab. The premiere of *Präsidentinnen* took place in the *Künstlerhaustheater*, Vienna, on 13 February 1990, directed by Günter Panak.

8. *Bericht der Bundespolizeidirektion Graz, Kriminalpolizeiliche Abteilung*, quoted according to Helmut Schödel, *Seele brennt. Der Dichter Werner Schwab* (Vienna: Deuticke, 1995) 108.

9. *Kleine Zeitung* [Graz] 4 January 1994; signed by Werner Krause and Frido Hütter.

10. The two anthologies are *Fäkaliendramen* (Graz, Vienna: Droschl, 1996); *Königskomödien* (Graz, Vienna: Droschl, 1996); and *Dramen III* (Graz, Vienna: Droschl, 1994). The single drama is DER REIZENDE REIGEN *nach dem Reigen des* REIZENDEN HERRN ARTHUR SCHNITZLER (Graz, Vienna: Droschl, 1996).

11. *Die Präsidentinnen* has been translated three times. All quotes for this article are taken from *First Ladies: Three Scenes, Werner Schwab: An Anthology of Plays*, trans. Michael Mitchell (Riverside, CA: Ariadne Press, 1999). The other two translations are *The Presidents*, trans. Ivo Schneider and Sarah Morrissette (Vienna: Thomas Sessler, 1991); and *Holy Mothers*, trans. Meredith Oakes (London: Casarotto Ramsay, 1999).

People-Annihilation or My Liver Is Senseless, trans. Michael Roloff, *Seven Contemporary Austrian Plays*, ed. Richard H. Lawson (Riverside, CA: Ariadne Press, 1995). All quotes for this article are taken from this translation.

ÜBERGEWICHT; *unwichtig: UNFORM* has been translated twice. All quotes for this article are taken from *OVERWEIGHT, unimportant: MISSHAPE: A European Supper* in *Werner Schwab: An Anthology of Plays*, trans. Michael Mitchell (Riverside, CA: Ariadne Press, 1999). The other translation is *OVERWEIGHT, unimportant: MISSHAPE: A European Supper*, trans. Michael Mitchell (Vienna: Thomas Sessler, no year). Subsequent quotes from these three dramas will be indicated within the article itself by page number and *First Ladies*, *People-Annihilation*, or *OVERWEIGHT* respectively.

12. The three cover dramas are *Troiluswahn und Cressidatheater*; *Faust :: Mein Brustkorb : Mein Helm*; and *DER REIZENDE REIGEN nach dem Reigen des REIZENDEN HERRN ARTHUR SCHNITZLER*.

13. Roland Koberg and Klaus Nüchtern, "Vernichten, ohne sich anzupatzen," *Falter* 9 September 1992: Beilage.

14. The English translation of this particular passage does not sufficiently convey the intended ambiguity and play on words of the German, which reads as follows:

"Erna: Ja, so ist das menschliche Leben. Da versucht man das ganze Leben lang einen ordentlichen Lebensweg zu gehen, und dann wenden sich die leibeigenen Kinder ab vom Leben und von der Menschlichkeit" (*Die Präsidentinnen* in *Fäkaliendramen*, 19).

"Erna: Yes, that's human life for you. You spend your whole life trying to live a decent life and your own children, your own flesh and blood, turn their backs on life and on humanity" (*First Ladies*, 9).

15. Elisabeth Krenn, *Gewalt und Agression in den Dramen von Werner Schwab* (Graz: Dipl.-Arb., 1995) 26.

16. Schödel, *Seele brennt* 106.

17. Quote taken from the drama *MESALLIANCE aber wir ficken uns prächtig*, contained in *Königskomödien*, 149. The reference to Jörg Haider, head of the Austrian Freedom Party at the time of the drama's writing, is obvious.

18. For example, family Kovacic in *People-Annihilation*, family Pestalozzi in *MESALLIANCE* or Mariedl's family in *Antiklimax*.
19. *Antiklimax*, in *Dramen III*, 287f.
20. See the results of Dieter Hornig's study "Werner Schwab: Groteske Körper / Obszöne Stimmen" (unpublished manuscript), 10: "The father role is a National Socialist role, a role of the *Volk*. [...] The fathers' bodies serve the ideology of the *Volk* and at the same time they are helplessly subjugated to femininity and the drive to reproduce, the drive of omnipotent mothers to give birth."
21. See Schödel, *Seele brennt* 107: "Schwab's bandits are not outsiders lurking about in places scorned by society; they do not occupy condemned houses or conspirators' apartments. They live as the population. It's a nightmare: *The entire country*!"
22. For a history of the reception of Schwab's dramas, see Barbara Schmiedl, *"Schrott mit einer schrottenen Halbwertszeit." Werner Schwab, seine Arbeitsmethode und die Rezeption seiner Werke in den Medien* (Graz: Dipl.-Arb., 1996).
23. Koberg and Nüchtern.
24. Lothar Lohs, "Der Schrottplatz, auf dem ich spiele," *Der Standard* 23/24 November 1991: 13.
25. Schödel, *Seele brennt*, 121f. Schödel, one of Schwab's "discoverers," seems to have taken on the task since Schwab's death of tracing biographical influences in his work and revising the dramatist's own biographical notes. Schwab's self-proclaimed ignorance concerning literary traditions, for example, is now being questioned – and justifiably so: "his dismissive attitude to the theatre, particularly his claim that he had hardly ever been to see a play, concealed a knowledge of twentieth-century dramatic tradition as profound and dynamic as that of any of his contemporaries." Quoted from Julian Preece, "Form, structure, and poetry in the varied plays of Werner Schwab," *Centre Stage. Contemporary Drama in Austria*, ed. Frank Finley and Ralf Jeutter (Amsterdam: Rodopi, 1999) 16.

26. See my essay: "Der österreichische Dramatiker Werner Schwab – der Shootingstar als Eintagsfliege?," *Jahrbuch der Österreich-Bibliothek in St. Petersburg*, Vol. 4 (1999/2000): forthcoming.
27. Preface of *Fäkaliendramen*, 10.
28. One of the most recent and insightful attempts to do exactly that is the article by Julian Preece cited above in *Centre Stage*.
29. *MESALLIANCE aber wir ficken uns prächtig*, in *Fäkaliendramen* 123.
30. See for example: Auguste Brunnthaler, *Werner Schwab – "Ein Sprach-Täter"* (Vienna: Dipl.-Arb., 1998); Dragutin Horvat, "Zersprachlichung der Wirklichkeit – Zerwirklichung der Sprache: Werner Schwab," *Zagreber Germanistische Beiträge. Jahrbuch für Literatur- und Sprachwissenschaft* Beiheft 2 (1994): 101-06; Elisabeth Krenn, *Gewalt und Aggression in den Dramen von Werner Schwab* (Graz: Dipl.-Arb., 1995); Jutta Landa, "'Königskomödien' oder 'Fäkaliendramen'? Zu den Theaterstücken von Werner Schwab," *Modern Austrian Literature* 26.3-4 (1993): 215-29; Gerda Elisabeth Moser, "Oswald Wiener – Werner Schwab. Anfang und Ende einer radikalen literarischen Sprachkritik," *ide (Informationen zur Deutschdidaktik)* 18.4 (1994): 97-109; Julian Preece, "The Use of Language in the Plays of Werner Schwab: Towards a definition of 'Das Schwabische,'" *Contemporary German Writers, Their Aesthetics and Their Language*, ed. Arthur Williams, Stuart Parkes, and Julian Preece (Bern, Berlin: Peter Lang, 1996) 267-82; Sandra Račko, *Das Schwabische und der Dreck. Zum Sprachgebrauch in Werner Schwabs 'Fäkaliendramen'* (Vienna: Dipl.-Arb., 1995); Hannelore Schlaffer, "Die Wörter des grotesken Körpers. Der Dramatiker Werner Schwab," *Merkur. Deutsche Zeitschrift für europäisches Denken* 48.538-549 (1994): 265-71; Birgit Wurm, *'Man kann eben nichts als die Sprache...'. Stilistische Untersuchungen an Werner Schwabs 'Fäkaliendramen'* (Vienna: Dipl.-Arb., 1997).
31. Michael Merschmeier, "'Alles Tote bin ich'. Über den Dramatiker Werner Schwab – und Aspekte des Theatermarkts," *Theater heute* 2 (1994): 1.

32. Peter von Becker, "Der Jung-Dramatiker des Jahres – Sätze wie Aussatz: 'Wir sind in die Welt gevögelt und können nicht fliegen'. Über Werner Schwabs Monster-Debüt *Übergewicht Unwichtig Unform*," *Theater 1991, Jahrbuch der Zeitschrift "Theater heute"*: 140.

33. This is undoubtedly the reason that Schwab's two early dramas have been translated more frequently than others. *First Ladies* and *People-Annihilation or My Liver Is Senseless*, both of which are linguistically more accessible than later works, have been translated into more than ten languages. Altogether, eight Schwab plays have appeared in translation. As of May 2000, the following remain untranslated: *OFFENE GRUBEN OFFENE FENSTER. EIN FALL von Ersprechen*; *HOCHSCHWAB: Das Lebendige ist das Leblose und die Musik*; *MESALLIANCE aber wir ficken uns prächtig*; *Troiluswahn und Cressidatheater*; and *Pornogeographie*.

34. *Mein Hundemund, Fäkaliendramen* 181.

35. Wurm 44.

36. Wurm 61. Emphasis in the original.

37. Wurm 60.

38. Krenn 99.

39. See for example Corina Caduff, "Kreuzpunkt Körper: Die Inszenierungen des Leibes in Text und Theater. Zu den Theaterstücken von Elfriede Jelinek und Werner Schwab," *Das Geschlecht der Künste*, ed. Corina Caduff and Sigrid Weigel (Cologne, Weimar, Vienna: Böhlau, 1996) 154-74; and Dieter Hornig; Hannelore Schlaffer, and Thomas Trenkler, "Die Krüppelwürmer. Der Defekt in den Dramen von Werner Schwab," *Germanistische Mitteilungen* 43/44 (1996): 165-74.

40. Caduff 160f.

41. Werner Schwab, "Das Grauenvollste – einfach wundervoll," *Theater heute* 12 (1991): 9.

42. Michael Merschmeier, "Talent trifft Talent – Graz meets Oberammergau. Vampir Familie oder Ödipus Farce. Werner Schwabs *Volksvernichtung oder Meine Leber ist sinnlos* an den Münchner Kammerspielen uraufgeführt," *Theater heute* 1 (1992): 32.

43. Hornig 2.
44. Hornig 3.
45. Preece, "Form, structure, and poetry" 27.
46. Günther Höfler, "'Stop making sense'. Werner Schwabs Pop-Stück *Mesalliance aber wir ficken uns prächtig* – ein modernes Volksstück?," *Jenseits des Diskurses – Literatur und Sprache in der Postmoderne*, ed. Albert Berger and Gerda Elisabeth Moser (Vienna: Passagen, 1994) 330.
47. Höfler 330f.
48. See for example the articles cited above by Dragutin Horvat, Jutta Landa, and Hannelore Schlaffer.
49. Höfler 332.
50. Thomas Trenkler and Wolfgang Kralicek, "Kunst wider den guten Geschmack," *Parnaß* 1 (1991): 70.
51. Unpublished interview with Werner Schwab, conducted by Wolfgang Kralicek on 26 November 1990, 5. The typescript of the interview is contained in the appendix of Elisabeth Krenn's *Diplomarbeit*.
52. Sigrid Löffler, "Meeting Mr. Kaltschnauz," *profil* 1 June 1992: 75.
53. Koberg and Nüchtern.
54. Koberg and Nüchtern.
55. Höfler 334.
56. Wolfgang Huber-Lang, "Der Rest ist Mißverständnis. Erst die Sprache, dann der Mensch: Das Theater des Grazer Senkrechtstarters Werner Schwab," *Die Presse* 21/22 December 1991.
57. "The funny thing is that the scenario is in fact realistic – what is more realistic than a restaurant? And the constellation of characters? – well, the woman is subjugated and the man is dominant. So the relationship and tension between characters are indeed realistic; but the language is the exact opposite." Unpublished interview with Schwab, conducted by Kralicek and contained in Krenn.

58. See Helmut Schödel, 122: "His publisher, too, apparently wanted to brush away the last crumbs of earthly soil from him. All trails to Kohlberg, Jagerberg, or even into Trink's cottage – paths that could have led to a better understanding of his work – were erased. He was to be a Sid Vicious of literature; he was to fall from the heavens like a meteor, only to smash to pieces."

59. Unpublished interview with Schwab, conducted by Kralicek and contained in Krenn.

60. See for example Hubert Winkels, "Heiße Hirnarbeit und kalter Mord. Werner Schwab metzelt seine Figuren dahin," *Die Zeit* 2 October 1992: 8: "His dramas have been conceived and created from linguistic materials (Schwab is from Graz). Everything else – the crudely crafted wooden figures and fragments of action – clatters along behind, loud and ugly. They must be performed, animated by voices and scenery. To read them is to quickly succumb to exhaustion."

61. Michael Merschmeier, "Theaterhauptstadt Wien im Winter: Die Kunst der Stunde. Eindrücke aus dem Burg- und Akademietheater, der Josefstadt, dem Schauspielhaus und dem Theater an der Wien," *Theater heute* 3 (1991): 47. See also the unpublished interview with Schwab, conducted by Kralicek, in Krenn. "The funny thing about it – and this happened with *First Ladies* too – is that you read it and think: This is awful, just terrible. And then you read it out loud … It was almost impossible to get through the trial reading because everyone was laughing so."

62. Caduff 173.

63. Preece, "The Use of Language" 276.

64. *Mein Hundemund*, in *Fäkaliendramen* 181.

65. Höfler perceives in the refusal to generate meaning "an anarchistic reproach directed toward cultural systems that insist on producing sense," 334.

66. Unpublished interview with Schwab, conducted by Kralicek, in Krenn.

Corpses and Gendered Bodies: The Theater of Marlene Streeruwitz

Helga W. Kraft

Marlene Streeruwitz is one of several contemporary Austrian playwrights who are challenging the German-speaking theater by destabilizing national and gender identity perception with their multilayered, postmodern plays. This writer has already received considerable scholarly attention although her plays began appearing on stage only in the early 1990s.[1] She drew attention immediately as she intrigued and shocked audiences with a new representation of a body politic. The subtle significance of her plays becomes clear if one considers recent studies addressing the problem of identity as related to the body in literature. For instance, Leslie Adelson in *Making Bodies, Making History. Feminism and German Identity* notes: "In the West German context of the last twenty years one could argue that the body in literature functions no longer as the mere object (victim) of history or as an allegorical emblem for the nation (or its moral conscience) but rather as the heterogeneous site of contested identities."[2] New theories regarding identity have entered scholarly discourse, and some of these theories want to obliterate the concept of identity altogether. Post-identity scholars articulate a set of strategies that acknowledge our simultaneous and ambivalent desire both to affirm our identities and to transcend them. In their study titled *after identity*, Danielsen and Engle summarize:

There are attempts both to recognize identity groups and to make them irrelevant. ... In response to the 'choice' between treating identity as a manifestation of essential difference or as an effect of social prejudice to be transcended, post-identity scholars articulate a set of strategies that acknowledge our simultaneous and ambivalent desire both to affirm our identities and to transcend them.[3]

Whereas some of these identity theories still proceed from "body-less," purely cerebral premises, Marlene Streeruwitz reifies such considerations by presenting the body on stage to probe the fractured identities relating to Austria's troublesome history. No longer is life staged as it is traditionally measured by the concept of a "life story." Instead of presenting such simulacrum of an imagined "reality" mimetically, the hidden structure of existing cultural identity is exposed. Only her early play, *Waikiki Beach.*, includes remnants of Aristotelian theater.[4] Usually, the playwright withholds any representation of dramatic tension with which the audience might identify. This is done, for instance, by staging the actors as embodied vessels of a clichéd language reflecting historically perpetuated untruths as well as entrenched and prevailing societal practices that lead to inhumanity, brutality, and exploitation. People do not communicate via language, but rather a "body of language" is communicated via people-actors-puppets.

In the past, the arts – including the theater – have often conspired in the dominant discourse. In Streeruwitz's theater, by contrast, identity is exposed as an assembly of traits furthered by unquestioned re-enactment benefiting prevailing powers, often anchored in romantic notions of love and duty. The so-called humanistic subject, a product of enlightenment thought, which was extolled over the last two hundred years, shows itself as exclusive and fictional. It was a bourgeois, androcentric creation. As the twentieth century progressed, the subversive capability of the subordinated object was increasingly explored in art and thought. Streeruwitz moves to center stage the concerns of those marginal groups that were left out of the ideal life story of the self in the Western world and shows them as pawns of power structures in which they themselves often unwittingly participate. This theater is highly political and attacks in particular the fascism of the writers' native country, not only by revealing the suppressed Nazi past but also by depicting the dangerous pervasiveness of fascism in contemporary society (Streeruwitz's *Elysian Park., New York. New York.*, and *Tolmezzo*).

No wonder that the plays of Streeruwitz did not have any world premieres in Austria until the year 2000. When Jörg Haider's right-wing FPÖ party entered the government coalition, the works of artists such as Streeruwitz were openly declared void of artistic quality on huge billboards to further political campaigns. Yet, such negative attention reinforced their impact on cultural politics.

In order to make underlying structures of a body politic visible, Streeruwitz shatters the traditional form of the theater. She follows in the footsteps of Brecht, Handke, and Jelinek in abandoning traditional theatrical rules and injects perspectives reminiscent of Kafka's work. For instance, she uses the alienation effect in a spatial sense. Her settings remind us in their sleaziness of Kafka's undignified locations (such as the basement in *The Castle* or the courtroom in *The Trial*). The play *New York. New York.* takes place in a Viennese public toilet turned into a modern Tartarus; *Waikiki Beach.* plays in the abandoned, dilapidated newspaper building of an unnamed city, undoubtedly Vienna; *Ocean Drive.* is set on a glacier mountain; and *Elysian Park.* is more like hell on earth. The author decorates her plays with glamorous geographical names that create a tension between their contents and their actual locations. The audience is forced to think about the discrepancy. Nothing is what it seems. From a theoretical point of view the Australian scholar Elizabeth Grosz explores identity in a similar vein in her study *Space, Time and Perversion: Essays on the Politics of Bodies* where she analyzes the gendered body in history.[5] For her and for Streeruwitz identities are not only destabilized in a geographical sense, they are also displaced in time and consequently in our perception of reality. The Jewish woman in *Tolmezzo.*, for instance, who returns to her native Vienna from the USA for a visit is alienated both in time and space. The people around her are just as anti-Semitic as they were in the Nazi era before she was forced into exile more than fifty years earlier. Streeruwitz mixes real-life people, such as this Jewish woman, with fictional characters brought alive, such as Spiderman and Barbie dolls, an import of male and female images from the US, that very same new homeland of the exiled woman. Austria has expanded its base of identity; after all, such trash is now globally dispersed. An intermixture of reality and virtual reality in a slapstick manner makes for a stunning theatrical effect. For instance, in *Elysian Park.* biological body identities are challenged. As crippled old fascists in wheel chairs suddenly jump up and break into a dance, the audience is shown the fluidity of the constructed body and the continuity of Nazi thought. These unexpected performative motions of the handicapped human beings on stage clarify the enactment of ideologies and social practices. Thus, Streeruwitz lets us witness how language infuses the body with unquestioned reasoning. At the same time she suggests that the restrictions through which the old Nazi ideologies are "crippled" are only temporary and can be removed at any time. In a Lacanian sense, the law of the father continues to rule through language in a dangerous way.

Clearly, the absence of the individual self is most blatant in the writer's treatment of the body. With great deliberation, she litters the stage with bodies and corpses in almost all of her plays. The dream of personal identity is shattered, yet the author expects the spectator to pick up the pieces, to recognize that the time has come where privileged identities should no longer benefit from others, that the enlightenment idea of the absolute subject has self-destructed by mutating into a killing machine. Streeruwitz's contribution to the new theater can be found in her emphasis on the body and the crippling effect on it by societal forces. She is one of the few writers who admits a feminist vision. The scenic ingeniousness and the compelling entertainment value of her plays no doubt contributed to their success on stage at a time some theoreticians call the "post-feminist" era. Perhaps this phenomenon is connected with the fact that gender theorists only started to focus intensively on the body in the late eighties and nineties. Elizabeth Grosz writes in another study titled *Volatile Bodies, Toward a Corporeal Feminism:*

> The body has remained a conceptual blind spot in both mainstream Western philosophical thought and contemporary feminist theory. Feminism has uncritically adopted many philosophical assumptions regarding the role of the body in social, political, cultural, psychical, and sexual life and, in this sense at least, can be regarded as complicit in the misogyny that characterizes Western reason.[6]

Grosz points out that some feminists, like Luce Irigaray, Judith Butler, and Monique Wittig, see the body as neither brute nor passive but interwoven with and constitutive of systems of meaning, signification, and representation. On the one hand it is a signifying and signified body; on the other, it is an object of systems of social coercion, legal inscription, and sexual and economic exchange.[7] I agree with Grosz who postulates that in order for women and minorities to develop autonomous modes of self-understanding and positions from which to challenge traditional patriarchal knowledges and paradigms, the specific nature and integration of the female body and female subjectivity and its similarities to and difference from men's bodies and identities need to be articulated in its historical rather than simply its biological concreteness.[8]

The "good female body" in traditional literature and art was oftentimes the dead body. A venture into anthropology, semiotics, psychoanalysis, art, and literature by Elisabeth Bronfen in her book *Over Her Dead Body* verifies this notion. Bronfen argues that

> femininity and death cause a disorder to stability, mark moments of ambivalence, disruption or duplicity and their eradication produces a recuperation of order, a return to stability. The threat that death and femininity posed is recuperated by representation, staging absence as a form of re-presence, or return, even if or rather precisely because this means appeasing the threat of real mortality, of sexual insufficiency, or lack of plentitude and wholeness.[9]

Bronfen examines the power, necessity, fascination, and danger inherent in the conjunction between femininity and death. She notes that these two concepts served as Western culture's privileged topoi and tropes for what is superlatively enigmatic. Freud names it the "uncanny." The de-mythification of the gendered body has been actively advanced during the last twenty to thirty years by many women dramatists who reject "traditional" androcentric theater because it serves merely the male enlightenment subject. When Marlene Streeruwitz speaks out to oppose what she calls *das Richtige Theater* (the "Correct Theater" with a capital "C"), she is rejecting a theater that does not reflect the life of people nowadays, neither for women nor for men. This "Correct Theater," she finds, "likes to limit itself to the argument of functioning connections in historicized life stories and searches for a general humanity which then turns out to be a masculine one. Bourgeois yearnings for fulfillment and desires for self-destruction are served."[10]

In the writer's opinion, in our present state of emancipated godlessness – which she views positively because it emancipated us from the concept of the patriarchal father-god – the theater cannot pursue the old question of redemption any longer, and she disdains the renaissance of old plays which proselytize this goal. She argues that we no longer should search for "the freezing of the eternal moment" that can only be found at the moment of death (e.g., in Goethe's *Faust*). Rather, the theater must stage "the anarchical quest for a happiness,"[11] the desire for which she believes rests in everyone. Such happiness can be repeated in our transitory life. An existence can be built of materiality, beneficial to the senses and the body. As she pointed out in an interview, Streeruwitz wants a theater committed to the living, and therefore she exposes on stage the dangerous tradition of emulating death which she sees in most literature since the eighteenth century. She considers the lingering of anachronistic yearnings for the last century as one of the unbearable burdens that we still carry, even though we have to live totally different lives. With her drama she deconstructs these yearnings and their pernicious influence on our present reality. As a consequence, the theater of Streeruwitz moves away from metaphysics and focuses on our material existence, the senses, the body. Unfortunately, very little happiness can be realized in such attempts, since the old societal system still reigns to hinder such practice. Therefore, it does not come as a surprise that in her plays the writer foregrounds and exaggerates torture of the body. She presents suicidal women and creates a stage strewn with corpses as people live out old, often unconscious patterns of a dichotomized identity.

Yet, her plays clarify what Elizabeth Grosz calls the need for a connection of the body to its dichotomized inner being. To symbolize this change, Grosz suggests a new paradigm for the human self to replace the worn-out Cartesian model where the mind reigns opposite and superior to the body, spirit over nature, man over woman. She favors as an alternative model the Moebius strip, where inside and outside flow together. Philosophically speaking it represents the identity of body and mind as one whole. Metaphysics have no place in this model, and the body is no longer inferior to the mind. The unfamiliar reader can better understand this model by visualizing a strip of paper, the far ends of which are twisted once and then connected to form a figure eight, or the infinity sign. Tracing the surface of the strip reveals that there is no polarity of inside and outside but a flowing connection. Thus

Grosz postulates such a fluid exchange between the inside and the outside of the body, or more precisely, between a person's biological-physical emanation and a person's spirit, mind, and emotions.[12] Streeruwitz, too, starts from the notion that soul, mind, feeling, and body are one, but that our society has devalued, split off, and misused the body for power purposes rooted in authoritative yet vague metaphysical so-called truths still perpetuated by an outdated enlightenment discourse.

The body's materiality – sexuality, sickness, pain, torture, and death – thus receives a new significance on the writer's stage. For instance, she explores sexuality in its gendered difference within our society. According to Streeruwitz, sexuality is largely obfuscated by romantic notions in women, while it is mainly fed by bodily cravings in men. In her study *Erklär mir Liebe* (Explain Love to Me), the cultural critic Susanne Baakmann comes to the conclusion that even nowadays "female stories about love describe the problem of being accepted as part of a couple in a social order which excludes the woman and her desire in many ways."[13] Although the playwright does not absolve women from complicity with the power game in society, more often than not they are seen as pawns in it since their "romantic" education blinds them.

Streeruwitz's heavy emphasis on violence against the human body includes incest with children, wife beating, rape, and kidnapping – the whole gamut of bodily harm including murder. With these demonstrations of violence the author visualizes the normative procedures of society in keeping individuals subjugated. It follows Nietzsche's notion that successful subjugation is connected to corporeal punishment,[14] which according to Foucault includes the punitive use of sexuality. Such violence is performed again and again to train memory and to keep or establish power relationships. These processes are usually hidden and unknown because historically they have been naturalized, that is, they are believed to be dictated by nature. Streeruwitz reveals in an extreme, grotesque manner that today such bodily and gendered punishment is still being exercised in society. For instance, the lifeless or unconscious puppet-like body of the prostitute Lulu in *New York. New York.* is slashed, beaten, raped, danced with, and generally mistreated throughout the first act in a public men's room in Vienna. The medical discourse which legitimized violence and pathologized women's existence (to different degrees at different times in history, as traced by Foucault as well) is embodied by a male figure who plays doctor and fondles Lulu's bloodied body. In a postmodern way Streeruwitz expresses the threat of an outbreak of such violence in war that is always looming in the background, as it did in actuality in the Middle East when she wrote these plays. In her plays men are not excepted from brutality; in *Sloane Square.* a punk is killed and thrown from a bridge onto a railroad platform. No one pays attention to this act. He appears to the audience as a cloth dummy oozing red. As this occurrence is repeated over and over and the bodies pile up, the indifference of everyone is evidence of a well-learned lesson in disregard. In *Bagnacavallo.*, where war is waged, corpse after corpse is dragged onto the stage until they form a large heap. The stage directions specify: "The corpses are rag dolls. They are filled with a disgusting red material, which is seeping out of the wounds of the corpses."[15] In a world without metaphysics, a body is just disgusting refuse that needs to be removed, a job usually reserved for women. The corpses of the dead punks in *Sloane Square.*, for instance, are cut apart by two women in a gathering that recalls the atmosphere of a quilting bee: "Both pull out from under their jackets huge scissors. Mrs. Marenzi watches how the cutting is done by the street-lady, and then she copies her."[16] They then carefully place the various body parts in designated plastic garbage bags. The disposal of the corpses is reminiscent of Gregor Samsa's final destiny in *The Metamorphosis* by Kafka.[17] Gregor, in the form of a dung beetle, is swept into the trash by the cleaning lady. However, whereas Gregor's disposed-of existence was at least an individual one, Streeruwitz's nameless masses of corpses exclude even any memory of individuality. In *Bagnacavallo.*, the fallen soldiers no longer receive the aura of glamour to validate them or the war for the glory of the nation. The slaughtered bodies document only the horror and senselessness of slaughter. Not even plundering the corpses, which occurs again and again on stage, yields anything of value or meaning. Siamese twins search every pocket of the many persons killed in war to steal useful items. However, nothing is found; their deaths are indeed useless for the people of their country. With the subsequent murderous wars on the Balkan, Streeruwitz's implied predictions came true.

In the play *New York. New York.*, another type of torture and plundering takes place. Here it is presented in a more abstract sense and relates to national identity and to concepts of mortality. The torture is inflicted off-stage in a room next to the abject public toilet that is the location of this play. It harbors "dear Mr. Prometheus" who remains invisible until the end of the play. He is sick and must be nursed by the toilet attendant Mrs. Horvath. A strange mixture of realism and a dreamlike, haunting glimpse into a hidden, guilt-ridden national conscience gone underground is achieved with the image of this mythological figure. The place is reminiscent of the underground sewer system in Vienna, the place where human refuse flows together. It is suggested that various unspecified and unseen persons, designated only by "they," who could be secret service agents, repeatedly visit and inflict pain on the ailing hidden creature. The audience must ask: Was Mr. Prometheus connected to the Nazi government? Could it be Hitler himself? Or is the movement of modernity laid to rest here? As in all her plays, Streeruwitz weaves a multilayered, grotesque web of images and allusions alerting the viewer to complex political and historical significance. In the secluded suffering of Mr. Prometheus, unembodied memories of the Austrian nation seem to be kept under lock and are abetted by Mrs. Horvath, the capitalist Cerberus guarding hell. As the "toilet lady" she can be seen as the attendant of the place where the excrements of culture are deposited. A visual image reinforces a connection between rationality and excrements: The figure of a professor and thinker insanely attempts to destroy all toilet bowls in the "Imperial Pissoir." Those implements of hygiene and with them the achievements of modernity are shattered in a culmination of rage. But the unseen Mr. Prometheus – or the Nazi past – seems to have trouble dying (or being flushed away), just like his mythical predecessor whose liver was pecked away every day anew by an eagle as punishment for stealing fire from heaven. Whatever his former transgressions, Mr. Prometheus's existence is to be kept from becoming public in a state that suppresses its memories. Eventually, however, the secret leaks out due to capitalist commercialism and globalization. For a large sum of money the greedy Mrs. Horvath grants a group of curious and eager Japanese tourists in Austrian folkloric dress – another faceless group with a grotesquely fluid identity – a glimpse of the dying Mr. Prometheus. Their "plundering of a corpse" consists of a barrage of photo flashes to record the moment of death.

The multiple significance of the Prometheus image cannot be equated only with Austria's Nazi past. It also is connected to the writer's notion of death, her rejection of traditional representations of human mortality. In *New York. New York.*, death manifests itself in grotesque and decidedly non-redemptive form as the bloody carcass of a horse! Streeruwitz satirizes the obsession with death in traditional literature. There seems to be an ironic intertextual reference to the American movie *The Godfather* where the decapitated head of a Mafioso's favorite horse is placed in the owner's bed as a death threat. In Streeruwitz's plays, the horse signifies fear of death as well. In an early play titled *Brahmsplatz.* (Brahms Square), an old woman desires to die alone behind a folding screen that displays on its front side the image of a fierce black stallion. The horse seems to jump out and scare everyone approaching the screen, i.e., approaching death. However, for the person located behind it, the screen offers a soothing vision of pink cloth. It suggests the "other side" of real life, a metaphysical afterlife, promising comfort. However, the screen breaks, thereby denying the old woman the protection it had afforded to other family members since 1871. She had lived her life for this moment and now finds herself betrayed. Streeruwitz deconstructs the Enlightenment illusion that man can conquer death by fixing it in space in all eternity. This thought is also expressed in *New York. New York.*. The tourists (all male) photograph the dead Prometheus over and over as if to eternalize the transition from life to death, from live spirit to dead matter. The fixation on the end of life, on death, is exposed as meaningless, for nothing is actually recorded on film but an animal carcass. Subversively, the writer points to the lost happiness during life caused by this fixation. The ultimate in substituting death for life is staged in Streeruwitz's 1999 play *Boccaleone*.. Here, the virtual world needs the human body only as corpse. A film company stages "lebende Bilder" (living pictures) in erotic poses using dressed up corpses that are delivered from a hospital which conveniently has people die in time for such demand by the media industry. Such film production provides the ultimate titillation for a paying audience to make up for a lost enjoyment of life.

Another way of exposing the truth of the body is depicted in the play *Tolmezzo*.. The playwright stages dolls to represent culturally accepted objectifications of human material robbed of any subjectivity: She brings not one but four actresses representing Barbie dolls on stage as well as four living Ken dolls. These puppets play background to a group of "real-life" Viennese persons. While the real characters are stuck in and live out traditional roles, unconscious for the most part of what motivates them, the eight doll-marionettes – who are obviously pure materiality – make visible to the audience the scenario of what Western culture imposes on the body through its invisible power agenda. At first, the Barbie dolls enter the stage made up and dressed as we know them from the toy store. Later on they appear without breasts, then without hair or without high-heeled shoes, thus robbed of the main attributes of their inscribed feminine identity.

When the Barbies turn away, the audience sees large moist spots on the backs of their dresses, clearly from the menstrual blood that marks women as outcasts. Their reproductive ability is put to shame and the impression of disgust in the audience is purposely created. Elizabeth Grosz, in her study *Volatile Bodies*, dedicates a whole chapter to an analysis of the solidity and fluidity of gendered bodies. She notes that the male represents the solid state, the individual with clear boundaries. Even his body fluids enter the discourse as solid since they have permanence as a goal (his spermatic fluid will produce a child), but women with their supposedly unclean fluids and their sticky viscosity present a danger that dissolves boundaries and can infest and infect.[18] The first line of Streeruwitz's play *New York. New York.* also refers to menstruation, which Mrs. Horvath, the old toilet attendant, dismisses vehemently: "I don't need it. No. I really don't need it. ... Even the smell. No. No blood, please. This smell, I couldn't. Never. My God."[19] Lack of menstruation signifies here that her body has lost value as a sexual object in the patriarchal economy. Precisely because of this fact, she is able to become one of "them," to participate in the male power structure without the threat that women's sexuality would pose. This disgust for her own blood and body expresses the self-estrangement necessary in society if a woman wants to profit from the system.

The disgust for feminine body functions is connected to the reality of procreation and the propensity of patriarchy to appropriate female power. Thus, the act of birth from the womb is devalued and considered disgusting or pathological. It is replaced by spiritually "clean" birth through baptism that is sacred and is executed by men in power. Although such discourse is breaking down as historical circumstances change, birth is still pathologized and considered possible only through the interference of mainly male obstetricians. In Streeruwitz's plays, the whole discourse of birth and motherhood is included in the question of the devalued body of women. Several pregnant women appear in Streeruwitz's plays, among them the Barbies in *Tolmezzo..* The play *Sloane Square.* centers on a young unmarried woman who is carrying an unborn child. At first, all family members feign to be pleased and a marriage is planned in order to reinvent family life as imagined by parents and grandparents. However, an unfamiliar environment – the train station Sloane Square in a foreign country – signifies transition and fosters alienation from the accustomed life goals. The spatial displacement precipitates the breakdown of the anticipated traditional idyll. Slowly the truth leaks out: The prospective young father does not want the child and the grandmother breaks her lifelong silence about the naked reality of her family life. Although she purportedly only lived for her children, she now boldly expresses her regret at ever having given birth to them. Her uncaring husband tortured her psychologically by carrying on an affair with her sister for years and, furthermore, he never took part in the child-rearing process. She had looked the other way and stayed in denial all her life. Hers is a fate shared by many of Streeruwitz's women and hence one staged by the dramatist with matter-of-factness, lacking drama. As life flows on normally again – here through the arrival of the train rectifying the spatial displacement – such moments of recognition and revelation are forgotten.

Several women in the writer's other plays who can no longer stand their brutalization, abuse, and domestic exploitation turn violence against themselves. They annihilate their own body through suicide. King Lear's daughter Goneril – sexually abused by her father – in the play *Dentro.* kills herself. She says: "If god is a father, we better not come to him."[20] Melisande in *Bagnacavallo.* faces a new fundamentalism prompting her to utter: "I can't bear it any longer. It can't go on."[21] No longer a virgin, Melisande is considered unsuitable for proper marriage. After the cynical suggestion that her suitor, significantly named Romeo, would marry her if she had her "damaged" body repaired by restoring her virginity through modern surgery, Melisande ends it all. For her, romantic love had been an empty promise. Streeruwitz works with exaggeration techniques to make a point. After all, in many parts of the Western world, the loss of virginity is no longer severely punished. However, laws and rules regulating women's reproductive capabilities (abortion, birth control) are still strongly intact.

Streeruwitz likes to incorporate intertextual references to trigger allusions with which to question generally accepted truths, such as the value of romantic love in *Bagnacavallo.*. The audience might link the names of Romeo, Melisande, and Genoveva to

Shakespeare's *Romeo and Juliette* and – if well-read – to Maeterlinck's *Pelleas and Melisande* and Hebbel's *Genoveva*. The intertextual signifiers provide associations to certain traits that our society has embraced, and the writer creates a tension between historical eras and societal shifts. Some of these figures do not complete their traditional stories, but go alternative emancipatory routes. Two women, Genoveva and the prostitute Anitra, turn their back to the audience and walk away together at the end, leaving behind the men who beg them to stay as they literally stand knee-deep in corpses piled up on stage. These women no longer clean up their messes. Such new possibilities for women in Streeruwitz's plays are an exception. On the whole, she displays bodies that are irreparably damaged by the ideological excrements of the human mind.

However – as already noted – women are not the only victims in this society hostile to the body. At one point in *Tolmezzo*. the Ken dolls are displayed as bloodied figures in the pose of St. Sebastian while the Barbies rejoice. This image fits Streeruwitz's belief that for centuries men as a gender have been prepared for sacrifice in war. Women cheered them on. The author remarked in an interview: "Generation after generation of men have been prepared through education and culture for this one heroic moment. For most of them it took place in World War One."[22] *Tolmezzo*. suggests that society allows men to rape women in war as a perverse recompense (one is again reminded of practices in the recent Yugoslavian civil war). In this play, the closer the women come to the beauty standards of society, the more likely they are to become victims. Only the stylized Barbie dolls win the beauty contest – the "real" women on stage cannot measure up to the female ideal – thus revealing the objectification of the female. Furthermore, the fact that only women deemed beautiful, i.e., the Barbie doll types, will be raped clearly conveys the cruelty and perversion of what beauty signifies. It should be added here that studies have shown that women – beautiful or not – are raped in our society. However, in the popular imagination such a connection exists.[23] "War" for women goes on beyond a declared war, as for instance in Streeruwitz's new play, *Sapporo.*, where an actress is gang-raped by drunk media men on whom she depends for a job. At the end of *Tolmezzo*, all the Barbies, in an advanced stage of pregnancy, reappear in debutante gowns next to their Kens in tuxes. The audience is simultaneously dazzled and revolted by a grotesque mixture of rape, marriage ritual, brutality, and family idyll that cannot hide strong cynical overtones. As Streeruwitz has shown before in *Sloane Square*. here, too, impending motherhood constitutes a questionable happy end.

Here and throughout her dramas, the playwright deconstructs basic concepts and myths of society that are based on patriarchal thought. An additional example is offered at the beginning of *Tolmezzo*. when a group of men want to enter a Viennese coffee house which is identified as "paradise." The fact that the key to the door is missing is blamed on the raging hormones of the menopausal female owner of the establishment. Women's sexuality prevents men from entering this biblical Eden. Subsequently, the men steal the key and invade the metaphorical paradise in a colonial manner. But sadly, the alcohol they confiscate in "paradise" is an elixir for the body designed only to numb their miserable corporeal existence through intoxication. This makeshift paradise must alleviate the anguish of one of the men who suffers from impotence and the cravings of another for sexual conquests in his need for aggrandizement. The Kleistian probe, articulated in the writer's famous essay on the marionette theater,[24] is not an option in Streeruwitz's plays. Kleist postulates that one needs to go through full consciousness before one can obtain the graceful materiality of the marionettes and reenter paradise through the backdoor, an achievement that Kleist deemed impossible for mankind. Streeruwitz, even more clearly than Kleist, denies a metaphysical origin – paradise – and points to the earthly substitutes as she deconstructs the gendered body/mind discourses of our society.

One of her deconstructive strategies is to fracture the narrative through stylistic means. By staging puppets Streeruwitz follows Kleist's tradition. By doubling the marionettes and bringing cartoon figures to the stage, the author also emulates the dark humor of Kafka's double figures who draw attention to the lack of individuality and the unseen stereotypical forces of society. In an early postmodern play (1971), Gerlind Reinshagen tripled her title figure of the drama *Leben und Tod der Marilyn Monroe*[25] (Life and Death of Marilyn Monroe) to help her trace the development of the Hollywood actress into a cultural icon and thereby reveal the mechanism of body politics. A culmination of such efforts seems to be the abundance of multiple figures in Streeruwitz's plays: the flock of Japanese tourists with cameras in *New York. New York.*, a number of green Martian travelers and two Siamese clowns in *Bagnacavallo.*, three fat ladies and three senile men in *Waikiki Beach.*, and three punks together with a group of women wearing black dresses and men with striped suits in *Sloane Square.*. These multiple bodies usually act in a pantomimic fashion. When they do speak, however, they spew out damaging clichés, the fruit of consciousness and culture gone awry. In *Waikiki Beach.*, for instance, when the male protagonist leaves the female protagonist to be killed, her death will not be investigated for unsubstantiated political reasons rendered in a highly poetic language by the old men, a caricature of a Greek chorus. Streeruwitz notes in her stage directions: "The three senile men failed again and have protected the guilty ones – as they have done for a thousand years."[26]

Paradoxically, Streeruwitz presents language and body as interlinked and at the same time as alienated. As language is produced by the speaking body, its functions or non-functions become evident. In *Waikiki Beach.* a skinhead speaks with a stutter. In *New York. New York.* the author features a mute young male who nevertheless has the patriarchal language inscribed onto his body. It can be expressed through pantomime just as well, as for instance when he batters a woman. When a mock romantic love scene is staged between the mute man and a pregnant woman, he suddenly lip-syncs karaoke style words that are transmitted by a loudspeaker replaying a pre-programmed romantic movie scene. Spoken language is also taken away entirely at times, as in the case of a senile man in *Elysian Park.*. He is silenced by medical injection and can mumble only incomprehensible phrases, thus preventing him from implicating corrupt authorities. In stark contrast, simplistic, fragmented everyday language emanates from the mouths of most stage figures when they communicate without the help of canned verbiage. Half sentences dominate, indicating that reality and emotions oftentimes can neither be grasped nor articulated if clichés or predigested words and sayings are not available or desired. Everything which is false, which has nothing to do with the reality of people's life and which conveys the performativity of social practices is quoted intertextually from high literature such as Goethe and Shakespeare or from popular sources such as films and popular songs. This practice is made visible by an absurd juxtaposition of sparse, almost inarticulate daily communicative attempts on the one hand and the smooth, poetic language or prefab images, imitations of so-called high or popular culture and art, on the other hand.

Language, according to Streeruwitz's theater, must be deconstructed and relearned through the body. At the same time the body must be freed from unreflected language which colonializes our consciousness and cripples our identity. Only then can the subject be her/his own agent to pursue happiness in the here and now. The dramatist states: "We don't have a heaven for which we should wait. We can look at our present now. ... Object of the classical writers was death; object of the modern drama was dying. I am occupied with life."[27] The pessimistic elements of Streeruwitz's theater reflect the difficulty of her continuing endeavor.

Recent reactionary political events in Austria vouch for the necessity of the author's continuing efforts. Streeruwitz's last play, *Sapporo.* (world premiere at the *steirischer herbst* festival in Graz, 2000), deconstructs the still existing Austrian atmosphere of *Heimat* kitsch which hides a fascist undercurrent supportive of traditional hierarchies. Yet, it becomes clear that even in this play Austria also represents our global situation. Streeruwitz continues to deconstruct political texts used for demagoguery in her widely published essayistic work. In each of her new plays she exposes a different aspect of language that prevents people from pursuing happiness in the here and now. She considers her texts to be "texts of searching,"[28] but she is well aware of the limitations to expressing herself in language. In her *Frankfurter Poetikvorlesungen* (Frankfurt Lectures on Poetics) she puts it this way: "The big problem to achieve de-colonization lies in the fact that – despite modernity – there exists no language with which to recount the history of violence without again doing violence and without passing on the order to kill."[29] The staging of her plays allows her to go beyond language. In addition, the writer's frequent participation in the ongoing Thursday demonstrations in Vienna against the new government coalition that includes the rightist FPÖ party offers her a possibility to counteract the subliminal and objectionable political language of the parties and the media by bringing in her bodily existence as a protest.

Notes

1. Streeruwitz's plays, with date of writing and date and place of world premiere:
New York. New York. (1987); world premiere 30 January 1993; *Kammerspiele*, Munich.
Waikiki Beach. (1988/89); world premiere 24 April 1992; *Schauspielhaus*, Cologne.
Sloane Square. (1990); world premiere 3 July 1992; *Schauspielhaus*, Cologne.
Ocean Drive. (1991); world premiere 17 December 1993; *Schauspielhaus*, Cologne.
Elysian Park. (1992); world premiere 17 June 1993; *Deutsches Theater*, Berlin.
Troyes. (1992); world premiere 20 May 1993; *St. Brieuc / Festival D'Avignon.*
Tolmezzo. Eine symphonische Dichtung. (1994); world premiere 11 June 1994; *Festwochen*, Vienna.

Bagnacavallo. (1995); world premiere 17 October 1995; *Schauspielhaus*, Cologne.
Dentro. Was bei Lears wirklich geschah. (1995); premiere anticipated in 2001.
Boccaleone. (1998).
Sapporo. Eine Revue. (2000); world premiere 26 October 2000, *steirischer herbst*, Graz.

2. Leslie A. Adelson, *Making Bodies, Making History. Feminism and German Identity* (Lincoln, London: University of Nebraska Press, 1993) 36.

3. Dan Danielsen and Karen Engle, *after identity* (New York, London: Routledge, 1995) xviii.

4. The following plays of Streeruwitz are under consideration in this article: *Bagnacavallo. Brahmsplatz. Zwei Stücke* (Frankfurt/M.: Suhrkamp, 1988); *Waikiki Beach. Sloane Square. Zwei Stücke* (Frankfurt/M.: Suhrkamp, 1992); *Tolmezzo. Eine symphonische Dichtung* (Frankfurt/M.: Suhrkamp, 1994); *New York. New York. Elysian Park. Zwei Stücke* (Frankfurt/M.: Suhrkamp, 1993). These plays, as well as *Dentro* and *Boccaleone*, were also published in *Waikiki Beach. Und andere Orte. Die Theaterstücke* (Frankfurt/M.: Fischer Taschenbuch, 1999).

5. Elizabeth Grosz, *Space, Time, and Perversion: Essays on the Politics of Bodies* (New York, London: Routledge, 1995).

6. Elizabeth Grosz, *Volatile Bodies. Toward a Corporeal Feminism* (Bloomington: University of Indiana Press, 1994) 6.

7. Grosz, *Volatile Bodies* 18.

8. Grosz, *Volatile Bodies* 19.

9. Elisabeth Bronfen, *Over Her Dead Body. Death, Femininity and the Aesthetic* (New York: Routledge, 1992) xii.

10. Marlene Streeruwitz, "Passion. Devoir. Kontingenz. Und keine Zeit," *Theater heute* (1992): 28ff. Translated by Helga Kraft.

11. Streeruwitz, "Passion" 28ff.

12. Grosz, *Volatile Bodies*, especially chapter 8 "Sexed Bodies," 187ff.
13. Susanne Baackmann: *Erklär mir Liebe. Weibliche Schreibweisen von Liebe in der Gegenwartsliteratur* (Hamburg: Argument, 1995) 16. Quotation translated by Helga Kraft.
14. Friedrich Nietzsche, *Beyond Good and Evil. Prelude to a Philosophy of the Future*, trans. Walter Kaufmann (New York: Vintage Books, 1966) 61.
15. Streeruwitz, *Bagnacavallo*. 63. This quotation translated by Helga Kraft, as are all subsequent ones from Streeruwitz's works.
16. *Sloane Square*. 125.
17. Franz Kafka, "Die Verwandlung," *Erzählungen* (Frankfurt/M.: S. Fischer, 1967).
18. Lately, other women writers have focused on female identity as connected to their different body fluids. See for example: Christa Wolf, first page of *Medea: Stimmen: Roman* (Munich: Luchterhand, 1996), or Elfriede Jelinek, *Krankheit oder Moderne Frauen* (Cologne: Prometh, 1987).
19. *New York. New York.* 11.
20. *Dentro.* in *Waikiki Beach. Und andere Orte.* 429.
21. *Bagnacavallo.* in *Waikiki Beach. Und andere Orte.* 396.
22. Streeruwitz, "Passion" 29.
23. Streeruwitz's suggestion must be challenged since research has shown that rape is not a crime of sexual desire (triggered by beauty, etc.) but of violence. Perhaps the writer attempts to surrealistically conflate sexual drives with violence since the act of rape is similar. See for instance, Elizabeth Wright, *Feminism and Psychoanalysis. A Critical Dictionary* (Oxford, Cambridge: Blackwell Publishers, 1992) 367 ff.
24. Heinrich von Kleist, "Über das Marionettentheater," *Werke in einem Band*, ed. Helmut Sembdner (Munich: Hanser, 1966).
25. Gerlind Reinshagen, "Leben und Tod der Marilyn Monroe," *Die Grüne Tür* (Frankfurt/M.: Suhrkamp, 1999).
26. *Waikiki Beach.* 73.

27. *Theater heute* (1992) 31.
28. Marlene Streeruwitz, *Collagenband 1996-2000 Und. Überhaupt. Stop.* (Vienna: edition selene, 2000).
29. Marlene Streeruwitz, *Können. Mögen. Dürfen. Sollen. Wollen. Müssen. Lassen. Frankfurter Poetikvorlesungen* (Frankfurt/M.: Suhrkamp, 1998).

Ocean Drive.:
Marlene Streeruwitz's Fractal Mise en Scène

Willy Riemer

Locations, whether real or generic, evoke moods and memories. The dramas of Marlene Streeruwitz and also her most recent narrative are entitled to draw on such associations. *Majakowskiring*. (2000), for example, is set in one of the high-security residential compounds of the GDR leadership. Built in the Nazi era, the house in Pankow was inhabited after 1945 by a general of the Red Army and then for a time by Otto Grotewohl, the first Minister President of the GDR. It was subsequently converted to a government guest house and later became the home for the writers' union of the GDR. Surveillance and control in public and in private life figure importantly in this narrative. As the protagonist despairs of yet another dissipated relationship and betrayal of affection by her "absent dictator" (93), she reflects on her past and remembers that the separation from her husband long ago had at least produced strong emotions: she had felt the urge to jab a knitting needle, finely honed, into his eye.[1] In *Ocean Drive*. (1994) this murderous impulse is carried out. Recognizing that she had been manipulated by the man she had just come to trust with her most intimate secret, Elizabeth Maynard in anguish thrusts the blade of a Swiss Army knife into the eye of her wily biographer.

Ocean Drive.: Marlene Streeruwitz's Fractal Mise-en-Scène

Up and down the East and West Coast of America there are numerous streets called "Ocean Drive"; perhaps the best known is in Miami. In the image constructed by the media this urban center in Florida connotes the business of crime, vice, and tourism. In *Ocean Drive.* a splendidly attired drug dealer makes an appearance in James Bond style and gloats over a hostile take-over maneuver that was made possible by closely monitoring the whereabouts of wealthy heiress and media celebrity Elizabeth Maynard. His display of entrepreneurial Darwinism suggests that the control mechanisms and exercise of power in the global market are not that different from the patterns of dominance found in *Majakowskiring.*. Streeruwitz is especially concerned, however, with exposing the petty aggressions and debilitating concessions that are to be found in daily life, and with deconstructing the so-called grand narratives that are put forth to legitimize such behavior. But how is it possible for Streeruwitz to critique such paradigms and their insidious consequences without in turn assuming a privileged vantage? I will consider the variants of power and control in *Ocean Drive.* and approach the structural basis of the text with this question in mind.

In the isolation of a pristine glacier near a mountain top Elizabeth Maynard, a glamorous film star past her prime, meets the star journalist Leonard Perceval to arrange for him to write her biography. In the course of their conversation and as the play unfolds to its gruesome end, a profusion of intertexts from ancient myths and the great classics to the slogans and pop culture of today is intercut. Kitsch and cliché, simulacra and caricatures, Shakespearean lines and surrealistic interludes, high finance, the drug trade, pollution, and health fads all have their moment on center stage in this fast-paced neon spectacle. Numerous side appearances keep interrupting the interview of Maynard and Perceval, but have no direct part in its progress. Fragmentation and complexity are the key features of *Ocean Drive.*.

Both protagonists, Lore in *Majakowskiring.* and Maynard in *Ocean Drive.*, have had successful careers that in their decline now also bring forebodings of an end and death. Lore is tempted to venture out to the bar scene of the "Hackeschen Höfe" in Berlin, but instead heads for Tegel and a flight that will take her back to the mundane reality she had thought of escaping. For Maynard the encounter with Perceval leads to a flickering moment of attraction, perhaps a delicate love unfurling out of season. Perceval's manipulation strikes all the harder. But his tragic death is a death rendered less tragic by being recorded on video tape. Maynard is led away to face uncertain consequences. As was the case for Lore, there is no escaping the established system.

The plays and narratives of Streeruwitz are complex and provocative. Though some reviewers are irritated by her concerns and style, her work has met with strong resonance. Her breakthrough came in 1992, when she received the prestigious critics' award from the journal *Theater heute*. The highly successful performances of *Waikiki Beach.*[2] and *Sloane Square.*[3] in Cologne made Marlene Streeruwitz the rising star on the German theater circuit. However, the subsequent production of her formally more ambitious *Ocean Drive.* had few enthusiasts.[4] Perhaps the setting was not sufficiently lavish; some critics suggested that Torsten Fischer's stage direction lacked verve, that he played too close to the text. Most of the reviews, however, also convey a sense of disorientation. Andreas Rossmann refers to *Ocean Drive.* as a product of postmodern craftsmanship; for *Die Welt* it is an example of arbitrary pluralism; its characters show neither depth nor development, claims Cornelie Ueding of the *Neue Zürcher Zeitung*; Ulrich Schreiber of the *Frankfurter Rundschau* considers the story to be drifting apart; whereas *Der Spiegel* complains of the tangled knots of action.[5] The critics do not so much comment on what was offered on stage, but rather on what was missing: what was missing in the performance was a conventional plot development with a clear turning point and closure in a neat psychological framework. And that is precisely what Streeruwitz does not provide in *Ocean Drive.*.

Except for the stations in her career and marriages, not much is revealed about Maynard. The many iterations of the theme of power and control, however, suggest the texture of her professional milieu. Her escort at the end compares her unspecified prospects to his own: "There is no getting away. Coercion at every turn. Within and out. Right from the start ... They are all waiting for you. Madam" (94).[6] Indeed, Maynard explains that her rise to fame and power was out of self-defense; she had grown weary of being victimized as a woman. It turns out, however, that even her refuge on the remote glacier does not provide shelter from manipulation. Her often interrupted sparring with Perceval is a struggle for control of her biography, and thus of her public identity. Identity includes the power to set markers and to influence the perception and response of others. In its episodic encounters *Ocean Drive.* presents variants of power and control that have to do with possession, imposed order, violence, and surveillance.

To escape influence and impositions of all kinds, Maynard had bought a mountain so remote that it could be assumed to be untouched by people and by pollution of any kind. No environmental messages had been inscribed by the global economy, no adventuresome antagonist had set foot on it, and no paparazzi were scavenging for little scandals. In its isolation the mountain was to be hers alone. It was an immaculate location for beginning her biography.

As Maynard soon comes to witness in dismay, ownership is not the same thing as control. In plain view and ignoring Maynard's outraged calls, a stalwart figure out of German folklore rams a signpost into the snow and ice. A caricature of a scientist pokes about with his instruments. Some delinquents are trooped past. Several tourists appear, aggressively littering at their rest stop and claiming that in a promotion they had acquired the right of access to the mountain – now called "Rainbow Warrior" – with its surrogate abominable snowman. Maynard's mountain has been developed as a cut-rate tourist attraction. The global economy spares no location from its creeping commercialization.

The mountain can be taken as a correlative of Maynard's biography. As she had intended to preserve the glacial purity of the location, she planned to control the contents of her personal grand narrative. But as the trespassers and Maynard's biographer clearly demonstrate, even in such private niches the impositions of the dominant discourse prevail. Indeed, Streeruwitz has some of the characters who had emptied their trash on the snow now complain about the deplorable conditions on the glacier and the lack of order. They sentimentally recall the good old times when there indeed was plenty of discipline and order and people knew where they belonged in society; one of the tourists reminisces about her father's time when strong measures could be used to assure order. If need be, such dominant order is imposed with violence.

For all the absurd images, banter, and incidental satire at the beginning of *Ocean Drive.*, there is an undercurrent of aggression in the encounters on the glacier. On one occasion an encounter erupts into raw violence. An aid worker leads a group of rowdy delinquents and an armed guard across the glacier; the experience, he explains, is intended as therapy to counteract their aggressive impulse and to build self-esteem. The delinquents urinate on the snow, they smoke, and they torment one of their own. When he finally escapes, the aid worker runs after him. They are both machine-gunned by the guard. Not violence itself seems in question by the authorities, but whether it is sanctioned and thus socially acceptable. For unwarranted acts of aggression the dominant discourse provides mechanisms for reestablishing order. After dumping a glass of a vegetarian concoction into the unblemished snow, Perceval sees Maynard's disapproval, realizes his faux pas and apologizes as a matter of course. Seeing and how one is seen play an important role in this chain of actions, as surveillance does for control.

In the very short opening scene of *Ocean Drive.*, Maynard and Perceval not so much meet as set up their confrontation. The stage instructions have them scrutinize each other, waiting with the obligatory smile, stalking and assessing each other. It is the preparation for doing battle. In all subsequent encounters the gaze structures the patterns of dominance; seeing is the prerequisite for exercising control. Once again a comparison to *Majakowskiring.* is instructive. Were the "friends of the GDR" lodged at the guest house under surveillance? How could they not be? "Since everything and everybody was being observed. And. Still was being observed" (32). The mountain top was no more of a refuge than the guest house in Pankow: Perceval suggests to Maynard that no doubt their meeting was being registered from some satellite. The gaze has become instrumentalized. In the end Maynard is prevented from departing with the helicopter. There is the evidence of a video tape recorded by a camera on the summit: "Everything up here is always under surveillance" (94). Cutting into Perceval's eye thus releases Maynard from his manipulation, but not from dominance.

If not the actual life, then its construction as a biography promises a degree of control. It determines what others will see and know. In a programmatic text Streeruwitz refers to the desire for a biography: "*Passion* and *devoir*, of course, continue to be the reef-bound shores between which we have to navigate our life ... in this inner turmoil the longing for biographical coherence is great."[7] The actress who for the screen has performed the stories of others, now wants her own.

After listing Maynard's divorces, settlements, and stations in her professional and financial career, Perceval sums up in a formula: so that's who you are. Maynard differentiates some details. She reflects on her career in film, pointing out that there are few film roles for actresses past forty and that television series provide some opportunity on the way down. But a recurrent motif in Streeruwitz's writings suggests that the longing for a biography is matched by the impossibility of achieving one. In *Nachwelt* (1999, Posterity), for example, the protagonist sets out to write the biography of Anna Mahler. After gathering bits of information and probing the recollections of contemporaries, she ultimately gives up on the attempt at retrieving origins and producing a coherent context.[8] Maynard similarly suggests some significant deficiencies in Perceval's account. She had never been loved the way she herself had loved; she has no children: "That is not much. In the end" (87). When asked why she wants to commission a biography, Maynard – a not very reliable informant – explains that she would like to be remembered; the biography is to be a monument for posterity.

In a recent interview, Streeruwitz maintains that the construction of identities has political motivation: the complexities of life are simplified so that it can be described and thereby influenced and subjected to control.[9] In Maynard's case, the biography has an inverse function. Maynard has engaged Perceval for his critical reputation; he is to give an aura of legitimacy and truthfulness to the biography. She, however, attempts to retain control over her personal grand narrative and thereby of the public image that it will project. While she, no doubt, wants to be remembered by her dwindling throng of admirers, she is also concerned with commercial prospects and the commodification of the story of her life.

The writing of a biography is an elaborate act of signification. Immediately after the dispute over control of contents, the arbitrariness of the process is illustrated. A man with signposts appears on the glacier and studies their inscription. He pounds one with the direction "Top" into the snow and ice; the signpost, however, points downward, towards the valley. This subsequently becomes the central place where meanings are negotiated and their power is asserted. One mountaineering couple comes to the sign. The man insists that the instruction must be wrong; it is contrary to natural law: summits go up, not down. His wife lectures him on the authority of those who had the signpost erected. They surely know what they are doing. The couple continues, downhill. Another couple is also persuaded that this is the way down to the summit.

The wrangling and sparring mostly concerns such signifying conflicts. What does the mountain mean to the various characters? They each have a singular explanation. For Maynard, the mountain is a refuge, all her own. For others, it is a mountaineering destination, a tourist trap, or a place for motivational therapy. As in some iterative scheme, people come and go, but the mountain, it seems, has always been there. A basic strategy of a postmodern literary work involves the denial of privileged explanations, resisting particularly the expectation of linear coherence, causal structure, and of closure. In its complexity and pluralistic representation *Ocean Drive.* is thus decidedly postmodern, though its characters with their propensity for singular explanations are not.

The stage instructions give Maynard the trappings of a film star. She embraces Perceval with a film kiss and assumes the glamour pose expected of her for a picture. But in its mise en scène, too, *Ocean Drive.* resembles the practices of mainstream film. The opening scene, for example, could just as easily be the spectacular establishing shot for a Dolby-equipped multiplex theater. Against the vast expanse of the glacier the roar of an approaching helicopter is heard; amid the flurry of snow a silvery ladder descends and Elizabeth Maynard makes her showy entry. A silvery reclining chair and a silver-dotted white parasol follow. The visual impact is that of a Hollywood film with its high production value and a dramaturgy of effects.

In its classical era, the female star was an important marketing instrument for Hollywood films. Her private life was constructed as an extension of her film role. Lighting and framing were carefully designed to enhance her glamorous appearance. For example, more close-ups were lavished on her than on the rest of the cast. In her centrality the star gave coherence to the film. In every regard Elizabeth Maynard fulfills the expectations of a film's star value. The stage space is divided into two distinct areas. On their rocky ledge Maynard and Perceval are separated from the other characters on the glacier; they are closer to the audience by comparison to the long shot distance of the location on the glacier. At the end Maynard bridges the gap and disappears into the larger space. *Ocean Drive.* has affinities to other conventions of mainstream film as well, particularly in the use of cross-cutting introduced by the stage instruction "meanwhile." In keeping with the trend of the 1990s, *Ocean Drive.* foregrounds violence.

Ocean Drive., however, is not all glitter and show, nor does it follow the grand narratives and seamless patterns of Hollywood genre commodities. Its diegesis is fragmentary, the episodes are delightfully unpredictable, and a more incongruous assemblage of characters is hard to imagine. Fragmentation operates at the language level as well; indeed ellipsis and aposiopesis are the signature devices used by Streeruwitz to counteract the pressure to conform in speech and thought. The grand narrative operating within individual sentences is no less coercion than the control and surveillance over the actions of the characters in the play. According to Streeruwitz, a sentence in its completion is a pretense or lie.[10] Punctuation can break off linear continuity and hence destabilize predictability and control behavior. In its incompletion the gap between the period and the beginning of the next sentence provides a space for the active participation of the reader.[11] Sigrid Berka explains this strategy as "part of Streeruwitz' formal solution of having to write without a voice of her own, of having to create places that are non-places, u-topoi."[12]

Disruptive punctuation, the omission of words and grammatical ambiguities all serve to expose worn speech patterns and patterns of dominance. A part of a sentence is left out as being self-evident, but then the very self-evidence is put in question, puts in question why one would have found such a ready and well-practiced answer. An example will illustrate this. Maynard explains that she will not put up with betrayal and deception from anyone.

"Long ago. I could then not believe. Cheated ... But today. I swim along quite well with sharks. In the meantime" (32). Between the period after "sharks" and the time reference lie the day-to-day aggressions and little betrayals that made Elizabeth Maynard who she is; in the space inbetween lies her life, not as a rounded and complete biography, but rather loosely generated in the imagination of the reader. The period that truncates a sentence thus prevents an idea, a thought from being closed shut and parceled off. The reality of Streeruwitz's dramas is porous.

The power of dominant language practice becomes evident on the stage. At the performance of *Ocean Drive.* in Cologne the director had the retarding punctuation smoothed out. Where the gaps did appear, they were articulated to sound like the spontaneous breaks of normal speech.[13] The text was sanitized for ready consumption of its story value.

Grand narratives provide comprehensive paradigms that in their exclusionary practice can form the basis for control and dominance. Streeruwitz rejects the finality of models that put forth such universalist claims. Instead of explanation she seeks description: "What still can be described is life as an exemplary interface of all complex structures that form us and which in turn we have a hand in constituting."[14] *Ocean Drive.*, however, is not simply a jumble of little episodes and interrupted thoughts. Its complex structure is not so much a cognitive cage as a construct resembling a musical score: rhythms and tonalities are explored, themes and motifs are introduced and taken through variations that reveal the dreadful emptiness under the shimmering glitter of Maynard's performance. The fragmentation at all levels and the recurrence of motifs, however, can also be seen in terms of deterministic chaos, an approach to the description of reality that rejects the constraints of conventional theories.

Of course, one may object that the uncritical transfer and application of concepts based on analogy may be inappropriate, since in the assimilation process each discipline necessarily changes the meaning of the concepts, so that exact equivalence is not possible.[15] N. Katherine Hayles alludes to Gregory Bateson's *Steps to an Ecology of Mind* (1972) and argues persuasively that scientific and literary theories constitute an ecology of ideas; they are isomorphic "because their central ideas form an interconnected network."[16] The ideas shared between sites are similar, yet recognizably distinct. Literary texts, to be sure, have neither the completeness nor the recursive precision of an algorithm: they depend on signification, they thrive on ambiguity, and they are open to intertextuality at every level. They have few iterative cycles compared to the normal practice of chaos theory, and even these are blurred by competing narrative devices. Nonetheless, I suggest that iteration and strange attractors can be taken to be isomorphic with recursive processes in *Ocean Drive.*.

For deterministic chaos, the vector of individual events or fragments is unpredictable; however, a recursion of similar events produces an assembly of such seemingly random results, each different, but all patterned around some focus or strange attractor. Such bundled results or fractals determine the behavior of the system. It is the study of such strange attractors that is at the heart of chaos theory.

Iteration is an important process in generating the fractal mise en scène of *Ocean Drive.*. Maynard is first to arrive on the glacier and last to leave; she makes herself comfortable and from this vantage point then observes the comings and goings of various people at the signpost mentioned earlier. There is almost no interaction between the groups that come here, and they certainly do not in a direct way affect the course of the play. But to each of the eight iterations and to each context Maynard brings the impression of previous engagements. It is as if very different constellations of people re-enact a basic scenario, the iterations of a force field looping around a dark compulsion for dominance and violence, the strange attractor for the various iterations. The journalist asks Maynard what her motivation in life might be, the reason behind it all. Her reply is simple and to the point: money. It is always money that matters. Money makes the world go round and violence is its most effective instrument (20). Other participants in the iteration have equally revealing observations. The man who was skeptical about following the signpost considers winning to be the most important thing (29). The aid worker explains the behavior of the delinquents: to inflict pain and to kill is the only strategy that they know for dealing with their frustration (42). The aid worker hopes that the therapy will diminish their aggressive drive for power. The most splendid formulation comes from the drug dealer: "The world is mine. I its ruler" (63). And then he embellishes the idea with some Nietzschean thought: "Apollo's chariot only if to himself a god" (70). The iterations suggest that the world in *Ocean Drive.* is fueled by the impulse to dominance, to ruthless egotism, with possession as instrument, and with aggression if need be. As Maynard departs from her magnificent mountain, the helicopter noise has a meaning different from that at the beginning.

Marlene Streeruwitz offers no uplifting solutions and utopian directives in her writings. Instead she writes against the hypocrisies of institutionalized oppression, against the grand narratives of the bourgeois mind, and against its chauvinist myths. She criticizes not by inventing yet another authoritative paradigm, but by exploring the complex details that every day brings. With her fractal mise en scène she suggests what matters: not the grand narrative nor an impressive biography, but the modest moments of personal happiness. That is Maynard's insight towards the end of *Ocean Drive..*

Notes

1. Marlene Streeruwitz, *Majakowskiring*. (Frankfurt/M.: S. Fischer, 2000) 36.

2. Marlene Streeruwitz, *Waikiki-Beach.* (Frankfurt/M.: Suhrkamp, 1992).

3. Marlene Streeruwitz, *Sloane Square.* (Frankfurt/M.: Suhrkamp 1992).

4. *Ocean Drive.* premiered at the *Schauspielhaus* in Cologne on 18 December 1993.

5. Andreas Rossmann, "Luftblasenlawine. Uraufführung in Köln: *Ocean Drive.* von Marlene Streeruwitz," *Frankfurter Allgemeine* 22 December 1993; "Mit dem Gletscher-Yeti im Klischee. Beliebiger Pluralismus: Uraufführung von Marlene Streeruwitz' *Ocean Drive.* in Köln," *Die Welt* 21 December 1993; Cornelie Ueding, "In der Schneeöde. Uraufführung von Marlene Streeruwitz' *Ocean Drive.* in Köln," *Neue Zürcher Zeitung* 23 December 1993; Ulrich Schreiber, "Emphatisches Gipfeltreffen im Schnee. *Ocean Drive.* von Marlene Streeruwitz in Köln uraufgeführt," *Frankfurter Rundschau* 22 December 1993; "Wirres vom Gletscher. Noch ein Abgesang auf die Männerwelt, aber mit Krach: Kölner Uraufführung des neuen Stücks von Marlene Streeruwitz," *Der Spiegel* 20 December 1993: 159-60.

6. All translations by W. Riemer.

7. Marlene Streeruwitz, "Passion. Devoir. Contingency. And No Time," trans. Willy Riemer, *After Postmodernism: Austrian Literature and Film in Transition*, ed. Willy Riemer (Riverside, CA: Ariadne Press, 2000) 210.

8. Marlene Streeruwitz, *Nachwelt. Ein Reisebericht.* (Frankfurt/M.: S. Fischer, 1999).

9. Willy Riemer and Sigrid Berka, "'Ich schreibe vor allem *gegen*, nicht für etwas.' Ein Interview mit Marlene Streeruwitz," *German Quarterly* 71.1 (1998): 55.

10. Marlene Streeruwitz, *Sein. Und Schein. Und Erscheinen. Tübinger Poetikvorlesungen* (Frankfurt/M.: Suhrkamp, 1997) 76.

11. Riemer and Berka 59.

12. Sigrid Berka, "The (non)Position of Woman in Marlene

Streeruwitz' Work," *After Postmodernism* 228.

13. Matthias Norquet, "Ein Graf haust als Yeti in einsamen Höhen. Vom Ausverkauf hehrer menschlicher Gefühle," *Salzburger Nachrichten* 27 December 1993.

14. Streeruwitz, *Sein. Und Schein. Und Erscheinen.* 60.

15. Rainer Paslack, "'… da stellt ein Wort zur rechten Zeit sich ein:' Die Karriere des Chaos zum Schlüsselbegriff," *Kursbuch* 98 (1989): 121-39.

16. N. Katherine Hayles, *Chaos Bound. Orderly Disorder in Contemporary Literature and Science* (Ithaca: Cornell UP, 1990) 184.

Contributors

Katherine Arens is Professor of Germanic Studies and Comparative Literature at the University of Texas at Austin. She has published widely on the intellectual and cultural history of Austria and Germany from 1750 on, including essays on philosophers, psychologists, and authors of literature, as well as on their impact on twentieth-century theory debates. Her most important book publications are *Austria and Other Margins: Reading Culture* (Camden House, 1996); *Structures of Knowing: Psychologies of the Nineteenth Century* (Reidel, 1989); and a forthcoming monograph on Fritz Mauthner's fiction.

Linda C. DeMeritt is Professor of German language and literature at Allegheny College, where she has been teaching since 1982. Her areas of research include contemporary Austrian literature and culture and the postmodern novel. She has published a German grammar textbook and numerous articles on contemporary authors, including Elisabeth Reichart, Elfriede Jelinek, Peter Henisch, Gert Jonke, and Peter Handke. She has also translated works by Reichart (*La Valse and Foreign*, SUNY Press, 2000) and Renate Welsh (*A House of Cards*, Ariadne Press, 2002).

Bernhard Doppler, born 1950 in Graz, Austria, is currently a Professor of German literature at the University of Paderborn, Germany, as well as a theater critic for DeutschlandRadio in Berlin. He has numerous publications covering various aspects of the literature and literary life of the nineteenth and twentieth centuries as well as of contemporary literature, concentrating on Catholic and erotic Austrian literature.

Rachel Freudenburg earned her Ph.D. in German literature from Harvard University in 1995. She currently teaches in the Department of German Studies at Boston College. In addition to pursuing her fascination with Thomas Bernhard, she researches fairy tales, illustration, feminist literary history, and gender studies. Current projects focus on the construction of masculinity in twentieth-century German culture.

Todd C. Hanlin is Professor of German at the University of Arkansas. His main area of research is twentieth-century Austrian literature and culture. His most recent publications include articles on Felix Mitterer, Peter Turrini, and Peter Henisch, an edition of Charles Sealsfield's *Austria as it is*, and the translation titled *The Best of Austrian Science Fiction*.

Beate Hochholdinger-Reiterer, Dr. phil., studied theater and German philology at the University of Vienna. She currently holds the position of Assistant Professor at the Vienna Institute for Theater, Film, and Media Studies. Her research interests include drama of the nineteenth and twentieth centuries (in particular, issues related to gender), reception history and image formation, and historical works on film and theater.

Helga Kraft is Professor of Germanic Studies and Head of the Department of Germanic Studies at the University of Illinois at Chicago. She has published in the area of Germanic studies and gender studies. Her most recent books are *Ein Haus aus Sprache: Dramatikerinnen und das andere Theater* (Metzler Verlag, 1996) and *Mütter Töchter Frauen. Weiblichkeitsbilder in der Literatur*, co-editor Elke Liebs (Metzler Verlag, 1993).

Kirsten A. Krick-Aigner, Assistant Professor of German language and literature at Wofford College in South Carolina, has written on the works of leading twentieth-century Austrian writers such as Ingeborg Bachmann and Elisabeth Reichart, Jewish Austrian writers, and women's history.

Margarete Lamb-Faffelberger, Ph.D., was born in Austria and has been teaching in the United States since the early 1980s. In 1992, she joined the Lafayette College faculty where she is Associate Professor of German. Her research deals primarily with contemporary Austrian prose, theater, film, and culture studies. She is also working on an extensive research project concerning literature, media, and issues of identity in contemporary Eastern Germany.

Jutta B. Landa (aka McLaughlin) received her Ph.D. from the University of Southern California and her Magister Philosophiae from the University of Vienna. She has been a member of the faculty at the Department of Germanic Languages at UCLA since 1985. Her research emphasis is on Austrian contemporary literature, and German and Austrian film. She authored a book on strategies of provocation in Austrian drama titled *Bürgerliches Schocktheater* (1987) and is the editor and co-author of *"I Am Too Many People": Peter Turrini, Playwright, Poet, Essayist*, published in 1998. She has written numerous articles on German and Austrian literature, the avant-garde, and film.

Dagmar C. G. Lorenz, Professor of German at the University of Illinois at Chicago, focuses in her research on Austrian and German Jewish literary and cultural issues and Holocaust Studies with an emphasis on history and social thought, aesthetics, and minority discourses. Recent book publications include *Keepers of the Motherland: German Texts by Jewish Women Writers* (1997) and *Verfolgung bis zum Massenmord. Diskurse zum Holocaust in deutscher Sprache* (1992). Edited volumes include *Contemporary Jewish Writing in Austria* (1999); *Transforming the Center, Eroding the Margins: Essays on Ethnic and Cultural Boundaries in German Speaking Countries*, co-editor Renate S. Posthofen (1998); and *Insiders and Outsiders. Jewish and Gentile Culture in Germany and Austria* (1994).

Jennifer E. Michaels is Samuel R. and Marie-Louise Rosenthal Professor of Humanities and Professor of German at Grinnell College. She received her M.A. from Edinburgh University and an M.A. and Ph.D. from McGill University in Montreal. She has taught at Grinnell College since 1975. She has published four books and numerous articles on aspects of twentieth-century German and Austrian literature.

Roxana Nubert received her Ph.D. from the University of Bucharest in 1993. She currently is a professor in the German Department at the University of West Timisoara, where she teaches contemporary German literature, German-language literature in the Romanian culture, and interdisciplinary literature. Her areas of research include modern Austrian literature, the modern and postmodern novel, and Romanian German culture and literature. She has published four books and numerous articles in these areas, and has been editor of the *Temeswarer Beiträge zur Germanistik* since 1997.

Laura Ovenden studied at the Universities of London and Nottingham, England. She has published several articles and recently submitted her doctoral thesis on the work of Elisabeth Reichart. Her research interests include the work of Reichart, Yoko Tawada, contemporary Austrian literature, and comparative literary analysis. She is at present a guest researcher at Nagoya City University, Japan.

Willy Riemer teaches German literature and Film Studies at the University of Delaware. He has published primarily on Austrian literature and film, including Thomas Bernhard, Marlene Streeruwitz, Broch, Doderer, and Michael Haneke. He edited the volume *After Postmodernism: Austrian Literature and Film in Transition* (Ariadne Press). He is currently completing a book on Michael Haneke.

Gerlinde Ulm Sanford teaches in the German program at Syracuse University. Her academic interests are modern Austrian Literature, Goethe, Schiller, and Baroque literature. She has published a Concordance on Schiller's esthetic and philosophical writings, a dictionary of Viennese professional names, an edition of Gryphius's tragedy *Aemilius Paulus Papinianus*. Furthermore, she has published a good number of articles on modern Austrian writers, including Mitterer, Schindel, Schwab, Turrini, and Weinheber. Presently, she is working on the correspondence between Goethe and his son August.

Gerd K. Schneider received his M.A. in German from the University of Washington in 1963 and his Ph.D. in German literature from the same institution in 1968. He has been teaching at Syracuse University since 1966 and was promoted to the rank of Full Professor in 1994. He has published a number of pedagogical articles and studies on Friedrich Nietzsche, Tankred Dorst, Willi Heinrich, Inge Merkel, Anna Mitgutsch, Johannes Mario Simmel, Dieter Wellershoff, and others. He is the editor of *Das Leben*. His latest book is titled *Die Rezeption von Arthur Schnitzlers Reigen: 1897-1994* (Ariadne Press, 1995).

Name and Title Index

A

Achleitner, Friedrich 7, 8, 290
Adorno, Theodor 291
Aichinger, Ilse 71
Alexander, Patrick 56
Arendt, Hannah 214, 215
 Eichmann in Jerusalem 214-15
Artaud, Antonin 311-12
Artmann, H.C. 7, 34-50, 290
 No Pepper for Czermak (*Kein Pfeffer für Czermak*) 7, 34, 42
 with black ink (*med ana schwoazzn dintn*) 37, 42
 the dear fairy pocahontas (*die liebe fee pocahontas*) 41

B

Bachler, Klaus 294
Bachmann, Ingeborg 71, 170-84, 290
 Death Styles (*Todesarten*) 171, 172, 174, 182
 Malina (*Malina*) 172, 174-81
Bacon, Francis 312
Bauer, Wolfgang 6, 8, 291
Bayer, Konrad 7, 8, 39, 290
 kasperl in the electric chair (*kasperl am elektrischen stuhl*) 39
Becher, Ulrich 3
Beckett, Samuel 94, 312
Beethoven, Ludwig van
 Fidelio 2, 4
Bernhard, Thomas 10, 11-13, 15, 17, 38, 50, 71, 79-82, 92-111, 114-29, 178, 277, 278, 280, 300, 312, 319
 Death Women (*Die Totenweiber*) 95
 Eve of Retirement (*Vor dem Ruhestand*) 80-81
 The Force of Habit (*Die Macht der Gewohnheit*) 100-02, 117

370 Name and Title Index

The Goal Attained (*Am Ziel*) 12
Heads (*Köpfe*) 95
Heldenplatz (*Heldenplatz*) 12, 80-81, 83, 136, 277, 280
Historionics (*Der Theatermacher*) 12, 115, 119, 122, 125-28, 280
The Hunting Party (*Die Jagdgesellschaft*) 92, 99, 102-10
The Ignoramus and the Madman (*Der Ignorant und der Wahnsinnige*) 12, 97, 103, 108
Immanuel Kant (*Immanuel Kant*) 115, 124-25
Minetti: Portrait of the Artist as an Old Man (*Minetti: Ein Portrait des Künstlers als alter Mann*) 115, 116-23, 129
The Mountain (*Der Berg*) 95
A Party for Boris (*Ein Fest für Boris*) 12, 95, 97, 104, 120
Ritter, Dene, Voss (*Ritter, Dene, Voss*) 12
Roses of Loneliness (*Rosen der Einöde*) 95
World-Improver (*Weltverbesserer*) 115, 120, 123-24, 128
Brecht, Bertolt 220, 330
Brenner, Eva 19-20, 181, 283
Bronfen, Elisabeth 332

Bruncken, Thirza 261
Brus, Günter 9, 291
Butler, Judith 115, 245, 332

C

Canetti, Elisa 263, 312
Canetti, Veza 19
The Ogre (*Der Oger*) 19, 214-32

D

Druskowitz, Helene von 241-44

E

Endres, Ria 115, 123
Ernst, Gustav 6

F

Falk, Gunther 8
Fischer, Klaus 180
Foucault, Michel 242, 335, 336
Franzobel 294
Frischmuth, Barbara 8, 39
Frohner, Alfred 312

G

Goethe, Johann Wolfgang von
  Egmont 4
  Faust 139, 334
  Faust II 193
Goldoni, Carlo 40
Goll, Claire
  The Glass Garden (*Der gläserne Garten*) 219, 220
Gottsched, Johann Christoph 40
Grass, Günter 39
Grillparzer, Franz 44
  Hero and Leander (*Des Meeres und der Liebe Wellen*) 2, 158
  King Ottocar, His Rise and Fall (*König Ottokars Glück und Ende*) 4

H

Haenel, Günther 3
Hahn, Margit 20
Haider, Jörg 23, 178, 265, 294, 330
Handke, Peter 7, 8, 9, 10, 13-14, 15, 17, 23, 34-50, 133-49, 280, 282, 286-88, 301, 330
  The Art of Asking (*Das Spiel vom Fragen*) 14, 137, 138-41, 280, 281, 286
  The Hour We Knew Nothing of Each Other (*Die Stunde, in der wir nichts voneinander wußten*) 14, 138, 139, 141, 143-44, 148, 280, 287
  Kaspar (*Kaspar*) 7, 13, 34, 45, 46, 50, 136
  The Ward Wants to Be the Guardian (*Das Mündel will Vormund sein*) 45
  Offending the Audience (*Publikumsbeschimpfung*) 8, 45, 46, 119, 133, 136, 282
  Preparations for Immortality (*Zurüstungen*) 14, 138, 139, 140, 141, 144-46, 280, 286, 288
  Prophecy (*Weissagung*) 136
  The Ride across Lake Constance (*Der Ritt über den Bodensee*) 14
  Self-Accusation (*Selbstbezichtigung*) 136
  The Trip with the Outrigger (*Die Fahrt im Einbaum*) 14, 138, 142, 146-48, 280, 288
Hartinger, Ingram
  Survival Texts (*Texte zum Überleben*) 20
Heidegger, Martin 83, 283, 290
Helfer, Monika 294
Heusinger, Brigitte 238
Hochhuth, Rolf 71
  The Deputy (*Der Stellvertreter*) 74

Hochwälder, Fritz 6, 7, 10, 54-67, 71-78
  Donadieu (*Donadieu*) 55
  The Holy Experiment (*Das heilige Experiment*) 55
  Holocaust (*Holokaust*) 72-74
  The Inn (*Die Herberge*) 55
  Meier Helmbrecht (*Meier Helmbrecht*) 55
  Orders (*Der Befehl*) 7, 54-67, 72, 76-77
  The Public Prosecutor (*Der öffentliche Ankläger*) 55
  The Raspberry Picker (*Der Himbeerpflücker*) 7, 55, 72, 74-76, 78
  Thursday (*Donnerstag*) 55
Hoffer, Hans 260
Hofmannsthal, Hugo von 290
Hollmann, Hans 259, 260
Horkheimer, Max 291
Horváth, Ödön von 6, 44, 219, 291, 312
Hrdlicka, Alfred 312

I

Ionesco, Eugen 94
Irigaray, Luce 323

J

Jarry, Alfred 311

Jelinek, Elfriede 10, 15, 17, 20-23, 38, 71, 83-84, 135, 178, 179, 220, 257-73, 277, 278, 279, 282-84, 301, 310, 330
  Burgtheater (*Burgtheater. Posse mit Gesang*) 83-84, 259
  Clara S. Musical Tragedy (*Clara S.*) 21, 259
  Cloud.Cuckoo.Land (*Wolken. Heim*) 21, 260, 279, 284
  Death and the Girl (*Der Tod und das Mädchen*) 20
  Death/Valley/Summit (*Totenauberg*) 21, 83, 260, 265, 281, 283
  The Good-Bye (*Das Lebewohl*) 23
  he not as he (*er nicht als er*) 22, 281
  Malady or Modern Women (*Krankheit oder Moderne Frauen*) 21, 260
  Never Mind (*Macht nichts*) 23
  The Piano Player (*Die Klavierspielerin*) 263
  Stick, Staff, and Pole (*Stecken, Stab und Stangl*) 22, 261
  A SportsPlay (*Sportstück*) 22, 258, 261, 265-73, 279, 281, 283
  Truck Stop (*Raststätte*) 22, 260, 279

What Happened after Nora Left Her Husband (*Was geschah, nachdem Nora ihren Mann verlassen hatte*) 21, 258, 279, 283

K

Kafka, Franz 119, 330, 336, 344
Kaiser, Georg 54, 60
Karajan, Herbert von 5
Karge, Manfred 260
Kipphardt, Heinar 71
Kleist, Heinrich von 343
Kolleritsch, Alfred 8
Kraus, Karl 263, 312
The Last Days of Mankind (*Die letzten Tage der Menschheit*) 219
Kreisky, Bruno 9
Kroetz, Franz Xaver 311

L

Lampersberger, Gerhard 290
Lang, Fritz 214
Lernet-Holenia, Alexander 4
Loher, Dea 294

M

Mahler, Gustav 39
Mann, Thomas 119

Mayröcker, Friederike 8
Merz, Carl 35, 43
Mitterer, Felix 6, 10, 18-19, 71, 84-87, 191-208, 214-32
Abraham (*Abraham*) 192, 207
Children of the Devil (*Die Kinder des Teufels*) 193, 207, 228-29
Discord in the House of God (*Krach im Hause Gott*) 19, 191-208
Don't Understand a Thing (*Man versteht nichts*) 18
Dragon's Thirst (*Drachendurst*) 192, 193, 207
An Everyman (*Ein Jedermann*) 194
In the Lion's Den (*In der Löwengrube*) 86, 192
Jailbird (*Verbrecherin*) 18
Lost Homeland (*Verlorene Heimat*) 193
Mouth (*Munde*) 192
No Place for Idiots (*Kein Platz für Idioten*) 18, 192
Siberia (*Sibirien*) 192
Stigma (*Stigma*) 193, 207, 228
There's No Finer Country (*Kein schöner Land*) 84, 192, 193
Visiting Hours (*Besuchszeit*) 192

The Wild Woman (*Die Wilde Frau*) 19, 192, 193, 214-32
The Woman in the Car (*Die Frau im Auto*) 192
Mozart, Wolfgang Amadeus 2
The Marriage of Figaro 2
Magic Flute 5, 98, 144
Mühl, Otto 9, 291
Müller, Heiner 143
Mulack, Christa 19, 191-96, 203, 205
Musil, Robert
The Man without Qualities (*Der Mann ohne Eigenschaften*) 5

N

Nestroy, Johann 2, 34, 39, 43-44, 72, 139, 310, 312
The Difficult One (*Der Schwierige*) 2
Nietzsche, Friedrich 245, 335
Nitsch, Hermann 9, 291
Nordey, Stanislas 25
Nurser, Hans 8

O

Opel, Adolf 171
Overlie, Mary 27

P

Pevny, Wilhelm 16
Peymann, Claus 8, 12, 14, 17-18, 22, 80, 117, 134-35, 137, 139, 146, 148-49, 153, 170-84, 260, 270, 277-81, 288, 292
Ingeborg Bachmann. Wer? 17, 170-84
Preses, Peter
Der Bockerer 3

Q

Qualtinger, Helmut 7, 35
Herr Karl (*Der Herr Karl*) 35, 43, 291

R

Raimund, Ferdinand 34, 39, 43-44, 72, 139, 145
Reichart, Elisabeth 20, 236-53
Africa (*Afrika*) 236
Aphrodite's Final Appearance (*Aphrodites letztes Erscheinen*) 20
Come across the Lake (*Komm über den See*) 237
February Shadows (*Februarschatten*) 236, 237, 238, 240-41, 246, 248, 252

Foreign (*Sakkorausch*) 20,
   236-53
The Forgotten Smile of
   Amaterasu (*Das vergessene
   Lächeln der Amaterasu*) 237
Furies (*Furien*) 236
Reinshagen, Gerlind
   Life and Death of Marilyn
   Monroe (*Leben und Tod der
   Marilyn Monroe*) 344
Richter, Emmy 278
Ronzoni, Michaela 294
Rühm, Gerhard 7, 35, 38,
   290

S

Santayana, George 86
Sass, Kai-Oliver 238
Schildknecht, Kurt Josef 258
Schleef, Einar 22, 257, 261,
   270-73, 279
Schroeter, Werner 175, 179
Schwab, Werner 23-25, 277,
   278-79, 282, 284-86, 291,
   300-20
   Animal Skull (*Tierschädel*) 25
   Anti-Climax (*Antiklimax*)
   306
   Fecal Dramas
   (*Fäkaliendramen*) 24, 284,
   302
   First Ladies (*Präsidentinnen*)
   24, 25, 280, 302, 304, 307,
   310, 314
   Heaven My Love My Dying
   Loot (*Der Himmel mein Lieb
   meine sterbende Beute*) 24,
   286
   Hochschwab (*Hochschwab*)
   285
   MESALLIANCE, but We
   Do Fuck Spendidly
   (*MESALLIANCE, aber
   wir ficken uns prächtig*) 314,
   316, 318
   My Dog Mouth (*Mein
   Hundemund*) 285
   Open Ditches Open
   Windows (*Offene Gruben
   offene Fenster*) 279, 281, 285
   *OVERWEIGHT;
   unimportant: MISSHAPE
   (ÜBERGEWICHT;
   unwichtig: UNFORM)* 301,
   305, 314-15
   *People-Annihilation
   (Volksvernichtung)* 24, 279,
   286, 301, 302, 303-04, 306,
   307, 314
   Royal Comedies
   (*Königskomödien*) 24, 284,
   302
Schwarzkogler, Rudolf 291
Strauß, Botho 138, 146
Streeruwitz, Marlene 20, 25-
   27, 232, 328-46, 350-61
   Bagnacavallo (*Bagnacavallo.*)
   336, 341, 344
   Boccaleone (*Boccaleone.*) 27,
   339

376 Name and Title Index

Brahms Square (*Brahmsplatz.*) 338
Dentro (*Dentro.*) 342
Elysian Park (*Elysian Park.*) 25, 330, 331, 344
Majakowskiring (*Majakowskiring.*) 350, 351, 355
New York, New York (*New York. New York.*) 330, 336, 337-40, 344
Ocean Drive (*Ocean Drive.*) 25, 26, 330, 350-61
Posterity (*Nachwelt*) 356
Sapporo (*Sapporo.*) 27, 342, 345
The 1st 40 years I kept Looking for my God 27
Tolmezzo (*Tolmezzo.*) 330, 331, 339, 340, 342, 343
Waikiki Beach (*Waikiki Beach.*) 25, 329, 330, 344, 352
Sloane Square (*Sloane Square.*) 25, 336, 340, 343, 344, 352
Stückl, Christian 24

T

Tabori, George 22
Toscanini, Arturo 5
Turrini, Peter 6, 10, 14-17, 23, 71, 78-79, 135, 153-66, 178, 221, 278, 279, 282, 288-94, 301
Alpine Glow (*Alpenglühen*) 16, 154, 279, 288-89
Alpine Saga (*Alpensaga*) 16
The Battle for Vienna (*Die Schlacht um Wien*) 16, 162-64, 165, 166, 279, 281, 288-89
Death and the Devil (*Tod und Teufel*) 16, 279
Enough (*Endlich Schluß*) 16, 279, 289
Grillparzer in the Sex Shop (*Grillparzer im Pornoladen*) 157-59, 166
I Love This Country (*Ich liebe dieses Land*) 17
Joseph and Mary (*Josef und Maria*) 16, 155-57, 165
Kasino (*Kasino*) 16
Love in Madagascar (*Die Liebe in Madagaskar*) 16, 279
Pig Slaughter (*Sauschlachten*) 15, 78-79
Shooting Rats (*Rozznjagd*) 15
The Slackers (*Die Minderleister*) 159-62, 166
Workers' Saga (*Arbeitersaga*) 16

U

Unger, Heinz R. 6, 311

W

Waldheim, Kurt 12, 71
Walser, Robert 22
Walter, Bruno 5
Weigel, Hans 33
Weiss, Peter 71
  The Investigation (*Die Ermittlung*) 74
  Marat/Sade (*Marat/Sade*) 153

Wieler, Jossi 23
Wiener, Oswald 7, 8, 290
Wiener Gruppe 7, 8, 9, 33-50, 290, 312
Wittgenstein, Ludwig 290
Wittig, Monique 332

Z

Zankl, Horst 259

About the Book

Postwar Austrian Theater is an excellent scholarly volume, matched by no other work in the English language of comparable intention and size. Its articles on dramatists like Bernhard, Handke, Jelinek, Streeruwitz, Turrini, and Mitterer are insightful and make us aware of the cultural changes in Austria in regard to coping with the Nazi past, confronting contemporary gender issues and overcoming provincialism in the future. The editors' introduction is a concise outline of a literary history of postwar Austrian theater.

Paul Michael Lützeler
Rosa May Distinguished University Professor in the Humanities
Graduate Director, European Studies Program
Director, Max Kade Center for Contemporary German Literature
Washington University

For the widely recognized ascent of a new generation of Austrian writers in the late 20th century, theater has played a central role. This volume succeeds in capturing the avant-garde spirit of theatrical productions which fanned the flames of Austria's own brand of cultural wars in the 1980s and 1990s. The lively and well researched contributions of established experts set valid parameters for a new understanding of writers like Bernhard, Jelinek, Hochwälder, Handke, Streeruwitz, and Turrini. The preeminent position of the Viennese Burgtheater under Peymann is well documented as is the prominent role of women writers.

Frank Trommler
University of Pennsylvania

About the Editors

Linda C. DeMeritt is Professor of German at Allegheny College and current President of the Modern Austrian Literature and Culture Association (MALCA).

Margarete Lamb-Faffelberger is Associate Professor of German at Lafayette College and General Editor of the Austrian Culture Series at Peter Lang Publishing, Inc.